OVERVIEW OF THE YEAR'S SEQUENCE

WRITING WITH SKILL, LEVEL ONE

LEVEL 5 OF THE COMPLETE WRITER

by

Susan Wise Bauer

STUDENT TEXT

This book is to be used in conjunction with *Writing With Skill, Level One: Level 5 of The Complete Writer, Instructor Text*

Level 1 ISBN 978-1-933339-52-8

Available at www.peacehillpress.com or wherever books are sold

Cover design by Mollie Bauer.

Publisher's Cataloging-In-Publication Data
(Prepared by The Donohue Group, Inc.)

Bauer, S. Wise.
Writing with skill. Level one, Student workbook / by Susan Wise Bauer.

p. : ill. ; cm. — (The complete writer ; level 5)

"This book is to be used in conjunction with *Writing With Skill, Level One: Level 5 of The Complete Writer, Instructor Text*."—T.p. verso.
Interest grade level: 5-8.
ISBN: 978-1-933339-53-5

1. English language—Composition and exercises—Study and teaching (Elementary) 2. English language—Rhetoric—Study and teaching (Elementary) I. Title. II. Title: Writing with skill. Level one, Student text.

LB1576 .B383 2012
372.62/3

TABLE OF CONTENTS

GENERAL INSTRUCTIONS

Each day's work is divided into several steps. Complete each step before moving on to the next. It is your responsibility to read the instructions and follow them carefully. Go slowly, and make sure that you don't skip lines or sections.

Whenever you see this symbol, ✦, you're about to see the answer to a question asked in the text. Stop reading until you've answered the question yourself. It's usually best to answer the question out loud—this forces you to put the answer into specific words (rather than coming up with a vague idea of what the answer might be). Only after you've answered the question out loud should you read the answer below the line.

Whenever you have trouble, ask your instructor for help. Many of the assignments tell you to "Check your work with your instructor." Before you show any work to your instructor, read through it a final time, checking for basic grammar and punctuation mistakes.

If you are writing by hand, make sure that your handwriting is legible! If you are working on a word processor, print out your work and read it through on paper before handing it in. (Sometimes it is difficult to see mistakes when you are reading on a screen.)

You will need to keep a Composition Notebook. Use a three-ring notebook divided into six sections. You will label each section as the year goes on.

Plan to work on your writing four days per week.

Part I

BASIC SKILLS
WEEKS 1–3

Overview of Weeks 1–3

Instead of immediately starting to write compositions, you'll begin by working on skills that need to be in place *before* you begin to write. The first three weeks of this course will review and practice three very basic skills: finding the main idea in a story, finding the main idea in a paragraph, and using a thesaurus to find synonyms.

Begin by labelling the first section of your notebook "Narrations" and the second "Outlines." You will use the other four sections later in this course.

Narrations. First, you'll review how to write narrations. The ability to summarize a piece of narrative fiction (storytelling) in three or four sentences is a basic skill which should be in place before you begin to work on outlining.

Summarizing forces you to identify the central story, or plot, of a narrative. When you summarize, you have to discard details, dialogue, and action, and just keep the basic story-line. This story-line is the *skeleton* of a narrative fiction; it lies underneath all of the details, dialogue, and actions, and organizes them into a particular order.

Finding the story-line in narrative fiction will make it easier for you, later on, to write your own compositions. When you write, you will need to be able to hold the basic story-line in your head as you flesh it out with details, dialogue, and actions. This will help you put all of those details, speeches, and events in the proper order.

The first week of the course walks you step by step through the process of summarizing and writing down a narration. These skills should be review for you. If you have a great deal of difficulty with the narrations, you may need to spend a few weeks working on this skill before continuing with *Writing with Skill*. Additional narration practice is provided in *Writing with Ease, Level Four*.

When you finish your narrations, place them in the first section of your notebook.

Outlines. Your narration practice will prepare you to write your own narratives. But not all compositions are organized following a story-line; there are many other ways to organize compositions.

You will learn some of these ways as you go through this program. However, before you start to write your own compositions, you will study how other writers organize *their* work—what order they put their information in. You will learn how to *outline* their work—how to note down the main idea in each section of their compositions. This will teach you the basic skills of outlining. When you then begin to write your own works, outlining will help you put your information down in the correct order.

When you've finished these outlines, place them in the second section of your notebook.

In the third week, you'll practice using the thesaurus as you write both a narration and an outline. The best choice is probably the most recent version of the classic *Roget's International Thesaurus*. Avoid condensed or pocket-sized thesaurii, since these are less complete. Free online thesaurii, as well as the "thesaurus" tool in most word processors, are also very incomplete. (With reference books, you get what you pay for.) Use a print thesaurus instead.

Week 1: Narrative Summaries

Day One: Original Narration Exercise

Focus: Summarizing a narrative by choosing the main events and listing them chronologically

Remember: you are responsible for reading and following the instructions! Your instructor is available to check your work, and to help if you if you have difficulty, but you should be able to do most of your work independently.

STEP ONE: **Read**

Read the following excerpt from the beginning of the first chapter of *The Pepins and Their Problems* by Polly Horvath.

At the end of the excerpt, you will see a small number that sits up above the last word. This small number is called a *superscript* number. *Super* means "above, over," so a superscript number sits up above the regular script, or print.

When you see the superscript number, look down at the bottom of the page. You will see a line of smaller type beginning with the same number. This is called a *footnote,* because it is a note at the foot, or bottom, of the page. The footnote tells you the title of the book that the excerpt comes from, the author, the publisher, the year of publication, and the page numbers in the book where the excerpt is found.

— — —

> There are always problems in the lives of Mr. and Mrs. Pepin; their children, Petunia and Irving; their dog, Roy; their cat, Miranda; and their very fine neighbor Mr. Bradshaw. Now, all families have problems, and all families, one hopes, eventually solve them, but the Pepins and their very fine neighbor Mr. Bradshaw have problems of such a bizarre nature that they are never able to find a solution and get on with their lives without the help of you, dear reader.
>
> Just recently the Pepins awoke to find toads in their shoes. This was quite a puzzler.

"What shall we do?" asked Mrs. Pepin, who needed to put her shoes on so she could catch the 8:05 train to her part-time job at the Domestic Laboratory, on the outskirts of beautiful downtown Peony, where she led the field in peanut butter experiments. The Domestic Laboratory was not a strict company, but it did require its workers to arrive shod.

"What shall we do?" asked Mr. Pepin, who needed his shoes so he could drive them both to the train station. There he would catch the 8:10 to work at the cardboard factory, where he was in charge of corrugation.

"I am not putting my foot in a toad-filled shoe," said Petunia, who was in the fifth grade, where she wasn't in charge of anything.

"Maybe we should go next door and ask Mr. Bradshaw if he has toads in his shoes," said Irving, who was a sixth-grade genius and in charge of leading all charges.

In the end, that is what the Pepins did. They went next door to their very fine neighbor Mr. Bradshaw, who was eating corn twinklies and hadn't looked at his shoes yet. The Pepins explained to Mr. Bradshaw what the problem was, and together they went to examine Mr. Bradshaw's very fine shoes. There were toads in every single pair. Even in the galoshes.

"Thank you for calling this to my attention," said Mr. Bradshaw, and then, because he was an exemplary host as well as a very fine neighbor, he poured bowls of corn twinklies all round.

The Pepins and Mr. Bradshaw could not imagine what to do with their toad-filled shoes. How had the toads gotten into the all the shoes, and how were the Pepins to get them out? They thought for a very long while, but even Irving the genius was unable to think of a solution.[1]

STEP TWO: **Note important events**

This is a short and simple passage—a warm-up for you!

When you summarize a narrative, it's often best to start by jotting down a few phrases or short sentences that remind you of things that happened in the story. Although you may not need to do this with such a short passage, practice this now. On scratch paper, write down four or five phrases or short sentences that will remind you of the things that happened in the passage. *Do not use more than five phrases or short sentences!*

Be sure to write the events down in the same order that they happen in the story.

If you have trouble with this assigment, ask your instructor for help.

---

1. Polly Horvath, *The Pepins and Their Problems* (Square Fish, 2008), pp. 3–5.

STEP THREE: **Write summary sentences**

After you've written down your four or five phrases or sentences, try to combine them into two or three sentences. You can do this by putting two phrases in the same sentence (for example, "Toads in their shoes" and "They couldn't put on their shoes" could be combined into "They couldn't put on their shoes because there were toads in the shoes"). Or you may find that one or more of your jotted notes turns out to be unnecessary. (If you leave out the detail that Mr. Bradshaw was eating corn cereal, the summary will still make sense!)

Say your two or three sentences out loud several times before writing them down. After you've written the sentences down, ask your instructor to check them. Remember to proofread the sentences first. Reading them out loud *after* you've written them is an excellent way to check your own work.

If you have trouble, ask your instructor for help.

Day Two: Original Narration Exercise

Focus: Summarizing a narrative by choosing the main events and listing them chronologically

Now that you've had a chance to warm up, you'll summarize a slightly more difficult passage.

STEP ONE: **Read**

Read the following excerpt from *The Wolves of Willoughby Chase* by Joan Aiken. In this passage, young Sylvia is travelling to stay with her wealthy cousin Bonnie at the country house known as Willoughby Chase. She has not had enough to eat, and her clothes are old and thin, so she is both hungry and cold—but she knows that she should be suspicious of the strange man who is sharing the railway carriage with her. When he offers her a box of chocolates, she refuses, even though her mouth waters.

> "Now come along — do," said the man coaxingly. "All little girls like sweeties, *I* know."
>
> "Sir," said Sylvia coldly, "if you speak to me again I shall be obliged to pull the communication cord."
>
> He sighed and put away the box. Her relief over this was premature, however, for he turned round next minute with a confectioner's pasteboard carton filled with every imaginable variety of little cakes—there were jam tarts, maids of honour, lemon cheese cakes, Chelsea buns, and numerous little iced confections in brilliant and enticing colors.

"I always put up a bit of a tiffin for a journey," he murmured, as if to himself, and, placing the box on the seat directly opposite Sylvia, he selected a cake covered with violet icing and bit into it. It appeared to be filled with jam. Sylvia looked straight ahead and ignored him, but again she had to swallow.

"Now, my dear, how about one of these little odds and ends?" said the man. "I can't possibly eat them all by myself, can I?"

Sylvia stood up and looked for the communication cord. It was out of her reach.

"Shall I pull it for you?" inquired her fellow-traveller politely, following the direction of her eyes upwards. Sylvia did not reply to him. She did not feel, though, that it would be ladylike to climb up on the seat or arm-rest to pull the cord herself, so she sat down again, biting her lip with anxiety. To her inexpressible relief the stranger, after eating three or four more cakes with every appearance of enjoyment, put the box back in his portmanteau, wrapped himself in a richly furred cloak, retired to his own corner, and shut his eyes. A subdued but regular snore soon issuing from his partly-opened mouth presently convinced Sylvia that he was asleep, and she began to breathe more freely. . . .

Presently she grew drowsy and fell into uneasy slumber, but not for long; it was bitterly cold and her feet in their thin shoes felt like lumps of ice. She huddled into her corner and wrapped herself in the green cloak, envying her companion his thick furs and undisturbed repose, and wishing it were ladylike to curl her feet up beneath her on the seat. Unfortunately she knew better than that.

She dreamed, without being really asleep, of arctic seas, of monstrous tunnels through hillsides fringed with icicles. Her travelling companion, who had grown a long tail and a pair of horns, offered her cakes the size of grand pianos and coloured scarlet, blue, and green; when she bit into them she found they were made of snow.

She woke suddenly from one of these dreams to find that the train had stopped with a jerk.

"Oh! What is it? Where are we?" she exclaimed before she could stop herself.

"No need to alarm yourself, miss," said her companion, looking unavailingly out of the black square of window. "Wolves on the line, most likely—they often have trouble of that kind hereabouts."

"Wolves!" Sylvia stared at him in terror.

"They don't often get into the train, though," he added reassuringly. "Two years ago they managed to climb into the guard's van and eat a pig, and once they got the engine-driver—another had to be sent in a relief-engine—but they don't often eat a passenger, I promise you."

As if in contradiction of his words a sad and sinister howling now arose beyond the windows, and Sylvia, pressing her face against the dark pane, saw that they were passing through a thickly wooded region where snow lay deep on the ground. Across this white carpet she could just discern a ragged multitude pouring, out of which arose, from time to time, this terrible cry. She was almost petrified with fear. . . . At length she summoned up strength to whisper:

"Why don't we go on?"

"Oh, I expect there are too many of 'em on the line ahead," the man answered carelessly. "Can't just push through them, you see—the engine would be derailed in no time, and then we should be in a bad way. No, I expect we'll have to wait here till daylight now—the wolves get scared then, you know, and make for home. All that matters is that the driver shan't get eaten in the meantime—he'll keep 'em off by throwing lumps of coal at them, I dare say."

"Oh!" Sylvia exclaimed in irrepressible alarm, as a heavy body thudded suddenly against the window, and she had a momentary view of a pointed grey head, red slavering jaws, and pale eyes gleaming with ferocity.

"Oh, don't worry about that," soothed her companion. "They'll keep up that jumping against the windows for hours. They're not much danger, you know, singly; it's only in the whole pack you've got to watch out for 'em."

Sylvia was not much comforted by this. She moved along to the middle of the seat and huddled there, glancing fearfully first to one side and then to the other. The strange man seemed quite undisturbed by the repeated onslaught of the wolves which followed. He took a pinch of snuff, remarked that it was all a great nuisance and they would be late, and composed himself to sleep again.

He had just begun to snore when a discomposing incident occurred. The window beside him, which must have been insecurely fastened, was not proof against the continuous impact of the frenzied and ravenous animals. The catch suddenly slipped, and the window fell open with a crash, its glass shivering into fragments.

Sylvia screamed. Another instant, and a wolf precipitated itself through the aperture thus formed. It turned snarling on the sleeping stranger, who started awake with an oath, and very adroitly flung his cloak over the animal. He then seized one of the shattered pieces of glass lying on the floor and stabbed the imprisoned beast through the cloak. It fell dead.

"Tush," said Sylvia's companion, breathing heavily and passing his hand over his face. "Unexpected—most."[2]

STEP TWO: **Note important events**

On scratch paper, write down five or six phrases or short sentences that will remind you of the things that happened in the passage. *Do not use more than six phrases or short sentences!* There are many vivid details in this passage (like the "jam tarts, maids of honour, lemon cheese cakes,

2. Joan Aiken, *The Wolves of Willoughby Chase* (Yearling, 1962), pp. 17–21.

Chelsea buns, and numerous little iced confections"). Remember that details should not be included in a summary—try to stay focused on the main events.

Be sure to write the events down in the same order that they happen in the story.

If you have trouble with this assigment, ask your instructor for help.

STEP THREE: **Write summary sentences**

After you've written down your five or six phrases or sentences, try to combine them into three or four sentences. Remember: you can do this by putting two phrases or sentences together (for example, "Sylvia was uncomfortable" and "The man offered her cakes but she refused" could be combined into "Sylvia was uncomfortable with the man, so when he offered her cakes she refused"). Or you may find that one or more of your jotted notes turns out to be unnecessary. (If you completely leave out the information that the man offered her cakes, the summary will still make sense!)

Say your three or four sentences out loud several times before writing them down. After you've written the sentences down, ask your instructor to check them. Remember to proofread the sentences first by reading them out loud.

If you have trouble, ask your instructor for help.

Day Three: Original Narration Exercise

Focus: Summarizing nonfiction by choosing the main events and listing them chronologically

In Days One and Two, you wrote narrations summarizing two excerpts from novels—long works of creative fiction. However, you can also use a narration to summarize nonfiction (history, science, biography, etc.).

STEP ONE: **Read**

The following passage about the Russian czar Peter the Great, who ruled 1682–1725, comes from *The Story of the World, Volume 3: Early Modern Times* by Susan Wise Bauer.

> Peter had always been fascinated by the West. But not very many Europeans traveled to Russia, and those who settled in Russia lived apart from the Russians, in special colonies for "foreigners." Peter had spent hours in these colonies, talking to the Westerners who lived there. He had even found an old, rotten English sailboat in a shed—and was fascinated by it. Peter wanted ships like the English

had. He wanted to build a navy that could sail to Europe. He wanted a fleet of merchant ships that could take Russian honey, wax, and furs to Europe.

But Peter knew that Russia would never be able to visit the West without a good port for ships to sail in and out of. Russia's northern coast was so cold and icy that ships couldn't even reach it for most of the year. And Peter's only port city, the city of Archangel, was so far north that it was frozen solid for half the year. During the cold dark Arctic winters, the sun only rose for five short hours a day. And the air was so cold that if you spat on the ground, your spit would freeze before it landed!

Russia needed a warmer port, and Peter had his eye on one: the port of Azov. The Sea of Azov led right into the Black Sea, which led to the Mediterranean. Azov belonged to the Ottoman Turks, but Peter was sure that the Russian army could defeat the Turks in battle and claim Azov for Russia.

So Peter marched his army down to Azov and laid a siege around the fortress that protected the port. He wrote out a demand for surrender, attached it to an arrow, and ordered an archer to shoot it into the city. But the Turks simply laughed at Peter's demand. Peter soon saw why. Turkish ships could sail right into Azov to bring food and weapons to the Turks inside the fortress. Meanwhile, the Russians camped outside the walls began to run out of food and ammunition. And the weather was growing colder. A savage winter was coming.

Peter realized that he would never be able to capture Azov unless he could stop Turkish ships from reaching it. So he withdrew his army and ordered his men to build twenty-five warships and hundreds of barges—all before spring! The Russian soldiers labored all winter, building this huge fleet and learning to sail it. When spring came, the brand-new Russian navy drove away the Turkish galleys that arrived to save Azov. Meanwhile, Russian soldiers began to build a pile of rubble high against Azov's walls. When the mound was high enough, soldiers poured over it into the fortress. The Turks waved their turbans in surrender. Azov had fallen![3]

STEP TWO: **Note important events**

On scratch paper, write down six or seven phrases or short sentences that will remind you of the things that happened in the passage. Do not use more than seven phrases or short sentences! Make sure that you focus on the main events in the passage (like the Russian army's conquest of Azov) rather than the smaller details (the weather started to grow colder).

Be sure to write the events down in the same order that they happen in the story.

If you have trouble with this assignment, ask your instructor for help.

3. Susan Wise Bauer, *The Story of the World, Volume 3: Early Modern Times* (Peace Hill Press, 2004), pp. 166–167.

STEP THREE: **Write summary sentences**

After you've written down your six or seven phrases or sentences, try to combine them into four sentences. Remember: you can do this by putting two phrases or sentences together, or you may find that one or more of your jotted notes turns out to be unnecessary.

Say your sentences out loud several times before writing them down. After you've written the sentences down, ask your instructor to check them. Remember to proofread the sentences first by reading them out loud.

If you have trouble, ask your instructor for help.

Day Four: Challenge Exercise

Focus: Summarizing a complete narrative by choosing the main events and listing them chronologically

In the final review exercise of this week, you'll practice summing up an entire story, from beginning to end.

STEP ONE: **Read**

This traditional folktale is German in origin—but it is so old that no one knows for sure where it came from (or what it means). The Brothers Grimm included it in their 1812 collection of fairy tales, but this version is from Andrew Lang's classic collection *The Red Fairy Book*.

— — —

"The Golden Goose"

There was once a man who had three sons. The youngest of them was called Dullhead, and was sneered and jeered at and snubbed on every possible opportunity.

One day it happened that the eldest son wished to go into the forest to cut wood, and before he started his mother gave him a fine rich cake and a bottle of wine, so that he might be sure not to suffer from hunger or thirst.

When he reached the forest he met a little old grey man who wished him "good-morning" and said, "Do give me a piece of that cake you have got in your pocket, and let me have a draught of your wine—I am so hungry and thirsty."

But this clever son replied, "If I give you my cake and wine I shall have none left for myself; you just go your own way." And he left the little man standing there and went further on into the forest. There he began to cut down a tree, but before long he made a false stroke with his axe, and cut his own arm so badly that he was obliged to go home and have it bound up.

Then the second son went to the forest, and his mother gave him a good cake and a bottle of wine as she had to his elder brother. He too met the little old grey man, who begged him for a morsel of cake and a draught of wine.

But the second son spoke most sensibly too, and said, "Whatever I give to you I deprive myself of. Just go your own way, will you?" Not long after, his punishment overtook him, for no sooner had he struck a couple of blows on a tree with his axe, than he cut his leg so badly that he had to be carried home.

So then Dullhead said, "Father, let me go out and cut wood." But his father answered, "Both your brothers have injured themselves. You had better leave it alone; you know nothing about it."

But Dullhead begged so hard to be allowed to go that at last his father said, "Very well, then—go. Perhaps when you have hurt yourself, you may learn to know better." His mother only gave him a very plain cake made with water and baked in the cinders, and a bottle of sour beer.

When he got to the forest, he too met the little grey old man, who greeted him and said, "Give me a piece of your cake and a draught from your bottle; I am so hungry and thirsty."

And Dullhead replied, "I've only got a cinder-cake and some sour beer, but if you care to have that, let us sit down and eat."

So they sat down, and when Dullhead brought out his cake he found it had turned into a fine rich cake, and the sour beer into excellent wine. Then they ate and drank, and when they had finished the little man said, "Now I will bring you luck, because you have a kind heart and are willing to share what you have with others. There stands an old tree; cut it down, and amongst its roots you'll find something." With that the little man took leave.

Then Dullhead fell to at once to hew down the tree, and when it fell he found amongst its roots a goose, whose feathers were all of pure gold. He lifted it out, carried it off, and took it with him to an inn where he meant to spend the night.

Now the landlord of the inn had three daughters, and when they saw the goose they were filled with curiosity as to what this wonderful bird could he, and each longed to have one of its golden feathers.

The eldest thought to herself, "No doubt I shall soon find a good opportunity to pluck out one of its feathers," and the first time Dullhead happened to leave the room she caught hold of the goose by its wing. But, lo and behold! her fingers seemed to stick fast to the goose, and she could not take her hand away.

Soon after the second daughter came in, and thought to pluck a golden feather for herself too; but hardly had she touched her sister than she stuck fast as well. At last the third sister came with the same intentions, but the other two cried out, "Keep off! for Heaven's sake, keep off!"

The younger sister could not imagine why she was to keep off, and thought to herself, "If they are both there, why should not I be there too?"

So she sprang to them; but no sooner had she touched one of them than she stuck fast to her. So they all three had to spend the night with the goose.

Next morning Dullhead tucked the goose under his arm and went off, without in the least troubling himself about the three girls who were hanging on to it. They just had to run after him right or left as best they could. In the middle of a field they met the parson, and when he saw this procession he cried, "For shame, you bold girls! What do you mean by running after a young fellow through the fields like that? Do you call that proper behaviour?" And with that he caught the youngest girl by the hand to try and draw her away. But directly he touched her he hung on himself, and had to run along with the rest of them.

Not long after the clerk came that way, and was much surprised to see the parson following the footsteps of three girls. "Why, where is your reverence going so fast?" cried he. "Don't forget there is to be a christening to-day!" And he ran after him, caught him by the sleeve, and hung on to it himself. As the five of them trotted along in this fashion one after the other, two peasants were coming from their work with their hoes. On seeing them the parson called out and begged them to come and rescue him and the clerk. But no sooner did they touch the clerk than they stuck on too, and so there were seven of them running after Dullhead and his goose.

After a time they all came to a town where a King reigned whose daughter was so serious and solemn that no one could ever manage to make her laugh. So the King had decreed that whoever should succeed in making her laugh should marry her.

When Dullhead heard this he marched before the Princess with his goose and its appendages, and as soon as she saw these seven people continually running after each other she burst out laughing, and could not stop herself. Then Dullhead claimed her as his bride, but the King, who did not much fancy him as a son-in-law, made all sorts of objections, and told him he must first find a man who could drink up a whole cellarful of wine.

Dullhead bethought him of the little grey man, who could, he felt sure, help him. So he went off to the forest, and on the very spot where he had cut down the tree he saw a man sitting with a most dismal expression of face.

Dullhead asked him what he was taking so much to heart, and the man answered, "I don't know how I am ever to quench this terrible thirst I am suffering from. Cold water doesn't suit me at all. To be sure I've emptied a whole barrel of wine, but what is one drop on a hot stone?"

"I think I can help you," said Dullhead. "Come with me, and you shall drink to your heart's content." So he took him to the King's cellar, and the man sat down before the huge casks and drank and drank till he drank up the whole contents of the cellar before the day closed.

Then Dullhead asked once more for his bride, but the King felt vexed at the idea of a stupid fellow whom people called "Dullhead" carrying off his daughter, and he began to make fresh conditions. He required Dullhead to find a man who could eat a mountain of bread. Dullhead did not wait to consider long but went straight off to the forest, and there on the same spot sat a man who was drawing in a strap as tight as he could round his body, and making a most woeful face the while. Said he, "I've eaten up a whole oven full of loaves, but what's the good of that to anyone who is as hungry as I am? I declare my stomach feels quite empty, and I must draw my belt tight if I'm not to die of starvation."

Dullhead was delighted, and said, "Get up and come with me, and you shall have plenty to eat," and he brought him to the King's court.

Now the King had given orders to have all the flour in his kingdom brought together, and to have a huge mountain baked of it. But the man from the wood just took up his stand before the mountain and began to eat, and in one day it had all vanished.

For the third time Dullhead asked for his bride, but again the King tried to make some evasion, and demanded a ship which could sail on land or water. "When you come sailing in such a ship," said he, "you shall have my daughter without further delay."

Again Dullhead started off to the forest, and there he found the little old grey man with whom he had shared his cake, and who said, "I have eaten and I have drunk for you, and now I will give you the ship. I have done all this for you because you were kind and merciful to me."

Then he gave Dullhead a ship which could sail on land or water, and when the King saw it he felt he could no longer refuse him his daughter.

So they celebrated the wedding with great rejoicings; and after the King's death Dullhead succeeded to the kingdom, and lived happily with his wife for many years after.[4]

STEP TWO: **Note important events and write summary sentences**

You can summarize a long story like this in one of two ways.

If you're able to, just list the six or eight most important events in the story, in the same order that they happen in the story. But because there are so many details in the story, you might have to write down *each* event first—even though this will make a much longer list. However, once you've written down the longer list, you should be able to group events together and condense them so that you end up with only six or eight *main* events.

4. Andrew Lang, *The Red Fairy Book* (Longmans, Green & Co., 1891), pp. 340–345.

Here's an example. You might be able to look at the first five paragraphs of the story and sum them up in a single sentence:

Dullhead had two older brothers who refused to share their food with a stranger.

But you might have to list each event instead, like this:

Dullhead was the youngest of three sons.
All three brothers met a little man in the the forest.
He asked them to share their food and drink.
The two oldest would not share their food with him.
The two oldest brothers hurt themselves after they refused to share.

Then you would need to work at condensing those five sentences into one or two sentences. You could start by crossing out the repetition:

Dullhead was the youngest of three sons.
~~All three brothers~~ met a little man in the the forest.
He asked them to share their food and drink.
The two oldest ~~would not share their food with him.~~
~~The two oldest brothers~~ hurt themselves after they refused to share.

Then, cross out the details that aren't necessary for the understanding of the story.

Dullhead was the youngest of three sons.
met a little man ~~in the the forest~~
He asked them to share their food ~~and drink.~~
The two oldest
~~hurt themselves after they refused~~ to share

Now, the first part of your summary might sound like this:

Dullhead was the youngest of three sons who met a little man. He asked to share their food, but the two oldest refused.

Your finished summary should not be more than eight sentences in length.

You should expect this exercise to take you some time, so don't get frustrated! When you have finished your summary, read it aloud. If it is still too long, read through it a second time, looking for unnecessary information or repeated phrases. Cross these out and try to combine sentences.

If you have trouble with this assignment, ask your instructor for help. And when you are finished with your summary, check your work with your instructor.

Week 2: One-Level Outlines

Day One: Introduction to Outlining

Focus: Understanding the basic principles of outlining

For the last week, you have practiced writing narrations—brief summaries of stories and nonfiction narratives.

Now you'll begin to work on a new form of summary writing: outlining. But before you begin outlining, you should be familiar with two terms: *paragraph* and *topic sentence*.

STEP ONE: **Understand paragraphs**

A paragraph is a group of sentences that are all related to a single subject. You can recognize a paragraph because the first sentence is *indented* (begins half an inch farther to the right than all the other sentences).

Look at the following paragraph from the book *Inside of a Dog: What Dogs See, Smell, and Know*:

> For five minutes these dogs tumble, grab, bite, and lunge at each other. The wolfhound throws himself onto his side and the little dog responds with attacks to his face, belly, and paws. A swipe by the hound sends the Chihuahua scurrying backward, and she timidly sidesteps out of his reach. The hound barks, jumps up, and arrives back on his feet with a thud. At this, the Chihuahua races toward one of those feet and bites it, hard. They are in mid-embrace—the hound with his mouth surrounding the body of the Chihuahua, the Chihuahua kicking back at the hound's face—when an owner snaps a leash on the hound's collar and pulls him upright and away. The Chihuahua rights herself, looks after them, barks once, and trots back to her owner.[5]

5. Alexandra Horowitz, *Inside of a Dog: What Dogs See, Smell, and Know* (Scribner, 2009), pp. 1–2.

All of the sentences in this paragraph are related to one subject: the fight between the wolfhound and the Chihuahua. (Notice that the first sentence is indented.)

Now read the following three paragraphs, found in *Understanding Light: The Science of Visible and Invisible Rays:*

> Of all the instruments man uses in connection with light, the most marvelous and the most complex is the human eye. It sees size, shape, and color. It registers degrees of brightness and darkness. It adjusts itself for distance and direction. It dispatches reports of what it sees to the brain. It is provided with a case which closes automatically to protect it in times of danger. And all this is accomplished by an object as big as a large marble.
>
> In ancient times, the work of the eye was believed to be an extension of the sense of feeling. Some invisible something came out of the eye, traveled to the object, felt it, and reported its findings. Today we are more likely to describe the eye in terms of the camera. This is a convenient method, for most of us are familiar with the working of a camera, but it is also valuable, since the mechanical operations of both the eye and the camera are similar.
>
> The human eye is shaped somewhat like a balloon full of air. On one side is the slightly bulging *cornea*; on the other side, the *optic nerve*. But unlike a balloon, the inside of the eye contains a good deal more than air.[6]

The sentences in these three paragraphs are also all related to a single subject. What object does the paragraph describe?

✦

All of the paragraphs tell us something about *the human eye.* But you can't just use "The human eye" as the subject for each paragraph, because *all* of the paragraphs talk about the human eye.

Instead, each paragraph tells us about a different part or function of the human eye. In the first paragraph, all of the sentences are related to the subject "What the human eye can do." In the second paragraph, all of the sentences are related to the subject "What people understand about how the human eye works." What is the subject of the third paragraph? Remember: it will have something to do with the human eye.

The subject of the third paragraph is "The structure of the human eye" or "What the human eye looks like."

When you start to outline, you will try to summarize the subject of each paragraph in one or two phrases or in one sentence. Your summary sentence or phrases should be specific

6. Beulah Tannenbaum and Myra Stillman, *Understanding Light: The Science of Visible and Invisible Rays* (McGraw-Hill, 1960), p. 101.

enough to show how the paragraph is different from other paragraphs that might have the same *general* subject.

STEP TWO: **Understand topic sentences**

Sometimes, paragraphs have *topic sentences.* A topic sentence does your work for you, because it states the subject of the paragraph outright. Topic sentences are usually found near the beginning or end of a paragraph.

Read the following four paragraphs. In each paragraph, the topic sentence is in bold print.

> **In 1513, a Spanish planter named Balboa discovered the Pacific Ocean.** Balboa and his followers marched from the shore of the Caribbean Sea through the dense forests of the Isthmus of Panama, taking twenty-two days to go forty-five miles. From the hill-tops they finally discovered a vast sea stretching south and west. Balboa called it the South Sea, and this name was much used. The ocean which Balboa saw, Magellan soon afterward crossed.[7]

> Galaxies themselves cluster together. The galaxies in our own neighborhood go by the uninspiring name of the "Local Group." The local group has about 30 members, including the Milky Way, the Magellanic Clouds and the Andromeda galaxy. Some clusters of galaxies contain thousands of members. **The Universe appears to be filled with a vast network of clusters of galaxies.**[8]

> **The story of cameras goes back a long way.** Hundreds of years ago people learned that an image coming through a tiny hole in the side of a tent or building makes an upside-down image on the opposite wall. Eventually, scientists learned that silver salts are sensitive to light. Then they learned to coat surfaces with these salts and capture images striking them through a lens. The development of negatives followed, so the photographer could make as many pictures from a single negative as he or she wanted. Then came roll film late in the 1880s, and with this invention, photography was off on its race to become the world's favorite hobby.[9]

> **Magic is successful because it is nine-tenths simple distraction.** Magicians call this diversion of a spectator's attention "misdirection." In

7. Henry Eldridge Bourne and Elbert Jay Benton, *A History of the United States* (D. C. Heath and Co., 1913), p. 5.
8. Slightly adapted from C. Gareth Wynn-Williams, *The Fullness of Space: Nebulae, Stardust, and the Interstellar Medium* (Cambridge University Press, 1992), p. 2.
9. George Laycock, *The Complete Beginner's Guide to Photography* (Doubleday, 1979), p. 3.

> using misdirection, the performer is simultaneously engaged in two series of actions. One series is obvious to the audience, the other is disguised.[10]

The first paragraph is about the discovery of the Pacific Ocean by Balboa—which is exactly what the topic sentence tells you. The second paragraph is about the clusters of galaxies in the universe. The third paragraph tells the story of the camera. And the fourth paragraph is all about distraction.

In each of these paragraphs, the topic sentence sums up the subject of the paragraph. But many paragraphs do not have a single topic sentence. Look again at the three paragraphs from *Understanding Light* that you looked at in Step One. Beside each paragraph, you will see the summary phrases or sentence that explain the paragraph's main subject.

Of all the instruments man uses in connection with light, the most marvelous and the most complex is the human eye. It sees size, shape, and color. It registers degrees of brightness and darkness. It adjusts itself for distance and direction. It dispatches reports of what it sees to the brain. It is provided with a case which closes automatically to protect it in times of danger. And all this is accomplished by an object as big as a large marble.	*What the human eye can do*
In ancient times, the work of the eye was believed to be an extension of the sense of feeling. Some invisible something came out of the eye, traveled to the object, felt it, and reported its findings. Today we are more likely to describe the eye in terms of the camera. This is a convenient method, for most of us are familiar with the working of a camera, but it is also valuable, since the mechanical operations of both the eye and the camera are similar.	*What people understand about how the human eye works*
The human eye is shaped somewhat like a balloon full of air. On one side is the slightly bulging *cornea*; on the other side, the *optic nerve*. But unlike a balloon, the inside of the eye contains a good deal more than air.[11]	*What the human eye looks like*

These are perfectly good paragraphs—but none of them have a single topic sentence that sums up the main subject. Not every good paragraph has a topic sentence, but in every good paragraph, all of the sentences relate to a single main subject.

You will not be required to identify or write topic sentences in this year of study. However, you will often see the term *topic sentence* used, so you should know what it means.

---

10. Vincent H. Gaddis, *The Wide World of Magic* (Criterion Books, 1967), p. 176.
11. Tanenbaum and Stillman, p. 101.

STEP THREE: **Understand basic outlining**

In the final step of today's lesson, you'll study the basic principles of outlining.

When you outline a passage of writing, you begin by finding the main idea in each paragraph and assigning it a Roman numeral. Your goal is not to write a single sentence that incorporates *all* (or even most) of the information in the paragraph. Instead, you should try to write a sentence (or several phrases) that sums up the paragraph's central theme, or subject.

You can often find the central subject of the paragraph by asking two questions for each paragraph:

1. What is the main thing or person that the paragraph is about?
2. Why is that thing important?

Read the following paragraph from *The Story of Canada* by Janet Lunn and Christopher Moore.

> Five hundred years ago, 60 million bison—or buffalo, as they are more often called—roamed the grasslands of North America. They meant life itself to plains nations like the Blackfoot of what is now southern Alberta. The Blackfoot moved slowly across the land, following the herds and carrying with them everything they had. They hunted deer and antelope, they grew tobacco, and they gathered wild turnips and onion. But for centuries it was the buffalo that provided for the Blackfoot people. Buffalo hides made their tipis and their clothing. Buffalo sinews were their thread. Buffalo bones made clubs and spoons and needles. They even used dried buffalo dung as fuel for their campfires. To the Blackfoot, buffalo meat was "real" meat and nothing else tasted so good. They trusted the buffalo to keep them strong.[12]

Now answer the following questions before looking at the answers.

What is the main thing that the paragraph is about?

Buffalo. The paragraph does talk about the Blackfoot people as well—but notice that the paragraph begins with the *buffalo,* and that all of the references to the Blackfoot people are made to explain how the *buffalo* were used.

Why is the buffalo important?

Because the Blackfoot people used it for food, clothing, and other purposes.

---

12. Janet Lunn and Christopher Moore, *The Story of Canada* (Key Porter Books, 1992), p. 313.

If you were to put together these two answers in one sentence, it would look something like this:

I. The Blackfoot people used buffalo for food, clothing, and many other purposes.

(Notice that I is the Roman numeral for "1" or "first paragraph.")

You might be tempted to write a whole list of things that the Blackfoot people used buffalo for ("The Blackfoot used the buffalo for meat, tipis and clothing, thread, clubs, spoons, needles, and fuel"), but when you are constructing an outline, you should *not* include *all* of the information in the paragraph. Instead, you should summarize.

The next paragraph in *The Story of Canada* reads:

> The Blackfoot had always gone on foot, using dogs to help carry their goods, for there were no horses in North America until Spanish colonists brought them in the 1500s. Soon after that, plains people captured animals that had gone wild, or stole them in raids. They traded the horses northward and early in the 1700s, horses came to the northern plains. Suddenly the Blackfoot were a nation on horseback. How exciting it was, learning to ride a half-wild mustang and galloping off to the horizon!

Ask the question: What is the main thing that the paragraph is about?

✦

Horses.

Why are horses important?

The Blackfoot tribe learned how to ride them in the 1700s.

So your sentence would sound like this:

II. The Blackfoot tribe learned to use horses in the 1700s.

(Note that II is the Roman numeral for "2" or "second paragraph.")

Remember: you are not trying to summarize every detail in the entire paragraph. You are finding the central idea in it.

In the next day's work, you'll try to find the central idea in each paragraph for yourself.

Day Two: Outlining Exercise

Focus: Finding the main idea in each paragraph of a passage about history

STEP ONE: **Read**

This excerpt is from a biography called *Hatshepsut: Egypt's First Female Pharaoh* by Pamela Dell.

You'll find the passage easier to understand if you have a little background information. Hatshepsut's father, Thutmose I, died around 1492 BC and left two heirs: his daughter Hatshepsut and his son Thutmose II. Hatshepsut had the best claim to the throne, because she was the daughter of Thutmose I's most important wife. But Thutmose I wanted his son, Thutmose II, to be the next ruler of Egypt instead. Unfortunately, Thutmose II was the son of a much less important wife.

To make Thutmose II more acceptable to the people as the next pharaoh, Thutmose I arranged for him to marry Hatshepsut—his half-sister. The Egyptian royal pharaohs often did this. They believed that their blood was divine, so they were reluctant to marry anyone from outside the royal family—that would be like mixing divine and human blood.

No one knows for sure whether Hatshepsut and Thutmose II were married when their father died. But at the time of their marriage, neither of them was an adult. Hatshepsut was probably between 12 and 15, and Thutmose was probably a few years older or younger.

Hatshepsut took the traditional vows to be "feminine to a divine degree, to exude fragrance as she walked, and speak in tones that filled the palace with music." The most important vow was "to make herself loved," and to do so, she pledged to "tend her lord with love and affection."

In her life as an unmarried royal princess, Hatshepsut had held the simple title of King's Daughter. But with her brother-husband's coronation, she took on the important role of King's Great Royal Wife. She also held the titles of God's Wife of Amen and King's Sister.

As king, Thutmose II carried on his father's tradition as best he could. Historians believe he was a frail and possibly sickly man. He was successful at some minor military operations, but compared with his father's great achievements. Thutmose II's military successes were insignificant. It is possible, however, that the records of his battles have been lost.

It seems to have been a time of peace, and Thutmose apparently put his efforts into other things besides warfare. He directed the building of monuments and other works. These included adding to the huge temple complex at Karnak on the east side of the Nile in Egypt's southern capital of Thebes.

Thutmose's ancient monuments indicate that Hatshepsut performed her royal wifely duties as a humble King's Wife. In many works depicting her with Thutmose, she appears in a secondary position, as a proper wife and queen would. She is usually dressed in a long, fitted sheath and a crown. Where her mother appears, Hatshepsut is portrayed standing behind both her mother and her husband, as was the tradition.

She also fulfilled her role as mother. During the New Kingdom, royal daughters were many and surviving royal sons were few. Hatshepsut gave birth to a daughter, but as far as history reveals, she and Thutmose had no sons. Whether they had a second daughter is another unanswered question. With infant mortality so high, it is possible that Hatshepsut bore another daughter who did not live to see adulthood.[13]

STEP TWO: **Begin to construct a one-level outline**

The passage selected for today's outlining exercise has short, easy paragraphs. Remember, you should begin by asking one simple question:

1. What is the main thing or person that this section is about?

In this passage, every single paragraph is about Hatshepsut, Thutmose II—or both of them.

Begin your outline by deciding whether each paragraph is about Hatshepsut, Thutmose II, or both. Write your answers on the outline below, remembering that each Roman numeral stands for a paragraph of the reading. The first point is done for you.

I. Hatshepsut and Thutmose II B
II. Hatshepsut's vows H
III. Hatshepsut as a wife H
IV. Thutmos II ~~as king~~ battles T
V. Thutmos II builds T
VI. Statues portraying Hatshepsut H
VII. their children B

When you are finished, check your work with your instructor.

13. Pamela Dell, *Hatshepsut: Egypt's First Female Pharaoh* (Compass Point Books, 2009), pp. 41–43.

STEP THREE: **Finish constructing a one-level outline**

Now finish your outline by asking the second question: In each paragraph, what did these people *do?* Or to put it another way: What event or part of their lives or accomplishment does the entire paragraph talk about?

Remember, you should not be listing individual details from the paragraphs. Instead, try to think of the single word or phrase that sums up what all the details have in common.

Consider the first paragraph:

> No one knows for sure whether Hatshepsut and Thutmose II were married when their father died. But at the time of their marriage, neither of them was an adult. Hatshepsut was probably between 12 and 15, and Thutmose was probably a few years older or younger.

You wouldn't finish out the first main point on your outline by writing:

I. Hatshepsut and Thutmose II may have married before their father died, were both very young

Both the timing of their marriage, and the *age* at which they were married, are details. But both of those details tell you more about their *marriage.* So your first point should be:

I. Hatshepsut and Thutmose II and their marriage

or

I. Hatshepsut and Thutmose II's marriage

Try now to finish your outline by finding the main subject of each paragraph. You can use the answer above for I.

If you have trouble, ask your instructor for help. When you are finished, check your work with your instructor.

Day Three: Outlining Exercise

Focus: Finding the main idea in each paragraph of a passage about science

You'll continue to practice basic outlining skills for the rest of this week.

STEP ONE: **Read**

This excerpt, from the basic geology text *The Round World* by Michael Dempsey, discusses the metals found in the crust of the Earth (the outermost layer of the Earth).

> Pure metals are rarely found in the Earth's crust. Nearly always they are combined with other elements, forming metallic compounds. Iron, for instance, may combine with oxygen or sulphur to form oxides or sulphides.
>
> The quantity of metals in the crust is relatively small. If they were scattered at random, there would never be sufficient concentration of one kind to make extraction worthwhile. Enormous quantities of rock would have to be treated to get a very small quantity of metal.
>
> Fortunately there have been a number of geologic processes during the past history of the Earth which have concentrated the metallic compounds. When a rock contains enough to make extraction worthwhile it is called an *ore*.
>
> There are three kinds of rock, *igneous* (cooled from a molten state), *sedimentary* (built up of weathered fragments of earlier rock) and *metamorphic* (rock altered by temperatures and pressures). All three may be orebearing, though the methods by which the metal becomes concentrated vary.[14]

STEP TWO: **Understand how to outline science writing**

When you outline science writing, you may need to ask slightly different versions of the questions suggested at the beginning of this week. Remember, those questions are:

1. What is the main thing or person that the paragraph is about?
2. Why is that thing important?

For a science text, you might sometimes find it more useful to ask:

14. Dempsey, Michael. *The Round World: Foundations of Geology and Geomorphology* (Sampson Low, Marston & Co., 1966), pp. 112–113.

1. What is being described or defined in this paragraph?
2. Is there one central thing which is most important about it?

Look at the first paragraph again and ask yourself: What is being described or defined in this paragraph?

This isn't an easy question to answer, because the paragraph starts out with a *negative* definition. What is *not* (or rarely) found in the Earth's crust?

Pure metals.

This paragraph is centered around describing what is found in the Earth's crust *instead of* pure metals. Pure metals aren't found in the Earth's crust—what is found instead?

Metals combined with other elements.

That answers both questions—metals are being described in this paragraph, and the most important thing about those metals is that they're combined with other elements.

So the first point in your outline would look like this:

I. Metals combined with other elements

There may be more than one good way to phrase a main point. If, for example, you wrote

I. The makeup of metals in the crust

that could also sum up the main idea of the paragraph—which then goes on to define exactly *what* the makeup of metals in the crust is.

STEP THREE: **Construct a one-level outline**

Now finish your outline by finding the main point for each of the remaining three paragraphs.

If you have difficulty, use the hints below. When you are finished, check your work with your instructor.

I. The makeup of metals in the crust (this point was already covered for you!)
II. This point has to do with amounts.
III. This paragraph has a definition in it. What is being defined? (You don't have to give the *content* of the definition.)
IV. How many kinds of what?

Day Four: Outlining Exercise

Focus: Finding the main topic in each paragraph of a passage about science

STEP ONE: **Understand topical outlines**

In the last passage you outlined, each paragraph talked about the same basic topic: metals in the Earth's crust. But even though *every* paragraph talked about metals in the Earth's crust, you couldn't outline it by writing:

I. Metals
II. Metals
III. Metals
IV. Metals

Instead, you had to identify what was being *said* about metals in each paragraph. The first paragraph talked about metals combined with each other, the second about how *much* metal was in the crust, the third about metal in rock (ore), and the fourth about the kinds of rock that have metal in them.

But sometimes a writer will use each paragraph of an essay to talk about a different topic. Look at the following paragraphs, adapted from a popular book about birds published at the beginning of the last century:

> The road runner is distinguished by curiously marked plumage, the possession of a long bill and a disproportionally long tail. As a result of its strange appearance, and stranger antics, the road runner is made the hero of many a fable. Among other wonders it is claimed that it can outrun the swiftest horse and kill the biggest rattlesnake. It is said to accomplish the latter feat by surrounding the reptile while asleep with a rampart of cactus spines on which the enraged reptile impales itself. Its food consists of a great variety of harmful insects, among which the snout beetles or weevils are conspicuous. It devours also mice, horned lizards, centipedes, land shells and small snakes; probably a young rattlesnake would fare no better than any other small snake. 
>
> Petrels are commonly known everywhere as "Mother Carey's Chickens." They are ocean wanderers who spend almost their whole lives on the billows of the deep. Always they follow in the wake of ships, quickly pouncing upon any refuse that may be thrown overboard. Petrels delight in a storm, for

it usually brings them food in plenty and they seem to know when one is coming. Petrels, it is said, get their name from their habit of walking on the water like Peter of old. However, they only appear to patter over the surface with their long, slender, black legs and little web feet, for in truth, they are supported by the constant motion of their wings. At night, when these restless birds have finally managed to tire themselves with their endless game of cross-tag and their excursions far and wide on every side of the swiftly running ship, they tuck their heads under their wings and settle down upon the waves to slumber peacefully.

Crows are usually affectionate, almost as much so as dogs. Once a crow becomes attached to you he will always be your friend. Leave him, and, while he will make one friendship during your absence, he will come back to you as soon as you return. Crows are naturally clean. When they are eating, if the tiniest particle sticks to their plumage they immediately stop to remove it.

The dusky grouse has gray, white, and black plumage, darkest on the back and tail. They build their nests under fallen trees or at the base of standing ones. They lay from six to ten eggs of a buff color, spotted and blotched with shades of brown. Its flesh is delicious eating and the mountain camper rarely loses an opportunity to feast on it. In spring the loud and sonorous hooting of the grouse comes from some giant pine in ravine and canyon, and can be heard for long distances. The male is a lazy father.[15]

Each one of these paragraphs describes a different bird. The simplest way to outline the passage is:

I. The road runner
II. Petrels
III. Crows
IV. The dusky grouse

This topical outline doesn't try to find the most *important* thing about the road runner, petrels, crows, or the dusky grouse. Since the paragraphs go on to give a whole list of facts about each bird, it would be almost impossible to figure out which fact is the most "central." What's central in each paragraph is the bird itself.

So the topical outline simply lists the topics: one kind of bird for each paragraph.

STEP TWO: **Read**

This excerpt is taken from the science book *Real Things in Nature* by Edward S. Holden. After you've read the passage, you will construct a basic topical outline of its paragraphs.

The sun is a huge globe nearly 870,000 miles in diameter. It is intensely hot and is made of gases and vapors. All the metals that we know—iron,

15. Adapted from *Birds and Nature in Natural Colors* (A. W. Mumford, 1914), pp. 341–346.

gold, copper, silver—are in the sun but they are not solid. They are vapors. The clouds in the sun are made up of drops of melted iron, gold, silver and so forth, just as our clouds are made up of drops of water. These fiery clouds are inconceivably hot; and they are driven to and fro by terrific hurricanes and winds. If you look into an iron furnace where the white-hot iron is boiling you get a kind of a picture of the sun's surface. The boiling lava in a volcano is a little like the surface of the sun, only not nearly so hot. The sun is 5,000 times more brilliant than white-hot boiling iron.

Outside of the boiling surface of the sun with its atmosphere of white-hot metallic clouds there is another envelope, something like another atmosphere. It is called the corona—the crown—of the sun. We see it only at the time of a solar eclipse.

The universe is full of swarms of meteors—clouds of stones travelling in orbits of their own. Many such swarms travel in orbits about the sun, as the planets do. They are usually quite invisible. We know they exist, though, because whenever the earth passes through one of these swarms we have showers of shooting stars.

If you will watch the sky, any clear night, patiently you will be sure to see several shooting stars every hour. You will see a little spot of light like a star suddenly appear and move across the sky, often leaving a bright trail of light. Each of these shooting stars is caused by a stone from a meteor swarm which enters the earth's atmosphere and falls towards the earth. As it falls (at the rate of about 20 miles a second) it becomes hot and bursts into flame and fire. Even a rifle bullet, which only goes half a mile a second, gets very hot in its passage through the air. A meteor becomes so hot that it burns up completely unless it is very large.

Comets usually come from the spaces outside our solar system and move round the sun once and then go off again, never to return. Comets are crowds of stones moving in a swarm. If you ever see a swarm of mayflies round the globe of an electric street-lamp, go off a little distance and you will see that the swarm looks like a whitish cloud. The rings of Saturn and comets are swarms of stones. If you go near to the electric-light you can see the separate flies. If you could go near enough to a comet (or to the rings of Saturn) you could see the separate stones. Comets give out light of their own, perhaps due to electricity.[16]

STEP THREE: **Construct a one-level topical outline**

Now write a one-level outline for the passage, listing only the main topic discussed in each paragraph. If you have difficulty, ask your instructor for help.

When you are finished, check your work with your instructor.

16. Slightly condensed from Edward Singleton Holden, *Real Things in Nature* (Macmillan, 1921), pp. 34–39.

Week 3: Using the Thesaurus

Day One: Original Narration Exercise

Focus: Summarizing first-person nonfiction

This week, you'll review the skills of narration and outlining, as well as adding one more tool to your toolbox: the use of a thesaurus.

STEP ONE: **Read**

Read the following excerpt from *The Story of My Life,* the autobiography (a biography written by the person herself) of Helen Keller. Helen Keller was born in 1880. She lost both her hearing and sight after a serious illness when she was 19 months old. Because she could neither see nor hear, she couldn't communicate with others. When she was six years old, her parents asked the Perkins Institution for the Blind in Boston to help them by sending Helen a teacher. The teacher who came was Anne Sullivan, aged 20. Sullivan took on the job of trying to communicate with Helen. In this part of the autobiography, Helen describes the moment when her teacher suddenly found a way to make contact with her.

— — —

> The morning after my teacher came she led me into her room and gave me a doll. The little blind children at the Perkins Institution had sent it and Laura Bridgman had dressed it; but I did not know this until afterward. When I had played with it a little while, Miss Sullivan slowly spelled into my hand the word "d-o-l-l." I was at once interested in this finger play and tried to imitate it. When I finally succeeded in making the letters correctly I was flushed with childish pleasure and pride. Running downstairs to my mother I held up my hand and made the letters for doll. I did not know that I was spelling a word or even that words existed; I was simply making my fingers go in monkey-like imitation. In the days that followed I learned to spell in this uncomprehending way a great many words, among them *pin, hat, cup* and—a few verbs like *sit, stand* and *walk.*

But my teacher had been with me several weeks before I understood that everything has a name.

One day, while I was playing with my new doll, Miss Sullivan put my big rag doll into my lap also, spelled "d-o-l-l" and tried to make me understand that "d-o-l-l" applied to both. Earlier in the day we had had a tussle over the words "m-u-g" and w-a-t-e-r." Miss Sullivan had tried to impress it upon me that "m-u-g" is *mug* and that "w-a-t-e-r" is *water,* but I persisted in confounding the two. In despair she had dropped the subject for the time, only to renew it at the first opportunity. I became impatient at her repeated attempts and, seizing the new doll, I dashed it upon the floor. I was keenly delighted when I felt the fragments of the broken doll at my feet. Neither sorrow nor regret followed my passionate outburst. I had not loved the doll. In the still, dark world in which I lived there was no strong sentiment or tenderness. I felt my teacher sweep the fragments to one side of the hearth, and I had a sense of satisfaction that the cause of my discomfort was removed. She brought me my hat, and I knew I was going out into the warm sunshine. This thought, if a wordless sensation may be called a thought, made me hop and skip with pleasure.

We walked down the path to the well-house, attracted by the fragrance of the honeysuckle with which it was covered. Some one was drawing water and my teacher placed my hand under the spout. As the cool stream gushed over one hand she spelled into the other the word *water,* first slowly, then rapidly. I stood still, my whole attention fixed upon the motions of her fingers. Suddenly I felt a misty consciousness as of something forgotten—a thrill of returning thought; and somehow the mystery of language was revealed to me. I knew then that "w-a-t-e-r" meant the wonderful cool something that was flowing over my hand. That living word awakened my soul, gave it light, hope, joy, set it free! There were barriers still, it is true, but barriers that could in time be swept away.

I left the well-house eager to learn. Everything had a name, and each name gave birth to a new thought. As we returned to the house every object which I touched seemed to quiver with life. That was because I saw everything with the strange, new sight that had come to me. On entering the door I remembered the doll I had broken. I felt my way to the hearth and picked up the pieces. I tried vainly to put them together. Then my eyes filled with tears; for I realized what I had done, and for the first time I felt repentance and sorrow.

I learned a great many new words that day. I do not remember what they all were; but I do know that *mother, father, sister, teacher* were among them—words that were to make the world blossom for me, "like Aaron's rod, with flowers." It would have been difficult to find a happier child than I was as I lay in my crib at the close of that eventful day and lived over the joys it had brought me, and for the first time longed for a new day to come.[17]

17. Helen Keller, *The Story of My Life* (Doubleday, Page & Company, 1903), pp. 22–24.

STEP TWO: **Understand the use of first and third person**

You will notice that the passage is written in the *first person*—from the point of view of Helen Keller herself. Look at the following quote from the story and circle each bolded pronoun. These are first person pronouns.

> **We** walked down the path to the well-house, attracted by the fragrance of the honeysuckle with which it was covered. Some one was drawing water and **my** teacher placed **my** hand under the spout. As the cool stream gushed over one hand she spelled into the other the word *water,* first slowly, then rapidly. **I** stood still, **my** whole attention fixed upon the motions of her fingers.

Now read another version of the quote, in which the first person pronouns have been changed to third person pronouns and names.

> **Helen and Miss Sullivan** walked down the path to the well-house, attracted by the fragrance of the honeysuckle with which it was covered. Some one was drawing water and **Helen's** teacher placed **her** hand under the spout. As the cool stream gushed over one hand she spelled into the other the word *water,* first slowly, then rapidly. **Helen** stood still, **her** whole attention fixed upon the motions of her fingers.

When you write your summary, you may either use the first person (as though *you* were Helen, summarizing her own story) or the third person point of view. Whichever you choose, be sure to use the same point of view all the way through the summary.

STEP THREE: **Note important events**

Now jot down six or seven phrases or short sentences that remind you of the main events in the passage. Remember, you can use either the first or third person. You can write

Miss Sullivan gave Helen a doll

or

Miss Sullivan gave me a doll

as long as you keep the same point of view in every phrase or sentence.

Do not use more than seven phrases or short sentences! Be sure to write the events down in the same order that they happen in the passage.

If you have trouble with this assignment, ask your instructor for help.

STEP FOUR: **Write summary sentences**

After you've written down your six or seven phrases or sentences, try to combine them into four sentences. Remember: you can do this by putting two phrases or sentences together, or you may find that one or more of your jotted notes turns out to be unnecessary.

Say your sentences out loud several times before writing them down. After you've written the sentences down, ask your instructor to check them. Remember to proofread the sentences first by reading them out loud.

If you have trouble, ask your instructor for help.

Day Two: Thesaurus Use

Focus: Understanding and using the thesaurus

STEP ONE: **Understand thesaurus use**

A thesaurus is a reference book that groups together words with similar but different shades of meaning. (A dictionary, on the other hand, contains definitions of single, particular words.) When you write, you can use the thesaurus to find the exact word you need. (Note: The numbers in the following description are based on the fourth edition of *Roget's International Thesaurus*. You will probably use a different edition, but the organization of your thesaurus will be the same even if the numbers are a little different.)

A thesaurus contains two types of lists.

The first half of the thesaurus contains words grouped by meaning and part of speech. These word groups all have numbers. For example, the list headed

475. Knowledge

might contain:

1. **nouns** that name different kinds of knowledge (information, facts, experience, perception, insight, understanding, wisdom, literacy), as well as names for fields of knowledge (literature, science, art, technology) and names of people who know things (scientist, scholar, authority, expert, intellectual),
2. **verbs** for the act of knowing (know, perceive, recognize, discern, be learned in, be expert in), and
3. **adjectives** that describe both people who are knowledgeable (informed, instructed, trained, familiar with, learned, educated, bookish) and things which are known (well-known, recognized, familiar, grasped, common, public).

The second half of the thesaurus contains an alphabetical listing of thousands of vocabulary words. This is the part of the thesaurus that you'll go to first as you write.

In the last lesson, you learned that Helen Keller "left the well-house eager to learn." Suppose that, while writing your summary, it seemed most natural to write "After Helen Keller learned that words stood for things, she was eager to learn." That's true, but when writing a summary you should try not to copy the exact wording in the passage. So instead, you could turn to the second half of your thesaurus and look up *eager* in the *e* section.

Beneath the word *eager,* you would find a series of other adjectives with different shades of meaning, each followed by a number: for example,

consenting *775.4*
desirous *634.21*
willing *622.5*
zealous *635.9*

Which of these comes closest to the meaning of *eager,* as Helen Keller used it? Probably not "consenting," because that just implies that she wouldn't *refuse* to learn if offered the opportunity—but in the passage, Keller is anxious to learn. "Willing" also fails to show how eager Keller was. But "desirous" and "zealous" both imply a real desire and need to learn.

If you decide that "zealous" is the closest to "eager," you would then turn back to the group of words numbered 635 in the first half of the thesaurus. That group of words is headed "Eagerness," so all of the nouns, adjectives, and verbs in it will have something to do with being eager. Glancing down the group, you would see that Section 635 has 15 different subgroups. The first six subgroups contain nouns; the next two contain verbs; the five after that, adjectives; and the final two, adverbs.

Since the word "zealous" was followed by the number 635.9, you would then look down to subgroup 9 of Section 635. There, you would find a series of adjectives closely related to the adjective *zealous:*

eager, anxious, avid, keen, prompt, ready, lively, vital, champing at the bit,

and many more.

You could choose one of these adjectives to substitute for *eager* and write one of the following:

She was anxious to learn.
She was keen to learn.
She was champing at the bit to learn.

Sometimes you'll find that the word you chose to follow leads you to a section where none of the words seem to fit. That's normal; using a thesaurus is sometimes a process of trial and error. But reading through the lists will help expand your vocabulary and fill your memory with words.

STEP TWO: **Practice thesaurus use**

Begin to practice your thesaurus skills now, using two sentences from Helen Keller's memoir.

For each underlined noun, adjective, and verb, find four synonyms in your thesaurus. List those synonyms on the lines provided. Remember that you must provide noun synonyms for nouns, adjective synonyms for adjectives, and verb synonyms for verbs.

When you look up a verb, remember that you'll need to look it up in the present tense. "Felt" is in a past tense. The present tense of "felt" is "feel." "Feel" is the word you'd look up in the second half of the thesaurus.

After you've found the synonyms, rewrite each sentence one time on your own paper, choosing from among the listed synonyms. Do not repeat any of the synonyms. When you've finished, read your sentences out loud and listen to how the sound and rhythm change. Remember to put your verbs back in the past tense!

If you're not sure which subsections of the thesaurus you should go to, ask your instructor for help.

When you're finished, show your work to your instructor.

Suddenly I felt a misty consciousness as of something forgotten—a thrill of returning thought; and somehow the mystery of language was revealed to me.

felt encountered experienced ____________ ____________

misty Foggy hazy Murky cloudy

mystery puzzle riddle problem secret

Neither sorrow nor regret followed my passionate outburst.

sorrow Sadness misery gloom unhappiness

regret remorse shame guilt ____________

outburst cry shout Explosion ____________

Day Three: Outlining Exercise

Focus: Finding the main idea in each paragraph of a passage about science

STEP ONE: **Read**

The following passage has two parts. The first four paragraphs all deal with the same topic (earthworms); each paragraph explores a different part or feature of the earthworm. The last three paragraphs describe different relatives of the earthworm, so each one has a different topic.

The earthworms are the commonest members of the branch of animals next below the insects in organization. Many people confuse the larvae of insects with worms, but a glance will at once distinguish them. The worms have no distinct head, while the larvae have. The former have no legs, while the larvae have jointed legs. Although both consist of a series of ring-like divisions, the larvae have a constant number, while earthworms have a varying number, forty or more.

There are two interesting things about the earthworm. In the first place it is of great benefit to the soil, owing to the fact that it is continually bringing the sub-soil to the surface by passing it through its body. It digests the vegetable matter in the soil and ejects the indigestible portion. Thus the soil is loosened, aired and enriched by the same process. Look for the "casts" of the earthworm on the bare ground, especially after a wet night.

The other interesting fact is that when an earthworm is cut in two, each part becomes an independent worm, and two worms grow where there was only one before. . . . The advantage of this power of resisting death is evident, inasmuch as the earthworm lives in surface soil, through which sharp-edged instruments, *e.g.*, hoe, plough-share, etc., often pass.

The structure of the animal is very simple and it has few special organs. It has no breathing organs. The blood is aerated through the body-wall. There is no heart, but the whole blood system is contractile. It has no eyes, but is provided with a very rudimentary organ of hearing.

Hairworms are interesting relatives of the earthworm. They are found in shallow water in ponds and in lakes. Owing to their resemblance to hairs, it is erroneously believed that they are really horse-hairs which have fallen into the water and have somehow become animated. The fact that they become torpid when the water dries up and revive with the return of water, has been accepted as conclusive evidence of their origin from hairs. Needless to say, they have no connection with hairs of any kind, except in appearance.

The lugworm lives in the sand of the sea-shore, and performs the same work on sand that the earthworm does on soil. Its "casts" may be seen on the surface of the sand.

The leech is a wormlike animal often found in pools. It fixes itself to other animals by means of disks, one at each end, and then extracts the blood after cutting through the skin. After one good meal it can live for months without any further food. The medicinal leech comes from Germany. It was formerly highly prized by physicians for the purpose of bleeding patients.[18]

18. S. Silcox, *Modern Nature Study* (George N. Morang & Company, 1902), pp. 188–189.

STEP TWO: **Construct a one-level outline**

Now write a one-level outline for the passage on the worksheet below.

Because the passage shifts from a detailed discussion of earthworms to a more topical description of other worms, you should also shift your outlining style when you get to the last three paragraphs. For the first four paragraphs, use the questions

1. What is being described or defined in this paragraph?
2. Is there one central thing which is most important about it?

to find the main point. For the last three paragraphs, simply list the topic covered.

Two of the points are done for you.

I. The difference between earthworms and insect larvae

II. 

III. cutting an Earthworm

IV. structure of Earthworm

V. Hairworms

VI. lugworms

VII. leeches

If you have difficulty, ask your instructor for help. And when you're finished, check your work with your instructor.

Day Four: Thesaurus Use

Focus:
Using the thesaurus

STEP ONE: **Practice thesaurus use**

For each underlined noun, adjective, and verb, find four synonyms in your thesaurus. (You only need to find two for "loosened.") List those synonyms on the lines provided. Remember that you must provide noun synonyms for nouns, adjective synonyms for adjectives, and verb synonyms for verbs.

When you look up a verb, remember that you'll need to look up the active form and the the present tense. "Is loosened" is the past tense and passive form of "loosen." "Is aired" is the past tense and passive form of "air." (Make sure you look at the *verb* "air," not the *noun* "air"!) What is the active, present form of "is enriched"?

After you've found the synonyms, rewrite each sentence one time on your own paper, choosing from among the listed synonyms. Do not repeat any of the synonyms. When you've finished, read your sentences out loud and listen to how the sound and rhythm change. Remember to put your verbs back in the past tense!

When you are finding synonyms for science writing, you should be particularly careful to pick words close in meaning. Leeches are found in pools, not oceans—even though "pool" and "ocean" may both be found in the same section of your thesaurus. In this exercise, work hard to find the *right* synonyms.

When you're finished, show your work to your instructor.

Thus the <u>soil</u> is <u>loosened</u>, <u>aired</u> and <u>enriched</u> by the same process.

soil	Dirt	ground	terrain	mud
loosened	Slackened	Un-tightened		
aired	Ventilated	aerated	refreshened	vented
enriched	enhanced	boosted	improved	supplemented

The leech is a wormlike <u>animal</u> often <u>found</u> in pools.

animal	Creature	Insect	organism	beast
found	located	Spotted	discovered	noticed

Part II

BUILDING BLOCKS FOR COMPOSITION WEEKS 4–15

Overview of Weeks 4–15

Begin by labelling the third section of your Composition Notebook "Topoi." Leave the next two sections blank; you'll be using them later in the year. Label the last section "Reference."

In the next 12 weeks of this course, you'll be doing three things.

Narrations. First, you'll review how to write narrations. The ability to summarize a story in three or four sentences is a basic skill which should be in place before you begin to work on outlining. Eleven of these first 12 weeks begin with a one-day narration exercise; when these exercises are completed, place them in the first section of your notebook.

If you have a great deal of difficulty with the narrations, you may need to spend a few weeks working on this skill before continuing with *Writing with Skill.* Additional narration practice is provided in *Writing with Ease, Level Four.*

Outlines. Instead of immediately starting to write compositions, you'll begin by working on skills that need to be in place *before* you begin to write.

Writing involves two difficult tasks. First, you have to figure out what you're writing about—the general topic, the information you should include, and where to find that information. Second, you have to put that information into the correct order before you can start setting it down on paper.

Instead of asking you to do both difficult tasks at the same time, this curriculum will give you the chance to practice them separately. You'll begin by practicing the second task: setting information down in order.

On the second day of each week, you'll complete an outlining exercise. Outlining helps you put information in the correct order; once you've ordered your facts, you can begin to write about them. When you practice outlining, you're developing your ability to carry out the second task in writing. (And because you're outlining someone else's writing, you don't have to come up with original ideas while you're practicing.)

When you've finished these outlines, place them in the second section of your notebook.

Topoi. Now that you've practiced putting information into the correct order, how do you practice the first step in the writing process—figuring out *what* to write about?

On the third and fourth days of each week, you'll study topoi (the plural form of the Greek word *topos*, from which we get the English word "topic"). In classical rhetoric—the study of writing in ancient and medieval times—topoi helped writers come up with arguments. If, for example, you were an Athenian and you wanted to convince your readers that the leaders of Athens were better than the rulers of Rome, you might first have told the story of what happened to Rome when it had insane or evil emperors. Then, you might have explained that the reason why Athens was flourishing was because it had sane, virtuous leaders.

Both parts of your argument are topoi. The first (telling the story of what happened to Rome) is a topos called "chronological narrative"—a story told from beginning to end in the same order that it happened in time. The second is a topos called "cause and effect sequence"—connecting something that happened (Athens flourished!) with whatever caused it (sane, virtuous leaders).

Topos literally means "place," and topoi are places that you go to find something to write about. If your assignment in history is "Read this chapter about the Great Pyramid and then write a brief composition," having a list of topoi in mind helps you come up with the subject of the composition. You might think to yourself "Can I tell a story about the Great Pyramid from beginning to end? Yes, I could write about its construction." (That would be a chronological narrative on a historical topic.) Or you might think "Can I explain cause and effect about the Great Pyramid? Yes, I could write about Egyptian views on the afterlife, and how those views caused the Great Pyramid to be built." (That would be a cause and effect sequence for a historical event.)

File any compositions written during the third and fourth days of your work under "Topoi" in the third section of your notebook.

Week 4: Chronological Narrative of a Past Event

Day One: Original Narration Exercise

Focus: Summarizing a narrative by choosing the main events and listing them chronologically

STEP ONE: **Read**

Read the following excerpt from Edith Nesbit's short story "The Deliverers of Their Country," found in *The Book of Dragons*.

It all began with Effie's getting something in her eye. It hurt very much indeed, and it felt something like a red-hot spark—only it seemed to have legs as well, and wings like a fly. Effie rubbed and cried—not real crying, but the kind your eye does all by itself without your being miserable inside your mind—and then she went to her father to have the thing in her eye taken out. Effie's father was a doctor, so of course he knew how to take things out of eyes—he did it very cleverly with a soft paintbrush dipped in castor oil.

When he had gotten the thing out, he said: "This is very curious." Effie had often got things in her eye before, and her father had always seemed to think it was natural—rather tiresome and naughty perhaps, but still natural. He had never before thought it curious.

Effie stood holding her handkerchief to her eye, and said: "I don't believe it's out." People always say this when they have had something in their eyes.

"Oh, yes—it's out," said the doctor. "Here it is, on the brush. This is very interesting."

Effie had never heard her father say that about anything that she had any share in. She said: "What?"

The doctor carried the brush very carefully across the room, and held the point of it under his microscope—then he twisted the brass screws of the microscope, and looked through the top with one eye.

"Dear me," he said. "Dear, dear me! Four well-developed limbs; a long caudal appendage; five toes, unequal in lengths, almost like one of the *Lacertidae*, yet there are traces of wings." The creature under his eye wriggled a little in the castor oil, and he went on: "Yes; a batlike wing. A new specimen, undoubtedly. Effie, run round to the professor and ask him to be kind enough to step in for a few minutes."

"You might give me sixpence, Daddy," said Effie, "because I did bring you the new specimen. I took great care of it inside my eye, and my eye *does* hurt."

The doctor was so pleased with the new specimen that he gave Effie a shilling, and presently the professor stepped round. He stayed to lunch, and he and the doctor quarreled very happily all the afternoon about the name and the family of the thing that had come out of Effie's eye.

But at teatime another thing happened. Effie's brother Harry fished something out of his tea, which he thought at first was an earwig. He was just getting ready to drop it on the floor, and end its life in the usual way, when it shook itself in the spoon—spread two wet wings, and flopped onto the tablecloth. There it sat, stroking itself with its feet and stretching its wings, and Harry said: "Why, it's a tiny newt!"

The professor leaned forward before the doctor could say a word. "I'll give you half a crown for it, Harry, my lad," he said, speaking very fast; and then he picked it up carefully on his handkerchief.

"It is a new specimen," he said, "and finer than yours, Doctor."

It was a tiny lizard, about half an inch long—with scales and wings.

So now the doctor and the professor each had a specimen, and they were both very pleased. But before long these specimens began to seem less valuable. For the next morning, when the knife-boy was cleaning the doctor's boots, he suddenly dropped the brushes and the boot and the blacking, and screamed out that he was burnt.

And from inside the boot came crawling a lizard as big as a kitten, with large, shiny wings.

"Why," said Effie, "I know what it is. It is a dragon like the one St. George killed."

And Effie was right. That afternoon Towser was bitten in the garden by a dragon about the size of a rabbit, which he had tried to chase, and the next morning all the papers were full of the wonderful "winged lizards" that were appearing all over the country. The papers would not call them dragons, because, of course, no one believes in dragons nowadays—and at any rate the papers were not going to be so silly as to believe in fairy stories. At first there were only a few, but in a week or two the country was simply running alive with dragons of all sizes, and in the air you could sometimes see them as thick as a swarm of bees. They all looked alike except as to size. They were green with scales, and they had four legs and a long tail and great wings like bats' wings, only the wings were a pale, half-transparent yellow, like the gear-boxes on bicycles.

They breathed fire and smoke, as all proper dragons must, but still the newspapers went on pretending they were lizards, until the editor of the *Standard* was picked up and carried away by a very large one, and then the other newspaper people had not anyone left to tell them what they ought not to believe. So when the largest elephant in the Zoo was carried off by a dragon, the papers gave up pretending—and put ALARMING PLAGUE OF DRAGONS at the top of the paper.

You have no idea how alarming it was, and at the same time how aggravating. The large-size dragons were terrible certainly, but when once you had found out that the dragons always went to bed early because they were afraid of the chill night air, you had only to stay indoors all day, and you were pretty safe from the big ones. But the smaller sizes were a perfect nuisance. The ones as big as earwigs got in the soap, and they got in the butter. The ones as big as dogs got in the bath, and the fire and smoke inside them made them steam like anything when the cold water tap was turned on, so that careless people were often scalded quite severely. The ones that were as large as pigeons would get into workbaskets or corner drawers and bite you when you were in a hurry to get a needle or a handkerchief. The ones as big as sheep were easier to avoid, because you could see them coming; but when they flew in at the windows and curled up under your eiderdown, and you did not find them till you went to bed, it was always a shock. The ones this size did not eat people, only lettuce, but they always scorched the sheets and pillowcases dreadfully.

Of course, the County Council and the police did everything that could be done: It was no use offering the hand of the Princess to anyone who killed a dragon. This way was all very well in olden times—when there was only one dragon and one Princess; but now there were far more dragons than Princesses—although the Royal Family was a large one. And besides, it would have been a mere waste of Princesses to offer rewards for killing dragons, because everybody killed as many dragons as they could quite out of their own heads and without rewards at all, just to get the nasty things out of the way. The County Council undertook to cremate all dragons delivered at their offices between the hours of ten and two, and whole wagonloads and cartloads and truckloads of dead dragons could be seen any day of the week standing in a long line in the street where the County Council had their offices. Boys brought barrowloads of dead dragons, and children on their way home from morning school would call

> in to leave the handful or two of little dragons they had brought in their satchels, or carried in their knotted pocket handkerchiefs. And yet there seemed to be as many dragons as ever. Then the police stuck up great wood and canvas towers covered with patent glue. When the dragons flew against these towers, they stuck fast, as flies and wasps do on the sticky papers in the kitchen; and when the towers were covered all over with dragons, the police inspector used to set fire to the towers, and burnt them and dragons and all.
>
> And yet there seemed to be more dragons than ever. The shops were full of patent dragon poison and anti-dragon soap, and dragonproof curtains for the windows; and indeed, everything that could be done was done.
>
> And yet there seemed to be more dragons than ever.[19]

STEP TWO: **Note important events**

You will now summarize the passage in three or four sentences and write those sentences down on your own paper.

Before you can write a brief summary of a lengthy passage, you'll need to identify the most important events in the passage. On your scratch paper, write down five or six phrases or short sentences that will remind you of the things that happened in the story. *Do not use more than six phrases or short sentences!* Remember, you're not supposed to write down *everything* that happens in the story—just the most important events. The most important events are the ones that help the story make sense; if you took them out of the original passage, you wouldn't understand the rest of the story. (For example, if you left out the fact that the dragons were everywhere, would the reactions of the people make sense to you?)

Be sure to write the events down in the same order that they happen in the story.

Here's a head start: begin with the sentence "Effie got a dragon in her eye."

If you have trouble with this assigment, ask your instructor for help.

STEP THREE: **Write summary sentences**

After you've written down your five or six phrases or sentences, try to combine them into three or four sentences. You can do this by putting two phrases in the same sentence (for example, "Effie got a dragon in her eye" and "Her brother got a dragon in his tea" could be combined into "Effie and her brother both found small dragons"). Or you may find that one or more of your jotted notes turns out to be unnecessary. (If you wrote down "Everyone killed the dragons" as well as "Police caught dragons and burned them," you don't really need the second sentence. If everyone was killing the dragons, that includes the police.)

Try to avoid listing minor details; instead, stick to main events. If you took a main event out of the original story, the rest of the story wouldn't make sense. It doesn't really matter what

---

19. Edith Nesbit, "The Deliverers of Their Country." From *The Book of Dragons* (Dover, 2004), pp. 41–45. Originally published by Harper & Brothers, 1900.

the newspapers first called the dragons—without that detail, the story still makes sense. But if we didn't know that the dragons were everywhere, we wouldn't understand why they were such a big problem.

Say your three or four sentences out loud several times before writing them down. After you've written the sentences down, ask your instructor to check them.

If you have trouble, ask your instructor for help.

Day Two: Outlining Exercise

Focus: Finding the main idea in each paragraph of a historical narrative

STEP ONE: **Read**

Read the following excerpt from *The Story of Mankind* by Hendrik van Loon. You will see *ellipses* (. . . .) after the first paragraph. The ellipses tell you that after the period at the end of "They had invented the art of writing," some of the text has been cut. (The paragraph which we removed was unrelated to the Egyptians; it was about cats, dogs, puppies, kittens, and writing. If you're curious, go check the book out of the library and read the whole chapter yourself.)

> The Egyptians have taught us many things. They were excellent farmers. They knew all about irrigation. They built temples which were afterwards copied by the Greeks and which served as the earliest models for the churches in which we worship nowadays. They had invented a calendar which proved such a useful instrument for the purpose of measuring time that it has survived with a few changes until today. But most important of all, the Egyptians had learned how to preserve speech for the benefit of future generations. They had invented the art of writing. . . .
>
> In the first century before our era, when the Romans came to Egypt, they found the valley full of strange little pictures which seemed to have something to do with the history of the country. But the Romans were not interested in "anything foreign" and did not inquire into the origin of these queer figures which covered the walls of the temples and the walls of the palaces and endless reams of flat sheets made out of the papyrus reed. The last of the Egyptian priests who had understood the holy art of making such pictures had died several years before. Egypt deprived of its independence had become a store-house filled with important historical documents which no one could decipher and which were of no earthly use to either man or beast.

Seventeen centuries went by and Egypt remained a land of mystery. But in the year 1798 a French general by the name of Bonaparte happened to visit eastern Africa to prepare for an attack upon the British Indian Colonies. He did not get beyond the Nile, and his campaign was a failure. But, quite accidentally, the famous French expedition solved the problem of the ancient Egyptian picture-language.

One day a young French officer, much bored by the dreary life of his little fortress on the Rosetta river (a mouth of the Nile) decided to spend a few idle hours rummaging among the ruins of the Nile Delta. And behold! he found a stone which greatly puzzled him. Like everything else in Egypt it was covered with little figures. But this particular slab of black basalt was different from anything that had ever been discovered. It carried three inscriptions. One of these was in Greek. The Greek language was known. "All that is necessary," so he reasoned, "is to compare the Greek text with the Egyptian figures, and they will at once tell their secrets."

The plan sounded simple enough but it took more than twenty years to solve the riddle. In the year 1802 a French professor by the name of Champollion began to compare the Greek and the Egyptian texts of the famous Rosetta stone. In the year 1823 he announced that he had discovered the meaning of fourteen little figures. A short time later he died from overwork, but the main principles of Egyptian writing had become known.[20]

STEP TWO: **Construct a one-level outline**

Instead of simply summarizing this passage, you will outline it.

Let's review the outlining process. You'll begin by looking for the main idea in each section of text. The passage above is divided into four sections (there's an extra space between each section). For each section, try to come up with a single sentence that states the main idea.

20. Hendrik van Loon, *The Story of Mankind* (Boni and Liveright, 1921), pp. 17–19.

In previous lessons, you did this for single paragraphs; often, though, a single main idea will be explored in more than one paragraph.

Don't try to include as much information as possible in this single sentence. Ask yourself two sets of questions:

1. What is the main thing or person that this section is about? *Or* Is the section about an idea?
2. Why is that thing or person important? *Or* What did that thing or person do/what was done to it? *Or* What is the idea?

Try that for the first section. What is the main thing or person that this section is about? If you're not sure, ask yourself: Who was responsible for all the inventions and discoveries in that first paragraph?

The Egyptians.

Now look at everything else in the passage, which tells you why the Egyptians were important: they were important because of all the things they did.

You can't list each individual invention or discovery, because you're not trying to include *all* the information in a single sentence. If you knew someone who played basketball, football, soccer, volleyball, and field hockey, you wouldn't summarize by saying "She plays basketball, football, soccer, volleyball, and field hockey." You'd say "She plays many sports."

Try finishing your sentence now. What did you come up with?

Your sentence should sound like one of these:

I. The Egyptians invented and discovered many things. OR

I. The Egyptians made many inventions and discoveries.

(Be sure not to simply copy the first sentence in the paragraph. Remember, this is supposed to be a summary in *your own words.*)

Now work on coming up with a summary sentence for each one of the remaining four sections. (You can use the sentence we gave you for the first section.) When you write an outline, you should use Roman numerals for the summary sentences, like this:

I. The Egyptians made many inventions and discoveries.
II. Second sentence
III. Third sentence
IV. Fourth sentence

For this assignment, try to use complete sentences (although this isn't always necessary in an outline).

If you have difficulty, ask your instructor for help. And when you are finished, check your assignment with your instructor.

Day Three: Analyzing the Topos

Focus: Understanding the form of a chronological narrative of a past event

The passage you outlined in your last writing session is an example of this week's topos*:* a **chronological narrative of a past event** (the deciphering of Egyptian writing). Remember, a topos is a form of writing.

When you write a chronological narrative of a past event, you explain *what happened in the past*, and *in what sequence*. A chronological narrative can stand on its own as a history composition or can be a smaller part of a larger paper.

Today's assignment is to examine how a chronological narrative is put together.

STEP ONE: **Examine model passages**

When you set out to write a chronological narrative in history, you aim to answer two simple questions:

*Who did what to whom? (*Or *What was done to what?)*

In what sequence?

Look again at the outline you made of the passage from *The Story of Mankind*. The exact words you used will be different, but the outline probably looks something like this:

I. The Egyptians invented and discovered many things.
II. Egyptian writing could not be read.
III. A French officer discovered a stone with writing on it.
IV. Champollion discovered the main principles of Egyptian writing.

Notice that each one of these main points answers the first question: *Who did what to whom? (*Or *What was done to what?)*

I. *Who?* The Egyptians *Did what?* invented and discovered *To what?* many things.
II. *What?* Egyptian writing *What was done to it?* could not be read.
III. *Who?* A French officer *Did what?* discovered *what?* a stone with writing on it.
IV. *Who?* Champollion *Did what?* discovered *To what?* the main principles of Egyptian writing.

The points are also put into chronological order (in other words, the oldest event comes first, the next oldest second, and so on). First, Egyptians invented writing. After that, the ability to read the writing faded away. Long after that, a French officer discovered the stone. And after the discovery of the stone, Champollion cracked the code of Egyptian writing.

Here is a second example of a **chronological narrative of a past event,** from *Albert Einstein and the Theory of Relativity* by Robert Cwiklik. It describes a village festival that Albert Einstein went to when he was four years old.

> As the celebration wound on, darkness fell. Everyone sensed that the event they were waiting for was about to happen. The crowd grew tense with excitement.
>
> Suddenly, the gas lamps along the avenue were dimmed. The street was almost totally dark.
>
> The band stopped playing. The people grew so quiet that they could hear the sausages roasting.
>
> Then, from somewhere unseen, a switch was thrown.
>
> In a great flash, the huge theater exploded in a blaze of bright, white light. The light spilled onto the crowd. The horses in the avenue shied and dogs yelped and howled, startled by the sudden brighteness. But the people raised up a great cheer and began to applaud loudly. They stared at the theater in astonishment and wonder.
>
> All around the theater building lamps were burning—not with smoky wicks and gas, but with clean, new electric lights.[21]

This chronological narrative of a past event introduces a discussion about Albert Einstein's early interest in electricity. Because chronological narratives sound like stories, they seize the reader's attention.

Glance back over the four sections and notice the order of events.

In the first section, nothing has happened yet; the crowd is just waiting for an event. With your pencil, underline "the crowd" (the *who*) once. Underline the phrase "they were waiting" twice (this answers the question *did what?*).

The second section happens right after the first section. You know this because of the word "suddenly." Draw a box around "suddenly." Underline "gas lamps" once and "dimmed" twice. These words answer the question *What did what?*

In the third section, underline "The band" and "The people" (the *who*) once. Underline the phrase "grew so quiet" twice (this answers the question *did what?*).

21. Robert Cwiklik, *Albert Einstein and the Theory of Relativity* (Barron's Educational Series, Inc., 1987), pp. 2–3.

In the final section, draw a box around "then." This time word tells you that the last section comes *after* the events listed earlier. Underline "electric lights" once and "exploded in a blaze" twice. These words answer the question *What did what?*

Now look at the summary below:

At first, the crowd was waiting.
Suddenly the gas lamps dimmed.
The band and the people grew quiet.
Then electric lights exploded in a blaze.

The original narrative has a lot more details in it—but this summary shows you exactly how the writer tells each main event in chronological order.

STEP TWO: **Write down the pattern of the topos**

Now copy the following chart onto a blank sheet of paper in the "Reference" section of your Composition Notebook. You will be adding to this page as you learn more about chronological narratives, so leave plenty of room at the bottom of the page; also leave blank space under the "Remember" column.

Chronological Narrative of a Past Event

Definition: A narrative telling what happened in the past and in what sequence

Procedure	Remember
1. Ask *Who did what to whom?* (Or *What was done to what?)*	
2. Create main points by placing the answers in chronological order.	

Day Four: Practicing the Topos

Focus: Learning how to write a chronological narrative of a past event

A chronological narrative of a past event can be used in many different kinds of writing. If you're asked to write about history, you can decide to tell, in order, what happened during a battle, or when a king died and his heir fought for the throne, or when an explorer set off to find a new land. But you can also use a short chronological narrative as the introduction to a scientific composition, or as a way to grab the reader's interest in a composition on any other subject. Here's the beginning of Susan Casey's book *The Wave: In Pursuit of the Rogues, Freaks, and Giants of the Ocean:*

> *57.5° N, 12.7° W, 175 miles off the coast of Scotland*
> February 8, 2000
> The clock read midnight when the hundred-foot wave hit the ship, rising from the North Atlantic out of the darkness. Among the ocean's terrors a wave this size was the most feared and the least understood, more myth than reality—or so people had thought. This giant was certainly real. As the RRS *Discovery* plunged down into the wave's deep trough, it heeled twenty-eight degrees to port, rolled thirty degrees back to starboard, then recovered to face the incoming seas. . . . Captain Keith Avery steered his vessel directly into the onslaught, just as he had been doing for the past five days. . . . He stood barefoot at the helm, the only way he could maintain traction after a refrigerator toppled over, splashing out a slick of milk, juice, and broken glass (no time to clean it up—the waves just kept coming). . . . [The] waves suddenly grew even bigger and meaner and steeper. Avery heard a loud bang coming from *Discovery's* foredeck. He squinted in the dark to see that the fifty-man lifeboat had partially ripped from its two-inch-thick steel cleats and was pounding against the hull.[22]

That's a much more interesting beginning than "The significant wave height, an average of the largest 33 percent of the waves, was sixty-one feet, with frequent spikes far beyond that," which the writer gets to after the story is over.

Today, you'll start to practice putting together a chronological narrative of your own. In later weeks, the "Practicing the Topos" exercise will be completed in a single session. Since this is the first time you have attempted to use this skill, this first exercise will be divided between today and the first day of next week's lesson.

STEP ONE: **Plan the narrative**

Your first step is to plan out the narrative by choosing a theme (this will also serve as your title) and selecting the events you'll write about.

On the next page, you'll see a list of events, written out chronologically for you, from the life of Alexander the Great. The bolded entries are main events; the indented entries are further details about those main events. (These details are taken from Plutarch's "Life of Alexander," written in AD 75.)

Your assignment is to write a chronological narrative based on these events. This chronological narrative can be one paragraph or several paragraphs, but it must be at least 150 words long and no longer than 300 words.

You may choose where your narrative begins and ends, but the narrative must progress chronologically forward at all times. Do not try to include all of the events! Instead, you will

22. Susan Casey, *The Wave: In Pursuit of the Rogues, Freaks, and Giants of the Ocean* (Doubleday, 2010) pp. 3–4.

need to select which events to use and which ones to leave out. This will force you to pick a "theme" for your chronological narrative.

For example: if you decide that your chronological narrative will be about "Alexander's Invasions," you might want to start your chronological narrative at 334 BC, the invasion of Persia, and only include the following events:

Invaded Persia in 334 BC
Invaded Egypt in 332 BC
Defeated Darius for a second time
Declared himself king of Persia
Invaded India in 326 BC

because all of those events have something to do with Alexander's invasions.

If, on the other hand, you wanted to write a chronological narrative about "Alexander's Early Life," you might choose the following events:

Born in 356 BC
Son of Philip II, king of Macedon
Tamed the horse Bucephalus at age 10
Taught by Aristotle from ages 13 to 16
Fought at his father's side beginning in 338 BC

and ignore the Persians completely.

Because this is the first time you've written a chronological narrative, you may use either of the lists above. Here are other possible themes:

"The Beginning of Alexander's Reign"
"The End of Alexander's Life"
"Alexander and Persia"

Choose a theme and select four or five main (bolded) events to use in your chronological narrative. (You can also come up with a theme of your own.)

If you have difficulty, ask your instructor for help.

EVENTS IN ALEXANDER THE GREAT'S LIFE

Born in 356 BC
Mother, Olympia
Son of Philip II, king of Macedon
Philip conquered most of Greece
Greek cities added to Macedonian kingdom
Tamed the horse Bucephalus at age 10
Philip intended to buy horse
Horse: wild, unmanageable
Alexander asked to ride the horse
Promised his father: If I can't ride it, I'll pay for it
Horse was afraid of shadow
Turned horse towards sun, rode horse

Taught by Aristotle from ages 13 to 16
- Most famous philosopher in the world at this time
- Gave Alexander lifelong thirst for knowledge
- Interested in medicine, philosophy, history

Fought at his father's side beginning in 338 BC
- Led his father's army to victory, Battle of Chaeronea

Father assassinated in 336 BC
- Assassin was bodyguard, Pausanias
- Pausanias then killed by rest of bodyguard

Succeeded his father to the throne
- Twenty years old
- Had all of his rivals to the throne murdered
- Greek cities rebelled, had to reconquer them

Invaded Persia in 334 BC
- Went to the city of Gordium
- Learned myth about Gordian knot (who untied it would rule the world)
- Cut the knot
- Defeated the Persian king Darius at the Battle of Issus
- Darius fled, left his wife, mother, and daughters behind
- Alexander treated the women with respect

Invaded Egypt in 332 BC
- Proclaimed pharaoh
- Founded Alexandria

Defeated Darius for a second time
- Darius and army defeated at the Battle of Gaugamela
- Darius once again forced to flee
- Alexander captured Babylon and Susa
- Darius was assassinated by his own kinsman, Bessus

Declared himself king of Persia

Invaded India in 326 BC
- Crossed the Indus River
- Fought against Indian king Porus and troop of elephants
- Troops mutinied and refused to go any farther
- Alexander, furious, shut himself into his tent
- Finally Alexander agreed to go home

Returned to Babylon
- Marched back through the Gedrosian Desert
- Famine, thirst, disease killed 3/4 of men before he got home

Died in 323 BC
- Came down with a fever in early June
- Fever lasted for weeks

In the last few days, unable to speak or name a successor
Died on June 28th
Kingdom divided among his generals

STEP TWO: **Become familiar with time and sequence words**

Remember, when you write a chronological narrative of a past event, you ask: Who did what to whom? (Or What was done to what?) In this exercise, most of this information is supplied so that you can concentrate on making the narrative flow smoothly forward in chronological order. (In later assignments, after you've had a little more practice, you'll take more responsibility for finding the information as well.)

In this first chronological narrative assignment, concentrating on using **time** and **sequence** words to turn the listed events into clear, straightforward prose. For example, if you were writing a narrative that included this main event:

Invaded Persia in 334 BC
Went to the city of Gordium
Learned myth about Gordian knot (who untied it would rule the world)
Cut the knot
Defeated the Persian king Darius at the Battle of Issus
Darius fled, left his wife, mother, and daughters behind
Alexander treated the women with respect

one part of your narrative might end up sounding like this:

> Alexander invaded Persia in 334. **Eventually,** he travelled to the city of Gordium. In the city was a knot known as the Gordian knot; according to myth, whoever could untie the knot would rule the world. **As soon as** he heard the myth, Alexander drew his sword and cut the knot instead.
>
> **After some time,** Alexander met the Persian king, Darius, and the Persian army at the Battle of Issus. He defeated Darius in battle. **Immediately afterwards,** Darius fled. He fled so quickly that he left his wife, mother, and daughters behind him. But **when** Alexander realized this, he treated the women with respect.[23]

Look back at the words in bold print. All of them are **time** and **sequence** words—words that you use in a chronological narrative to show the order in which events happen.

---

23. Note: If you know other details about Alexander (more about the Gordian knot, or the Battle of Issus, or the Persian king Darius), you may certainly use them to make the narrative more interesting. But remember: this isn't required, and you can't go over 300 words for the entire composition.

Plan on using the following list of time and sequence words as you construct your chronological narrative. Try to use at least three of them, without repeating any. Finish today's work by reading the time words out loud.

TIME AND SEQUENCE WORDS
For chronological narratives [SET AS 2 COLUMNS]

Words for events that happen before any others
First
At first
In the beginning
Before

Words for events that happen at the same time
When
At that point
At that moment
While

Words for an event that happens very soon after a previous event
When
As soon as
Soon
Shortly/shortly afterwards
Presently
Before long
Not long after
Immediately

Words for an event that happens after a previous event—but you're not exactly sure whether a long or short period of time elapsed first
Next
Afterwards
After
After some time
Subsequently
Following/following that
Furthermore
Then

Words for an event that happened long after another event
Eventually
Later/later on
Finally

Words for an event that happened after another event—AND was caused by the previous event
As a result
As a consequence
Since
Because
Seeing that

You've finished a long assignment today. At the beginning of next week, you'll return to your list of events and use it to write a brief chronological narrative.

Week 5: Chronological Narrative of a Scientific Discovery

Day One: Finishing the Chronological Narrative of a Past Event

Focus: Learning how to write a chronological narrative of a past event

At the end of last week, you began to work on writing a chronological narrative of a past event. You selected events from a list, and also read through time and sequence words.

Today, you'll finish this narrative.

STEP ONE: **Review the topos**

Turn to the Chronological Narrative of a Past Event chart in your Composition Notebook. Add the bolded points below under the "Remember" column.

Chronological Narrative of a Past Event

Definition: A narrative telling what happened in the past and in what sequence

Procedure	Remember
1. Ask *Who did what to whom?* (Or, *What was done to what?*)	**1. Select your main events to go with your theme.**
2. Create main points by placing the answers in chronological order.	**2. Make use of time words.**

You will find a copy of the Time and Sequence Words reference sheet in Appendix I. Take it out and place it in the Reference section of your Composition Notebook, just after the Chronological Narrative of a Past Event page.

STEP TWO: **Write the narrative**

Now use the events list you worked on at the end of last week and write your own chronological narrative, based on it.

Here's a summary of your assignment:

1. This chronological narrative can be one paragraph or several paragraphs, but it must be at least 150 words long and no longer than 300 words.
2. You may choose where your narrative begins and ends, but the narrative must progress chronologically forward at all times.
3. Do not try to include all of the events! Instead, you will need to select which events to use and which ones to leave out. This will force you to pick a "theme" for your chronological narrative.
4. Use three or more time words in your narrative.

Try not to use the identical words of the events list. For example, if you are using the following events:

Son of Philip II, king of Macedon
Philip conquered most of Greece
Greek cities added to Macedonian kingdom

try not to write:

*Alexander was the **son** of Philip II, **king** of Macedon. Philip conquered most of Greece. He added the **Greek cities** to the **Macedonian kingdom**.*

Changing the common nouns and their adjectives (the words in bold print) is a simple and straightforward way to make your narrative sound different:

*Alexander was the **heir** of Philip II, **ruler** of Macedon. Philip conquered most of Greece. He added the **city-states of Greece** to **his realm**.*

If you have difficulty, ask your instructor for help. And when you're finished, show your composition to your instructor.

Day Two: Outlining Exercise

Focus: Finding the main idea in each paragraph of a scientific narrative

STEP ONE: **Read**

Read the following excerpt from *100 Greatest Science Discoveries of All Time* by Kendall Haven.

Andreas Vesalius was born in Brussels in 1515. His father, a doctor in the royal court, had collected an exceptional medical library. Young Vesalius pored over each volume and showed immense curiosity about the functioning of living things. He often caught and dissected small animals and insects.

At age 18 Vesalius traveled to Paris to study medicine.

Physical dissection of animal or human bodies was not a common part of accepted medical study. If a dissection *had* to be performed, professors lectured while a barber did the actual cutting. Anatomy was taught from the drawings and translated texts of Galen, a Greek doctor whose texts were written in 50 BC.

Vesalius was quickly recognized as brilliant but arrogant and argumentative. During the second dissection he attended, Vesalius snatched the knife from the barber and demonstrated both his skill at dissection and his knowledge of anatomy, to the amazement of all in attendance.

As a medical student, Vesalius became a ringleader, luring his fellow students to raid the boneyards of Paris for skeletons to study and graveyards for bodies to dissect. Vesalius regularly braved vicious guard dogs and the gruesome stench of Paris's mound of Monfaucon (where the bodies of executed criminals were dumped) just to get his hands on freshly killed bodies to study.

In 1537 Vesalius graduated and moved to the University of Padua (Italy), where he began a long series of lectures—each centered on actual dissections and tissue experiments. Students and other professors flocked to his classes, fascinated by his skill and by the new reality he uncovered—muscles, arteries, nerves, veins, and even thin structures of the human brain.

This series culminated in January 1540, with a lecture he presented to a packed theater in Bologna, Italy. Like all other medical students, Vesalius had been trained to believe in Galen's work. However Vesalius had long been

> troubled because so many of his dissections revealed actual structures that differed from Galen's descriptions.
>
> In this lecture, for the first time in public, Vesalius revealed his evidence to discredit Galen and to show that Galen's descriptions of curved human thighbones, heart chambers, segmented breast bones, etc., better matched the anatomy of apes than humans. In his lecture, Vesalius detailed more than 200 discrepancies between actual human anatomy and Galen's descriptions. Time after time, Vesalius showed that what every doctor and surgeon in Europe relied on fit better with apes, dogs, and sheep than the human body. Galen, and every medical text based on his work, were wrong.[24]

STEP TWO: **Construct a one-level outline**

Begin to outline this passage by looking for the main idea in each section of text. You'll see that the passage above is divided into five sections (there's an extra space between each section). For each section, try to come up with a single sentence that states the main idea.

Remember, you shouldn't try to include as much information as possible in this single sentence. Ask yourself two sets of questions:

1. What is the main thing or person that this section is about? *Or* Is the section about an idea?
2. Why is that thing or person important? *Or* What did that thing or person do/what was done to it? *Or* What is the idea?

Try that for the first section. What is the main thing or person that this section is about? (That should be easy—whose name is mentioned three times?)

✦

Vesalius (of course).

Now look at everything else in the passage, which tells you a number of different facts about Andreas Vesalius's early life—where he was born, what he read, what he did, what field of study he decided to pursue. All of these facts don't belong in your sentence. But the last three (he read medical books, he dissected animals, he went to medical school) all tell you about a single quality that Vesalius had—a quality that makes him important. He was important because he was. . .

Try finishing that sentence now.

What did you come up with? It should sound like one of these:

I. Vesalius was curious about living things.

24. Kendall Haven, *100 Greatest Science Discoveries of All Time* (Libraries Unlimited, 2007), pp. 7–8.

I. Vesalius was interested in living things.
I. Vesalius was curious about how living things functioned.

Now work on coming up with a summary sentence for each one of the remaining four sections. (You can use the sentence we gave you for the first section.) Continue to use Roman numerals for the summary sentences, like this:

I. Vesalius was curious about living things.
II. Second sentence
III. Third sentence
IV. Fourth sentence
V. Fifth sentence

For this assignment, try to use complete sentences (although this isn't always necessary in an outline).

If you have difficulty, ask your instructor for help. And when you are finished, check your assignment with your instructor.

Day Three: Analyzing the Topos

Focus: Understanding the form of a chronological narrative about a scientific discovery

The passage you outlined in your last writing session is an example of this week's topos: a **chronological narrative of a scientific discovery** (Vesalius's disproving Galen's theories about anatomy).

When you write a chronological narrative about a scientific discovery (or event), you explain *what happened* and *in what sequence*—just as you do when you write a chronological narrative of a past event, as you did last week. There are two major kinds of scientific events that you can narrate chronologically:

1. a scientific discovery or advance, and
2. a scientific process that happened in the past.

Vesalius's disproving of Galen's theories is an example of the first kind of scientific event. The birth of a star, the retreat of glaciers, and the fossilization of a fallen *T. rex* are examples of the second kind.

Later in the year, you'll work on chronological narratives about scientific processes. This week, you'll examine how a chronological narrative about a scientific *discovery* is put together.

STEP ONE: **Examine model passages**

When you set out to write a chronological narrative about a scientific discovery, you aim to answer two questions:

What steps or events led to the discovery?

In what sequence did these steps or events happen?

Look again at the outline you made of the passage from *100 Greatest Science Discoveries of All Time*. The exact words you used will be different, but the outline probably looks something like this:

I. Vesalius was curious about living things.
II. Dissection was not done in medical school.
III. Vesalius learned through dissection.
IV. Vesalius then gave lectures based on dissection.
V. Vesalius showed that Galen was wrong.

Notice that each one of these main points, except for the second, lists a step or event that led to Vesalius's contradiction of Galen. The points are also put into chronological order. First, young Vesalius was curious; because he was curious, he dissected and learned; after he learned, he lectured; finally, the lectures showed that Galen was wrong.

So what is the second point doing in the narrative?

Because a chronological narrative about a scientific discovery tells us how a scientist moves from one understanding of the world to another (in this case, from Galen's old understanding of anatomy to Vesalius's new understanding), you will often need to provide a paragraph or section that explains what the old understanding of the world was *before* the discovery. The second point in the narrative tells us about the old approach to anatomy; we need to know this so that we can appreciate just how different Vesalius's new ideas were.

So a chronological narrative about a scientific discovery usually includes a "background point" somewhere near the beginning—a paragraph that gives necessary background information.

Here is a second example of a **chronological narrative of a scientific discovery,** from *Seven African-American Scientists* by Robert C. Hayden and Richard Loehle. You may not be familiar with the term "Far East," which generally refers to China, Japan, Korea, and other eastern Asian countries.

> The peanut harvest was a large one, but the market for peanuts was small. More peanuts were grown than could be sold. Besides, peanuts from the Far East were being imported and sold in America for less money than American-grown peanuts. Acres of peanuts rotted in the ground—and [George Washington] Carver received much criticism. He faced a real

dilemma. What could be done with all the surplus peanuts that he had talked the farmers into growing in place of cotton? Being the scientist that he was, Carver decided that he would take the peanut apart. He wanted to know what it was made of. What would it be good for? He sought to find new commercial uses for the peanut.

In his lab, George Carver began to shell peanuts by the handful. Saving the reddish peanut skins and broken shells, Carver ground the peanuts themselves into a fine powder. He heated the powder and then put this peanut mash under a hand press. An oily substance dripped into a cup beneath the press.

Carver then heated this oil at various temperatures to see what happened to it. The oil was broken down into other substances, which Carver used to make soap, cooking oil, and rubbing oil for the skin.

By adding certain chemicals to the dried peanut cake that remained in the press, Carver extracted a substance similar to cow's milk, though it had less calcium than animal milk. From this milk, he was able to make cheese.

Next, Carver removed the dried, crumbly, peanut cake left in the press and placed it into a glass vessel. He added water and enzymes. The enzymes were substances that would help break down any proteins in the peanut. This mixture was placed in a warm-water bath to activate the enzymes. By this technique, the different proteins in the peanut were separated, and Carver showed that a pound of peanuts contained the same amount of protein as a pound of beefsteak.[25]

In this chronological narrative of a scientific discovery, the very first paragraph is the "background point"—the one that gives you the information you need to understand *why* George Washington Carver set out to discover new uses for the peanut. With your pencil, underline "George Washington Carver" once and "faced a real dilemma" twice. Carver had talked farmers into growing peanuts instead of cotton—and now, they had too many peanuts.

Each of the following sections describes, in order, the steps Carver took to discover more about peanuts.

In the second section, draw a box around the word "began." This is the beginning—the first step Carver took. Now ask yourself: What did Carver begin to do? Did he discover anything? Use your pencil to underline the following verbs twice: "to shell," "ground," "heated," "put." These verbs show you that Carver's first step was simply to *process* the peanuts—to turn them into powder, mash, and oil.

---

25. Robert C. Hayden and Richard Loehle, *Seven African-American Scientists* (Twenty-First Century Books, 1992), pp. 120–122.

In the third section, draw a box around the word "then." This time word shows you that the third section happened, chronologically, after the second. Circle the word "oil" in the first sentence, and then circle "soap, cooking oil, and rubbing oil" in the second sentence. After Carver processed the peanuts, he was able to turn the oil into three other products.

In the fourth section, draw a box around the word "remained." Then circle "dried peanut cake" in the first sentence and "cheese" in the second sentence. Carver's next step, after he used the oil, was to make use of what was left *after* the oil was drained away; he made cheese out of the remaining peanut material.

In the fifth section, draw a box around the word "Next." This time word shows you that Carver's final actions took place *after* he made cheese from the peanut cake. Circle "peanut cake left in the press" in the first sentence and "protein" in the last sentence. The last thing Carver did with the leftover peanut cake was analyze it for protein.

Now look at the summary below:

> There were too many peanuts.
> Carver began by processing the peanuts.
> Then Carver drained off the oil and used it.
> Afterwards, Carver made cheese from the peanut cake.
> Next, Carver analyzed the leftover peanut cake for protein.

The original narrative has a lot more details in it—but this summary shows you exactly how the writer tells each step in Carver's discoveries in chronological order.

STEP TWO: **Write down the pattern of the topos**

Now copy the following onto a blank sheet of paper in the Reference section of your Composition Notebook. You will be adding to this page as you learn more about chronological narratives of scientific events, so leave plenty of room at the bottom of the page.

Chronological Narrative of a Scientific Discovery

Definition: A narrative telling what steps or events led to a discovery, and in what sequence

Procedure	Remember
1. Ask, *What steps or events led to the discovery?*	1. May need a background paragraph explaining the circumstances that existed before the discovery.
2. Ask, *In what sequence did these steps or events happen?*	
3. Create main points by placing the answers in chronological order.	

Day Four: Practicing the Topos

Focus: Learning how to write a chronological narrative about a scientific discovery

Like a chronological narrative about a past event, a chronological narrative about a scientific discovery can be used as a science composition on its own, or as an introduction to a paper which then goes on to examine scientific concepts. The astronomy textbook *In Quest of the Universe* begins like this:

> On the night of March 23, 1993, amateur astronomer David Levy photographed part of the sky near the planet Jupiter. His friends, fellow astronomers Carolyn Shoemaker and her husband Eugene Shoemaker, spotted something unusual in the picture: a comet that had broken up into about 20 pieces. The comet became known officially as Comet Shoemaker-Levy 9 (the ninth comet discovered by these three sky-watchers) and unofficially as the "string of pearls" comet.
>
> When astronomers announced the news of the comet on June 1, 1993, they had traced its path closely enough to tell that it had come under the influence of Jupiter's powerful gravitational field. They had deduced that the comet was pulled apart by Jupiter's gravity in July of 1992. They predicted that the comet would crash into Jupiter on or about July 25, 1994. . . .
>
> By the time of the predicted impacts, the entire world was watching, linked together by the Internet and the television. The Hubble Space Telescope was trained on Jupiter, as was the Galileo space probe then approaching the Jupiter system, as well as most major observatories around the world and untold numbers of amateur telescopes. It has been said that more telescopes were aimed at the same spot—Jupiter—than ever before or since, and the viewers were not disappointed.[26]

This is definitely a more gripping beginning than "Comets are thought to be material that coalesced in the outer solar system, the remnants of small eddies. These objects would feel the gravitational forces of Jupiter and Saturn, and many would fall onto those planets."[27]

Today, you'll practice putting together a chronological narrative of your own.

---

26. Theo Koupelis, *In Quest of the Universe,* sixth ed. (Jones and Bartlett, 2010), pp. 1–2.
27. Koupelis, p. 198.

STEP ONE: **Plan the narrative**

Your first step is to plan out the narrative.

You'll need to approach the chronological narrative about a scientific discovery a little differently than the narrative about a past event. Because a scientific discovery is reached by a related series of steps, you can't pick and choose among the main events as easily as you did when you wrote about Alexander the Great. (You could leave out Alexander's invasion of India and still have a good historical narrative—but if you left out Vesalius's determination to find corpses and dissect them, his new discoveries about human anatomy wouldn't make sense.)

Instead, when you write the narrative of a scientific discovery, you make three choices:

1. Where to begin and end.
2. How much detail to use.
3. Where to put the "background paragraph," and how much information to include in it.

Below, you'll see a list of events, written out chronologically for you, covering Edward Jenner's discovery of the smallpox vaccine. The information for this list was taken from *Doctors and Discoveries: Lives That Created Today's Medicine* (Houghton Mifflin, 2002) by John G. Simmons and *Diseases: Finding the Cure* by Robert Mulcahy (The Oliver Press, 1996).

Your assignment is to write a chronological narrative based on these events. This chronological narrative can be one paragraph or several paragraphs, but it must be at least 150 words long and no longer than 300 words.

1. Begin planning out your narrative by circling the events that belong in the "background information" paragraph of your composition.
2. Next, mark a beginning and ending place for your composition.
3. Each main event in bold print is followed by details about that main event. Draw a light line through the details you don't intend to include.

EVENTS LEADING TO JENNER'S DISCOVERY
OF THE SMALLPOX VACCINE

Smallpox was a great danger in the eighteenth century
Killed 40 million people in the eighteenth century
Half of the people who caught smallpox died
Smallpox victims kept in "smallpox houses"
No reliable way to avoid smallpox
Many doctors gave people mild cases of smallpox to protect them
The "mild cases" sometimes killed the patients
Edward Jenner born in 1749
Inoculated against smallpox as a child
Inoculation made him sick
Kept in a smallpox house while he was sick

- **Jenner began to train as a doctor in 1762**
  - Apprentice to a surgeon for eight years
  - Entered St. George's Hospital in 1770
  - Studied surgery and anatomy
- **Jenner began to practice medicine in his home town in 1773**
- **Jenner noticed that milkmaids were not getting smallpox**
  - Knew milkmaids often had cowpox
  - Cowpox gave cows blisters on their udders
  - Milkmaids sometimes got blisters on hands and arms
  - Cowpox gave patients a fever that lasted 4 days
  - Many local people believed that cowpox gave them immunity to smallpox
- **Jenner investigated relationship between smallpox and cowpox**
  - Kept records of cowpox outbreaks
  - Discovered two forms of cowpox
  - Decided only one form of cowpox gave immunity to smallpox
- **Jenner inoculated James Phipps on May 14, 1796**
  - James Phipps was eight years old
  - Jenner used pus from a cowpox blister
  - Jenner scraped Phipps's arm and put pus into it
  - Phipps had a small fever
  - Jenner tried to give Phipps a mild case of smallpox
  - Phipps was immune
- **Jenner tested his vaccine on 23 other people**
  - Did not know why vaccination worked
  - Believed his observations were correct
- **Jenner published his results**
  - At first, other doctors skeptical
  - Royal Society of Medicine refused to accept his findings
  - Some people afraid cowpox would make them act like cows
- **Vaccine slowly accepted**
  - Parliament gave Jenner money in 1802 to continue his research
  - 12,000 people vaccinated in 1804
  - British government began to give the vaccines in 1808
  - Deaths decreased to 600 per year

STEP TWO: Use time and sequence words

You'll use time and sequence words in this composition, just as you did in last week's assignment.

Turn to the Chronological Narrative of a Scientific Discovery chart in your Composition Notebook. Add the bolded point below under the "Remember" column.

Chronological Narrative of a Scientific Discovery
Definition: A narrative telling what steps or events led to a discovery, and in what sequence

Procedure

1. Ask, *What steps or events led to the discovery?*
2. Ask, *In what sequence did these steps or events happen?*
3. Create main points by placing the answers in chronological order.

Remember

1. May need a background paragraph explaining the circumstances that existed before the discovery.
2. **Make use of time words.**

Now pull out your Time and Sequence Words list and keep it in view as you write. Refer to your list of time words as you construct your chronological narrative. Try to use at least three of them, without repeating any.

STEP THREE: **Write the narrative**

Here's a summary of your assignment:

1. This chronological narrative can be one paragraph or several paragraphs, but it must be at least 150 words long and no longer than 300 words.

2. You may choose where your narrative begins and ends, but the narrative must progress chronologically forward at all times.

3. The only exception is your "background paragraph," where you describe what the world was like before the smallpox vaccine. This paragraph should come early in the composition (first or second).

4. Do not include all of the details.

5. Use three or more time words in your narrative.

6. Try not to use the identical words of the events list. As you did last week, change the common nouns and adjectives if necessary so that your narrative is not a direct copy of the events list.

If you have difficulty, ask your instructor for help. And when you're finished, show your composition to your instructor.

Week 6: Chronological Narrative of a Past Event

Day One: Original Narration Exercise

Focus: Summarizing a narrative by choosing the main events and listing them chronologically

STEP ONE: **Read**

Read the following excerpt from *The Once and Future King* by T. H. White. The "Once and Future King" is King Arthur; the first half of the novel describes Arthur's boyhood. White imagines that young Arthur (known as "the Wart" by his adoptive family) was tutored by the magician Merlin, who taught him about the natural world by turning him into different animals. Archimedes is Merlin's pet owl.

— — —

He was fast asleep when Archimedes came for him.

"Eat this," said the owl, and handed him a dead mouse.

The Wart felt so strange that he took the furry atom without protest, and popped it into his mouth without any feelings that it was going to be nasty. So he was not surprised when it turned out to be excellent, with a fruity taste like eating a peach with the skin on, though naturally the skin was not so nice as the mouse.

"Now, we had better fly," said the owl. "Just flip to the window-sill here, to get accustomed to yourself before we take off."

Wart jumped for the sill and automatically gave himself an extra kick with his wings, just as a high jumper swings his arms. He landed on the sill with a thump, as owls are apt to do, did not stop himself in time, and toppled straight out of the window. "This," he thought to himself, cheerfully, "is where I break my neck." It was curious, but he was not taking life seriously. He felt the castle walls streaking past him, and the ground and the moat swimming up. He kicked with his wings, and the ground sank again, like water in a leaking well. In a second that kick of his wings had lost its effect, and the ground was welling up. He kicked again. It was strange, going forward with the earth ebbing and flowing beneath him, in the utter silence of his down-fringed feathers.

"For heaven's sake," panted Archimedes, bobbing in the dark air beside him, "stop flying like a woodpecker. Anybody would take you for a Little Owl, if the creatures had been imported. What you are doing is to give yourself flying speed with one flick of your wings. You then raise on that flick until you have lost flying speed and begin to stall. Then you give another just as you are beginning to drop out of the air, and do a switch-back. It is confusing to keep up with you."

"Well," said the Wart recklessly, "if I stop doing this I shall go bump altogether."

"Idiot," said the owl. "Waver your wings all the time, like me instead of doing these jumps with them."

The Wart did what he was told, and was surprised to find that the earth became stable and moved underneath him without tilting, in a regular pour. He did not feel himself to be moving at all.

"That's better."

"How curious everything looks," observed the boy with some wonder, now that he had time to look about him.

And, indeed, the world did look curious. In some ways the best description of it would be to say that it looked like a photographer's negative, for he was seeing one ray beyond the spectrum which is visible to human beings. An infra-red camera will take photographs in the dark, when we cannot see, and it will also take photographs in daylight. The owls are the same, for it is untrue that they can only see at night. They see in the day just as well, only they happen to possess the advantage of seeing pretty well at night also. So naturally they prefer to do their hunting then, when other creatures are more at their mercy. To the Wart the green trees would have looked whitish in the daytime, as if they were covered with apple blossom, and now, at night, everything had the same kind of different look. It was like flying in a twilight which had reduced everything to shades of the same colour, and, as in the twilight, there was a considerable amount of gloom.

"Do you like it?" asked the owl.

"I like it very much. Do you know, when I was a fish there were parts of the water which were colder or warmer than the other parts, and now it is the same in the air."

"The temperature," said Archimedes, "depends on the vegetation of the bottom. Woods or weeds, they make it warm above them."

"Well," said the Wart, "I can see why the reptiles who had given up being fishes decided to become birds. It certainly is fun."

"You are beginning to fit things together," remarked Archimedes. "Do you mind if we sit down?"

"How does one?"

"You must stall. That means you must drive yourself up until you lose flying speed, and then, just as you feel yourself beginning to tumble—why, you sit down. Have you never noticed how birds fly upward to perch? They don't come straight down on the branch, but dive below it and then rise. At the top of their rise they stall and sit down."

"But birds land on the ground too. And what about mallards on the water? They can't rise to sit on that."

"Well, it is perfectly possible to land on flat things, but more difficult. You have to glide in at stalling speed all the way, and then increase your wind resistance by cupping your wings, dropping your feet, tail, etc. You may have noticed that few birds do it gracefully. Look how a crow thumps down and how the mallard splashes. The spoon-winged birds like heron and plover seem to do it best. As a matter of fact, we owls are not so bad at it ourselves."

"And the long-winged birds like swifts, I suppose they are the worst, for they can't rise from a flat surface at all?"

"The reasons are different," said Archimedes, "yet the fact is true. But need we talk on the wing? I am getting tired."

"So am I."

"Owls usually prefer to sit down every hundred yards."

The Wart copied Archimedes in zooming up toward the branch which they had chosen. He began to fall just as they were above it, clutched it with his furry feet at the last moment, swayed backward and forward twice, and found that he had landed successfully. He folded up his wings.[28]

STEP TWO: **Note important events**

On your scratch paper, write down four or five phrases or short sentences that will remind you of the things that happened in the story. *Do not use more than five phrases or short sentences!* Remember, you're not supposed to write down *everything* that happens in the story—just the most important events. The most important events are the ones that help the story make sense; if you took them out of the original passage, you wouldn't understand the rest of the story. (For example, if you left out the fact that the Wart turned into an owl, would the flying scenes make sense to you?)

Be sure to write the events down in the same order that they happen in the story.

If you have trouble with this assigment, ask your instructor for help.

28. T. H. White, *The Once and Future King* (Ace Books, 1958), pp. 162–165.

STEP THREE: **Write summary sentences**

After you've written down your four or five phrases or sentences, try to combine them into three or four sentences. You can do this by putting two phrases in the same sentence (for example, "Wart ate a magic mouse" and "Wart turned into an owl" could be combined into "Wart ate a magic mouse that turned him into an owl"). Or you may find that one or more of your jotted notes turns out to be unnecessary. (If you wrote down "Wart saw like an owl" and "Wart could see in the dark," you don't really need one of those sentences; both describe the same change.

Try to avoid listing minor details; instead, stick to main events. Minor details don't change the sense of the story. (It doesn't really matter that the Wart learned to flick his wings and stall—without that detail, we can still understand the story.)

Say your three or four sentences out loud several times before writing them down. After you've written the sentences down, ask your instructor to check them.

If you have trouble, ask your instructor for help.

Day Two: Outlining Exercise

Focus: Finding the main idea in each paragraph of a historical narrative

STEP ONE: **Read**

Read the following excerpt from *Historical Catastrophes: Hurricanes and Tornadoes* by Billye Walker Brown and Walter R. Brown. This passage is about Colonel Joseph Duckworth, the first man to fly a plane into a hurricane.

> [Colonel Joseph] Duckworth had grown up with airplanes. He began by flying freight along the southern coasts of the Great Lakes, before airplanes had many instruments at all. Flying so low that he could see the ground, he fought ice and wind for several years. Then, for the ten years before World War II began, he flew for Eastern Airlines, learning how to use each of the new instruments as it became available. During the war years, the Army Air Corps assigned him the command of the Instrument Flying School at Bryan, Texas.
>
> The Texas air was clear and bright in Bryan on the morning of July 27, 1943. Lt. Ralph O'Hair and Col. Duckworth sat enjoying their second cup of coffee when O'Hair mentioned that Galveston [a coastal Texas city] was

threatened again by a hurricane that was moving inland from the Gulf [of Mexico].

"Let's go down and get an AT-6,"[29] Duckworth suggested calmly. "I'd like to fly right into the center of that thing."

. . . Without knowing exactly how to approach the storm, Duckworth and O'Hair used their vast experience of flying around and through clouds to pick the easiest path through the tremendous winds around the hurricane. Even so, they were tossed around "like a stick in a dog's mouth," as they described it later.

They reached the eye over land, somewhere between Galveston and Houston. Reversing their course, they flew back to Bryan and landed.

There to meet them was the base's Weather Officer, Lt. William Jones-Burdick. He was excited by what the pilots told him.

"Sounds great, Colonel," Jones-Burdick said. "I certainly wish that I could have been along with you!"

Duckworth smiled broadly. "Okay," he said. "Hop in and we'll go back through."

This second flight, with a qualified meteorologist aboard, gave hurricane watchers their first instrument readings and expert observations from inside a major storm. Jones-Burdick carefully recorded the temperature of the air around him and described the clouds, turbulence, and rain.

Excited by Duckworth's success, the Weather Bureau requested the Air Force to send out three more flights during the 1943 hurricane season. . . and it was proven that hurricane air reconnaissance could gather some very valuable data for weather forecasters as well as the public.[30]

STEP TWO: **Construct a one-level outline**

Begin to outline this passage by looking for the main idea in each section of text. You'll see that the passage above is divided into five sections (there's an extra space between each section). For each section, try to come up with a single sentence that states the main idea. Remember:

---

29. An AT-6 was a single-engine airplane used for training pilots from the late 1930s through the 1950s. It was also known as the "North American T-6 Texan."

30. Billye Walker Brown and Walter R. Brown, *Historical Catastrophes: Hurricanes and Tornadoes* (Addison-Wesley, 1972), pp. 141–143.

don't try to include as much information as possible in this single sentence. Ask yourself two sets of questions:

1. What is the main thing or person that this section is about? *Or* Is the section about an idea?
2. Why is that thing or person important? *Or* What did that thing or person do/what was done to it? *Or* What is the idea?

You'll notice that this passage, unlike the others you've outlined, has dialogue in it; some parts of the passage are written more like a story. This dialogue makes the passage more interesting to read, but it shouldn't affect the answers to these questions.

Try asking the first question about the first section now. What is the main thing or person that this section is about?

The answer should be obvious:

✦

Joseph Duckworth.

Now look at everything else in the passage. There are many details about Joseph Duckworth's life—but you're not trying to include all of the information about Joseph Duckworth in a single sentence. Remember, you're trying to find the *main idea only.*

You may remember that you had a similar challenge in the first passage you outlined from *The Story of Mankind;* the passage contained a whole list of inventions and discoveries made by the Egyptians, and you summarized by saying something like "The Egyptians invented many things." In this passage, you need to take a similar approach. What important, single idea can you draw from all of these details about Joseph Duckworth?

If you're still puzzled, try finishing this sentence: "Joseph Duckworth was a very. . . ."

What did you come up with? Your sentence should sound like one of these:

I. Joseph Duckworth was a very experienced pilot. OR

I. Colonel Joseph Duckworth knew how to fly in many different situations.

Now work on coming up with a summary sentence or phrase for each one of the remaining sections. Don't worry about sticking to either sentences or phrases exclusively—use whichever form seems most natural. Remember to use Roman numerals.

If you have difficulty, ask your instructor for help. And when you are finished, check your assignment with your instructor.

Day Three: Analyzing the Topos

Focus: Understanding the form of a chronological narrative about a past event

The passage you outlined in your last writing session was a **chronological narrative of a past event.** You studied and practiced this form in the first week of this program; in this week, you'll review and practice some more.

STEP ONE: Review time and sequence words

Remember, a chronological narrative of a past event explains *what happened in the past* and *in what sequence.* Each one of the main points in your outline describes something that happened, and the passage itself presents these happenings in chronological order.

Your points probably sound something like the points below (although your exact words will be different):

I. ______________ Joseph Duckworth was a very experienced pilot.
II. ______________ A hurricane moves inland.
III. Presently______ Duckworth and O'Hair fly into the hurricane.
IV. Afterwords______ They make a second flight with a meteorologist.
V. later on______ Flights are made into other hurricanes.

Pull out your Time and Sequence Words sheet. Using your pencil, write an appropriate time word on the blank in front of each point. When you are finished, check your work with your instructor.

STEP TWO: Add dialogue and actions

In this passage, the authors *dramatize*—use dialogue (the words characters actually speak) and actions to move the narrative forward. First, they tell you about Duckworth's past. Then, when the narrative reaches the morning of the flight, the authors change techniques. Rather than simply listing events, they begin to tell a story.

Dialogue can make chronological narratives more interesting. Look at the following example from Harold Lamb's history of the Mongol invasions, *Genghis Khan and the Mongol Horde.* In this section, Genghis Khan's warriors are pursuing the defeated king Muhammad Shah, who has been driven from his country by the Mongol armies.

You will notice ellipses (. . .) in the passage below. Remember, ellipses show that words in the original have been left out of the excerpt.

> Muhammad Shah . . . decided to journey to other countries far in the west.
>
> Concealing his treasure in a strong tower, he started along the caravan road with his escort of nobles and warriors. . . He thought no army could follow as fast as his small company could ride. But within a few days he sighted the strange horsemen speeding through the dust at his heels. They scattered his followers and loosed a few arrows at him. . . .
>
> On his swift horse Muhammad escaped. Now he was really frightened. Leaving the highway, he doubled back toward the Caspian Sea. Only a few warriors remained with him.
>
> The once powerful Shah had become a fugitive, trying to save his life. And the few men who stayed with him lost respect for him. He was always running away!
>
> One night he found that arrows had passed through his tent. After that he slept out in a small shelter. "Is there no place on earth," he begged one of his officers, "where I can be safe from the Mongol thunderbolt?"
>
> Friends told him to hurry to the Caspian and take ship to a small island where he could hide.[31]

The author could have written "Muhammad Shah wondered if he would be safe anywhere." But instead, he gave Muhammad Shah dialogue—an actual speech that moves the narrative forward by showing why Muhammad Shah took sail to an island in the Caspian Sea (where he would die—although you should read the book if you want to find out how).

STEP THREE: Add to the pattern of the topos

Turn to the Chronological Narrative of a Past Event chart in your Composition Notebook. Add the bolded point below under the "Remember" column.

Chronological Narrative of a Past Event

Definition: A narrative telling what happened in the past and in what sequence

Procedure	Remember
1. Ask *Who did what to whom?* (Or *What was done to what?)*	1. Select your main events to go with your theme.
2. Create main points by placing the answers in chronological order.	2. Make use of time words.
	3. Consider using dialogue to hold the reader's interest.

31. Harold Lamb, *Genghis Khan and the Mongol Horde* (Random House, 1954), pp. 119–120.

Day Four: Practicing the Topos

Focus: Learning how to write a chronological narrative about a past event

Today, you'll practice putting together another chronological narrative about a past event.

STEP ONE: **Plan the narrative**

Below, you'll see a list of events, written out chronologically for you, about the sinking of the *Titanic.* The bolded entries are main events; the indented entries are further details about those main events. (Those details are taken from Logan Marshall's 1912 account, *The Sinking of the Titanic,* and Jack Winocour's *The Story of the Titanic: As Told by Its Survivors.*)

Your assignment is to write a chronological narrative based on these events. This chronological narrative can be one paragraph or several paragraphs, but it must be at least 150 words long and no longer than 300 words.

Remember that you should not try to include every event. For example, you could construct a narrative with only the following events:

Collision with the iceberg
Captain realized ship was sinking
Lifeboats launched
Ship sank between 2:05 and 2:20 AM

Leaving out the ice sightings, the initial flooding of the ship, and the sending of distress signals doesn't confuse the narrative at all; it is still clear that the ship collided with the iceberg, began to sink, and then sank after lifeboats were launched.

Look over the following events now, and mark three or four main (bolded) events to include in your narrative. If you have difficulty, ask your instructor for help.

EVENTS IN THE SINKING OF THE TITANIC

Ice sightings on April 14, 1912
- Captain Edward Smith received six ice warnings earlier
- Icebergs reported in *Titanic*'s path at 9:30 PM
- Report never reached captain
- *Titanic* continued at top speed
- Night was moonless and dark
- Lookouts had no binoculars
- Ice warning sent to *Titanic* from nearby ship *Californian*
- *Titanic* radio operator Jack Phillips ignored warning
  - "Shut up! Shut up! I am busy!" (Reported by *Californian*)

Collision with the iceberg

Iceberg sighted straight ahead at 11:40 PM
Lookouts telephoned first officer on the bridge
First officer (William Murdoch) ordered ship turned to port (left)
Ship collided with iceberg 37 seconds after sighting
Sharp edge of berg cut starboard (right) side of ship open
Passengers on deck played with ice chunks from berg

Ship began to flood

Officers told passengers there was no danger
"Oh, no, nothing at all, nothing at all. Just a mere nothing. We just hit an iceberg." (Reported by survivor Edith Louise Rosenbaum Russell)
Five separate compartments filled with water
Sixth compartment began to flood
Pumps in sixth compartment began to work
Pumps could remove 2,000 tons of water per hour
24,000 tons of water flooding into ship per hour

Captain realized ship was sinking

Shipbuilder Thomas Andrews told captain ship would sink in 1 1/2 hours
Captain Smith: "Give the command for all passengers to be on deck with life-belts on." (Reported by Logan Marshall)
Lifeboats readied just after midnight, in early hours of April 15
Lifeboats could only carry half the passengers on *Titanic*
Second officer Charles Lightoller asked captain for permission to fill boats
"Hadn't we better get the women and children into the boats, sir?" (Reported by Lightoller himself)
Lifeboats filled with women and children beginning 12:25 AM

Distress signals sent

White distress rocket launched 12:50 AM
Wireless operators sent out old distress signal CQD
"We have struck an iceberg. Badly damaged. Rush aid." (Reported by Logan Marshall)
Later also began to send new SOS signal as well
"Sinking by the head." (Reported by Jack Winocour)
Other ships received signal but were far away
Closest ship, *Carpathia,* responded but was four hours away
Signal transmitted to New York (*Titanic* destination)
Shipline official announced, "We are confident that there will be no loss of life." (Reported by Logan Marshall)

Lifeboats launched

First lifeboats launched beginning 1:10 AM
Passengers reluctant to leave ship
Many said, "This ship cannot sink; it is only a question of waiting until

another ship comes up and takes us off." (Reported by Jack Winocour)
First lifeboats only 1/4 full
Deck began to tilt, more passengers left ship
Later lifeboats overloaded
Last lifeboat launched 2:05 AM
Captain Smith went down with ship but told officers to save themselves.
"You have done your duty, boys. Now every man for himself." (Reported by survivor W. J. Mellers)

Ship sank between 2:05 and 2:20 AM
Propellers rose above water 2:05 AM
First funnel of ship fell into water
Water broke windows and flooded into bridge
Stern (rear) of ship rose above water
Electricity failed 2:18 AM
Second funnel fell
Ship split in half
Bow (front) section sank
Stern rose back up in water
Stern sank 2:20 AM
Only one lifeboat returned for people in water

Rescue arrived 4:10 AM
711 of 2,222 people in lifeboats
Carpathia arrived 4:10 AM
Carpathia picked up passengers until 8:50 AM
Five passengers died on board *Carpathia*
Carpathia set out for New York 8:50 AM

Survivors reached New York April 18

STEP TWO: Choose details and dialogue

When you write your chronological narrative, you won't include every detail listed under the main events; this would make your narrative too long and complicated. Instead, choose the details you want to highlight, and leave others out. Be sure that you include at least one line of dialogue.

For example, if you chose the following events:

Captain realized ship was sinking
Shipbuilder Thomas Andrews told captain ship would sink in 1 1/2 hours
Captain Smith: "Give the command for all passengers to be on deck with life-belts on." (Reported by Logan Marshall)
Lifeboats readied just after midnight, in early hours of April 15
Lifeboats could only carry half the passengers on *Titanic*

Second officer Charles Lightoller asked captain for permission to fill boats
"Hadn't we better get the women and children into the boats, sir?" (Reported by Lightoller himself)
Lifeboats filled with women and children beginning 12:25 AM

Lifeboats launched
First lifeboats launched beginning 1:10 AM
Passengers reluctant to leave ship
Many said, "This ship cannot sink; it is only a question of waiting until another ship comes up and takes us off." (Reported by Jack Winocour)
First lifeboats only 1/4 full
Deck began to tilt, more passengers left ship
Later lifeboats overloaded
Last lifeboat launched 2:05 AM
Captain Smith went down with ship but told officers to save themselves.
"You have done your duty, boys. Now every man for himself." (Reported by survivor W. J. Mellers)

you might write:

Captain Smith realized that the ship was sinking. The first lifeboats were launched at 1:10 AM, but many passengers refused to leave the ship. They said, "This ship cannot sink; it is only a question of waiting until another ship comes up and takes us off."

Or you might write:

The captain realized the Titanic *was doomed when the shipbuilder told him that the ship would sink in an hour and half. "Give the command for all passengers to be on deck with life-belts on," he ordered. The lifeboats were filled with women and children, and then were launched.*

Notice that only two or three details were included for one main event—and that another main event was simply stated with no details at all.

Read through your selected main events and mark which details and dialogue you intend to include. (You may find that you need to adjust your choices when you begin to write.)

STEP THREE: **Write the narrative**

As you begin to write, don't forget to include time and sequence words (as you learned in Week 4's lesson).

Here's a summary of your assignment:

1. This chronological narrative can be one paragraph or several paragraphs, but it must be at least 150 words long and no longer than 300 words.
2. The narrative must progress chronologically forward at all times.
3. Include at least one line of dialogue, but do not try to include all of the details!
4. Use two or more time words in your narrative.

5. If necessary, review the following rules about how to write dialogue:

Use quotation marks to surround a speaker's exact words.

If a dialogue tag ("he said," "Captain Smith said") comes before a speech, use a comma after the dialogue tag. The punctuation at the end of the speech itself goes *inside* the closing quotation mark.

Captain Smith said, "Put on your life jackets."

If the dialogue tag comes after the speech, place a comma, question mark, or exclamation point (but *not* a period) before the closing quotation mark.

"Put on your life jackets," Captain Smith said.

"Put on your life jackets!" Captain Smith said.

"Should we put on our life jackets?" Captain Smith said.

Do *not* write

"Put on your life jackets." Captain Smith said.

Dialogue should never just sit in the middle of a paragraph as an independent sentence, with no dialogue tag. Don't write

The ship began to sink. Captain Smith was concerned. "Put on your life jackets." The passengers began to obey.

Instead, write

The ship began to sink. Captain Smith was concerned. "Put on your life jackets," he told the passengers.

If you have difficulty, ask your instructor for help. And when you're finished, show your composition to your instructor.

Week 7: Chronological Narrative of a Scientific Discovery

Day One: Original Narration Exercise

Focus: Summarizing a narrative by choosing the main events and listing them chronologically

STEP ONE: **Read**

Read the following excerpt from *Tik-Tok of Oz* by L. Frank Baum. Baum wrote a whole series of books set in the magical land of Oz. In this chapter, Betsy Bobbin and her friend the Shaggy Man have joined up with the sky fairy Polychrome, daughter of the Rainbow (in Oz, the Rainbow is a person!), and the Princess Rose, who has been driven from her throne in the Rose Kingdom and is now in exile. Travelling together, the four find an old well. The Shaggy Man tries to draw water out of it using a windlass (a mechanism for cranking a bucket up out of a well), but the hook on the end of the windlass doesn't hold a bucket. Instead, the hook creaks up out of the well with a pile of copper junk on the end of it.

"Good gracious!" exclaimed Shaggy. "Here is a surprise, indeed!"

"What is it?" inquired Betsy, clinging to the windlass and panting for breath.

For answer the Shaggy Man grasped the bundle of copper and dumped it upon the ground, free of the well. Then he turned it over with his foot, spread it out, and to Betsy's astonishment the thing proved to be a copper man.

"Just as I thought," said Shaggy, looking hard at the object. "But unless there are two copper men in the world this is the most astonishing thing I ever came across."

At this moment the Rainbow's Daughter and the Rose Princess approached them, and Polychrome said:

"What have you found, Shaggy One?"

"Either an old friend, or a stranger," he replied.

"Oh, here's a sign on his back!" cried Betsy, who had knelt down to examine the man. "Dear me; how funny! Listen to this."

Then she read the following words, engraved upon the copper plates of the man's body:

SMITH & TINKER'S
Patent Double-Action, Extra-Responsive,
Thought-Creating, Perfect-Talking
MECHANICAL MAN
Fitted with our Special Clockwork Attachment.
Thinks, Speaks, Acts, and Does Everything but Live.

"Isn't he wonderful!" exclaimed the Princess.

"Yes; but here's more," said Betsy, reading from another engraved plate:

DIRECTIONS FOR USING:
For THINKING:—Wind the Clockwork
Man under his left arm, (marked No. 1).
For SPEAKING:—Wind the Clockwork
Man under his right arm, (marked No. 2).
For WALKING and ACTION:—Wind Clockwork Man
in the middle of his back, (marked No. 3).

N. B.[32]—This Mechanism is guaranteed to
work perfectly for a thousand years.

"If he's guaranteed for a thousand years," said Polychrome, "he ought to work yet."

"Of course," replied Shaggy. "Let's wind him up."

In order to do this they were obliged to set the copper man upon his feet, in an upright position, and this was no easy task. He was inclined to topple over, and had to be propped again and again. The girls assisted Shaggy, and at last Tik-Tok seemed to be balanced and stood alone upon his broad feet.

"Yes," said Shaggy, looking at the copper man carefully, "this must be, indeed, my old friend Tik-Tok, whom I left ticking merrily in the Land of Oz.

32. "N.B." is an abbreviation for the Latin phrase *nota bene,* which literally means "mark well." In English, the abbreviation N.B. stands for "Note this" or "Make a note of this fact."

But how he came to this lonely place, and got into that old well, is surely a mystery."

"If we wind him, perhaps he will tell us," suggested Betsy. "Here's the key, hanging to a hook on his back. What part of him shall I wind up first?"

"His thoughts, of course," said Polychrome, "for it requires thought to speak or move intelligently."

So Betsy wound him under his left arm, and at once little flashes of light began to show in the top of his head, which was proof that he had begun to think.

"Now, then," said Shaggy, "wind up his phonograph."

"What's that?" she asked.

"Why, his talking-machine. His thoughts may be interesting, but they don't tell us anything."

So Betsy wound the copper man under his right arm, and then from the interior of his copper body came in jerky tones the words: "Ma-ny thanks!"

"Hurrah!" cried Shaggy, joyfully, and he slapped Tik-Tok upon the back in such a hearty manner that the copper man lost his balance and tumbled to the ground in a heap. But the clockwork that enabled him to speak had been wound up and he kept saying: "Pick-me-up! Pick-me-up! Pick-me-up!" until they had again raised him and balanced him upon his feet, when he added politely: "Ma-ny thanks!"

"He won't be self-supporting until we wind up his action," remarked Shaggy; so Betsy wound it, as tight as she could—for the key turned rather hard—and then Tik-Tok lifted his feet, marched around in a circle and ended by stopping before the group and making them all a low bow.[33]

STEP TWO: Note important events

On your scratch paper, write down five or six phrases or short sentences that will remind you of the things that happened in the story. *Do not use more than six phrases or short sentences!* Remember, you're not supposed to write down *everything* that happens in the story—just the most important events. The most important events are the ones that help the story make sense; if you took them out of the original passage, you wouldn't understand the rest of the story.

Be sure to write the events down in the same order that they happen in the story.

If you have trouble with this assigment, ask your instructor for help.

STEP THREE: Write summary sentences

After you've written down your five or six phrases or sentences, try to combine them into three or four sentences. You can do this by putting two phrases in the same sentence, or you may find that one or more of your jotted notes turns out to be unnecessary.

---

33. L. Frank Baum, *Tik-Tok of Oz* (Reilly & Britton, 1914), pp. 72–74.

Try to avoid listing minor details; instead, stick to main events. Minor details don't change the sense of the story. (It doesn't really matter that when Tik-Tok first walked, he went in a circle; without that detail, we can still understand the story.)

Say your three or four sentences out loud several times before writing them down. After you've written the sentences down, ask your instructor to check them.

If you have trouble, ask your instructor for help.

Day Two: Outlining Exercise

Focus: Finding the main idea in each paragraph of a scientific narrative

STEP ONE: **Read**

Read the following excerpt from *Discoverer of the Unseen World: A Biography of Antoni van Leeuwenhoek* by Alma Smith Payne. In this passage, Payne explains how Leeuwenhoek became the first scientist to see single-celled organisms. The "new contrivance" Leeuwenhoek wanted to test was a tiny, clear tube of glass that would allow him to examine a drop of water underneath the lens of his microscope.

"Leeuwenhoek" is pronounced "leh-ven-hook."

\- - -

> In considering various ways to test the new contrivance, he thought of the appearance of the fresh water in Berkelse Mere, the inland lake located "about two hours from Delft." Its water was always clear in winter. But during the summer it lost this clearness and became whitish in color with little green clouds floating through it. The country people believed the change in the water's appearance was caused by the dews that occurred at that time; for this reason they called it "honeydew."
>
> This was hearsay, Leeuwenhoek reasoned. He would have to see for himself. Accepting a belief as a fact, without being curious enough to test it, was just the kind of thing that had been going on for centuries. Here was a chance for him, one of the most curious amateurs of science, to satisfy his curiosity about the nature of the inland lake. In so doing, he might also make a contribution to science. And it would give him an opportunity to test the quality of his newly made microscope and the clearness of his glass pipettes.
>
> So he journeyed to Berkelse Mere, to the southeast of Delft. Here he scooped up a generous sample of the marshy water and put it into a container. It

was too late to examine the water when he returned home that night. So he put the container in the office-laboratory where he did all of his work and study.

The following night he assembled his simple equipment and prepared to observe the Berkelse Mere water by the light of a single candle. First he sucked a drop of water into a little glass pipette which he had glued onto the rod of his newest microscope. In reality the instrument was "a simple magnifying glass," and this is what he always called it. It consisted of two matched oblong sheets of metal, which encased a tiny bi-convex, or football-shaped, lens. The whole thing was smaller than a small oblong football ticket.

Leeuwenhoek carefully lifted the microscope and pressed the minute lens close to one eye. He could not believe what he saw. There before him was a veritable swimming pool of earthly particles, green streaks, and little "animalcules"! The streaks were spirally wound like serpents and "orderly arranged, after the manner of copper or tin worms, which distillers use to cool their liquors as they distill over." The amazing thing about these little figures was that they were only as thick as a strand of hair (the common form of green alga *Spirogyra*).[34]

STEP TWO: **Construct a one-level outline**

Begin to outline this passage by looking for the main idea in each section of text. You'll see that the passage above is divided into four sections (there's an extra space between each section). For each section, try to come up with a single sentence that states the main idea.

Remember, you shouldn't try to include as much information as possible in this single sentence. Ask yourself two sets of questions:

1. What is the main thing or person that this section is about? *Or* Is the section about an idea?
2. Why is that thing or person important? *Or* What did that thing or person do/what was done to it? *Or* What is the idea?

Try that for the first section. What is the main thing or person that this section is about?

If your answer was "Leeuwenhoek," look again. The details in the section don't tell you about Leeuwenhoek. What do they tell you about?

Once you've answered that question, answer the second: Why is it important?

Use the same strategies to come up with summary sentences for each of the remaining three sections. Remember to use Roman numerals for the summary sentences.

34. Alma Payne Ralston, *Discoverer of the Unseen World: A Biography of Antoni van Leeuwenhoek* (The World Publishing Company, 1966), pp. 16–18.

For this assignment, try to use complete sentences (although this isn't always necessary in an outline).

If you have difficulty, ask your instructor for help. And when you are finished, check your assignment with your instructor.

Day Three: Analyzing the Topos

Focus: Understanding the form of a chronological narrative about a scientific discovery

The passage you outlined in your last writing session is another example of this week's topos: a **chronological narrative of a scientific discovery**. You have already studied several examples of this (Vesalius's discoveries in anatomy, George Washington Carver's work with the peanut, the sighting of Comet Shoemaker-Levy 9). Today, you'll expand your knowledge of this form.

STEP ONE: **Review the pattern of the topos**

Turn to the Chronological Narrative of a Scientific Discovery page in your Composition Notebook. Read through the pattern of the narrative again.

STEP TWO: **Examine the model**

Your chart should have reminded you that a chronological narrative about a scientific discovery answers two questions:

What steps or events led to the discovery?
In what sequence did these steps or events happen?

and puts those answers in chronological order.

Look again at the outline you made of the passage from *Discoverer of the Unseen World*. The exact words you used will be different, but the outline probably looks something like this:

I. Berkelse Mere was a lake that changed color in the summer.
II. Leeuwenhoek decided to test the lake.
III. He collected a water sample to observe.
IV. He saw microscopic life forms.

Points II, III, and IV list, in chronological order, steps that led to the discovery of microscopic life forms.

Your chart should also have reminded you that you may need a paragraph giving background information. Point I gives you necessary background information; it describes an existing phenomenon (the cloudy lake) that no one in Leeuwenhoek's day understood.

Finally, your chart reminded you to make use of time and sequence words.

Below, you will see an expanded version of the passage about Leeuwenhoek's discovery. Read through the passage one more time and follow these simple instructions:

1. Look for the time and sequence words, which have been bolded.
2. When you read the additional paragraphs, ask yourself "What new element do these paragraphs bring into the narrative?"

> In considering various ways to test the new contrivance, he thought of the appearance of the fresh water in Berkelse Mere, the inland lake located "about two hours from Delft." Its water was always clear in winter. But during the summer it lost this clearness and became whitish in color with little green clouds floating through it. The country people believed the change in the water's appearance was caused by the dews that occurred at that time; for this reason they called it "honeydew."
>
> This was hearsay, Leeuwenhoek reasoned. He would have to see for himself. Accepting a belief as a fact, without being curious enough to test it, was just the kind of thing that had been going on for centuries. Here was a chance for him, one of the most curious amateurs of science, to satisfy his curiosity about the nature of the inland lake. In so doing, he might also make a contribution to science. And it would give him an opportunity to test the quality of his newly made microscope and the clearness of his glass pipettes.
>
> **So** he journeyed to Berkelse Mere, to the southeast of Delft. Here he scooped up a generous sample of the marshy water and put it into a container. It was too late to examine the water **when** he returned home that night. **So** he put the container in the office-laboratory where he did all of his work and study.
>
> The **following night** he assembled his simple equipment and prepared to observe the Berkelse Mere water by the light of a single candle. **First** he sucked a drop of water into a little glass pipette which he had glued onto the rod of his newest microscope. In reality the instrument was "a simple magnifying glass," and this is what he always called it. It consisted of two matched oblong sheets of metal, which encased a tiny bi-convex, or football-shaped, lens. The whole thing was smaller than a small oblong football ticket.
>
> Leeuwenhoek carefully lifted the microscope and pressed the minute lens close to one eye. He could not believe what he saw. There before him was a veritable swimming pool of earthly particles, green streaks, and little

> "animalcules"! The streaks were spirally wound like serpents and "orderly arranged, after the manner of copper or tin worms, which distillers use to cool their liquors as they distill over." The amazing thing about these little figures was that they were only as thick as a strand of hair (the common form of green alga *Spirogyra*).
>
> He saw other particles that had only the beginning of streaks. But all consisted of very small green globules joined together. Among these many odd-shaped particles were many little "animalcules." He did not know it, but undoubtedly at least some of these were Protozoa. Some were round in shape, others were elongated or oval.
>
> Some of the creatures had two little legs near the head and two fins at the end of their bodies (probably rotifers). Others were elongated and moved very slowly (probably ciliates).
>
> These "animalcules," as he referred to bacteria and Protozoa in all his observations, were of several colors, some being white and transparent, while others were green in the middle, banded by white (probably *Euglena viridis*); others sparkled with green scales, and still others were a kind of dove-gray. He wrote: "The motion of most of these animalcules in the water was so swift, and so various, upwards, downwards, and round about, that 'twas wonderful to see: and I judge that these little creatures were above a thousand times smaller [in volume, not in linear dimensions] than the smallest ones I have ever seen, upon the rind of cheese, in wheaten flour, mould and the like" (mites).[35]

You will notice that most of the time and sequence words occur in the middle of the passage, where Leeuwenhoek is actually going through the steps of the discovery.

What do you think the additional paragraphs add to the narrative?

They do add to the description of the microscopic world Leeuwenhoek discovered. But you should have noticed a new element in the final paragraph. It is bolded below:

> These "**animalcules**," as he referred to bacteria and Protozoa in all his observations, were of several colors, some being white and transparent, while others were green in the middle, banded by white (probably *Euglena viridis*); others sparkled with green scales, and still others were a kind of dove-gray. He wrote: "**The motion of most of these animalcules in the water was so swift, and so various, upwards, downwards, and round about, that 'twas wonderful to see: and I judge that these little creatures were above a thousand times smaller** [in volume, not in linear dimensions] **than the smallest ones I have ever seen, upon the rind of cheese, in wheaten flour, mould and the like**" (mites).

35. Payne, pp. 16–19.

The writer of this narrative has decided to use Leeuwenhoek's exact words, found in a letter Leeuwenhoek wrote to the scientists of the Royal Society.

Last week, you learned that dialogue—the words characters actually speak—can add interest to a chronological narrative about a past event. A chronological narrative about a scientific discovery can also become more vivid and real when dialogue is used.

Many scientists wrote letters, essays, and even books about their discoveries, so often you can find the exact words that scientists have used about their own work. Introducing a sentence or two from the scientist herself *about* her discovery adds color and interest to a chronological narrative about a scientific discovery.

Now add the bolded point below under the "Remember" column on your Chronolgoical Narrative of a Scientific Discovery chart:

Chronological Narrative of a Scientific Discovery
Definition: A narrative telling what steps or events
led to a discovery, and in what sequence

Procedure
1. Ask, *What steps or events led to the discovery?*
2. Ask, *In what sequence did these steps or events happen?*
3. Create main points by placing the answers in chronological order.

Remember
1. May need a background paragraph explaining the circumstances that existed before the discovery.
2. Make use of time words.
3. **If possible, quote directly from the scientist's own words.**

Day Four: Practicing the Topos

Focus: Learning how to write a chronological narrative about a scientific discovery

In your last lesson, you saw an example of a chronological narrative about a scientific discovery that made use of the scientist's own words. Here is another, from *Doctors and Discoveries: Lives That Created Today's Medicine* by John G. Simmons. This narrative tells how the sixteenth-century French surgeon Ambroise Pare learned to use antiseptic on wounds to keep them from getting infected. (The first paragraph gives background information.)

> The years of Pare's youth were marked by the ascendancy of Francis I, who, four years after becoming king in 1515, lost his bid to become emperor of the Holy Roman Empire. This led him into a series of wars with Charles of Hapsburg that were fought largely on the Italian peninsula. There, at the siege of Turin in 1537, Pare made his first and most famous innovation.

> As was customary, Pare and his fellow surgeons treated gunshot wounds by cauterizing[36] them with boiling oil of elder, which was thought to prevent death from "gunpowder poisoning." This method caused terrible agony and more damage to the flesh than the projectile had. At Turin, the oil ran out. As a stopgap, Pare covered the wounds with a salve composed of egg yolk, turpentine, and oil of roses. One night he wrote, "I could not sleep . . . for I was troubled in minde, and the dressing of the precedent day, (which I judged unfit) troubled my thoughts; and I feared that the next day I should finde them dead, or at the point of death by the poyson of the wound, whom I had not dressed with the scalding oyle." In fact, these patients were still alive and in better condition than the men who had been treated with cauterization. Pare continued to treat casualties in this way, he added, and "When I had many times tryed this in divers others I thought this much, that neither I nor any other should ever cauterize any wounded with Gun-shot."[37]

Today, you'll practice putting together a chronological narrative of your own, making use of direct quotes. If necessary, review last week's rules for writing dialogue.

STEP ONE: **Plan the narrative**

Your first step is to plan out the narrative. On the next page, you'll see a list of events, written out chronologically for you, covering Johannes Kepler's discovery that planets move in elliptical orbits. This information was taken from *Star Maps: History, Artistry, and Cartography* by Nick Kanas (Praxis, 2007); *Johannes Kepler and the New Astronomy* by James R. Voelkel; and *Tycho & Kepler: The Unlikely Partnership* by Kitty Ferguson (Bloomsbury, 2002).

You'll need to make three choices:

1. Which main events and details to use in your narrative.
2. Where to put the "background paragraph," and how much information to include in it.
3. Which time and sequence words to use.

Your chronological narrative can be one paragraph or several paragraphs, but it must be at least 150 words long and no longer than 300 words.

Begin to plan out your narrative now by following these three instructions:

1. Circle the events that belong in the "background information" paragraph of your composition.

---

36. Cauterization is the burning of tissue in order to seal off a wound and prevent infection.
37. John G. Simmons, *Doctors and Discoveries: Lives That Created Today's Medicine* (Houghton Mifflin, 2002), p. 120.

2. Draw a light line through the main events and details you do not intend to include. (Remember, you can eliminate an entire main event plus all its details. If you want to include a main event, you can also include only one of its details—or all of them.)
3. Consult your chart of Time and Sequence Words. Make an initial selection of four or five words that you might be able to use in your narrative (you'll only need to use two or three in your actual draft).

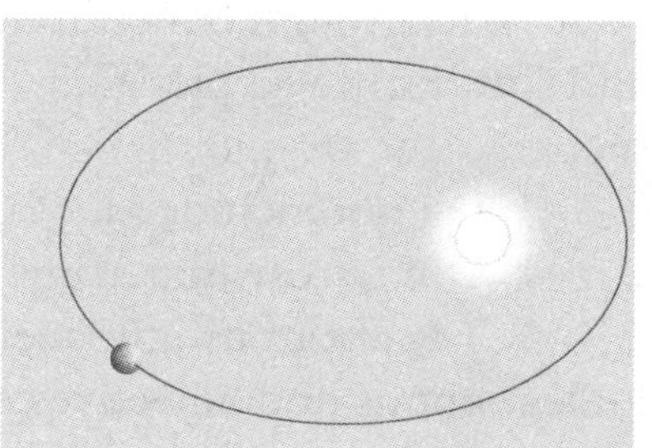

EVENTS LEADING TO KEPLER'S DISCOVERY OF ELLIPTICAL PLANETARY ORBITS

Johannes Kepler studied at university in the 1590s

He studied heliocentrism
One of his teachers was a follower of Copernicus

Heliocentric world view of Copernicus vs. geocentric world view

Heliocentrism=sun at center of solar system
Copernicus said sun at *exact* center of solar system
Copernicus said all orbits completely circular
Geocentrism=Earth at center of solar system
Geocentric world view still popular
Copernicus's theory still rejected by many
Most astronomers believed Earth at center of solar system
Geocentrism=Earth had no orbit because it remained still

Worked as assistant to astronomer Tycho Brahe 1600–1601

Helped Brahe observe orbits for planets
Assumed all orbits were circles
Observed Mars at different times
Mars seemed to speed up and slow down
Could not explain why the planet Mars moved as it did

Tycho Brahe died in 1601

Told Kepler to keep on trying to understand orbit

Kepler tried to find mathematical explanation for movement of Mars

Failed 40 times to find formula that explained Mars orbit
Struggled with Mars orbit for five years

In 1605, Kepler realized orbit must be an ellipse

Formulated "Kepler's first law of planetary motion"

Law: Planets move in elliptical orbits, sun is one focal point of orbit

Published findings in *Astronomia Nova* in 1609

Contained theory that all planets move in elliptical orbits
Planets move faster when close to sun, slower when farther away
Argued that sun pulls on planets
Intended to prove heliocentrism once and for all
Argued that Earth behaved like other planets

STEP TWO: **Write a draft of the narrative**

Your next step is to write a first draft of your narrative. Here's a summary of your assignment:

1. This chronological narrative can be one paragraph or several paragraphs, but it must be at least 150 words long and no longer than 300 words.

2. The narrative must progress chronologically forward at all times. The only exception is your "background paragraph," where you describe what most people believed about the Earth and sun during Kepler's day. This paragraph should come early in the composition (first or second).

3. Do not include all of the main events and details.

4. Use two or more time words in your narrative.

5. Try not to use the identical words of the events list. In previous lessons, you were told to look at nouns and adjectives and to change them if possible. This events list contains a number of verbs; when you write this narrative, concentrate on changing the verbs. For example, if you are writing a paragraph based on the following events:

Worked as assistant to astronomer Tycho Brahe 1600–1601

Helped Brahe observe orbits for planets

Assumed all orbits were circles

try not to write:

*Kepler **worked** as an assistant to the astronomer Tycho Brahe from 1600–1601. He **helped** Brahe **observe** orbits for planets. Both men **assumed** all orbits **were** circles.*

Instead try to use original verbs in place of the verbs (bolded) in the events list.

*Kepler **became** the assistant of the astronomer Tycho Brahe in 1600 and worked with Brahe for a year. His job was to **track** the orbits of the planets. Both men **believed** that all planets **orbited** the sun in a perfect circle.*

If you have difficulty, ask your instructor for help.

STEP THREE: **Add direct quotes**

Now that you've completed a rough draft of your narrative, consider how you might use Johannes Kepler's actual words to make some part of it more vivid.

Read through these five direct quotes from Kepler himself.

DIRECT QUOTES FROM KEPLER

"First, therefore, let my readers grasp that today it is absolutely certain . . . that all the planets revolve around the sun, with the exception of the moon, which alone has the Earth as its centre."[38]

38. Johannes Kepler and Charles G. Wallis, *The Harmonies of the World* (BiblioBazaar, 2008), p. 22.

"The planetary orbit is elliptical and the sun, the source of movement, is at one of the foci of this ellipse."[39]

"I was almost driven to madness considering and calculating this matter. I could not find out why the planet would rather go on an elliptical orbit."[40]

"I am moved by an exceedingly powerful desire for knowledge of the heavens."[41]

"If God is concerned with astronomy, which piety desires to believe, then I hope that I shall achieve something in this domain."[42]

Now look over your list of main events, and try to decide which main events each of these quotes belong to. (Some of the quotes might be usable in more than one part of the composition.)

For example, consider this quote: "I am moved by an exceedingly powerful desire for knowledge of the heavens." The quote tells you why Kepler spent his life studying the sky. So it might fit into a paragraph based on the following events:

Johannes Kepler studied at university in the 1590s
Worked as assistant to astronomer Tycho Brahe 1600–1601
Kepler tried to find mathematical explanation for movement of Mars

If the draft of your paragraph based on the first event read like this:

Johannes Kepler became a university student in the 1590s. He was taught heliocentrism, because one of his teachers believed Copernicus's theories of the universe.

you could add the quote as follows:

Johannes Kepler became a university student in the 1590s and studied astronomy. He said of his own studies, "I am moved by an exceedingly powerful desire for knowledge of the heavens." He was taught heliocentrism, because one of his teachers believed Copernicus's theories of the universe.

Now decide which quote you want to use and add it in to the appropriate paragraph. If you have difficulty, ask your instructor for help.

When you are finished, check your work with your instructor.

---

39. Kepler and Wallis, p. 25.
40. Quoted in Owen Gingerich, *The Eye of Heaven: Ptolemy, Copernicus, Kepler* (American Institute of Physics, 1993), p. 344.
41. Quoted in Max Caspar and Clarisse Doris Hellman, *Kepler* (Dover, 1993) pp. 120–121.
42. Caspar and Hellman, p. 123.

Week 8: Description of a Place

Day One: Original Narration Exercise

Focus: Summarizing a narrative by choosing the central details

STEP ONE: **Read**

Read the following excerpt from George MacDonald's modern fairy tale *The Princess and the Goblin.*

CHAPTER 1

Why the Princess Has a Story about Her

There was once a little princess whose father was king over a great country full of mountains and valleys. His palace was built upon one of the mountains, and was very grand and beautiful. The princess, whose name was Irene, was born there, but she was sent soon after her birth, because her mother was not very strong, to be brought up by country people in a large house, half castle, half farmhouse, on the side of another mountain, about half-way between its base and its peak.

The princess was a sweet little creature, and at the time my story begins was about eight years old, I think, but she got older very fast. Her face was fair and pretty, with eyes like two bits of night sky, each with a star dissolved in the blue. Those eyes you would have thought must have known they came from there, so often were they turned up in that direction. The ceiling of her nursery was blue, with stars in it, as like the sky as they could make it. But I doubt if ever she saw the real sky with the stars in it, for a reason which I had better mention at once.

These mountains were full of hollow places underneath; huge caverns, and winding ways, some with water running through them, and some shining with all colours of the rainbow when a light was taken in. There would not have been much known about them, had there not been mines there, great deep pits, with long galleries and passages running off from them, which had been dug to get at the ore of which the mountains were full. In the course of digging, the miners came upon many of these natural caverns. A few of them had far-off openings out on the side of a mountain, or into a ravine.

Now in these subterranean caverns lived a strange race of beings, called by some gnomes, by some kobolds, by some goblins. There was a legend current in the country that at one time they lived above ground, and were very like other people. But for some reason or other, concerning which there were different legendary theories, the king had laid what they thought too severe taxes upon them, or had required observances of them they did not like, or had begun to treat them with more severity, in some way or other, and impose stricter laws; and the consequence was that they had all disappeared from the face of the country. According to the legend, however, instead of going to some other country, they had all taken refuge in the subterranean caverns, whence they never came out but at night, and then seldom showed themselves in any numbers, and never to many people at once. It was only in the least frequented and most difficult parts of the mountains that they were said to gather even at night in the open air. Those who had caught sight of any of them said that they had greatly altered in the course of generations; and no wonder, seeing they lived away from the sun, in cold and wet and dark places. They were now, not ordinarily ugly, but either absolutely hideous, or ludicrously grotesque both in face and form. There was no invention, they said, of the most lawless imagination expressed by pen or pencil, that could surpass the extravagance of their appearance.

But I suspect those who said so had mistaken some of their animal companions for the goblins themselves—of which more by and by. The goblins themselves were not so far removed from the human as such a description would imply. And as they grew misshapen in body they had grown in knowledge and cleverness, and now were able to do things no mortal could see the possibility of. But as they grew in cunning, they grew in mischief, and their great delight was in every way they could think of to annoy the people who lived in the open-air storey above them. They had enough of affection left for each other to preserve them from being absolutely cruel for cruelty's sake to those that came in their way; but still they so heartily cherished the ancestral grudge against those who occupied their former possessions and especially against the descendants of the king who had caused their expulsion, that they sought every opportunity of tormenting them in ways that were as odd as their inventors; and although dwarfed and misshapen, they had strength equal to their cunning. In the process of time they had got a king and a government of their own, whose chief business, beyond their own simple affairs, was to devise trouble for their neighbours.

It will now be pretty evident why the little princess had never seen the sky at night. They were much too afraid of the goblins to let her out of the house then, even in company with ever so many attendants; and they had good reason, as we shall see by and by.[43]

STEP TWO: **Note central details**

You may notice that this passage is a little different than the narratives you've been summarizing. Instead of listing a series of chronological events, George MacDonald sets the stage for his story by describing the world Princess Irene lives in. The passage should have given you a clear picture in your mind.

On your scratch paper, write down five or six phrases or short sentences that identify the most important things about this world. If a detail doesn't add significantly to the mental picture of the princess's world, you should leave it out. (For example, it doesn't really matter that the people in the world mistook animals for the goblins. But if you don't mention that the goblins were "misshapen in body," your picture of the world will be incomplete.)

If you have trouble with this assignment, ask your instructor for help.

STEP THREE: **Write summary sentences**

After you've written down your five or six phrases or sentences, try to combine them into three or four sentences. You can do this by putting two phrases in the same sentence (for example, "Many mountains and valleys in kingdom" and "Mountains filled with caverns and mines" could be combined into "There were many mountains filled with caverns and mines in the kingdom"). Or you may find that one or more of your jotted notes turns out to be unnecessary (if you wrote down "Mountains filled with caverns and mines" and "Miners found caverns," you can eliminate one of those sentences).

Say your three or four sentences several times before writing them down. After you've written the sentences down, ask your instructor to check them.

If you have trouble, ask your instructor for help.

43. George MacDonald, *The Princess and the Goblin* (Blackie & Son, 1888), pp. 1–6.

Day Two: Outlining Exercise

Focus: Finding the central topic in each paragraph of a description

STEP ONE: **Read**

Read the following excerpt from *The Mississippi Bubble* by Thomas B. Costain.

You may find the following background information useful: In the seventeenth century, France, Spain, and England were competing for control of the new land on the North American continent. The French wanted to build a great city on the Mississippi River so that they could control which ships went up and down the river. But the English and Spanish navies might appear at any moment to attack a French settlement. So might the Native Americans, known to the French as Indians, who already lived along the Mississippi. So any settlement would need a strong fort to defend it.

The leader the text refers to, Sieur d'Iberville, was a famous French general sent by King Louis XIV to establish this French colony.

— — —

> The expedition had touched first at a place on the north of the Gulf which Iberville named Biloxi. They returned to Biloxi after their success in finding the mouth of the river and the commander decided that a fort should be built there. Temporarily it would serve as the headquarters of the French on the Gulf. The great city they hoped to build on the bend of the river would come later.
>
> Iberville had chosen well. Biloxi Bay was a safe harbor, well screened by Deer Island. The bay extended back into the mainland for several miles and Deer Island lay across the mouth of the bay, blocking it off except a channel at either end. This made a snug little harbor for the new settlement. There was always the danger of English or Spanish ships appearing on the green waters of the Gulf.
>
> The site that the great leader chose for the fort was ideal. It was a high bank on the east side of the bay near the mouth. Here the French guns could sweep the horizon and the lookout could keep a sharp eye on the beach, the water, and the country round about. There were deep ravines on two sides of the hill which run down to the bay; this made a natural fort of the hill. The weakest spot was on the forest side where the land sloped gently to the woods beyond. Iberville put his men to work immediately to build a strong entrenchment from one ravine to the other. He knew only too well how suddenly and swiftly the Indians could attack. . .

The fort they erected was similar to those which the French had always constructed in their pioneering efforts along the St. Lawrence River. There were several wooden buildings, the main one two stories in height, inside a high barricade of logs. The outer wall had bastions at each corner. These were made of squared logs, two to three feet thick, placed one upon another. The four bastions were surrounded by deep ditches, and they served as projections from which the defenders could meet the attacks of the enemy with raking fire in all directions. They could also keep the enemy from setting fire to the walls of the fort.[44]

STEP TWO: **Construct a one-level outline**

You've already practiced outlining passages that tell events in chronological order. For these outlines, you have been asking yourself two questions:

1. What is the main thing or person that this section is about?
2. Why is that thing or person important?

This passage is a little different; it describes a *place*. Although you can certainly use the same two questions when you outline a passage of description, you can also take a simpler approach. Instead of asking these two questions and writing a sentence that answers each one, you can ask yourself: What part of the place does this paragraph focus on?

Try that for the first section now.

Were you able to come up with an answer?

This first paragraph tells about Iberville's decision to build the fort and city at Biloxi. So the first section tells you about the *location* of the fort and city. Your first outline point would be:

I. The location

Look at the second section. This paragraph focuses on one specific part of the location. (Hint: it involves water.)

Did you come up with an answer?

44. Thomas Costain, *The Mississippi Bubble* (Random House, 1955), pp. 24–26.

This second paragraph tells you about the bay itself. Your second outline point can be either

II. Biloxi Bay itself

or

II. The bay and harbor

If you were doing a two-level outline of this paragraph (something you won't practice until later on), the subpoints—points that tell you more about the *main* point—would all describe the bay and the harbor formed by the bay.

Now try to complete this exercise by providing points III and IV. You can continue to use phrases rather than complete sentences. If you have difficulty, ask your instructor for help. And when you are finished, check your assignment with your instructor.

Day Three: Analyzing and Practicing the Topos, Part One

Focus: Understanding the form of a description of a place

The passage you outlined in your last writing session is an example of this week's topos: a **description of a place.** Today's assignment is to understand the elements that go into a good place description.

STEP ONE: **Understand the purpose of descriptions**

Like chronological narratives, descriptions of places can sometimes stand on their own; a detailed description of a medieval castle, an ancient city, or a modern submarine could be a short history composition in its own right. More often, though, a description of a place fits into a larger piece of writing. Thomas Costain's description of the fort in *The Mississippi Bubble* is part of a chapter about the bitter wars between European countries over the New World. The description of the fort's many walls, towers, ditches, and defenses helps give you an idea of just how hard the French were prepared to fight for control of the Mississippi River.

Here is another description of a place, this one from a book by Jonathan Kozol called *Savage Inequalities.* Kozol's book is about the dreadful condition of schools in poor, inner-city neighborhoods. In this passage, he is being driven through East St. Louis on his way to visit a neighborhood where the schoolchildren live.

> As we ride past blocks and blocks of skeletal structures, some of which are still inhabited, she slows the car repeatedly at railroad crossings. A seemingly endless railroad train rolls past us to the right. On the left: a

> blackened lot where garbage has been burning. Next to the burning garbage is a row of twelve white cabins, charred by fire. Next: a lot that holds a heap of auto tires and a mountain of tin cans. More burnt houses. More trash fires. The train moves almost imperceptibly across the flatness of the land.[45]

After you read the description of this bleak wasteland, you're not at all surprised when Kozol arrives at the school itself and finds disintegrating classrooms, no heat, no equipment, damaged textbooks, and bathrooms that don't work.

As you can see from the two examples you've looked at, a description of a place is more than just a listing of details. When you write a description, you decide what details to include. But you also decide what *emotion* the description should help the reader feel, or what *idea* the reader should begin to understand.

Read the following description of the field where the Battle of Hastings was fought in 1066.

> There is a little patch of a square mile or so, in the midst of the rich Sussex landscape in England. Through it, in low ground, sluggishly flows a small brook, and from the brook ridges slope up gently on either hand. It is covered for the most part with the green, thick English grass, dotted now and then by old elms and oaks. A gray, half-ruined wall, toothed with battlements at the summit, runs along one verge of the field; and there are two or three old towers, forlorn. . . . [with] wall and towers suggesting a splendor that has now departed.[46]

The writer goes on to contrast the peace of the field *now* with the struggle of the battle itself, *long ago.* He wants us to feel, sharply, the difference between the present and the past, so he uses quiet, slow, peaceful words in his description: *little, low, sluggishly, small, gently, forlorn.*

This is the first element in a well-written description: the writer has in mind a *specific purpose* that he wants the description to fulfill. Thomas Costain wanted the reader to understand just how strong and well defended the French fort on the Mississippi would be; Jonathan Kozol wanted the reader to focus on the poverty of East St. Louis; James Hosmer, who wrote the description of the field above, wanted the reader to appreciate the peace and quiet of the present-day spot.

STEP TWO: **Write down the pattern of the topos**

Now copy the following onto a blank sheet of paper in the Reference section of your Composition Notebook. You will be adding to this page as you learn more about chronological narratives, so leave plenty of room at the bottom of the page; also leave blank space under the "Remember" column.

---

45. Jonathan Kozol, *Savage Inequalities* (Harper Perennial, 1992), pp. 11–12.

46. James Kendall Hosmer, *A Short History of Anglo-Saxon Freedom* (Charles Scribner's Sons, 1890), p. 25.

The definition of this topos may seem very obvious. Copy it down anyway—you'll be learning, in later lessons, about descriptions that *aren't* simply physical and visual.

Description of a Place

Definition: A visual description of a physical place

Procedure	Remember
1. Ask, *What specific purpose should this description fulfill?*	

STEP THREE: **Practice the topos**

You'll end today's lesson by writing two brief descriptions, each with a different purpose.

Look closely at the second sentence in James Hosmer's description of the Battle of Hastings field:

Through it, in low ground, sluggishly flows a small brook, and from the brook ridges slope up gently on either hand.

Now imagine that Hosmer had wanted us to feel the urgency and danger of the Battle of Hastings himself. He might have written:

The sunken field was gashed by a thin stream of water, and from the stream's edges, ridges rose up on either hand.

What if Hosmer had written a description of the field without any particular purpose in mind? The sentence might sound like this:

A brook ran through the field. There were hills on both sides of the water.

which would have been incredibly boring (and not very descriptive). Descriptions that have purpose are always more vivid and engaging.

Your assignment is to take the following description and rewrite it twice. The first time, imagine that you're using this description of a room in the first chapter of a ghost story: make it creepy, frightening, or suspenseful. The second time, imagine that the description is coming at the conclusion of a romance in which the hero and heroine have finally fallen in love and decided to marry.

> *The room was large and the ceiling was high and vaulted. The windows were long and high, with arches at the tops. The floor was made of oak boards. The sun was setting outside, and the light that came through the windows was red and gold, but it did not reach all the way into the corners of the room. Curtains hung at the windows, and there was a lot of furniture in the room.*

As you write, remember that you can make use of adjectives (the "shining windows" or the "gloomy windows"), synonyms ("The room was large" could become either "The room was echoing" or "The room was spacious and welcoming"), and vivid verbs (did the light "flood" or "struggle" through the windows?).

If you need assistance, ask your instructor for help. And when you are finished, show your two descriptions to your instructor.

Day Four: Analyzing and Practicing the Topos, Part Two

Focus: Understanding the form of a description of a place

STEP ONE: Understand space and distance words and phrases

Read these three excerpts from the passages you've already examined this week. Notice which words are bolded.

> Biloxi Bay was a safe harbor, well screened by Deer Island. The bay extended **back** into the mainland for several miles and Deer Island lay **across** the mouth of the bay, blocking it off except a channel at either end.
>
> A seemingly endless railroad train rolls **past** us **to the right**. **On the left:** a blackened lot **where** garbage has been burning. **Next to** the burning garbage is a row of twelve white cabins, charred by fire.
>
> The windows were long, narrow, and pointed, and at so vast **a distance from** the black oaken floor as to be altogether inaccessible from **within.** Feeble gleams of encrimsoned light made their way **through** the trellised panes. . . Dark draperies hung **upon** the walls.

When you studied chronological narratives, you learned that time and sequence words can help you put events into chronological order. When you write a description, **space and distance words and phrases** can help you create a clear picture of a place.

Pull out the list of Space and Distance Words/Phrases found in Appendix I. This is not an exhaustive (complete) list, and many of the words on it can work in more than one way (if, for example, you wanted to explain that a tree stood three feet to the right of a house, you could say "The tree was next to the house" or "The tree was to the right of the house" or even "The tree was a short distance from the house"). But the categories on the list will give you a starting place as you write your descriptions.

Before you go on with the next step, look up from your paper and choose one object or piece of furniture in the room. Now look down your list of Space and Distance Words/Phrases and count how many of them could accurately describe your relationship to that object.

STEP TWO: **Add to the pattern of the topos**

These space and distance words and phrases can help you write a more precise, and so more interesting, description.

Read the following description and underline each of the space and distance words and phrases.

In a hole in the ground there lived a hobbit. Not a nasty, dirty, wet hole, filled with the ends of worms and an oozy smell, nor yet a dry, bare, sandy hole with nothing in it to sit down on or to eat; it was a hobbit-hole, and that means comfort.

It had a perfectly round door like a porthole, painted green, with a shiny yellow brass knob in the exact middle. The door opened on to a tube-shaped hall like a tunnel: a very comfortable tunnel without smoke, with panelled walls, and floors tiled and carpeted, provided with polished chairs, and lots and lots of pegs for hats and coats—the hobbit was fond of visitors. The tunnel wound on and on, going fairly but not quite straight into the side of the hill—The Hill, as all the people for many miles round called it—and many little round doors opened out of it, first on one side, and then on another. No going upstairs for the hobbit: bedrooms, bathrooms, cellars, pantries (lots of these), wardrobes (he had whole rooms devoted to clothes), kitchens, dining-rooms, all were on the same floor, and indeed on the same passage. The best rooms were all on the left-hand side (going in), for these were the only ones to have windows, deep-set round windows looking over his garden, and meadows beyond, sloping down to the river.[47]

When you are finished, ask your instructor to check your work.

Now turn to the Description of a Place chart in your Composition Notebook. Add the bolded point below under the "Remember" column.

Description of a Place

Definition: A visual description of a physical place

Procedure	Remember
1. Ask, *What specific purpose should this description fulfill?*	**1. Make use of space and distance words.**

47. J. R. R. Tolkien, *The Hobbit* (Random House, 1982), p. 1.

STEP THREE: **Practice the topos**

Look carefully at the picture of Neuschwanstein Castle in Germany. King Ludwig of Bavaria had it built between 1869 and 1884 on the ruins of a medieval castle. The palace was designed to have more than 200 rooms, but fewer than 20 were finished before the king's death. If the castle looks familiar to you, it may be because Disney used it as the model for the castle in *Sleeping Beauty*.

Write a description of at least four but not more than eight sentences describing this place. Use at least four different space and distance words and phrases in your description. Be sure to describe the castle itself *and* also to include some detail about the surrounding landscape.

The purpose of your description should be to convey how spectacular the castle is. If you need help with this purpose, ask your instructor.

When you are finished, ask your instructor to check your work.

Neuschwanstein Castle, Bavaria, Germany. Credit: Shutterstock.com

Week 9: Description of a Place

Day One: Original Narration Exercise

Focus: Summarizing a narrative by choosing the central details and actions

STEP ONE: **Read**

Read the following excerpt from *Mary Poppins in the Park* by P. L. Travers. Travers wrote a series of books about Mary Poppins, the magical British nanny, and her charges: Michael and Jane, the two older children in the Banks family; the twins John and Barbara; and baby Annabel. In this chapter, Michael and Jane are playing in the park, with Mary Poppins nearby—which always means that something mysterious is about to happen.

"Plasticine" is a kind of modelling clay.

In the story, Michael thinks that a statue looks like "Neleus." Neleus was a minor Greek god, one of the sons of the sea god Poseidon.

— — —

"What are you making?" he enquired, flinging himself on the grass beside her.

"A Park for Poor People," she replied. "Everyone is happy there. And nobody ever quarrels."

She tossed aside a handful of leaves and he saw, amid the wildweed, a tidy square of green. It was threaded with little pebbled paths as wide as a fingernail. And beside them were tiny flower-beds made of petals massed together. A summer-house of nettle twigs nestled on the lawn; flowers were stuck in the earth for trees; and in their shade stood twig benches, very neat and inviting.

On one of these sat a plasticine man, no more than an inch high. His face was round, his body was round, and so were his arms and legs. The only pointed thing about him

was his little turned-up nose. He was reading a plasticine newspaper and a plasticine tool-bag lay at his feet.

"Who's that?" asked Michael. "He reminds me of someone. But I can't think who it is!"

Jane thought for a moment.

"His name is Mr. Mo," she decided. "He is resting after his morning labours. He had a wife sitting next to him, but her hat went wrong, so I crumbled her up. I'll try again with the last of the plasticine—" She glanced at the shapeless, coloured lump that lay behind the summer-house.

"And that?" He pointed to a feminine figure that stood by one of the flower-beds.

"That's Mrs. Hickory," said Jane. "She's going to have a house, too. And after that I shall build a Fun Fair."

He gazed at the plump little plasticine woman and admired the way her hair curled and the two large dimples in her cheeks.

"Do she and Mr. Mo know each other?"

"Oh, yes. They meet on the way to the Lake."

And she showed him a little pebbly hollow where, when Mary Poppins' head was turned, she had poured her mug of milk. At the end of the lake a plasticine statue reminded Michael of Neleus.

"Or down by the swing—" She pointed to two upright sticks from which an even smaller stick hung on a strand of darning wool.

Michael touched the swing with his finger-tip and it swayed backwards and forwards.

"And what's that under the buttercup?"

A scrap of cardboard from the lid of the cake-box had been bent to form a table. Around it stood several cardboard stools and upon it was spread a meal so tempting that a king might have envied it.

In the centre stood a two-tiered cake and around it were bowls piled high with fruits—peaches, cherries, bananas, oranges. One end of the table bore an apple-pie and the other a chicken with a pink frill. There were sausages, and currant buns, and a pat of butter on a little green platter. Each place was set with a plate and a mug and a bottle of ginger wine.

The buttercup-tree spread over the feast. Jane had set two plasticine doves in its branches and a bumble-bee buzzed among its flowers.

"Go away, greedy fly!" cried Michael, as a small black shape settled on the chicken. "Oh, dear! How hungry it makes me feel!"

Jane gazed with pride at her handiwork. "Don't drop your crumbs on the lawn, Michael. They make it look untidy."

"I don't see any litter-baskets. All I can see is an ant in the grass." He swept his eyes round the tiny Park, so neat amid the wildweed.

"There never is any litter," said Jane. "Mr. Mo lights the fire with his paper. And he saves his orange peel for Christmas puddings. Oh, Michael, don't bend down so close, you're keeping the sun away!"

His shadow lay over the Park like a cloud.

"Sorry!" he said, as he bent sideways. And the sunlight glinted down again as Jane lifted Mr. Mo and his tool-bag and set them beside the table.

"Is it his dinner-time?" asked Michael.

"Well—no!" said a little scratchy voice. "As a matter of fact, it's breakfast!"

"How clever Jane is!" thought Michael admiringly. "She can not only make a little old man, she can talk like one as well."

But her eyes, as he met them, were full of questions.

"Did *you* speak, Michael, in that squeaky way?"

"Of course he didn't," said the voice again.

And, turning, they saw that Mr. Mo was waving his hat in greeting. His rosy face was wreathed in smiles and his turned-up nose had a cheerful look.

"It isn't what you call the meal. It's how it tastes that matters. Help yourself!" he cried to Michael. "A growing lad is always hungry. Take a piece of pie!"

"I'm having a beautiful dream," thought Michael, hurriedly helping himself.

"Don't eat it, Michael. It's plasticine!"

"It's not! It's apple!" he cried, with his mouth full.[48]

STEP TWO: **Note central details**

Like last week's story, this week's narrative contains a description. At the end of the description, something happens that moves the story forward.

On your scratch paper, write down six or or seven phrases or short sentences that describe Jane's Park for Poor People. You don't need to summarize the conversation between Jane and Michael (so, for example, you don't need to note "Michael asked Jane who the little plasticine woman was"), but you can use details within the conversation (so you might want to write "The little woman was named Mrs. Hickory").

After you've written down your phrases, add a final sentence describing the most important thing that happens at the end of the story.

If you have trouble with this assignment, ask your instructor for help

STEP THREE: **Write summary sentences**

After you've written down your phrases, try to combine them into three or four sentences. (Your last sentence doesn't count.) Because there are so many details about the park,

48. P. L. Travers, *Mary Poppins in the Park* (Harcourt Books, 1997), pp. 186–191.

experiment with putting three phrases into one sentence; for example, "Little house of twigs," "Flowers were trees," and "benches made of twigs" could all be combined into "Twig benches and a twig house were surrounded by trees made of flowers."

Say your three or four sentences several times before writing them down. When you've finished, add your last sentence to the end of your summary. You will probably need to use a time word to connect the last sentence to the summary, since the park itself and all of its details were already in existence *before* the event at the end of the story happened.

After you've written the sentences down, ask your instructor to check them. If you have trouble, ask your instructor for help.

Day Two: Outlining Exercise

Focus: Finding the central topic in each paragraph of a description

STEP ONE: **Read**

Read the following excerpt from *Life in a Medieval Castle* by Gary Blackwood. You have probably studied before about the "feudal system." Under this system, a lord granted land to farmers, who then became his *vassals* and owed him crops and military service.

The words in brackets [] have been inserted to make the excerpt clearer.

Castles of various sorts were common throughout Europe during the Middle Ages—in Belgium, Switzerland, the Netherlands, Germany, and Italy. They served a variety of purposes: as toll stations, arsenals, fortresses, and watchtowers. In terms of a fortified residence, the castle flourished above all in those countries where the feudal system was most firmly in place—in France and in Norman-occupied Britain. . . .

Before the Norman invasion [in the ninth century], European fortifications were crude for the most part, not much more than a ring of mounded-up earth surrounded by a ditch and topped by a fence, or palisade, of upright logs.

In the first half of the tenth century, structures that could properly be

considered castles began to appear. They were of this same basic "ringwork" design, except for the addition of a tower, or donjon, sometimes inaccurately called a keep. The donjon provided a stronghold that was more secure and could be more easily defended than the palisade.

Jean de Colmieu, writing in the early twelfth century, describes how such a castle was constructed:

> They throw up a little hill of earth as high as they can; they surround it by a fosse [ditch] of considerable width and awful depth. On the inside edge of the fosse they set a palisade of squared logs of wood. . . . If it is possible they strengthen this palisade by towers built at various points. On the top of the little hill they build a house, or rather a citadel, whence a man can see on all sides. No one can reach its door except by a bridge, which . . . gradually rises until it reaches the top of the little hill and the door of the house, from which the master can control the whole of it.

This fortified hill was called a motte, meaning "mound" in French (not to be confused with the word *moat*, another name for the ditch that was dug around the perimeter). Most mottes were 100 to 250 feet in diameter at the base and could be as high as 80 feet, not including the height of the tower, which might add another 30 or 40 feet.

The area within the palisade, which might cover from two to ten acres, was called the bailey. In some cases, the bailey entirely surrounded the motte. In others it was entirely separate, except for the wooden bridge described by de Colmieu that linked the two sections. In this case, the motte might have a smaller palisade of its own around the tower.

An ordinary Norman manor house of the time had a simple floor plan: the kitchen and storeroom were located at one end, the main living and dining room was in the center, and the lord's private chamber was at the other end. The layout of the typical donjon probably resembled a manor house turned up on end, so that the kitchen was on the ground floor, the main hall on the second floor, and the lord's chamber at the top. Considering that the towers of many motte and baileys were no more than twelve feet square and forty feet tall, life inside them must have been cramped, to say the least.[49]

---

49. Gary L. Blackwood, *Life in a Medieval Castle* (Lucent Books, 2000), pp. 15–17.

STEP TWO: **Construct a one-level outline**

As in last week's outlining assignment, this week's passage describes a place. Last week, you learned that although you can ask two questions about each section:

1. What is the main thing that this section is about?
2. Why is that thing or person important?

you can also ask a simpler question when outlining a passage of description:

What part of the place does this paragraph focus on?

As you work on finding the major points for your outline, you may want to use a combination of the two methods.

The reason is simple. When a passage of description is narrowly focused on one area, the single question "What part of the place does this paragraph focus on?" can give you a straightforward answer. But often, a passage of description will contain sections that have a slightly different focus.

Look at the first section in the description and ask yourself "What part of the place does this paragraph focus on?"

✦

What answer did you come up with?

You probably came up with a single word:

Castles

That's not a very good major point; it's too broad, too vague, and too general. Imagine that you were using an outline to write, and your first outline point merely said "Castles." How would you know what to write—or even where to start? This question doesn't work because although the passage goes on to describe each major part of a medieval castle, the first *section* of the passage is an introduction that talks about castles *generally.*

Try asking the two other questions now. What main thing is the section about?

✦

Castles.

Why are the castles important?

✦

Castles were common or *Castles served many purposes* (these two points are similar—they were common because they served many purposes). That's a good first main point for the passage.

Follow this rule as you look for a major point for the remaining sections: First, ask "What part of the place does the section focus on?" If the answer is a single common word, go back to the two-question procedure instead.

Now try to complete this exercise by providing points II through VII. You can mix phrases and sentences if necessary. If you have difficulty, ask your instructor for help. And when you are finished, check your assignment with your instructor.

Day Three: Analyzing and Practicing the Topos, Part One

Focus: Understanding the form of a description of a place

The passage you outlined in your last writing session is another example of this week's topos: a **description of a place.** You studied and practiced this form last week; this week, you'll study and practice some more.

STEP ONE: **Review the use of space and distance words and phrases**

Read the following descriptions and underline the space and distance words and phrases. The first description was written by the Greek historian Herodotus; the second, by the modern historian Stephen Blake; the third, by the secretary to the sixteenth-century Spanish conquistador Hernan Cortes.

When you are finished, check your work with your instructor. In the first two lines of the assignment, the space and distance words and phrases have been bolded as an example.

> The sanctuary is situated **in the center of** the city, and one can walk **around** it and look **down into** it from all sides, because the city has risen . . . with the accumulation of soil over time but the sanctuary has remained undisturbed since it was first built, and therefore it is possible to look down into it. Surrounding it is a dry wall carved with reliefs, and within that wall is a grove of very tall trees growing around a large temple which contains the cult statue. The sanctuary is square and measures 583 feet on each side. Extending from the entrance is a stone road about 1,750 long and 400 feet wide, leading through the marketplace to the east. Trees so tall that they seem to touch the sky grow on either side of the road, which continues until it reaches the sanctuary of Hermes. That is what the sanctuary of Boubastis looks like.[50]

50. Herodotus, *The Landmark Herodotus: The Histories,* trans. Robert B. Strassler (Random House, 2009), p. 180.

In its plan and build, Peking, like the other sovereign cities, reflected the dominance of the imperial household. At its very heart, a fortress within a fortress within a fortress, lay the Forbidden City, a 385-acre enclosure that contained audience halls, private apartments, religious shrines, and about 15,000 persons—the imperial family, personal servants, privileged retainers, and eunuchs. At the center of the Forbidden City stood the Hall of Supreme Harmony. In the middle of this hall on a great throne the Ming emperor exercised absolute power.[51]

Mexico-Tenochtitlan is completely surrounded by water, standing as it does in the lake. It can be approached by only three causeways: one, about half a league long, entering from the west; another from the north, about a league long. There is no causeway from the east, and one must approach by boat. To the south is the third causeway. . . . The lake upon which Mexico is situated, although it seems to be one, is really two, very different from each other, for one is saline, bitter, and stinking, and has no fish in it, while the other is of sweet water and does have fish, although they are small. The salt lake rises and falls, and has currents caused by the winds. The fresh-water lake is higher, so that the good water flows into the bad, and not the other way around, as some have thought. . . On its shores are more than fifty towns, many of them of five thousand houses, some of ten thousand, and one, Texcoco, as large as Mexico.[52]

STEP TWO: **Understand point of view**

If you were Herodotus, where would you be standing while describing the sanctuary of Boubastis?

Herodotus gives you a hint in the first sentence of the description, when he says "One can walk around and look down into it from all sides." As he describes the sanctuary, he is doing so from the point of view of someone who is above the place, looking down over it and seeing all of its different parts.

The second passage has a different point of view. Imagine that the narrator of this passage is walking through the walls of Peking, towards the center. He arrives at the Forbidden City, at the "heart" of the city, and walks through the walls of the Forbidden City, still heading towards the center. He arrives at the Hall of Supreme Harmony, at the center of the Forbidden Center, and walks through its door. Right at the middle of the Hall is the throne of the Ming emperor.

---

51. Stephen P. Blake, *Shahjahanabad: The Sovereign City in Mughal India 1639–1739* (Cambridge University Press, 2002), p. 206.

52. Francisco Lopez de Gomara, *Cortes: The Life of the Conqueror by His Secretary,* trans. Lesley Byrd Simpson (University of California Press, 1964), p. 159.

This point of view is of someone moving forward, getting closer and closer to the center. The first narrator can see the whole place he's describing all at once. The second narrator can't see the Hall, or the throne, until he arrives at it.

There are four basic points of view for a description:

1. From above, as though you were hovering over the place. This is sometimes called the "impersonal" point of view, because you're not directly involved in the place itself; you're looking over it as a detached observer.
2. From inside it, as though you were part of the place, standing still in the middle of it at a particular point and looking around.
3. From one side, as though you were standing beside the place looking at it from one particular angle.
4. Moving, as though you were walking through the place, or around it.

You can choose to use any one of these points of view when you write a description, but once you've settled on one, keep asking yourself: Am I still describing this place from the *same* point of view? You shouldn't (for example) be describing a mountain from above, and then suddenly leap into an inside cave without telling the reader how you got there.

Now look back at the third description. Try to figure out which point of view this passage is written from. When you've decided, check your answer with your instructor.

STEP THREE: **Add to the pattern of the topos**

Pull Appendix II, Points of View, from the back of your workbook. Place it in your Composition Notebook. (You will learn about the other points of view in Appendix II later.)

Now turn to the Description of a Place chart in your Composition Notebook. Add the bolded point below under the "Procedure" column.

Description of a Place
Definition: A visual description of a physical place

Procedure	Remember
1. Ask, *What specific purpose should this description fulfill?*	1. Make use of space and distance words and phrases.
2. Choose a point of view.	

Day Four: Analyzing and Practicing the Topos, Part Two

Focus: Understanding the form of a description of a place

STEP ONE: **Review point of view**

In the last assignment, you learned about the four basic points of view that descriptions can be written from. Glance at your Points of View appendix and review those now.

When you've finished, read the following three descriptions. The first comes from the French writer Rene Auguste Constantin de Renneville, who was imprisoned in the French prison known as the Bastille from 1702 to 1713. The second was written by the nineteenth-century English novelist Charles Dickens. The third is from American Jon Krakauer's account of climbing Mount Everest in 1996.

In the margin beside each description, write which point of view is being used. When you are finished, check your work with your instructor.

> The walls were dirty and soiled with filth; only the ceiling was still fairly clean and white. The furniture consisted of a small broken feeding table, a small collapsed chair of straw on which one could no longer safely sit; and the entire room was swarming with fleas; in a minute I was covered with them. The names of the prisoners were written on the unclean walls. Here a camp bed, a thin mattress, a feather pillow, a vile torn cover eaten by moths were laid down for me. I had never seen so much vermin, and I only kept myself free of it through constant effort to exterminate it. . . . I ate poorly, and slept even worse. In addition, the room was filled with rotten and unhealthy fumes, and every quarter of an hour, the sentry tolled a bell that was so close to my room that it seemed it was hanging from my ears.[53]

> Once upon a time—of all the good days in the year, on Christmas Eve—old Scrooge sat busy in his counting-house. It was cold, bleak, biting weather: foggy withal: and he could hear the people in the court outside, go wheezing up and down, beating their hands upon their breasts, and stamping their feet upon the pavement stones to warm them. The city clocks had only just gone three, but it was quite dark already—it had not been light all

53. Constantin de Renneville, quoted in *The Bastille: A History of a Symbol of Despotism and Freedom*, by Hans-Jurgen Lusebrink, trans. Rolf Reichardt (Duke University press, 1997), pp. 10–11.

> day—and candles were flaring in the windows of the neighbouring offices, like ruddy smears upon the palpable brown air. The fog came pouring in at every chink and keyhole, and was so dense without, that although the court was of the narrowest, the houses opposite were mere phantoms.[54]

> Plodding slowly up the last few steps to the summit, I had the sensation of being underwater, of life moving at quarter speed. And then I found myself atop a slender wedge of ice, adorned with a discarded oxygen cylinder and a battered aluminum survey pole, with nowhere higher to climb. A string of Buddhist prayer flags snapped furiously in the wind. Far below, down a side of the mountain I had never laid eyes on, the dry Tibetan plateau stretched to the horizon as a boundless expanse of dun-colored earth.[55]

STEP TWO: **Practice the topos**

Now you'll experiment with writing a description of the same place from three of the four points of view.

Choose the most interesting room in your house (or if you can go outside, the most interesting section of yard, park, field, or forest). Your goal will be to describe this place in no more than three or four sentences for each point of view, giving a sense of peace, calm, tranquility, belonging, and contentment.

The first time you describe the place, do so from an *abstract/impersonal* point of view. You should not be present in the description at all (in other words, you would write "Photographs hang along the living room wall," as opposed to "I can see pictures of my family on the wall"). Imagine that you're hovering above the place and can see everything in it simultaneously.

The second time you describe the place, do so from *one side or angle.* Choose a place to stand, and describe only what you can see from that particular spot. You should put yourself in the description (so you would write "A beech tree stands on my left, with a holly half-hidden behind it," as opposed to "There is a beech tree with a holly behind it").

Finally, describe the place one last time. This time, describe what you can see as you walk through it *or* as you walk around it. Be sure to list details in the same order that you see them as you move. You can choose to either put yourself in the description ("As I walk past the kitchen table, the refrigerator comes into view on my right") or leave yourself out ("The refrigerator stands on the right, just past the kitchen table").

When you are finished, check your work with your instructor.

54. Charles Dickens, *A Christmas Carol in Prose, Being a Ghost Story of Christmas* (Chapman & Hall, 1845), pp. 5–6.

55. Jon Krakauer, *Into Thin Air* (Anchor Books, 1999), p. 189.

WEEK 10: DESCRIPTION OF A PLACE

Day One: Original Narration Exercise

Focus: Summarizing a narrative by choosing the central events and details

STEP ONE: **Read**

Read the following excerpt from *A Christmas Carol* by Charles Dickens. You've already seen a description from *A Christmas Carol* in last week's lesson. Dickens was a master of vivid, detailed descriptions, and *A Christmas Carol* is probably his best-known work.

In this passage, the miser Scrooge is coming home in the dark after a long day's work—on Christmas Eve. He has just walked up the steps of his own house and is getting ready to open his own front door.

Jacob Marley was Scrooge's former partner, but when the story begins, he's been dead for seven years. "Livid" means ashen colored, pale, deathly white; you should also know that some bacteria found in decaying seafood can give off a very faint luminescent glow.

> Now, it is a fact that there was nothing at all particular about the knocker on the door, except that it was very large. It is also a fact that Scrooge had seen it, night and morning, during his whole residence in that place; also that Scrooge had as little of what is called fancy about him as any man in the City of London. . . . Let it also be borne in mind that Scrooge had not bestowed one thought on Marley since his last mention of his seven-years'-dead partner that afternoon. And then let any man explain to me, if he can, how it happened that Scrooge, having his key in the lock of the door, saw in the knocker, without its undergoing any intermediate process of change—not a knocker, but Marley's face.
>
> Marley's face. It was not in impenetrable shadow, as the other objects in the yard were, but had a dismal light about it, like a bad lobster in a dark cellar. It was not angry or ferocious, but looked at Scrooge as Marley used to look: with ghostly spectacles turned up on its ghostly forehead. The hair was curiously

stirred, as if by breath of hot air; and, though the eyes were wide open, they were perfectly motionless. That, and its livid colour, made it horrible; but its horror seemed to be in spite of the face, and beyond its control, rather than a part of its own expression.

As Scrooge looked fixedly at this phenomenon, it was a knocker again.

To say that he was not startled, or that his blood was not conscious of a terrible sensation to which it had been a stranger from infancy, would be untrue. But he put his hand upon the key he had relinquished, turned it sturdily, walked in, and lighted his candle.

He *did* pause, with a moment's irresolution, before he shut the door; and he *did* look cautiously behind it first, as if he half expected to be terrified with the sight of Marley's pigtail sticking out into the hall. But there was nothing on the back of the door, except the screws and nuts that held the knocker on, so he said, "Pooh, pooh!" and closed it with a bang.

The sound resounded through the house like thunder. Every room above, and every cask in the wine merchant's cellars below, appeared to have a separate peal of echoes of its own. Scrooge was not a man to be frightened by echoes. He fastened the door, and walked across the hall, and up the stairs: slowly, too: trimming his candle as he went. . . . Half-a-dozen gas-lamps out of the street wouldn't have lighted the entry too well, so you may suppose that it was pretty dark with Scrooge's dip.

Up Scrooge went, not caring a button for that. Darkness is cheap, and Scrooge liked it. But, before he shut his heavy door, he walked through his rooms to see that all was right. He had just enough recollection of the face to desire to do that.

Sitting-room, bedroom, lumber-room. All as they should be. Nobody under the table, nobody under the sofa; a small fire in the grate; spoon and basin ready; and the little saucepan of gruel (Scrooge had a cold in his head) upon the hob. Nobody under the bed; nobody in the closet; nobody in his dressing-gown, which was hanging up in a suspicious attitude against the wall. Lumber-room as usual. Old fire-guard, old shoes, two fish baskets, washing-stand on three legs, and a poker.

Quite satisfied, he closed his door, and locked himself in; double locked himself in, which was not his custom. Thus secured against surprise, he took off his cravat; put on his dressing-gown and slippers, and his nightcap; and sat down before the fire to take his gruel.

It was a very low fire indeed; nothing on such a bitter night. He was obliged to sit close to it, and brood over it, before he could extract the least sensation of warmth from such a handful of fuel. . . . As he threw his head back in the chair, his glance happened to rest upon a bell, a disused bell, that hung in the room, and communicated, for some purpose now forgotten, with a chamber in the highest story of the building. It was with great astonishment, and with a strange, inexplicable dread, that, as he looked, he saw this bell begin to swing. It swung so softly in the outset that it scarcely made a sound; but soon it rang out loudly, and so did every bell in the house.

This might have lasted half a minute, or a minute, but it seemed an hour. The bells ceased, as they had begun, together. They were succeeded by a clanking noise, deep down below, as if some person were dragging a heavy chain over the casks in the wine merchant's cellar. Scrooge then remembered to have heard that ghosts in haunted houses were described as dragging chains.

The cellar door flew open with a booming sound, and then he heard the noise much louder on the floors below; then coming up the stairs; then coming straight towards his door.[56]

STEP TWO: **Note central events and details**

This week's story contains a series of events, *and* at least one description which should be included in your narrative summary.

Begin by writing down on scratch paper five or six phrases or short sentences that will remind you, in order, of the things that happened in the story. After you've put these sentences down in order, ask yourself: If you hadn't read the story, would you need a few more *visual* details about any of these phrases or sentences? Underline one or two phrases or sentences that would be clearer if you provided a few more descriptive details. Draw a line from the phrase(s) or sentence(s) to the other side of your paper. At the end of this line, write down three or four central details about the place where the event happened.

If you have trouble with this assignment, ask your instructor for help.

STEP THREE: **Write summary sentences**

Now try to combine your phrases or sentences about the main events into three sentences (your narrative shouldn't be more than four sentences, and you'll need to keep one sentence for the additional descriptive details). Say your three sentences out loud several times. Then decide which details to include in your additional sentence. Write down all four sentences, putting the sentence with the additional details directly after the sentence that mentions the main event connected to those details. (If you can incorporate the details into one of other sentences, that's fine.)

After you've written the sentences down, ask your instructor for help. And if you have trouble, ask your instructor for help.

56. Dickens, pp. 19–25.

Day Two: Outlining Exercise

Focus: Finding the central topic in each paragraph of a description

STEP ONE: **Read**

Read the following excerpt from *The Travels of Marco Polo,* describing the palace of the Mongol khan Kublai Khan, who established the Yuan Dynasty in China. Marco Polo was a Venetian merchant who travelled to China between 1271 and 1295; when he returned, he wrote a book about his adventures.

— — —

The grand khan usually resides during three months of the year, namely, December, January, and February, in the great city of Kanbalu, situated towards the north-eastern extremity of the province of Cathay; and here, on the southern side of the new city, is the site of his vast palace . . . the most extensive that has ever yet been known.

It reaches from the northern to the southern wall [of the city], leaving only a vacant space (or court), where persons of rank and the military guards pass and repass. It has no upper floor, but the roof is very lofty. The paved foundation or platform on which it stands is raised ten spans above the level of the ground, and a wall of marble, two paces wide, is built on all sides, to the level of this pavement, within the line of which the palace is erected; so that the wall, extending beyond the ground plan of the building, and encompassing the whole, serves as a terrace, where those who walk on it are visible from without. Along the exterior edge of the wall is a handsome balustrade, with pillars, which the people are allowed to approach.

The sides of the great halls and the apartments are ornamented with dragons in carved work and gilt, figures of warriors, of birds, and of beasts, with representations of battles. The inside of the roof is contrived in such a manner that nothing besides gilding and painting presents itself to the eye. . . . The exterior of the roof is adorned with a variety of colour, red, green, azure, and violet, and the sort of covering is so strong as to last for many years. The glazing of the windows is so well wrought and so delicate as to have the transparency of crystal.

In the rear of the body of the palace there are large buildings containing several apartments, where is deposited the private property of the monarch, or his treasure in gold and silver bullion, precious stones, and pearls, and also his vessels of gold and silver plate. Here are likewise the apartments of his wives and concubines; and in this retired situation he despatches business with convenience, being free from every kind of interruption. . . .

Not far from the palace, on the northern side, and about a bow-shot distance from the surrounding wall, is an artificial mount of earth, the height of which is full a hundred paces, and the circuit at the base about a mile. It is clothed with the most beautiful evergreen trees; for whenever his majesty receives information of a handsome tree growing in any place, he causes it to be dug up, with all its roots and the earth about them, and however large and heavy it may be, he has it transported by means of elephants to this mount, and adds it to the verdant collection. From this perpetual verdure it has acquired the appellation of the Green Mount. On its summit is erected an ornamental pavilion, which is likewise entirely green. The view of this altogether—the mount itself, the trees, and the building, form a delightful and at the same time a wonderful scene.

In the northern quarter also, and equally within the precincts of the city, there is a large and deep excavation, judiciously formed, the earth from which supplied the material for raising the mount. It is furnished with water by a small rivulet, and has the appearance of a fish-pond, but its use is for watering the cattle. The stream passing from thence along an aqueduct, at the foot of the Green Mount, proceeds to fill another great and very deep excavation. . . . In this latter basin there is great store and variety of fish, from which the table of his majesty is supplied with any quantity that may be wanted. The stream discharges itself at the opposite extremity of the piece of water, and precautions are taken to prevent the escape of the fish by placing gratings of copper or iron at the places of its entrance and exit. It is stocked also with swans and other aquatic birds. . . Such is the description of this great palace.[57]

STEP TWO: **Construct a one-level outline**

This week's passage is one last example of a place description—Kublai Khan's palace in China. As in the first description you outlined, some sections in this passage can be outlined fairly easily if you simply ask "What part of the place does this paragraph focus on?" If this question doesn't give you a simple answer, you can instead ask:

1. What is the main thing this section is about?
2. Why is that thing or person important?

---

57. Marco Polo and John Masefield, *The Travels of Marco Polo, the Venetian* (J. M. Dent, 1908), pp. 166–171.

Use the following hints as you work through the sections.

Section 1. All of the sentences in this section refer to the same *thing.* This is an introductory section, giving the reader an overview of . . . what?

Section 2. The sentences in this section all refer to the same *quality* or *characteristic* shared by the parts mentioned.

Sections 3–5. These sections refer to specific parts of the place.

As in the last lesson, you can mix phrases and sentences if necessary. If you have difficulty, ask your instructor for help. When you are finished, check your assignment with your instructor.

Day Three: Analyzing and Practicing the Topos, Part One

Understanding the use of figurative language in a description of a place

You've already learned three things about the description of a place: it should serve a particular purpose, it should use space and distance words, and it should be written from a particular point of view. This week, you'll add one more element to your descriptions.

STEP ONE: **Understand metaphor and simile**

Look again at these excerpts from the descriptions you studied last week.

> Trees **so tall that they seem to touch the sky** grow on either side of the road, which continues until it reaches the sanctuary of Hermes. That is what the sanctuary of Boubastis looks like. (Herodotus)

> In addition, the room was filled with rotten and unhealthy fumes, and every quarter of an hour, the sentry tolled a bell that was so close to my room that **it seemed it was hanging from my ears.** (de Renneville)

> The city clocks had only just gone three, but it was quite dark already—it had not been light all day—and candles were flaring in the windows of the neighbouring offices, **like ruddy smears upon the palpable brown air.** The fog came pouring in at every chink and keyhole, and was so dense without, that although the court was of the narrowest, **the houses opposite were mere phantoms.** (Dickens)

All three of these descriptions use *figurative language.* Herodotus's trees don't really touch the sky; the bell wasn't really hanging from de Renneville's ears; and if you were in Dickens's London during a fog, you wouldn't see smears on palpable (touchable) brown air or phantom houses. Figurative language exaggerates some part of the description in order to make it even more vivid in the reader's mind.

There are two major categories of figurative language (or "figures of speech"). A simile compares two things *explicitly* by using "like" or "as," or otherwise spelling out for you that figurative language is being used:

like ruddy smears upon the palpable brown air
they seem to touch the sky

In the first simile, the word "like" says clearly, "Hey, this is figurative language!" The candle light isn't a smear; it's *like a smear.* In the second simile, the trees don't touch the sky. They just *seem* to touch the sky.

A metaphor doesn't announce itself by using the words "like" or "as," or by saying that one thing "seems like" or "resembles" another. Instead, the writer simply speaks about one thing in terms of another. When Dickens writes "palpable brown air," he is talking about the air as though it were a thing to be touched and held. This is his way of telling you that the air is smoggy and impossible to see through. If he were to spell the metaphor out, he might write,

like ruddy smears upon the air, which was like a thing that could be touched.

It's much simpler and more elegant for him to use an adjective which means "able to be touched" (palpable) and just apply it to the air. In the same way, he doesn't write

the houses opposite were almost invisible but not quite, like transparent ghosts.

Instead, he writes

the houses opposite were mere phantoms.

STEP TWO: Identify figurative language in descriptions

Read the following descriptions. Underline each metaphor and simile. In the margin, write "m" for metaphor and "s" for simile.

Remember this rule: A simile announces itself ("Look here! Figurative language being used!"). A metaphor simply speaks about one thing in terms of another.

If you have difficulty, ask your instructor for help. And when you are finished, check your work with your instructor.

> The summer heat has withered everything except the mesquite, the palo verde, the grease wood, and the various cacti. Under foot there is a little dry grass, but more often patches of bare gravel and sand roll in shallow beds that course toward the large valleys. In the draws and flat places the fine sand lies thicker, is tossed in wave forms by the wind, and banked

high against clumps of cholla or prickly pear. In the wash-outs and over the cut banks of the arroyos it is sometimes heaped in mounds and crests like driven snow.[58]

In the center . . . is the river Nile. On both sides of the river is the black rich soil of the land of Egypt. We can see the wide fields that have been planted by . . . men of the village. Those fields will soon be covered with a bright carpet of green and, later in the season, will be brilliant with waving grain. Farther to the westward are the sandstone mountains, which glitter in the bright sunshine.[59]

When approaching the Alps from the air, on a clear day, we look down on their highest point within the massive snows of Mont Blanc. We also identify the dark finger of the Matterhorn and the great north wall of the Bernese Alps. Beyond these familiar landmarks, virtually endless rows of snow peaks recede to a misty horizon. They resemble white-capped waves on a windblown sea.[60]

The land had meantime been thickly enveloped in its pure white mantle, and wreaths of snowdrifts lay over the rocks scattered over its surface. The light became fainter. Sometimes the precipitous faces of the glaciers seemed to glow in subdued rose through the leaden grey of the atmosphere. When new "ice holes" appeared, a frosty vapour rose and spread over the surface of the ice; the ship and surrounding objects were covered as if with down; even the dogs were frosted white.[61]

Mount Shasta rises in solitary grandeur from the edge of a comparatively low and lightly sculptured lava plain near the northern extremity of the Sierra. . . . Go where you may, within a radius of from fifty to a hundred miles or more, there stands before you the colossal cone of Shasta, clad in ice and snow, the one grand unmistakable landmark—the pole star of the landscape.[62]

---

58. John Charles Van Dyke, *The Desert: Further Studies in Natural Appearances* (Charles Scribner's Sons, 1913), p. 3.
59. Walter Scott Perry, *With Azir Girges in Egypt* (Atkinson, Mentzer & Co., 1913), p. 37.
60. Nicholas Shoumatoff and Nina Shoumatoff, *The Alps: Europe's Mountain Heart* (University of Michigan Press, 2001), p. 3.
61. Julius Payer, *New Lands Within the Arctic Circle* (Macmillan & Co., 1876), p. 294.
62. John Muir, *Nature Writings* (Library of America, 1997), p. 634.

STEP THREE: **Add to the pattern of the topos**

Turn to the Description of a Place chart in your Composition Notebook. Add the bolded point below under the "Remember" column.

Description of a Place
Definition: A visual description of a physical place

Procedure	Remember
1. Ask, *What specific purpose should this description fulfill?*	1. Make use of space and distance words and phrases.
2. Choose a point of view.	**2. Consider using vivid metaphors and similes.**

Day Four: Analyzing and Practicing the Topos, Part Two

Focus: Understanding the use of figurative language in a description of a place

STEP ONE: **Review the form of the description**

Read the following description of London, written by the nineteenth-century journalist Blanchard Jerrold. Jerrold teamed up with the French artist Gustave Dore to write a book about London that would combine written descriptions with engraved pictures of the city.

> At every corner there is a striking note for the sketch-book. A queer gateway, low and dark, with a streak of silver water seen through the stacks of goods beyond, and bales suspended like spiders from their web; a crooked narrow street with cranes over every window, and the sky netted with ropes as from the deck of a brig. . . . An apple stall surrounded by jubilant shoe-blacks and errand-boys. A closed, grass-grown church-yard, with ancient tomb stones lying at all angles like a witch's fangs.[63]

Now answer the following questions:

63. Blanchard Jerrold and Gustave Dore, *London: A Pilgrimage* (Anthem Press, 2005), pp. 22–24.

1. What is the point of view of the narrator?
2. How many space and distance words does the description use? Underline them.
3. What metaphors and similes does the description use? Underline them.
4. What quality of the city of London do you think the narrator is trying to bring out? (In other words, can you guess at the purpose of the description?)

Ask your instructor for help if you have difficulty with any of the questions. When you are finished, check your answers with your instructor.

STEP TWO: **Practice avoiding cliches**

Although metaphors and similes can make descriptions more vivid, using figurative language that's cliched (used too often) can have the opposite effect. When Herodotus wrote that a tree seemed to touch the sky, he wasn't using a cliche. But after Herodotus, thousands (maybe tens of thousands) of writers also wrote that trees seemed to touch the sky. After thousands of writers use the same simile or metaphor, it becomes a cliche.

When you write a description, you may be tempted to describe a peak as "sharp as a needle," a stream as "chattering merrily," or the sides of a limestone pyramid as "white as snow." But because these images are so often used, they don't cause the reader to stop and picture in his mind exactly what you're describing; his eye just skims over it and he moves on.

In the description above, did the sentence about the tomb stones lying at angles like witch's fangs make you stop for a moment to picture exactly what that would look like?

You can avoid using cliches by rejecting the first image that pops into your head; it's usually the most familiar one. Imagine that you want to express just how white something is. Your first thought will probably be "White as snow." Instead of using that metaphor, stop and think for a moment. Exactly what *sort* of whiteness are you trying to describe? Is it the hard, shiny whiteness of marble? Think about what else is not just white, but also hard and shiny. Pearls? Dried toothpaste? The paint on a Chevrolet?

Or maybe it is the soft, dull whiteness of cotton. What else is not just white, but also soft and dull? A marshmallow? Chicken feathers?

When you use figurative language, you have to think about the *exact* qualities you are trying to convey. Practice doing that now. In the sentences below, cross out each cliche. Then spend some time thinking about the exact quality described in brackets. Come up with a metaphor that's new and vivid, and write it in over the crossed-out cliche.

When you are finished, check your work with your instructor. And if you have difficulty, ask your instructor for help.

The beaches are as hot and white as snow, but the ocean is blue and numbingly cold.
[Too hot to walk on]

White beaches glistened like the sun.
[Brightness—glittering and reflective]

The gallant ship, surrounded by enemies, lay like a stone on the sea.
[Strength—impregnability, resistance]

Lower away in the south, there lay a black squall-cloud with a rounded outline, like a big ball.
[Roundness and puffiness]

Masses of beech and fir sheltered the castle on the north, and spread down here and there along the green slopes like a blanket.
[Extent—the way that the trees creep farther and farther down the slopes and cover more and more land]

Glare ice, black ice they call it, polished the road and reflected first my headlights and then the rising sun. The land stretched flat and frozen on either side, slicked with hoarfrost and gleaming like gold.
[Not just shininess, but also reflectiveness]

In front of the line of battle, the forest was cut down, and the trees left lying where they fell among the stumps, with tops turned outwards. The ground was covered with heavy boughs, overlapped and interlaced, with sharpened points bristling into the face of the assailant like pins and needles.
[Not just sharpness, but also the ability to keep people away]

Week 11: Combining Chronological Narrative of a Past Event and Description of a Place

Day One: Original Narration Exercise

Focus: Summarizing a narrative by choosing the main events and listing them chronologically

STEP ONE: **Read**

Read the following excerpt from Mark Twain's *Tom Sawyer.*

— — —

Monday morning found Tom Sawyer miserable. Monday morning always found him so—because it began another week's slow suffering in school. He generally began that day with wishing he had had no intervening holiday, it made the going into captivity and fetters again so much more odious.

Tom lay thinking. Presently it occurred to him that he wished he was sick; then he could stay home from school. Here was a vague possibility. He canvassed his system. No ailment was found, and he investigated again. This time he thought he could detect colicky symptoms, and he began to encourage them with considerable hope. But they soon grew feeble, and presently died wholly away. He reflected further. Suddenly he discovered something. One of his upper front teeth was loose. This was lucky; he was about to begin to groan, as a "starter," as he called it, when it occurred to him that if he came into court with that argument, his aunt would pull it out, and that would hurt. So he thought he would hold the tooth in reserve for the present, and seek further. Nothing offered for some little time, and then he remembered hearing the doctor tell about a certain thing that laid up a patient for two or three weeks and threatened to make him lose a finger. So the boy eagerly drew his sore toe from under the sheet and held it up for inspection. But now he did not know the necessary symptoms. However, it seemed

well worth while to chance it, so he fell to groaning with considerable spirit.

But Sid slept on unconscious.

Tom groaned louder, and fancied that he began to feel pain in the toe.

No result from Sid.

Tom was panting with his exertions by this time. He took a rest and then swelled himself up and fetched a succession of admirable groans.

Sid snored on.

Tom was aggravated. He said, "Sid, Sid!" and shook him. This course worked well, and Tom began to groan again. Sid yawned, stretched, then brought himself up on his elbow with a snort, and began to stare at Tom. Tom went on groaning. Sid said:

"Tom! Say, Tom!" [No response.] "Here, Tom! TOM! What is the matter, Tom?" And he shook him and looked in his face anxiously.

Tom moaned out: "Oh, don't, Sid. Don't joggle me."

"Why, what's the matter, Tom? I must call auntie."

"No—never mind. It'll be over by and by, maybe. Don't call anybody."

"But I must! DON'T groan so, Tom, it's awful. How long you been this way?"

"Hours. Ouch! Oh, don't stir so, Sid, you'll kill me."

"Tom, why didn't you wake me sooner? Oh, Tom, DON'T! It makes my flesh crawl to hear you. Tom, what is the matter?"

"I forgive you everything, Sid. [Groan.] Everything you've ever done to me. When I'm gone—"

"Oh, Tom, you ain't dying, are you? Don't, Tom—oh, don't. Maybe—"

"I forgive everybody, Sid. [Groan.] Tell 'em so, Sid. And Sid, you give my window-sash and my cat with one eye to that new girl that's come to town, and tell her—"

But Sid had snatched his clothes and gone. Tom was suffering in reality, now, so handsomely was his imagination working, and so his groans had gathered quite a genuine tone.

Sid flew down-stairs and said: "Oh, Aunt Polly, come! Tom's dying!"

"Dying!"

"Yes'm. Don't wait—come quick!"

"Rubbage! I don't believe it!"

But she fled up-stairs, nevertheless, with Sid and Mary at her heels. And her face grew white, too, and her lip trembled. When she reached the bedside she gasped out:

"You, Tom! Tom, what's the matter with you?"

"Oh, auntie, I'm—"

"What's the matter with you—what is the matter with you, child?"

"Oh, auntie, my sore toe's mortified!"

The old lady sank down into a chair and laughed a little, then cried a little, then did both together. This restored her and she said: "Tom, what a turn you did give me. Now you shut up that nonsense and climb out of this."

The groans ceased and the pain vanished from the toe. The boy felt a little foolish, and he said: "Aunt Polly, it SEEMED mortified, and it hurt so I never minded my tooth at all."

"Your tooth, indeed! What's the matter with your tooth?"

"One of them's loose, and it aches perfectly awful."

"There, there, now, don't begin that groaning again. Open your mouth. Well—your tooth IS loose, but you're not going to die about that. Mary, get me a silk thread, and a chunk of fire out of the kitchen."

Tom said: "Oh, please, auntie, don't pull it out. It don't hurt any more. I wish I may never stir if it does. Please don't, auntie. I don't want to stay home from school."

"Oh, you don't, don't you? So all this row was because you thought you'd get to stay home from school and go a-fishing? Tom, Tom, I love you so, and you seem to try every way you can to break my old heart with your outrageousness." By this time the dental instruments were ready. The old lady made one end of the silk thread fast to Tom's tooth with a loop and tied the other to the bedpost. Then she seized the chunk of fire and suddenly thrust it almost into the boy's face. The tooth hung dangling by the bedpost, now.

But all trials bring their compensations. As Tom wended to school after breakfast, he was the envy of every boy he met because the gap in his upper row of teeth enabled him to expectorate in a new and admirable way. He gathered quite a following of lads interested in the exhibition; and one that had cut his finger and had been a centre of fascination and homage up to this time, now found himself suddenly without an adherent, and shorn of his glory. His heart was heavy, and he said with a disdain which he did not feel that it wasn't anything to spit like Tom Sawyer; but another boy said, "Sour grapes!" and he wandered away a dismantled hero.[64]

STEP TWO: **Note important events**

You will now summarize the passage in three or four sentences and write those sentences down on your own paper.

On your scratch paper, write down five or six phrases or short sentences that will remind you of the things that happened in the story. *Do not use more than six phrases or short sentences!*

64. Mark Twain, *The Adventures of Tom Sawyer* (The American Publishing Company, 1881), pp. 60–63.

Remember, you're not supposed to write down *everything* that happens in the story—just the most important events.

Be sure to write the events down in the same order that they happen in the story.

If you have trouble with this assigment, ask your instructor for help.

STEP THREE: **Write summary sentences**

After you've written down your five or six phrases or sentences, try to combine them into three or four sentences. You can do this by putting two phrases in the same sentence (for example, "Tom Sawyer didn't want to go to school" and "Decided to pretend his sore toe hurt" could be combined into "Tom Sawyer didn't want to go to school, so he pretended that his toe hurt"). Or you may find that one or more of your jotted notes turn out to be unnecessary.

Say your three or four sentences out loud several times before writing them down. After you've written the sentences down, ask your instructor to check them.

If you have trouble, ask your instructor for help.

Day Two: Outlining Exercise

Focus: Finding the central topic in each paragraph of a chronological narrative that includes description

STEP ONE: **Read**

Read the following excerpt from *The History of Puerto Rico: From the Spanish Discovery to the American Occupation* by R. A. Van Middeldyk. "The Admiral" is Christopher Columbus, who made his first visit to Puerto Rico in November 1493. This was Columbus's second voyage to the Americas; he had returned from his first journey not long before and had convinced the Spanish government to pay for a second trip of exploration.

> The first island discovered on this voyage lies between 14° and 15° north latitude, near the middle of a chain of islands of different sizes, intermingled with rocks and reefs, which stretches from Trinidad, near the coast of Venezuela, in a north-by-westerly direction to Puerto Rico. They are divided in two groups, the Windward Islands forming the southern, the Leeward Islands the northern portion of the chain. . . .
>
> For an account of the expedition's experiences on that memorable voyage, we have the fleet physician Chanca's circumstantial description addressed to the

Municipal Corporation of Seville, sent home by the same pilot who conveyed the Admiral's first despatches to the king and queen. After describing the weather experienced up to the time the fleet arrived at the island "de Hierro," he tells their worships that for nineteen or twenty days they had the best weather ever experienced on such a long voyage, excepting on the eve of San Simon, when they had a storm which for four hours caused them great anxiety. At daybreak on Sunday, November 3d, the pilot of the flagship announced land. "It was marvelous," says Chanca, "to see and hear the people's manifestations of joy; and with reason, for they were very weary of the hardships they had undergone, and longed to be on land again."

The first island they saw was high and mountainous. As the day advanced they saw another more level, and then others appeared, till they counted six, some of good size, and all covered with forest to the water's edge. Sailing along the shore of the first discovered island for the distance of a league, and finding no suitable anchoring ground, they proceeded to the next island, which was four or five leagues distant, and here the Admiral landed, bearing the royal standard, and took formal possession of this and all adjacent lands in the name of their Highnesses. He named the first island Dominica, because it was discovered on a Sunday, and to the second island he gave the name of his ship, Marie-Galante.

"In this island," says Chanca, "it was wonderful to see the dense forest and the great variety of unknown trees, some in bloom, others with fruit, everything looking so green. We found a tree the leaves whereof resembled laurel leaves, but not so large, and they exhaled the finest odor of cloves. There were fruits of many kinds, some of which the men imprudently tasted, with the result that their faces swelled, and that they suffered such violent pain in throat and mouth that they behaved like madmen, the application of cold substances giving them some relief."

No signs of inhabitants were discovered, so they remained ashore two hours only and left next morning early (November 4th) in the direction of another island seven or eight leagues northward. They anchored off the southernmost coast of it, now known as Basse Terre, and admired a mountain in the distance, which seemed to reach into the sky (the volcano "la Souffrière"), and the beautiful waterfall on its flank. The Admiral sent a small caravel close inshore to look for a port, which was soon found. Perceiving some huts, the captain landed, but the people who occupied them escaped into the forest as soon as they saw the strangers. On entering the huts they found two large parrots (guacamayos) entirely different from those seen until then by the Spaniards, much cotton, spun and ready for spinning, and other articles, bringing away a little of each.[65]

65. Rudolph Adams Van Middeldyk, *The History of Puerto Rico: From the Spanish Discovery to the American Occupation* (D. Appleton and Company, 1903), pp. 9–11.

STEP TWO: **Construct a one-level outline**

This week's passage combines two of the topics you've been studying: the chronological narrative and the description of a place.

As in previous weeks, you'll need to find a major point for each section. Because the sections alternate between chronological narrative and description, you'll have to use both of the methods you've studied. If the section seems to be chronological narrative, ask:

1. What is the main thing or person that this section is about? *Or* What is the major event in this section?
2. Why is that thing, person, or event important?

If the section seems to be primarily descriptive, ask:

What part of the place does this paragraph focus on?

If you're not sure which method will work best, try both.

You may mix phrases and sentences if necessary. If you have difficulty, ask your instructor for help. And when you're finished, check your assignment with your instructor.

Day Three: Analyzing the Topos

Focus: Understanding the form of a chronological narrative that includes description

The passage you outlined in your last writing session was a **chronological narrative of a past event** that made use of a **description of a place**—a combination of two forms you have already learned. Today, you'll review the elements that make up both forms, and look at the ways in which writers combine them. Tomorrow, you'll write your own chronological narrative, making use of a place description.

STEP ONE: **Review the elements of a chronological narrative**

In studying the form of a chronological narrative of past events, you've learned:

1. A chronological narrative answers the questions: Who did what to whom? (Or what was done to what)? And in what sequence?
2. Time and sequence words make the narrative flow smoothly forward.
3. Dialogue and actions help hold the reader's interest.

Look back at your outline of the passage from *The History of Puerto Rico.* It probably looks something like this:

I. The islands discovered on the voyage
II. Chanca's description of their journey
III. Landing on the islands
IV. Fruits and trees on the island
V. Travelling to another island with people

The first and fourth sections contain descriptions, but points II, III, and V tell you who did what and in what order:

First, Chanca and the others made a journey.
Second, they landed on the islands.
Third, they travelled to other islands nearby.

The passage makes use of time and sequence words to help move the narrative forward—not just the time and sequence words on your chart, but also verbs and phrases that show the passage of time. Look at the sections below, and circle the bolded words, saying each word aloud as you circle it.

> **After** describing the weather experienced **up to the time** the fleet arrived at the island "de Hierro," he tells their worships that **for nineteen or twenty days** they had the best weather ever experienced on such a long voyage, excepting on the eve of San Simon, **when** they had a storm which **for four hours** caused them great anxiety. **At daybreak** on Sunday, November 3d, the pilot of the flagship announced land. "It was marvelous," says Chanca, "to see and hear the people's manifestations of joy; and with reason, for they were very weary of the hardships they had undergone, and longed to be on land again."
>
> The **first** island they saw was high and mountainous. **As the day advanced** they saw another more level, and **then** others appeared, **till** they counted six, some of good size, and all covered with forest to the water's edge. Sailing along the shore of the first discovered island for the distance of a league, and finding no suitable anchoring ground, they **proceeded** to the **next** island, which was four or five leagues distant, and here the Admiral landed, bearing the royal standard, and took formal possession of this and all adjacent lands in the name of their Highnesses. He named the **first** island Dominica, because it was discovered on a Sunday, and to the **second** island he gave the name of his ship, Marie-Galante.
>
> No signs of inhabitants were discovered, so they remained ashore **two hours only** and left **next morning early** (November 4th) in the direction of another island seven or eight leagues northward. They anchored off the southernmost coast of it, now known as Basse Terre, and admired a mountain in the distance, which seemed to reach into the sky (the volcano "la Souffrière"), and the beautiful waterfall on its flank. The Admiral sent a small caravel close inshore to look for a port, which was **soon** found.

> Perceiving some huts, the captain landed, but the people who occupied them escaped into the forest **as soon as** they saw the strangers. **On** entering the huts they found two large parrots (guacamayos) entirely different from those seen **until then** by the Spaniards, much cotton, spun and ready for spinning, and other articles, bringing away a little of each.

Finally, notice how the writer makes use of dialogue. Rather than putting in speeches made by Columbus and the other travellers, the writer chooses to use the exact words of someone who was on the voyage. When Chanca, the fleet physician, writes "It was marvelous to see and hear the people's manifestations of joy," we are brought much closer to the actual event than if the writer had simply put "The people were glad to see land."

STEP TWO: **Review the elements of a description of a place**

The writer of *The History of Puerto Rico* inserts passages of description into his narrative whenever he wants the reader to picture the places that the explorers are discovering. The first and fourth sections:

> I. The islands discovered on the voyage
> IV. Fruits and trees on the island

are place descriptions, but the final section also contains an important single-sentence description of a place.

Each description has a particular purpose. The first section acts as an introduction to the entire journey; it's a little like being given a map to look at as the story goes on. The fourth section makes clear to the reader just how strange and foreign the unfamiliar landscape looked to the explorers. And the sentence in the final section gives the reader a sense of the awe felt by the explorers when they saw the beauty of the new land.

Go through the descriptions below and circle the bolded space and distance words and phrases, saying each one out loud. As you read, think about the point of view of the narrator in each section. Is the narrator above the scene and uninvolved in it, inside it, looking at it from one side, or moving through it? (Each section has a different point of view.) Jot a note identifying the point of view beside each section before going on to read the explanations below the descriptions.

> *Introduction/map*
> The first island discovered on this voyage lies **between** 14° and 15° **north latitude, near** the **middle** of a chain of islands of different sizes, **intermingled** with rocks and reefs, which stretches **from** Trinidad, **near** the coast of Venezuela, **in a north-by-westerly direction to** Puerto Rico. They are divided in two groups, the Windward Islands forming the **southern**, the Leeward Islands the **northern** portion of the chain. . . .

A strange, foreign, unfamiliar land

"**In** this island," says Chanca, "it was wonderful to see the dense forest and the great variety of unknown trees, some in bloom, others **with** fruit, everything looking so green. We found a tree the leaves **whereof** resembled laurel leaves, but not so large, and they exhaled the finest odor of cloves. There were fruits of many kinds, some of which the men imprudently tasted, with the result that their faces swelled, and that they suffered such violent pain **in** throat and mouth that they behaved like madmen, the application of cold substances giving them some relief."

Awe at the natural beauty

They anchored **off** the **southernmost** coast of it, now known as Basse Terre, and admired a mountain **in the distance,** which seemed to reach **into** the sky (the volcano "la Souffrière"), and the beautiful waterfall **on** its flank.

Did you identify the point of view of each section? If so, read on.

The "introduction/map" section is very definitely written from above the scene. The narrator of this section is the writer of the history, Rudolph Adams Van Middeldyk. He's describing the scene as though looking down on a map, and he's certainly not personally involved with it.

The "unfamiliar land" section is written by Chanca, the fleet physician, and he seems to be inside the scene. You could also argue that he's moving through it, but we're not given any space or distance words that imply he's walking through the island as he describes it; he sounds more as if he's standing next to the tree with the laurel leaves, looking around.

In the "natural beauty" section, the narrators are the sailors who've just dropped anchor on the southern coast, and they are looking at the island as a whole from the side angle.

Finally, the "unfamiliar land" and "natural beauty" sections both contain figurative language. Chanca says that the sailors "behaved like madmen"; although this has more to do with the people than with the place itself, the simile certainly makes the scene vivid. In the final section, Van Middeldyk uses one of those cliches; you can do better when you write tomorrow.

STEP THREE: Analyze a model passage

Your final assignment for today is to go through the following chronological narrative and description and do the same analysis that was done for you above. You don't have to construct another outline, but you do have to:

1. Identify each paragraph as either *primarily* narrative or *primarily* description and write the label in the right-hand margin.
2. Circle each time and sequence word in the narrative paragraphs.

3. Underline each space and distance word in the description paragraphs.
4. In the left-hand margin, write the purpose and point of view of any descriptive paragraph.
5. Draw a box around any figurative language (this may occur either in the descriptive or narrative passages).
6. Underline any lines of dialogue twice.
7. Check your answers with your instructor.

This passage is from *Nelson's Trafalgar: The Battle That Changed the World* by Roy Adkins. The Battle of Trafalgar was fought on October 21, 1805, just off the coast of Spain. The British fleet was one one side; the French and Spanish (the "Combined Fleet") were allied on the other. Rear-Admiral Dumanoir [doom-ah-nwhar] commanded part of the French fleet. The *Victory* was the flagship of the British fleet and was commanded by Admiral Lord Nelson, who was killed during the battle. Captain Lucas, who commanded the *Redoubtable* (also spelled *Redoutable* in some histories), was a French officer.

> It was now a few minutes past one o'clock, just over an hour after the battle had begun. At the heart of the fighting, where the two British columns had cut the French and Spanish line, the flow of blood from the decks into the gutters and out through drain holes had left scarlet streaks down the sides of the ships. The sea itself was taking on a dull crimson cast alternately lit by flashes from the muzzles of the cannons and shaded by the pall of dust and smoke.
>
> The British, French, and Spanish ships were now shuffling positions in a kaleidoscope of fire, smoke, wreckage and blood, while the battle line of the Combined Fleet continued to degenerate into a confused mass as one after another of the British ships slid through it. Those British ships reaching the line were no longer running before the wind, which itself was very light, but were manoeuvring at very slow speeds, sometimes less than one mile per hour, to aim at selected targets. . . .

> Rear-Admiral Dumanoir with the leading ships of the French and Spanish line—representing a quarter of the fleet—continued to sail away northwards. In the meantime, the slowest-sailing ships of the British fleet were still desperately struggling to catch up and reach the now disintegrating line so as to support their leaders. This meant that some ships fought in the battle for a much longer time than others, and afterwards crews

would taunt each other on shore, "Oh! you belong to one of the ships that did not come up till the battle was nearly over."

With the *Victory* so close, Captain Lucas feared that there might be an attempt to board his own ship, the *Redoubtable*. . . . [H]e ordered the gun-ports to be closed on the side against the *Victory* in order to stop the British gaining access. His musketeers kept up a constant fire with bullets and grenades, concentrating on the *Victory*, but in the middle of this growing chaos, where the noise was by now deafening, all the officers continued to pace the decks, frequently choked and blinded by smoke, largely ignoring the increasing carnage and destruction around them. The guns of the *Victory* were continuing to pulverise the hull of the *Redoubtable*, and behind the shredded wooden wall of the French ship there was devastation—few men were left on the lower decks who had not been hurt.[66]

Day Four: Practicing the Topos

Focus: Learning how to write a chronological narrative of a past event that includes a description of a place

Today, you'll put together a chronological narrative of a past event; one of your paragraphs will also describe a place that's central to the event.

STEP ONE: **Plan the narrative**

On the next page, you'll see a list of events, written out chronologically for you, about the sixteenth-century Russian tsar Ivan IV ("Ivan the Terrible"). Bolded entries are main events; the indented entries are futher details about those main events. These details are taken from *The Cambridge History of Russia* (Cambridge University Press, 2006) edited by Maureen Perrie and from *Russia: The Once and Future Empire from Pre-History to Putin* by Philip Longworth (Macmillan, 2006).

Your chronological narrative will be based on these events. This chronological narrative must be at least 150 words long and no longer than 300 words.

As in previous assignments, you will not include every event. Look over the following events now, and mark three or four main (bolded) events to include in your narrative. **You must include the construction of St. Basil's Cathedral as one of your main events.**

After you have chosen your main events, mark which details and dialogue you intend to include. You won't include all of the details under any main event (pick and choose), but you must include at least one line of dialogue in your final composition.

66. Roy Adkins, *Nelson's Trafalgar: The Battle That Changed the World* (Viking, 2005), pp. 138–140.

EVENTS IN THE LIFE OF TSAR IVAN IV

Ivan's childhood

Born August 25, 1530
His father was Grand Prince of Moscow
Father died 1533
Ivan became Grand Prince at age 3
His mother ruled for him
Mother poisoned in 1538
Russian noblemen struggled over the throne
Ivan's family fought to keep the throne for Ivan
They drove out opposition by 1547

Crowned Emperor (Tsar) of Russia in 1547

First Russian ruler to use the title "tsar"
"Tsar" was Russian form of "Caesar," old Roman title
Believed he was God's anointed and should have complete power
The medieval history called the *Nikon Chronicle* says: "From that time on, the princes began to regard him with fear."

Enlarged his kingdom through conquest

Fought against the Mongols
Fought against his western neighbors
Fought north into Siberia
Conquered the Tatar city of Kazan in 1552 (Tatars=Turkish people group)
Russia now spread across vast territories
Russia now had many different races inside it

Ordered the building of a new church to celebrate his military victories

Commanded the church built in 1552
Construction began in 1555
Construction went on until 1679
The church was called Cathedral of the Intercession of the Virgin
Later its name was changed to honor Basil the Blessed
Church now known as St. Basil's Cathedral

Became known as "Ivan the Terrible"

"Terrible" really means "dreaded" or "awe-inspiring"
Given the title because of his punishment of wrongdoers

Began a "reign of terror" in 1564

Began to suffer from mental breakdown
Formed secret police to hunt out his enemies
Ivan wrote, "If a tsar's subjects do not obey him they will forever be at war with one another."
An Italian ambassador wrote home, "Since he tries to find out everything his subjects do, very few of them dare to say anything." He also wrote that the Russian

"people fear their lord, and are more obedient to their ruler than any other people in the world."

Secret police known as *oprichnina* wore black cloaks and carried brooms (brooms represented "sweeping clean")

Had political opponents murdered

Attacked his own city of Novgorod and massacred the population

Ivan IV said, "We are free to show favor to our servants and are free to put them to death."

Killed his own son in 1581

His son Ivan was 27

Argued with his son about the clothes his son's wife wore

Son contradicted him

Ivan the Terrible struck his son with an iron-tipped staff

Son was in coma for several days before dying

Died in 1584

Had been ill—could no longer walk and was carried in a litter

Was getting ready to play chess

Died suddenly

Left his country poorer and in chaos

STEP TWO: **Plan the description**

As part of your composition, include a description of St. Basil's Cathedral. On the next page, you will see some pictures of the cathedral. Use these images and write a brief description of the cathedral. (If possible, go online and do a search at images.google.com for "St. Basil's Cathedral." The domes and towers are painted bright colors; a description without this detail is acceptable, but the colors make the cathedral much more interesting.)

You will include this description in your narrative, either as part of the paragraph where you tell us that Ivan IV ordered the cathedral built, or as a separate paragraph following this main event.

Note that the pictures show the cathedral in its present form; it has been added onto, restored, and repainted since Ivan's day. When you write your description, you may want to mention that you are describing the cathedral as it now looks.

Write down a few phrases now that give details about the cathedral's size, shape, and appearance. Your final description should follow these guidelines:

1. It should be written from above, with an impersonal perspective.
2. It should include at least two space and distance words.
3. The cathedral's design was unusual and unique; the description should give a sense of the cathedral's being out of place, looking like nothing else in the city, shocking onlookers with its strangeness.
4. The description should contain at least one clear use of figurative language.

STEP THREE: **Write**

As you begin to write, don't forget to include time and sequence words and dialogue.

Don't forget to incorporate your description of the cathedral into your composition.

When you are finished, show your composition to your instructor.

All photo credits: Shutterstock.com

Week 12: Scientific Description

Day One: Original Narration Exercise

Focus: Summarizing a narrative that combines two narrative voices

STEP ONE: **Read**

Read the following excerpt from *The Hound of the Baskervilles* by Arthur Conan Doyle. In this passage, a country doctor named James Mortimer has come to London to see the great detective Sherlock Holmes and his friend, Dr. Watson at 221B Baker Street. James Mortimer has just finished explaining to Sherlock Holmes that he needs helping solving a mystery; his friend Sir Charles Baskerville died suddenly and tragically, three months before. His body was found lying on the moor (the high, open area of land) near his house, late at night. James Mortimer thinks that the death is connected, somehow, to the legend that the entire Baskerville family is cursed to be haunted and pursued by a giant, ghostly hound.

As this excerpt begins, James Mortimer has already told Holmes and Watson all about the legend. Now he is describing the circumstances of Charles Baskerville's death.

"Chimerical" means "unreal, imaginary, fantastic" (it comes from the name of a mythological Greek beast, the chimera, which had the head of a lion, the body of a goat, and the tail of a snake).

"Within the last few months it became increasingly plain to me that Sir Charles's nervous system was strained to the breaking point. He had taken this legend which I have read you exceedingly to heart—so much so that, although he would walk in his own grounds, nothing would induce him to go out upon the moor at night. Incredible as it may appear to you, Mr. Holmes, he was honestly convinced that a dreadful fate overhung his family, and certainly the records which he was able to give of his ancestors were not encouraging. The idea of some ghastly presence constantly haunted him, and on more than one occasion he has asked me whether I had on my medical journeys at night ever seen any strange creature or heard the baying of a hound. The latter question he put to me several times, and always with a voice which vibrated with excitement.

"I can well remember driving up to his house in the evening some three weeks before the fatal event. He chanced to be at his hall door. I had descended from my gig and was standing in front of him, when I saw his eyes fix themselves over my shoulder and stare past me with an expression of the most dreadful horror. I whisked round and had just time to catch a glimpse of something which I took to be a large black calf passing at the head of the drive. So excited and alarmed was he that I was compelled to go down to the spot where the animal had been and look around for it. It was gone, however, and the incident appeared to make the worst impression upon his mind. I stayed with him all the evening, and it was on that occasion, to explain the emotion which he had shown, that he confided to my keeping that narrative which I read to you when first I came. I mention this small episode because it assumes some importance in view of the tragedy which followed, but I was convinced at the time that the matter was entirely trivial and that his excitement had no justification.

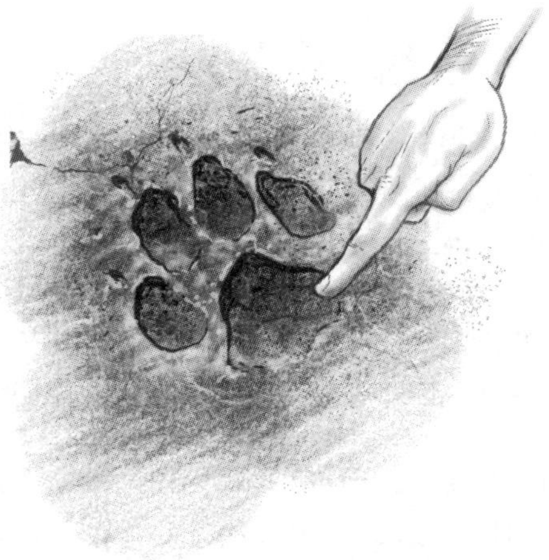

"It was at my advice that Sir Charles was about to go to London. His heart was, I knew, affected, and the constant anxiety in which he lived, however chimerical the cause of it might be, was evidently having a serious effect upon his health. I thought that a few months among the distractions of town would send him back a new man. Mr. Stapleton, a mutual friend who was much concerned at his state of health, was of the same opinion. At the last instant came this terrible catastrophe.

"On the night of Sir Charles's death Barrymore the butler, who made the discovery, sent Perkins the groom on horseback to me, and as I was sitting up late I was able to reach Baskerville Hall within an hour of the event. I checked and corroborated all the facts which were mentioned at the inquest. I followed the footsteps down the yew alley, I saw the spot at the moor-gate where he seemed to have waited, I remarked the change in the shape of the prints after that point, I noted that there were no other footsteps save those of Barrymore on the soft gravel, and finally I carefully examined the body, which had not been touched until my arrival. Sir Charles lay on his face, his arms out, his fingers dug into the ground, and his features convulsed with some strong emotion to such an extent that I could hardly have sworn to his identity. There was certainly no physical injury of any kind. But one false statement was made by Barrymore at the inquest. He said that there were no traces upon the ground round the body. He did not observe any. But I did—some little distance off, but fresh and clear."

"Footprints?"

"Footprints."

"A man's or a woman's?"

Dr. Mortimer looked strangely at us for an instant, and his voice sank almost to a whisper as he answered.

"Mr. Holmes, they were the footprints of a gigantic hound!"

I confess at these words a shudder passed through me. There was a thrill in the doctor's voice which showed that he was himself deeply moved by that which he told us. Holmes leaned forward in his excitement and his eyes had the hard, dry glitter which shot from them when he was keenly interested.

"You saw this?"

"As clearly as I see you."

"And you said nothing?"

"What was the use?"

"How was it that no one else saw it?"

"The marks were some twenty yards from the body and no one gave them a thought. I don't suppose I should have done so had I not known this legend."

"There are many sheep-dogs on the moor?"

"No doubt, but this was no sheep-dog."

"You say it was large?"

"Enormous."

"But it had not approached the body?"

"No."

"What sort of night was it?'

"Damp and raw."

"But not actually raining?"

"No."

"What is the alley like?"

"There are two lines of old yew hedge, twelve feet high and impenetrable. The walk in the centre is about eight feet across."

"Is there anything between the hedges and the walk?"

"Yes, there is a strip of grass about six feet broad on either side."

"I understand that the yew hedge is penetrated at one point by a gate?"

"Yes, the wicket-gate which leads on to the moor."

"Is there any other opening?"

"None."

"So that to reach the yew alley one either has to come down it from the house or else to enter it by the moor-gate?"

"There is an exit through a summer-house at the far end."

"Had Sir Charles reached this?"

"No; he lay about fifty yards from it."

"Now, tell me, Dr. Mortimer—and this is important—the marks which you saw were on the path and not on the grass?"

"No marks could show on the grass."

"Were they on the same side of the path as the moor-gate?"

"Yes; they were on the edge of the path on the same side as the moor-gate."

"You interest me exceedingly. Another point. Was the wicket-gate closed?"

"Closed and padlocked."

"How high was it?"

"About four feet high."

"Then anyone could have got over it?"

"Yes."

"And what marks did you see by the wicket-gate?"

"None in particular."

"Good heaven! Did no one examine?"

"Yes, I examined, myself."

"And found nothing?"

"It was all very confused. Sir Charles had evidently stood there for five or ten minutes."

"How do you know that?"

"Because the ash had twice dropped from his cigar."[67]

STEP TWO: **Note important events in the two different stories**

You will now summarize the passage in three or four sentences, and write those sentences down on your own paper.

This may be a challenge because there are actually two different stories in the excerpt. The first is the story that James Mortimer is telling about Charles Baskerville; the second is the story that the author, Arthur Conan Doyle, is telling about James Mortimer and Sherlock Holmes.

Begin by jotting down, on the left-hand side of your paper, five or six phrases or sentences that will remind you of the things that happened in James Mortimer's story. Draw a vertical line down the middle of the paper. On the right-hand side, jot down two or three phrases or sentences that will remind you of the things that happen in Arthur Conan Doyle's story.

If you have trouble with this assignment, ask your instructor for help.

STEP THREE: **Write summary sentences**

After you've written down your phrases and sentences, try to combine them into three or four sentences. The first part of your summary should begin with "According to Dr. Mortimer" (or

---

67. Arthur Conan Doyle, *The Hound of the Baskervilles: Another Adventure of Sherlock Holmes* (Mclure, Phillips & Co., 1902), pp. 23–29.

a similar phrase). The second part of your summary should begin with "After Dr. Mortimer finished his story" (or a similar phrase).

Say your three or four sentences out loud several times before writing them down. After you've written the sentences down, ask your instructor to check them.

If you have trouble, ask your instructor for help.

Day Two: Outlining Exercise

Focus: Finding the central topic in each paragraph of a scientific description

STEP ONE: **Read**

Read the following excerpt from *The Illustrated Encyclopedia of Astronomy and Space*, edited by Ian Ridpath. An astronomical unit is 92,955,807.27 miles (149,597,870.7 kilometers), approximately the same as the average distance between the Earth and the sun.

— — —

A comet is a small icy body embedded in a cloud of gas and dust moving in a highly elliptical orbit around the Sun. Comets spend most of their lives in frozen reaches far from the Sun, but periodically their orbits bring them close enough to be heated up and to release gas and dust clouds to form a hazy head, developing tails which always point away from the Sun. These have given comets their name: from the Greek meaning "long-haired one."

Comets were thought to be atmospheric phenomenona until Tycho Brahe demonstrated that the comet he discovered in 1577 showed no shift in position through parallax, proving it was far beyond the Moon. Isaac Newton demonstrated that comet Kirch, discovered in 1680, moved in an orbit around the Sun in accordance with his theory of gravity. Edmond Halley, and later Wilhelm Olbers, greatly improved methods of determining the orbits of comets. The study of their physical structure and behavior began in the mid-18th century and is now an increasingly important field of research. . . .

Despite the popular picture of a comet as a brilliant object with a fine tail, most comets are actually faint, diffuse, tail-less objects visible only with large telescopes. Comets consist of a nucleus, a head or *coma,* and a tail.

The nucleus is the only solid body, with a diameter of from 1 to 30 miles (1.6–48 km), a low overall density, and a mass from about 10 billion to 100 trillion tons. A comet's nucleus is made of dust particles loosely compacted with water ice, together with frozen carbon monoxide and methane. The Sun's heat melts the nucleus, releasing huge volumes of gas which carry away dust and ice particles.

This gas produces the head or *coma* of the comet consisting of water vapor, carbon monoxide, and OH (hydroxyl), with minor amounts of other molecules containing carbon, hydrogen, and nitrogen. These molecules are then broken up into smaller fragments to produce a plasma, or ionized gas. The coma is normally about 10,000 to 1000,000 miles (16,000–160,000 km) across; the record is 1.1 million miles (1.8 km) for comet Flaugergues 1811 I. Hydrogen, carbon, and oxygen atoms form an invisible enveloping cloud some 10 to 20 million miles (16 to 32 million km) across.

If a comet becomes very active, the solar wind carries away dust and gas to form its tail. Prominent tails develop only in large active comets close to the Sun, and always point away from the Sun. . . .

The total number of comets is enormous—about 10 million comets must have their perihelion points within the orbit of Neptune alone. Most new comets move sunward from a great distance, suggesting they originate in a vast cloud at a distance of 20,000 to 60,000 a.u. [astronomical units]. This is known as Oort's cloud, after the Dutch astronmer Jan Oort, and contains an estimated 100 billion comets.[68]

STEP TWO: **Construct a one-level outline**

This week's passage is a slightly different kind of description: a scientific description of an object or phenomenon.

When you first outlined a descriptive passage in Week 8, you learned that you can sometimes ask a simpler question of a descriptive paragraph than of a narrative paragraph. When you're reading a narrative, you're following a series of events, so you need to know not only what a paragraph is *about,* but what is happening in it. You have been finding this information by asking: What is the main thing or person that this section is about? Why is that thing or person important?

In a descriptive passage, though, a writer often describes a place or object one part or *aspect* at a time. "Aspect" refers to some specific characteristic or quality of the object that's not actually physical; so, for example, if a description of a fort began by discussing the fort's walls, that would be a *part* of the fort; if the description began by describing the *need* for the fort, or the importance of the fort, that would be an *aspect.*

68. *The Illustrated Encyclopedia of Astronomy and Space,* rev. ed., ed. Ian Ridpath (Thomas Y. Crowell Publishers, 1979), pp. 42–44.

Often you can find the central topic in a section of scientific description by asking: What aspect or part of the whole does this section describe?

Let's try this for the first paragraph of your description. First, experiment with the original method: What is the most important thing in this paragraph?

✦

The answer's obvious: *a comet.*

Why is that thing important?

This doesn't turn out to be a very useful question, because there are a number of important things listed (orbits, heads and tails, names) and they all seem to have equal importance in the passage. Instead, ask yourself: What aspect or part of the whole does this paragraph describe?

Think about this for a moment before looking at the next line.

The whole thing.

This paragraph tells you what a comet *is* by giving an overall description of the parts of a comet, where a comet comes from, and how a comet gets its name. If you were going to give this paragraph a title, it might be "Introduction to comets" or "All about comets." Often, a scientific description will start with an introductory paragraph that gives a basic definition and overview of the object (or phenomenon) under study.

So your first point might look like this:

I. *Definition of comets*

or

I. *What a comet is*

Now look at the second paragraph. Once again, asking "What's the most important thing in this passage?" would probably give you the answer "Comets." But which of the discoveries about comets listed in this paragraph would qualify as the *most important one?* Instead, ask yourself: What part or aspect of the comet does this paragraph describe? No specific parts are mentioned—but how about *aspect?* What is happening in this paragraph, all centered around the comet?

Or, to put this another way, what did Tycho Brahe, Isaac Newton, Edmond Halley, and Wilhelm Olbers all do?

They all studied comets. So your second point might look like this:

II. *The study of comets*

or

II. *How the study of comets developed*

Now go through the rest of the paragraphs, asking yourself: What part or aspect of the comet does this section describe?

If you have difficulty, ask your instructor for help. When you're finished, check your work with your instructor.

Day Three: Analyzing the Topos

Focus: Understanding the form of a scientific description of an object or phenomenon

The passage you outlined in your last writing session is an example of this week's topos: **a scientific description of an object or phenomenon** (a thing that can be seen). Today's assignment is to understand the elements that go into a good scientific description.

STEP ONE: **Examine model passages**

Look back at your outline. Although your exact wording won't be the same, your outline probably resembles this one:

I. What comets are
II. How the study of comets developed
III. The structure of a comet
IV. Nucleus
V. Head, or *coma*
VI. Tail
VII. Number of comets

Now look at the pattern this writer has followed:

I. What comets are	Brief definition
II. How the study of comets developed	History of discovery
III. The structure of a comet	Description of physical parts
IV. Nucleus	
V. Head, or coma	
VI. Tail	
VII. Number of comets	Amplitude (this is a general word for measures of size, height, width, quantity)

Sections III–VI make up the scientific description of the comet. Like a description of a place, a scientific description is often part of a longer composition; in this piece, the scientific description is part of a longer encyclopedia entry.

Here's another scientific description, this one from Bill Bryson's *A Short History of Nearly Everything.*

> Whatever their size or shape, nearly all your cells are built to fundamentally the same plan: they have an outer casing or membrane, a nucleus wherein resides the necessary genetic information to keep you going, and a busy space between the two called the cytoplasm. The membrane is not, as most of us imagine it, a durable, rubbery casing, something that you would need a sharp pin to prick. Rather, it is made up of a type of fatty material known as a lipid, which has the approximate consistency "of a light grade of machine oil," to quote Sherwin B. Nuland. . .
>
> If you could visit a cell, you wouldn't like it. Blown up to a scale at which atoms were about the size of peas, a cell itself would be a sphere roughly half a mile across, and supported by a complex framework of girders called the cytoskeleton. Within it, millions upon millions of objects—some the size of basketballs, others the size of cars—would whiz about like bullets. There wouldn't be a place you could stand without being pummeled and ripped thousands of times every second from every direction.[69]

You should see a similarity between this passage and the description of comets in the first section. Both descriptions are *structural:* They describe the different parts that make up the whole.

The description of the comet tells us about the nucleus, the head (or *coma*), and the tail; all three of those things together make up a comet. Look at the two paragraphs about the cell. In the first paragraph, Bryson describes three parts that make up a cell. What are those parts? Go back and underline them.

In the second paragraph, Bryson mentions one more element that goes into the structure of a cell (and helps support it). What is it? Underline it now.

✦

What did you underline?

In the first paragraph, you should have underlined outer casing or membrane, nucleus, and cytoplasm. In the second paragraph, you should have underlined cytoskeleton. These are the different parts that make up a cell.

When you write a scientific description, you can begin by describing each of the separate parts that make up the whole. Now look again at these sentences from this week's descriptions:

> *A comet's nucleus is made of dust particles loosely compacted with water ice, together with frozen carbon monoxide and methane.*
>
> *If a comet becomes very active, the solar wind carries away dust and gas to form its tail.*

69. Bill Bryson, *A Short History of Nearly Everything* (Random House, 2004), p. 377.

The membrane is not, as most of us imagine it, a durable, rubbery casing, something that you would need a sharp pin to prick. Rather, it is made up of a type of fatty material known as a lipid. . .

Each one of these sentences describes the nucleus, the tail, and the membrane by telling you *what it is made of.*

STEP TWO: **Understand the use of figurative language**

When you write a scientific description, you can describe the parts of an object and tell what each part is made of—and still not give the reader a clear picture of it. Read the following sentences:

Galaxies are made up of collections of stars, dust, nebulae, and other cosmic materials. Each one has a nucleus. The nucleus is a bulge consisting of very tightly packed groups of stars. Some galaxies have spiral arms; others are elliptical or irregular in shape.

The sentences tell you about the different parts of a galaxy, but they don't create a clear picture in your head. Compare those sentences with this paragraph, which begins by describing spiral galaxies like our Milky Way:

At the center of the nucleus of our galaxy . . . is an enormous black hole—perhaps one million times the size of the sun. Moving outward, we come to the "spiral arms". . . . Stars form in the spiral arms from clouds of dust and interstellar gas, and the entire galaxy rotates in space like a giant pinwheel. . . . Not all galaxies are like the Milky Way, however. Some are elliptical in shape, like giant footballs floating in space. Others are small, irregular things, like the dough left on a cookie tray after all the cookies have been cut.[70]

There are three useful similes in that paragraph. (Remember, a simile is figurative language that uses "like" or "as" to draw a comparison between two things.) Underline them now.

✦

Did you underline the following?

like a giant pinwheel
like giant footballs floating in space
like the dough left on a cookie sheet

All of these similes allow you to picture the appearance of the galaxies described.

70. James Trefil, ed., *Encyclopedia of Science and Technology* (Routledge, 2001), p. 211.

Bill Bryson also uses figurative language in his description of a cell. He could just write "Proteins, chemicals, and other agents move around through the cell." Instead, he imagines what the cell would look like if you could stand in it:

Blown up to a scale at which atoms were about the size of peas, a cell itself would be a sphere roughly half a mile across, and supported by a complex framework of girders called the cytoskeleton. Within it, millions upon millions of objects—some the size of basketballs, others the size of cars—would whiz about like bullets.

When you are writing a scientific description, you are often trying to give a picture of something that's outside of regular everyday experience. It's not easy to fully understand the structure of a galaxy, or a comet, or a cell if you've never actually *seen* one. Figurative language keeps scientific descriptions from being abstract and technical by giving the reader a vivid, simple picture.

STEP THREE: **Write down the pattern of the topos**

Copy the following onto a blank sheet of paper in the Reference section of your Composition Notebook. You will be adding to this page as you learn more about scientific descriptions, so leave plenty of room.

Scientific Description
Definition: A visual and structural description of an object or phenomenon

Procedure	Remember
1. Describe each part of the object or phenomenon and tell what it is made from.	1. Consider using figurative language to make the description more visual.

Day Four: Practicing the Topos

Focus: Learning how to write a scientific description of an object or phenomenon

Have you ever seen a human brain? If you haven't, maybe this scientific description will help:

The human brain, from the top, is something like a walnut, wrinkly and divided down the middle into two halves, or hemispheres, by a deep fissure. At the bottom of the fissure, the two halves are connected by a great bridge of nerve fibers called the corpus callosum. From a side view the brain is more like a mushroom, with the hemispheres forming the cap, and

> the lower parts of the brain forming a stem which connects below with the spinal cord.[71]

This description follows both of the guidelines you learned in the last writing session. It describes the parts of the brain (two hemispheres, a brain stem, the corpus callosum) and tells you that the corpus callosum is made out of nerve fibers. And it also uses *two* different similes to make the brain's appearance clear. From the top, it looks like a walnut; from the side, like a mushroom.

Today, you'll practice writing your own scientific description, following this pattern.

STEP ONE: **Plan the description**

Look carefully at the labelled diagram of the parts of the volcano. Then read the excerpts that follow. Your assignment is to write a description of a volcano that describes each important part of the volcano's structure by explaining what it is made of and what it looks like. This description should be at least 200 words but not more than 400.

You should not try to include details about every part of the volcano. As you read through the excerpts, decide which parts of the volcano your description will include, and which you will leave out. Cross lightly through the parts that you will not use in your description.

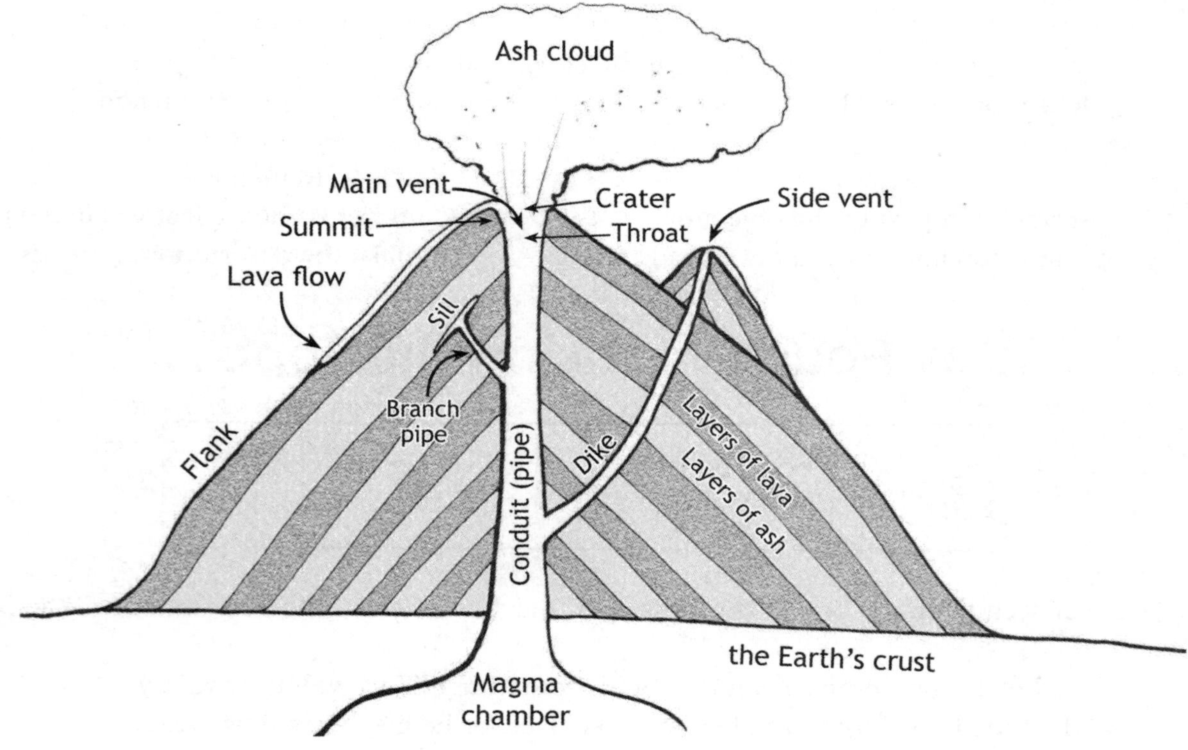

71. Daniel Goleman and Richard J. Davidson, *Consciousness: the Brain, States of Awareness, and Alternate Realities* (Irvington Publishers, 1979), p. 20.

Alexander E. Gates and David Ritchie, *Encyclopedia of Earthquakes and Volcanoes* (Facts on File, 2007)

> Lava is molten rock that flows out onto Earth's surface. . . . The word *lava* appears to be derived from the Italian word *lavare,* "to wash away" . . . its use is generally confined to fluid, molten rock reaching Earth's surface and to the formations produced by such rock during volcanic eruptions. Where lava solidifies after flowing for some distance, the resulting deposit is called a lava flow. (p. 146)
>
> Molten rock underground is generally known as magma, as distinct from lava, which is molten rock that has emerged onto the surface from a volcanic vent. . . . Magma is ever-present in these large chambers up to a kilometer beneath the surface. It can remain there for long periods of time without an eruption taking place. However, if it is charged with additional magma . . . or it is squeezed by local stress, the magma may ascend to the volcano. This process produces an eruption. (p. 157)

Robert Wayne Decker and Barbara Decker, *Volcanoes* (W. H. Freeman, 1981)

> The craters on volcanoes . . . are created in many different ways. Funnel-shaped craters usually result from an initial enlargement of the vent by volcanic explosions, followed by the collapse of loose debris back into the crater at the end of the eruption. After gas escapes from magma, the reduction in volume sometimes allows the magma to drain back down the vent, forming a deep cylindrical crater on the volcano's summit. (164)
>
> Sometimes an explosive eruption produces a cloud of volcanic debris so full of fragments that it is too heavy to rise very high into the atmosphere. Such an emulsion of gas and fragments forms a pyroclastic flow, the most dangerous kind of volcanic hazard. Pyroclastic flows can travel at speeds of more than 100 kilometers per hour, flattening and burning almost everything in their paths. Small pyroclastic flows often race down the valleys on a volcano's flanks, but larger masses that are expelled at high speeds . . . can sweep over small hills or across large flat areas. (125)

Sir Archibald Geikie, *Textbook of Geology* (P. F. Collier, 1902)

> At its exit from the side of a volcano, lava glows with a white heat, and flows with a motion which has been compared to that of honey or of melted iron. It soon becomes red, and, like a coal fallen from a hot fireplace, rapidly grows dull as it moves along, until it assumes a black, cindery aspect.

> At the same time the surface congeals, and soon becomes solid enough to support a heavy block of stone. . . . Viscous [thick] lavas, like those of Vesuvius, break upon the surface into rough brown or black cinder-like slags, and irregular ragged cakes, which, with the onward motion, grind and grate against each other with a harsh metallic sound, sometimes rising into rugged mounds or getting seamed with rents and gashes, at the bottom of which the red-hot glowing lava may be seen. (p. 219)
>
> As the molten mass rises within the chimney of the volcano, continued explosions of vapour take place from its upper surface. The violence of these may be inferred from the vast clouds of steam, ashes, and stones hurled to so great a height into the air. . . . As soon as the molten rock reaches the surface the superheated water or steam imprisoned within its mass escapes copiously, and hangs as a dense white cloud over the moving current. (p. 222)

STEP TWO: **Choose a metaphor or simile**

As you write your description, you should include at least one metaphor or simile.

Jot down at least one metaphor or simile that could help describe each of the following:

The ash cloud
The layers inside the volcano
The magma chamber and main conduit

If you have difficulty, ask your instructor for help.

STEP THREE: **Write the description**

Here's a summary of your assignment:

1. This description can be one paragraph or several paragraphs, but it must be at least 200 and not more than 400 words.
2. You may choose which parts of the volcano to include in your description.
3. As part of your description, explain what the selected parts are made from.
4. Use at least one metaphor or simile in your description.

If you have difficulty, ask your instructor for help. And when you're finished, show your composition to your instructor.

Week 13: Scientific Description

Day One: Original Narration Exercise

Focus: Summarizing a narrative with several parts

STEP ONE: **Read**

Read the following complete folktale, "Why the Sea Is Salt." This tale is a pourquoi story— a genre (type) of story that tells why something in nature is as it is. "Pourquoi" is pronounced *puh-quaa*, with the accent on the second syllable, and means "why" in French. You may be familiar with the *Just-So Stories* by Rudyard Kipling; these are also pourquoi stories.

— — —

Why the Sea Is Salt
A Norwegian Folktale

Once upon a time, many, many years ago, there lived two brothers, one of whom was very rich, and the other very poor. When Christmas evening came, the poor man had nothing in his house for Christmas dinner, and so he went to his brother and asked him for some food. The rich man was greatly displeased, as it was not the first time that he had been asked to give his brother food. But Christmas is a time when even selfish people give gifts. So he gave his brother a fine ham, but told him never to let him see his face again.

The poor man thanked his brother for the ham and started for home. On his way home he had to pass through a great forest, and when he had reached the thickest part of the forest he suddenly came to a place where there was a bright light. Near this bright light he saw an old man with a white beard chopping logs to make firewood.

"Good evening," said the poor man to the old man.

"Good evening to you. Where are you going at this late hour?" said the old man.

"I am taking this ham home for my Christmas dinner," answered the poor man.

"It is lucky for you," returned the old man, "that you met me. If you will take that ham into the land of the dwarfs, you can make a good bargain with it. The entrance to the land of the dwarfs lies just under the roots of this tree. The dwarfs are very fond of ham and they seldom get any, but you must not sell the ham for money; instead, get the magic mill which stands behind the door, and when you come out again, I will teach you how to use it."

The poor man thanked his new friend, who then showed him the door under a stone below the roots of a tree. By this door the poor man entered the land of the dwarfs, and when he got in, all the little people swarmed around him like ants in an anthill, and each one of them tried to buy the ham.

"I ought to keep it for my Christmas dinner," said the poor man, "but I will sell it to you if you will give me the magic mill which stands there behind the door."

At first they would not agree to this. They offered him gold and silver, but he refused all such offers. Finally, some of the dwarfs said, "Let him have the old mill. He does not know how to use it. Let him have it, and we will take the ham."

At last the bargain was made. The poor man took the magic mill, which was a little thing, not half so large as the ham, and then returned to his old friend the woodchopper, who showed him how to start it and also how to stop it. The poor man then thanked the old man again and started off with all speed for home. But all this had taken a great deal of time, and it was nearly midnight before he reached home.

"Where have you been?" said the poor man's wife. "I have been waiting, waiting, waiting, and we have neither wood for the fire nor food for our Christmas dinner."

The house was cold and dark, but the poor man told his wife to wait and see what would happen. He then placed the little magic mill on the table and told it to grind light and heat. As soon as the mill started, the room became brilliantly lighted by candles, and a bright and cheerful fire was blazing on the hearth. He then told the mill to grind a tablecloth, dishes, spoons, knives, and forks. He next told it to grind meat, and everything else that was good for a Christmas Eve supper; and the mill ground all that he ordered.

He was astonished at his good luck, as you may believe; and his wife was almost beside herself with joy. His wife wanted to know where he got the mill, but he would not tell her that. They had a splendid supper and a very merry Christmas.

On the third day, the poor man invited all his friends to come to a feast. What a feast it was! The table was covered with a cloth as white as snow, and the dishes were all silver or gold. The rich brother could not, in his great house and with all his wealth, set such a table.

"There is something very strange in all this," said every one.

"Something very strange indeed," said the rich brother. "On Christmas evening you were so poor that you came to my house and begged for food, and now you give a feast as if you were a king! Where did you get all these things?"

The poor brother then brought out the magic mill and made it grind first one thing and then another. The magic mill ground out boots and shoes, coats and cloaks, stockings, gowns, and blankets, and the poor man's wife gave all of these things to the poor people who had gathered about the house to get a sight of the grand feast that the poor brother had made for the rich one.

The rich brother wanted to borrow the mill, intending, for he was not an honest man, never to return it. But his brother would not lend it, for the old man with the white beard had told him never to sell it or lend it to any one.

Years passed by, and at last the owner of the mill built himself a grand castle on a rock near the sea. He covered this castle with plates of gold. The castle windows and the golden plates, reflecting the golden sunset, could be seen far out from the shore. This wonderful castle soon became a noted landmark for sailors. Strangers often came to see this castle of gold and the wonderful mill, of which the strangest tales were told far and wide.

After some time, there came a great merchant, who wished to see the magic mill. He asked whether it would grind salt; and, being told that it would, he wanted to buy it; for he traded in salt, and thought that if he owned the mill, he could supply all his customers without having to take long and dangerous voyages.

The man would not sell it, of course. He was so rich now that he did not want to use it for himself; but every Christmas he ground out food and clothes and coal for the poor, and nice presents for the little children; so he rejected all the offers of the rich merchant.

The merchant, however, made up his mind to steal the mill. He bribed one of the man's servants to let him into the castle at night, and he stole the magic mill and sailed away with it in triumph.

When he had gone a little way out to sea, he took the mill out on the deck and decided to set it to work.

"Now, mill, grind salt," said he; "grind salt with all your might! — salt, salt, nothing but salt!" So the mill began to grind salt and the sailors began to fill the sacks with it; but all of the sacks were soon full, and in spite of all that could be done, the salt began to fill the ship.

When the ship was filled the dishonest merchant was very much frightened, and wanted to stop the mill. But the mill would not stop grinding. The merchant knew how to start the mill, but he did not know how to stop it; no matter which way he turned it, it went on grinding and grinding. The heap of salt grew higher and higher, until at last the ship went down, making a great whirlpool where it sank.

The ship soon went to pieces, but the mill stands on the bottom of the sea, and day after day, year after year, it grinds "salt, salt, nothing but salt!" And this is the reason, say the peasants of Denmark and Norway, why the sea is salt.[72]

STEP TWO: **Find the different stories in the narrative**

You will now summarize the passage in five or six sentences, and write those sentences down on your own paper.

Last week, your narrative had two different stories told by two different people—one told by a character within the story (Dr. Mortimer), and the other told by the writer himself, Arthur Conan Doyle, *about* Dr. Mortimer, Sherlock Holmes, and Dr. Watson. This week, your narrative only has one point of view and one narrator—but there is still more than one story in it. Each story has many different details, so whittling the summary down to the most central events will be a challenge.

There are actually three different narrative strands, or stories, in this tale. Try to locate them now. Jot down the major characters in each narrative strand. Use these two hints:

Hint #1: The same major character occurs in the first two stories, but not in the third.

Hint #2: The second story in the narrative occurs in the *middle* of the first story (or, to put it another way, the first story begins, the second story begins and finishes, and then the first story ends).

Don't hestitate to ask your instructor for help. Show your instructor your answers before continuing on.

STEP THREE: **Note the main events in each story**

Now that you've found the three stories in the narrative, write down *only the two central events* in each story. If you cannot find them, ask your instructor for help.

STEP FOUR: **Write summary sentences**

Use your notes to write a summary with no more than six sentences. You may put each main event into its own sentence, but you may also combine two events into a single longer sentence.

Remember that you will need to place the two events in the second story *between* the first and second event in the first story!

When you are finished, show your work to your instructor.

---

72. Calvin N. Kendall and Marion Paine Stevens, *Fourth Reader* (D. C. Heath and Co., 1920), pp. 37–42.

Day Two: Outlining Exercise

Focus: Finding the central topic in each paragraph of a scientific description combined with a chronological narrative

STEP ONE: **Read**

Read the following excerpt from *The Greely Arctic Expedition: As Fully Narrated by Lieut. Greely, U.S.A., and Other Survivors.* This passage comes from Greely's account of his disastrous 1881 expedition to the Arctic, which ended with 19 of his 25-man crew dead. The account was first published in 1884.

When the writer uses the word "fantasia" in the fourth paragraph, he means that the crashing of the ice sounds unreal, fantastic, strange.

In the fifth paragraph, Point Barrow is a headland (a piece of land surrounded by water on three sides) on the northern coast of what is now Alaska. It is the northernmost point in the United States. Many Arctic expeditions used Point Barrow as a starting point for their journeys toward the North Pole. Point Barrow is blocked by ice for as much as nine months of the year.

There is also some technical language in the fifth paragraph. To "steam up a long lead" means to follow a particular path through the water under steam power. "Grounded ice" is an ice wall, found in shallow water, which rests on the ground beneath the surface. An "ice cape" or ice cap is a blanket of ice that covers less than 50,000 square kilometers (31,000 square miles) of land (if a blanket of ice covers more than that, it is called an "ice sheet"). A "fathom" is a nautical measurement six feet long (so 15 fathoms is the same as 90 feet).

In the sixth paragraph, "the pack" refers to pack ice or drift ice; this is floating ice which has been blown by the wind into a large single cluster.

The icebergs are like floating rocks whirled along a rapid current. The crystal mountains dash against each other backward and forward, bursting with a roar like thunder and returning to the charge until, losing their equilibrium, they tumble over in a cloud of spray, upheaving the ice-fields, which fall afterward like the crack of a whip-lash on the boiling sea. The sea-gulls fly away screaming, and often a black, shining whale comes for an instant puffing to the surface. When the midnight sun grazes the horizon the floating mountains and the rocks seem immersed in a wave of purple light.

The cold is by no means so insupportable as is supposed. We passed from a heated cabin at 30° above zero to 47° below zero in the open air without inconvenience. A much higher degree of cold becomes, however, insufferable if there is wind. At 15° below zero a steam, as if from a boiling kettle, rises from the water. At once frozen by the wind, it falls in a fine powder. This phenomenon is called ice-smoke.

At 40° [below zero] the snow and human bodies also smoke, which smoke changes at once into millions of tiny particles like needles of ice, which fill the air and make a light, continuous noise like the rustle of a stiff silk. At this temperature the trunks of trees burst with a loud report, the rocks break up, and the earth opens and vomits smoking water. Knives break in cutting butter. Cigars go out by contact with the ice on the beard. To talk is fatiguing. At night the eyelids are covered with a crust of ice, which must be carefully removed before one can open them. . . .

The song of the icy sea is a very peculiar one, and can scarcely be described so as to convey any clear idea of its nature. It is not loud, yet it can be heard to a great distance. It is neither a surge nor a swash, but a kind of slow, crashing, groaning, shrieking sound, in which sharp silvery tinklings mingle with the low, thunderous undertone of a rushing tempest. It impresses one with the idea of nearness and distance at the same time, and also that of immense forces in conflict. When this confused fantasia is heard from afar through the stillness of an Arctic night the effect is strangely weird and almost solemn, as if it were the distant hum of an active, living world breaking across the boundaries of silence, solitude and death.

On June 25th the steam whaler *North Star*, the first ship of the season to reach Point Barrow, steamed up a long lead, which ran in a northeast direction about six miles from the shore, until she came opposite the signal station, when she made fast to the grounded ice. On the 8th of July she made her way into a small inlet in the shore ice, about three miles from shore, with the hope that the projecting ice capes, grounded in fifteen fathoms, would withstand the pressure and protect her until the current should change, or a favorable opportunity for making her escape should occur.

It soon, however, became certain that this hope was vain, for the pack kept on its way slowly and steadily, but as relentless as fate. The ice capes were ground into powder, and melted away before the resistless pressure as if they were not a straw's weight instead of millions of tons. The grounded mass around the ship soon followed, and the ill-fated *Star* was caught and ground to pieces as if she were no stronger than a child's cardboard toy. Never was destruction more complete. Her great masts and massive ribs of solid timber cracked and broke as if they were pipe-stems, and in an hour from the time the pressure first reached her nothing remained of the great ship that looked so beautiful and strong in the bright sunshine a few minutes before but two or three boats, a little hard bread, a few bags of flour and forty-eight homeless men.[73]

STEP TWO: **Construct a one-level outline**

This week's passage, like last week's, is a scientific description of an object or phenomenon. The thing being described is *the Arctic Ocean*, which is both an object and a phenomenon; it is an object filled with ice, but it is also incredibly cold (that is the phenomenon).

You can find the central topic in the first four paragraphs by asking yourself, as you did last week, "What aspect or part of the whole does this paragraph describe?" Remember; a part is a physical element of the whole; an aspect is a characteristic or quality.

In the fifth and sixth paragraphs, the writer illustrates one particular aspect of the Arctic Ocean (its danger) by changing techniques. Instead of continuing with his scientific description, he inserts a brief chronological narrative. When you outline a chronological narrative, you should ask:

1. What is the main thing or person that this section is about? *Or* Is the section about an idea?
2. Why is that thing or person important? *Or* What did that thing or person do/what was done to it? *Or* What is the idea?

Try this for the last two paragraphs in the excerpt.

If you have difficulty, ask your instructor for help. When you're finished, check your work with your instructor.

Day Three: Analyzing the Topos

Focus: Understanding the form of a scientific description of an object or phenomenon

The passage you outlined in the last writing session was a scientific description of an object or phenomenon, combined with a brief chronological narrative. But today you won't be practicing a combination. Instead you'll study another way of putting together a scientific description.

Last week, you learned that when you write a scientific description, you can describe each separate part of the object or phenomenon and tell what it is made from; you can also use figurative language to make the description more visual. Today, we'll add another element to that pattern.

---

73. A. W. Greely, George L. Barclay, and Winfield Scott Schley, *The Greely Arctic Expedition* (Barclay & Co., 1884), pp. 85–87.

STEP ONE: **Understand point of view in scientific description**

Look again at this excerpt from *The Greely Arctic Expedition:*

> At this temperature the trunks of trees burst with a loud report, the rocks break up, and the earth opens and vomits smoking water. Knives break in cutting butter. Cigars go out by contact with the ice on the beard. To talk is fatiguing. At night the eyelids are covered with a crust of ice, which must be carefully removed before one can open them.

These sentences describe an aspect of the Arctic Ocean—the cold—in a very specific way; they tell the reader how the cold looks, sounds, and feels to an observer.

When you write a scientific description, you can always explain what an object (or phenomenon) is made from. But you should also consider describing exactly how an observer would *see, hear,* or *sense* the object or phenomenon.

Read the following description of an atom, written by physicist Hans Christian Von Baeyer after he has travelled to the National Institute of Standards and Technology in Colorado to see the "atom trap" used by scientist David Wineland to catch and view atoms.

> Right in the middle of the trap a little star appeared. Tentatively at first, amid the flickering reflections all around, and then with increasing intensity, the mercury atom poured out its light. Held in a tight grip by electrical forces between its own charge and the metal walls of the trap; it did not budge; its trembling motion in the trap was far too minute to be noticeable. It looked firmly anchored, and indeed it was. . . . So here it was, an atom in captivity.
>
> It was then, as I watched spellbound, that I began to notice that the atom was blinking. At first I thought that this was just part of the general flickering of the screen, but it soon became apparent that the mercury atom was definitely turning off and on, at the rate of several times a second. This was surely the most astonishing thing I had ever seen . . . a powerful reminder that atoms are active, dynamic systems, capable of the most intricate internal transformations and convolutions, and not in the least bit like the immutable, eternal kernels of matter the ancients had imagined them to be.[74]

Later in the book, Von Baeyer describes the parts of an atom. But in this passage, he describes how *he,* the observer, *experiences* the atom. He tells us where he was while he was looking at the atom, exactly how it appeared to him, and what his thoughts were as he watched it.

Like place descriptions, scientific descriptions have a point of view. When you studied place descriptions, you learned that a place can be described from four different points of view:

---

74. Hans Christian Von Baeyer, *Taming the Atom: The Emergence of the Visible Microworld* (Dover Publications, 2000), p. xix.

1. From above (impersonal)
2. From inside
3. From one side or angle
4. Moving through or around

A scientific description is a little bit different. When you describe each part of an object or phenomenon and tell what it is made of, you are using a removed point of view. Look again at this paragraph from last week's description of a comet:

> The nucleus is the only solid body, with a diameter of from 1 to 30 miles (1.6–48 km), a low overall destiny, and a mass from about 10 billion to 100 trillion tons. A comet's nucleus is made of dust particles loosely compacted with water ice, together with frozen carbon monoxide and methane. The Sun's heat melts the nucleus, releasing huge volumes of gas which carry away dust and ice particles.

Try to picture where the author of this passage might be standing while he describes a comet. Where do you think he is?

If you can't quite figure it out, you're on the right track. The writer isn't standing *anywhere* while he looks at the comet. He's describing it from a removed position—as though he's home, in his study, looking at diagrams, scientific studies, charts, and tables.

This can be a very effective way to describe a scientific object or phenomenon. When you're writing about science, you'll often find yourself describing something you haven't actually seen—like a cell, or an atom. Even if you've seen a comet through a telescope, it was probably indistinct and fuzzy. And although you may have seen a volcanic eruption on television, you probably haven't *been* at one, so you haven't smelled, heard, or felt the effects of an eruption.

But sometimes you'll find it more effective to describe an object or phenomenon as though you are actually present: seeing, hearing, smelling, and feeling what you're describing. Maybe you'll be lucky enough to see the thing you're describing with your own eyes, like Hans Christian Von Baeyer did. If not, you'll have to use the information and photographs you find in books, plus your imagination. The authors of the popular health guide *100 Questions & Answers about Influenza* probably never saw a flu virus with their own eyes, but here's what they wrote:

> . . . A flu virus looks like a mere fluff of protein stippled with a multitude of tiny spikes. Imagine a miniature mace, the medieval weapon, a metal ball with dozens of spikes—that's basically a flu virus up close and personal.[75]

Even if the writers haven't actually looked at a flu virus through an electron microscope, in this description they are imagining what they would see through the lens. This description is written from the point of view of someone who is present, in the same place as the flu virus, looking at it.

---

75. Delthia Ricks and Marc Siegel, *100 Questions & Answers About Influenza* (Jones & Bartlett Learning, 2008), p. 13.

STEP TWO: **Identify point of view in scientific description**

Read the following descriptions, which are taken from the nature books *Trees That Every Child Should Know* by Julia Ellen Rogers and *The Yosemite* by John Muir. In the margin next to each description, write "Removed" or "Present." Remember, in a "present" point of view, the narrator is describing what he sees as he stands and looks at a particular object. In a "removed" point of view, the narrator tells you what an object is like and what it is made of—but he is writing as if he were home in his study, looking at reference books and charts.

You may have some difficulty with this assignment—it is supposed to be challenging! Don't worry too much about how many you get "right" or "wrong"; you're just trying to develop a deeper understanding of what makes an effective description.

When you're finished, show your work to your instructor. Your instructor will discuss your answers with you.

> Of all the world's eighty or ninety species of pine trees, the Sugar Pine (*Pinus Lambertiana*) is king, surpassing all others, not merely in size, but in lordly beauty and majesty. . . . The trunk is a remarkably smooth, round, delicately-tapered shaft, straight and regular as if turned in a lathe, mostly without limbs, purplish brown in color and usually enlivened with tufts of a yellow lichen. Toward the head of this magnificent column long branches sweep gracefully outward and downward, sometimes forming a palm-like crown, but far more impressive than any palm crown I ever beheld.[76]

> First, willows have slender, flexible twigs that give the tree tops grace and lightness. Second, willow leaves are nearly always long and slim to match the supple twigs. They are always simple, and short-stemmed. The wood is light and soft, so the trees break easily in storms of wind and ice. An old willow tree is likely to be crippled, but its scars and wounds are covered in summer by the arching branches and the abundant foliage.[77]

> The manzanita [shrub] never fails to attract particular attention. The species common in the Valley is . . . round-headed with innumerable branches, red or chocolate-color bark, pale green leaves set on edge, and a rich profusion of small, pink narrow-throated urn-shaped flowers, like those of arbutus. The knotty, crooked, angular branches are about as rigid as bones, and the red bark is so thin and smooth on both trunk and branches, they look as if they had been peeled and polished and painted.[78]

---

76. John Muir, *The Yosemite* (Century, 1912), pp. 97–98.
77. Julia Ellen Rogers, *Trees That Every Child Should Know: Easy Tree Studies for All Seasons of the Year* (Doubleday, 1909), p. 164.
78. Muir, *The Yosemite*, p. 151.

The scrawny, grey, digger pines, with cones as big as a man's head, grew on the lower foot hills. Next came the great yellow pines, and still higher up, the grand sugar pines, along the highest level of the stage road. They stood oftenest in close ranks so that their tops were small, because of the crowding. And here they had stood for centuries. The road was no wider than the broad stumps of some that had been cut down, and their prostrate trunks were longer than any log I have ever seen before.[79]

The white ash is a tall, handsome, stately tree, with a trunk like a grey granite column. The white in its name is from the pale leaf linings, that illuminate the tree top in summer. The twigs are pale, and the bark is often as pale grey as that of a white oak. The slender, dart-like seeds are one to two inches long, with a wing which is twice the length of the round, tapering seed. They hang in thick clusters, paler green than the leaves, and often flushed with a rosy tinge in late summer.[80]

STEP THREE: **Add to the pattern of the topos**

Turn to the Scientific Description chart in your Composition Notebook. Add the bolded point below under the "Procedure" column.

Scientific Description
Definition: A visual and structural description of an object or phenomenon

Procedure	Remember
1. Describe each part of the object or phenomenon and tell what it is made from.	1. Consider using figurative language to make the description more visual.
2. Choose a point of view.	

Day Four: Practicing the Topos

Focus: Learning how to write a scientific description of an object or phenomenon

STEP ONE: **Review point of view**

Last week, you read this description of a pyroclastic flow from the reference book *Volcanoes* by Robert Wayne Decker and Barbara Decker:

79. Rogers, pp. 112–114.
80. Rogers, p. 204.

> Sometimes an explosive eruption produces a cloud of volcanic debris so full of fragments that it is too heavy to rise very high into the atmosphere. Such an emulsion of gas and fragments forms a pyroclastic flow, the most dangerous kind of volcanic hazard. Pyroclastic flows can travel at speeds of more than 100 kilometers per hour, flattening and burning almost everything in their paths. Small pyroclastic flows often race down the valleys on a volcano's flanks, but larger masses that are expelled at high speeds . . . can sweep over small hills or across large flat areas.

Compare this to the following description of a pyroclastic flow, written by the Roman lawyer Pliny the Younger after he lived through the eruption of Mount Vesuvius in the year 79.

> Ashes were already falling, not as yet very thickly. I looked round: a dense black cloud was coming up behind us, spreading over the earth like a flood. . . . We had scarcely sat down to rest when darkness fell, not the dark of a moonless or cloudy night, but as if the lamp had been put out in a closed room. You could hear the shrieks of women, the wailing of infants, and the shouting of men; some were calling their parents, others their children or their wives, trying to recognize them by their voices. . . . A gleam of light returned, but we took this to be a warning of the approaching flames rather than daylight. However, the flames remained some distance off; then darkness came on once more and ashes began to fall again, this time in heavy showers. We rose from time to time and shook them off, otherwise we should have been buried and crushed beneath their weight.[81]

The first description is written from the removed point of view, the second from the present point of view. The removed point of view tells you about the makeup, behavior, and qualities of a pyroclastic flow. The present point of view tells you what a pyroclastic flow looks and feels like.

(You may notice that the second description is organized almost like a chronological narrative. The forms of a description and a chronological narrative can overlap, but we will study this a little later. For now, just pay attention to the difference betwen a removed and a present point of view.)

STEP TWO: **Understand the aspects of a present point of view**

A description written from the present point of view tells the reader what the narrator is seeing, hearing, feeling, smelling, and even tasting. When you write a description from the present point of view, you should think of each one of these senses: sight, sound, touch, smell, and

81. Pliny the Younger, *The Letters of the Younger Pliny*, trans. and ed. Betty Radice (Penguin Books, 1963), Book VI.

taste. A description written from the present point of view won't include all of them—but it will include at least two or three.

Read the following sentences from present point-of-view descriptions of a forest fire. Write in the margin which of the five senses (sight, smell, taste, feeling, hearing) is being used. More than one sense may be used in the same sentence.

> When the back fire and the crown (primary) fire met, a terrific roar blasted past us, while smoke and flame erupted hundreds of feet into the air.
>
> As we scrambled after the crown fire, the blue smoke tang of the fire gritted between our teeth.
>
> The fire was rushing through the trees with a tremendous cloud of black smoke rising up above it.
>
> The acrid stink of burning logs lingered in the blackened ground.
>
> The ground still radiated heat upwards, even after the fire had swept past and disappeared.

After you've written the answers, check them with your instructor.

STEP THREE: **Write the description**

Your last assignment for this week is to rewrite last week's description so that it comes from a present, rather than a removed, point of view.

Pull out last week's description now. Look at each part of the volcano described. For each one, ask yourself: If I were standing right there, looking at the volcano itself, what would this part look, sound, smell, feel, and taste like? Then rewrite your description as though you were standing next to the volcano, using all five senses.

This description can be one paragraph or several paragraphs, but it must be at least 150 and not more than 300 words. You do not need to use all of the senses in your description, but you must use at least three of the five.

For your reference, the senses are:

sight
smell
taste
touch
sound

If you have difficulty, ask your instructor for help. And when you're finished, show your composition to your instructor.

Week 14: Scientific Description

Day One: Original Narration Exercise

Focus: Summarizing a narrative by choosing the central events and details

STEP ONE: **Read**

Read the following excerpt from the first chapter of *The Adventures of Baron Munchausen. The Adventures of Baron Munchausen* is a collection of tall tales about a real man, Karl Friedrich Hieronymous, Baron Munchausen. He was born in Germany in 1720 and, after joining the Russian army in 1739, rose to the rank of captain. Munchausen died in 1797.

Baron Munchausen was well known for telling exciting stories about his adventures. Between 1781 and 1783, a series of stories about Baron Munchausen's exploits appeared, anonymously, in the German magazine *Vademecum für lustige Leute*. However, although some of the adventures described were based on Munchausen's own stories, others were actually drawn from folktales told about other German heroes long before Munchausen was even born.

Although no one knows for sure, the anonymous writer may have been the German writer and scientist Rudolf Erich Raspe, who was a friend of Munchausen's but had moved from Germany to England in 1775. In 1785, Raspe published an English version of the *Adventures of Baron Munchausen* in which he expanded and added to many of the tales—over Munchausen's strong objections. A year later, Raspe's friend Gottfried August Burger borrowed Raspe's book, with his approval, and translated the stories back into German—adding yet more fantastic detail as he did so.

So although the adventures are based on the life of a real German soldier, there is no longer any good way to tell what parts of the story are true and what parts are not. Some of the stories are obviously invented—but others aren't quite so clear.

Your excerpt is taken from the 1902 English translation of Burger's adaptation of Raspe's translation of the anonymous 1781 stories! It includes the following preface. No one knows *who* wrote this preface.

— — —

To the Public.

Having heard, for the first time, that my adventures have been doubted, and looked upon as jokes, I feel bound to come forward and vindicate my character *for veracity,* by paying three shillings at the Mansion House of this great city for the affidavits hereto appended.

This I have been forced into in regard of my own honor, although I have retired for many years from public and private life; and I hope that this, my last edition, will place me in a proper light with my readers.

AT THE CITY OF LONDON, ENGLAND.

We, the undersigned, as true believers in the *profit,* do most solemnly affirm, that all the adventures of our friend Baron Munchausen, in whatever country they may *lie,* are positive and simple facts. *And,* as we have been believed, whose adventures are tenfold more wonderful, *so* do we hope all true believers will give him their full faith and credence.

GULLIVER. x
SINBAD. x
ALADDIN. X
Sworn at the Mansion House
9th Nov. last, in the absence
of the Lord Mayor.
JOHN *(the Porter)*

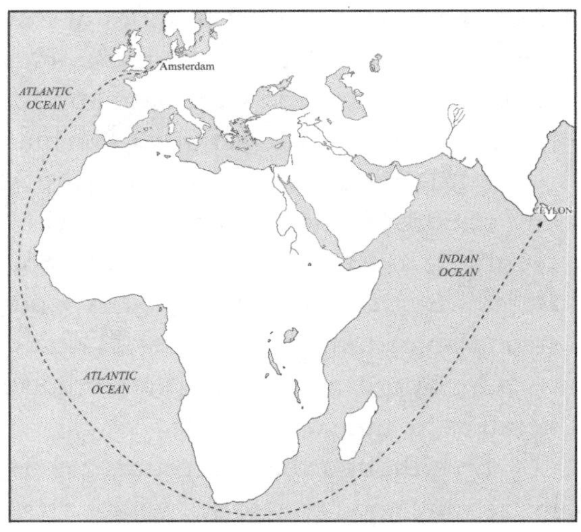

Some years before my beard announced approaching manhood, or, in other words, when I was neither man nor boy, but between both, I expressed in repeated conversations a strong desire of seeing the world, from which I was discouraged by my parents, though my father had been no inconsiderable traveller himself, as will appear before I have reached the end of my singular, and, I may add, interesting adventures. A cousin, by my mother's side, took a liking to me, often said I was a fine forward youth, and was much inclined to gratify my curiosity. His eloquence had more effect than mine, for my father consented to my accompanying him in a voyage to the island of Ceylon, where his uncle had resided as governor many years.

We sailed from Amsterdam with despatches from their High Mightinesses the States of Holland. The only circumstance which happened on our voyage worth relating was the wonderful effects of a storm, which had torn up by the roots a great number of trees of enormous bulk and height, in an island where we lay at anchor to take in wood and water. Some of these trees weighed many tons, yet they were carried by the wind so amazingly high, that they appeared like the feathers of small birds floating in the air, for they were at least five miles above the earth. However, as soon as the storm subsided they all fell perpendicularly into their respective places, and took root again, except the largest which happened, when it was blown into the air, to have a man and his wife, a very honest old couple, upon its branches, gathering cucumbers (in this part of the globe that useful vegetable grows upon trees). The weight of this couple, as the tree descended, over-balanced the trunk, and brought it down in an horizontal position. It fell upon the chief man of the island, and killed him on the spot; he had quitted his house in the storm, under an apprehension of its falling upon him, and was returning through his own garden when this fortunate accident happened.

The word fortunate, here, requires some explanation. This chief was a man of a very avaricious and oppressive disposition, and though he had no family, the natives of the island were half-starved by his oppressive and infamous impositions.

The very goods which he had thus taken from them were spoiling in his stores, while the poor wretches from whom they were plundered were pining in poverty. Though the destruction of this tyrant was accidental, the people chose the cucumber-gatherers for their governors, as a mark of their gratitude for destroying, though accidentally, their late tyrant.

After we had repaired the damages we sustained in this remarkable storm, and taken leave of the new governor and his lady, we sailed with a fair wind for the object of our voyage.

In about six weeks we arrived at Ceylon, where we were received with great marks of friendship and true politeness. The following singular adventures may not prove unentertaining.

After we had resided at Ceylon about a fortnight I accompanied one of the governor's brothers upon a shooting party. He was a strong, athletic man, and being used to that climate (for he had resided there some years), he bore the violent heat of the sun much better than I could. In our excursion he had made a considerable progress through a thick wood when I was only at the entrance.

Near the banks of a large piece of water, which had engaged my attention, I thought I heard a rustling noise behind. On turning about I was almost petrified (as who would not?) at the sight of a lion, which was evidently approaching with the intention of satisfying his appetite with my poor carcase, and that without asking my consent.

What was to be done in this horrible dilemma? I had not even a moment for reflection; my piece was only charged with swan-shot, and I had no other about me. However, though I could have no idea of killing such an animal with that weak kind of ammunition, yet I had some hopes of frightening him by the report, and perhaps of wounding him also. I immediately let fly without waiting till he was within reach, and the report did but enrage him, for he now quickened his pace, and seemed to approach me full speed. I attempted to escape, but that only added (if an addition could be made) to my distress; for the moment I turned about I found a large crocodile, with his mouth extended almost ready to receive me. On my right hand was the piece of water before mentioned, and on my left a deep precipice, said to have, as I have since learned, a receptacle at the bottom for venomous creatures; in short I gave myself up as lost, for the lion was now upon his hind-legs, just in the act of seizing me. I fell involuntarily to the ground with fear, and, as it afterwards appeared, he sprang over me.

I lay some time in a situation which no language can describe, expecting to feel his teeth or talons in some part of me every moment. After waiting in this prostrate situation a few seconds I heard a violent but unusual noise, different from any sound that had ever before assailed my ears; nor is it at all to be wondered at, when I inform you from whence it proceeded. After listening for some time, I ventured to raise my head and look round, when, to my unspeakable joy, I perceived the lion had, by the eagerness with which he sprung at me, jumped forward, as I fell, into the crocodile's mouth! which, as before observed, was wide open. The head of the one stuck in the throat of the other, and they were struggling to extricate themselves! I fortunately recollected my *couteau de chasse,* which was by my side; with this instrument I severed the lion's head at one blow, and the body fell at my feet! I then, with the butt-end of my fowling-piece, rammed the head farther into the throat of the crocodile, and destroyed him by suffocation, for he could neither gorge nor eject it.

Fowling-piece

Soon after I had thus gained a complete victory over my two powerful adversaries my companion arrived in search of me; for finding I did not follow him into the wood, he returned, apprehending I had lost my way, or met with some accident. After mutual congratulations, we measured the crocodile, which was just forty feet in length.

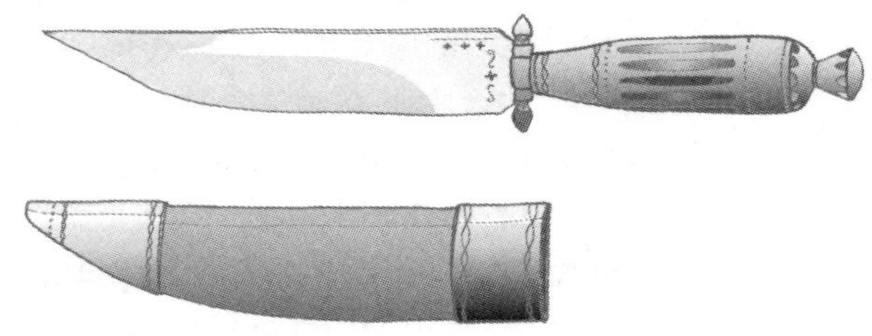

Couteau de chasse

As soon as we had related this extraordinary adventure to the governor, he sent a wagon and servants, who brought home the two carcases. The lion's skin was properly preserved, with its hair on, after which it was made into tobacco pouches, and presented by me, upon our return to Holland, to the burgomasters, who, in return, requested my acceptance of a thousand ducats.

The skin of the crocodile was stuffed in the usual manner, and makes a capital article in their public museum at Amsterdam, where the exhibitor relates the whole story to each spectator, with such additions as he thinks proper.

Some of his variations are rather extravagant; one of them is, that the lion jumped quite through the crocodile, when, as soon as his head appeared, Monsieur the Great Baron (as he is pleased to call me) cut it off, and three feet of the crocodile's tail along with it. Nay, so little attention has this fellow to the truth, that he sometimes adds, as soon as the crocodile missed his tail, he turned about, snatched the *couteau de chasse* out of Monsieur's hand, and swallowed it with such eagerness that it pierced his heart and killed him immediately!

The little regard which this impudent knave has to veracity makes me sometimes apprehensive that my *real facts* may fall under suspicion, by being found in company with his confounded inventions.[82]

STEP TWO: **Find the different stories in the narrative**

You will now summarize the story in three or four sentences, and write those sentences down on your own paper.

Like last week's narrative, this passage has more than one story in it. Try to locate them now. Use the following hint: what are the unlikeliest events in the passage? Each one marks the center of a different story.

Once you've found the different stories, draw lines through the passage above to separate the stories. When you've finished, show your work to your instructor.

If you have difficulty, ask your instructor for help.

STEP THREE: **Note the main events in each story**

Now write down only three events from each story. You may *not* write down more than three! If you have difficulty, ask your instructor for help.

STEP FOUR: **Write summary sentences**

Use your notes to write a summary with no more than six sentences. You may put each main event into its own sentence, but you may also combine two events into a single longer sentence.

When you are finished, show your work to your instructor.

---

82. Rudolf Erich Raspe, *The Adventures of Baron Munchausen* (Thomas Y. Crowell & Co., 1902), pp. 1–8.

Day Two: Outlining Exercise

Focus: Finding the central topic in each paragraph of a scientific description

STEP ONE: **Read**

Read the following excerpt from Anna Botsford Comstock's classic guide to observing and understanding nature, *Handbook of Nature Study.*

— — —

Take a dozen dead twigs from almost any sumac or elder, split them lengthwise, and you will find in at least one or two of them a little tunnel down the center where there was once pith. In the month of June or July, this narrow tunnel is made into an insect apartment house, one little creature in each apartment, partitioned off from the one above and the one below. The nature of this partition reveals to us whether the occupants are bees or wasps; if it is made of tiny chips, like fine sawdust glued together, a bee made it and there are little bees in the cells; if it is made of bits of sand or mud glued together, a wasp was the architect and young wasps are the inhabitants. Also, if the food in the cells is pollen paste, it was placed there by a bee; if paralyzed insects or spiders are in the cells, a wasp made the nest.

The little carpenter bee *(Ceratina dupla)* is a beautiful creature, scarcely one quarter of an inch in length, with metallic blue body and rainbow tinted wings. In spring, she selects some twig of sumac, elder, or raspberry which has been broken, and thus gives her access to the pith; this she at once begins to dig out, mouthful by mouthful, until she has made a smooth tunnel several inches long; she gathers pollen and packs beebread in the bottom of the cell to the depth of a quarter-inch, and then lays upon it a tiny white egg. She brings back some of her chips of pith and glues them together, making a partition about one-tenth of an inch thick, which she fastens firmly to the sides of the tunnel; this is the roof for the first cell and the floor of the next one; she then gathers more pollen, lays another egg, and builds another partition.

Thus she fills the tunnel, almost to the opening, with cells, sometimes as many as fourteen; but she always leaves a space for a vestibule near the door, and in this she makes her home, while her family below her are growing up.

The egg in the lowest cell of course hatches first; a little bee grub issues from it and eats the beebread industriously. This grub grows by shedding its skin when it becomes too tight, then changes to a pupa, and later to a bee resembling its mother. But, though fully grown, it cannot get out into the sunshine, for all its younger brothers and sisters are blocking the tunnel ahead of it; so it simply tears down the partition above it and kicks away the little pieces. The little grub bides its time until the next youngest brother or sister tears down the partition above its head and pushes the fragments into the very face of the elder, which, in turn, pushes them away. Thus, while the young bees are waiting, they are kept more or less busy pushing behind them the broken bits of all the partitions above them. Finally, the youngest gets its growth, and there they all are in the tunnel, the broken partitions behind the hindmost at the bottom of the nest, and the young bees packed closely together in a row with heads toward the door. When we find the nest at this period, we know the mother because her head is toward her young ones and her back to the door.

A little later, on some bright morning, they all come out into the sunshine and flit about on gauzy, rainbow wings, a very happy family, out of prison.[83]

STEP TWO: **Construct a one-level outline**

This week's passage is yet another example of scientific description. For each section, decide whether it would be more productive to ask yourself "What aspect or part of the whole does this section describe?" or "What is the main thing that this section is about? Why is that thing important?"

If you have difficulty, ask your instructor for help. When you're finished, check your work with your instructor.

Day Three: Analyzing the Topos

Focus: Understanding the form of a scientific description of an object or phenomenon

The scientific description that you outlined last week mixed together the removed and present point of view. Today, you'll study mixing points of view.

STEP ONE: **Understand combined points of view in scientific description**

Look again at the first paragraph of the description from *The Handbook of Nature Study.* It begins with the personal point of view, as though you and the narrator were both standing together, looking at the twig containing the "apartment house":

83. Anna Botsford Comstock, *Handbook of Nature Study,* rev. ed (Cornell University Press, 1986), pp. 386–387.

Take a dozen dead twigs from almost any sumac or elder, split them lengthwise, and you will find in at least one or two of them a little tunnel down the center where there was once pith.

However, as it continues, the writer shifts to a removed point of view, telling us about the parts of the "apartment house" and what each part is made of:

[I]f it is made of tiny chips, like fine sawdust glued together, a bee made it and there are little bees in the cells; if it is made of bits of sand or mud glued together, a wasp was the architect and young wasps are the inhabitants.

If you're writing a description of a place, it is usually a good idea to keep a consistent point of view; the reader can easily understand what it might be like to look down on a pyramid from above, or at an Incan city from the side, and it can be very disorienting if the viewpoint suddenly shifts. (Not always; as you become a more skilled writer, you may find that you need to suddenly change your point of view as you describe a place. But for now, "don't change point of view" is a good rule to follow.)

When you're writing a scientific description, though, you're often attempting to give a clear picture of something that the reader has never seen—and in many cases, will *never* see. (How many of us will get to see an atom? A magma chamber? The inside of a cell?) Describing the parts of an atom, or a cell, will give the reader an idea of what the object is like, but not necessarily a clear and *vivid* idea.

Compare these two descriptions of a cell. The first is an impersonal, removed description, from the popular science book *How We Live and Why We Die: The Secret Lives of Cells* by Lewis Wolpert; the second is Bill Bryson's description of a cell, which you read back in Week 12.

> Cells can do a remarkable number of different things: skin cells cover and protect us, muscles contract, nerve cells conduct impulses, gut cells absorb food; cells form the vessels of the circulatory system, cells in the kidney filter the blood, immune system cells protect us from foreign invaders, blood cells carry oxygen, bone and cartilage cells give us support; and so on. Yet, in spite of the apparent differences between, for example, a nerve cell and a skin cell, they work by the same basic principles. Each cell is surrounded by a thin and flexible membrane that controls what can get into and out of the cell. In many cases this membrane is in tight contact with neighbouring cells which are held together to form extensive sheets of cells, such as our skin and blood vessels. Inside each cell there are two major regions: the nucleus and the cytoplasm. A bit like a flattish disc, the nucleus is the most prominent structure and is itself bounded by a membrane that controls what can enter or leave the nucleus.[84]

> Whatever their size or shape, nearly all your cells are built to fundamentally the same plan: they have an outer casing or membrane, a nucleus wherein resides the necessary genetic information to keep you going, and a busy space between the two called the cytoplasm. . . . If you could visit

84. Lewis Wolpert, *How We Live and Why We Die: The Secret Lives of Cells* (W. W. Norton, 2009), pp. 2–3.

> a cell, you wouldn't like it. Blown up to a scale at which atoms were about the size of peas, a cell itself would be a sphere roughly half a mile across, and supported by a complex framework of girders called the cytoskeleton. Within it, millions upon millions of objects—some the size of basketballs, others the size of cars—would whiz about like bullets. There wouldn't be a place you could stand without being pummeled and ripped thousands of times every second from every direction.[85]

Even though Bill Bryson isn't actually looking at a cell, he uses his imagination. After he uses the removed point of view to describe the parts of the cell and what they're made of, he thinks about what a cell might look like if it were large enough for someone to stand inside. Then he finishes his description from the personal point of view.

Lewis Wolpert's description of a cell is clear and useful. But Bryson's is more vivid, more gripping, and more likely to keep the reader's attention.

STEP TWO: **Identify combined points of view**

In the following descriptions, underline the sentences which come from a personal point of view.

> There are mountains and volcanoes on Venus, and evidence of plate tectonics that have shifted vast sections of the crust. There must be Venus-quakes, as well. Imagine trying to walk on the surface of Venus! The very ground is red-hot. The atmosphere is so thick that it warps light like a fisheye lens. The sky is perpetually clouded. Yet there is no real darkness: even during the long Venusian night there is an eerie, sullen glow from the red-hot ground.[86]

> The red cells [carry oxygen] for about one hundred eighty days, then they die. The white blood cells roam around looking for intruders, like bacteria and viruses, to attack and kill. There are also platelets . . . sticky plugs that often take on amorphous shapes and are reformed every seven days. Imagine that you've just been created in bone marrow. But instead of being limited to being a red cell, white cell, or platelet, you belong to an elite cadre of cells, unique and gifted, because you have the power to become any cell you desire. . . . You're called a "pluripotential-stem" cell. Most of your life is spent bathed in blood in the marrow. But every once in a while you may slip away into freely circulating blood and travel through the body.[87]

> . . . Jupiter is a liquid world that has no surface. The gaseous atmosphere blends gradually with the liquid hydrogen interior. Below the clouds of Jupiter lies the largest ocean of the solar system—and it has no surface and no waves. When you look at Jupiter, all you see are clouds. These cloud layers

---

85. Bryson, p. 377.
86. Ben Bova, *Venus* (Tor, 2000), p. 11.
87. Mehmet Oz, *Healing from the Heart* (Dutton, 1998), p. 17.

> lie deep inside a nearly transparent atmosphere of hydrogen and helium. You can detect this hydrogen atmosphere by noticing that Jupiter has limb darkening. . . . When you look near the limb of Jupiter (the edge of its disk) the clouds are much dimmer . . . because it is nearly sunset or sunrise along the limb. If you were on Jupiter at that location, you would see the sun just above the horizon, and it would be dimmed by the atmosphere. In addition, light reflected from clouds must travel out at a steep angle through the atmosphere to reach Earth, dimming the light further. Jupiter is brighter near the center of the disk because the sunlight shines nearly straight down on the clouds.[88]

> Hot springs are defined as springs of water that issue onto the earth's surface at temperatures "appreciably" above the average temperature of the air at their exit point. This means that if you sat in one in Hawaii you might be boiled like a lobster, whereas in Minnesota you could be turned into a giant ice cube.[89]

> The process that caused Antarctica—and all the other continents—to drift over time is known as plate tectonics. Understanding plate tectonics starts with knowing Earth's basic structure. If you could slice through our planet, you'd find it is made up of three major layers. The innermost layer is a very hot core of iron and nickel. The inside of this core is solid, and the outside is liquid. The middle layer, the mantle, is composed of rock that flows very, very slowly, like toothpaste. The outermost layer is the crust. Oceanic crust forms the ocean floor, while continental crust forms the continents. The crust and the upper part of the mantle, which is cooler and more rigid than the mantle's deeper parts, together make up what geologists call the lithosphere. The lithosphere is broken up into more than a dozen huge rocky slabs called tectonic plates. These plates are slowly moving.[90]

STEP THREE: **Add to the pattern of the topos**

Turn to the Scientific Description chart in your Composition Notebook. Add the bolded point below under the "Remember" column.

Scientific Description

Definition: A visual and structural description of an object or phenomenon

Procedure	Remember
1. Describe each part of the object or phenomenon and tell what it is made from.	1. Consider using figurative language to make the description more visual.
2. Choose a point of view.	**2. Consider combining points of view.**

---

88. Michael A. Seeds, *The Solar System,* 6th ed. (Thomson Brooks/Cole, 2008), pp. 515–516.

89. Ron L. Morton, *Music of the Earth: Volcanoes, Earthquakes, and Other Geological Wonders* (Plenum Press, 1996), p. 125.

90. Rebecca L. Johnson, *Plate Tectonics* (Lerner Publications, 2006), p. 6.

Day Four: Practicing the Topos

Focus: Learning how to write a scientific description of an object or phenomenon

Today, you'll write a scientific description that mixes points of view. This description should have three elements:

1. A section that describes, from a removed point of view, each part of an object or phenomenon and tells what it's made from.
2. A section that also describes at least one part of the object or phenomenon from a present, personal point of view, using at least three of the five senses (smell, taste, touch, hearing, sight).
3. A metaphor, simile, or some other use of figurative language that makes some part of the object or phenomenon more vivid and real to the reader.

In the last session, you read two descriptions of planets (Venus and Jupiter) that combined removed and present points of view. Your assignment is to write a similar description of the planet Mars. Remember: your description should also include figurative language; there is only one minor example of figurative language ("like a fisheye lens") in the previous descriptions.

STEP ONE: Write a draft of the description of Mars

Look carefully at the labelled diagrams of the planet Mars on the next page. Then, read the facts and excerpts that follow. Finally, write a rough draft of a description of Mars. This should describe each important part of the planet by explaining what it is made of and what it looks like. You should not try to include details about every part of Mars; you can focus on the exterior, the interior, or a few selected major features of both. This description should be at least 200 words but not more than 400.

You will insert the present point of view into this rough draft in the second step of your lesson.

FACTS ABOUT MARS

Taken partly from Patrick Moore, editor, *The International Encyclopedia of Astronomy*, and Ian Ridpath, editor, *The Illustrated Encyclopedia of Astronomy and Space*

Planet Overall

Fourth planet from the sun

Diameter of 4,200 miles (about half of Earth)

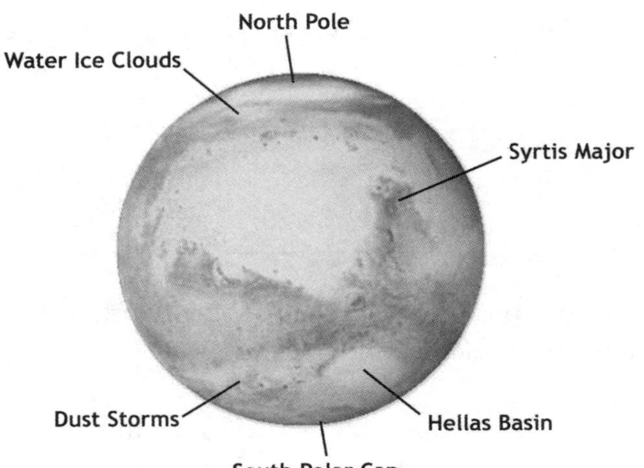

- Martian year (time it takes orbit to go all around the sun) is 686 days.
- Martian day 24 hours 37 min. long
- Orange/red color with blue-gray markings and white polar caps
- Two moons, Phobos and Deimos
    - Phobos rises in the west and sets in the east.
    - Deimos rises in the east and sets in the west 2.7 Mars days later.

Atmosphere

- 95% carbon dioxide, 2.7% nitrogen, 1.6% argon (a gas which doesn't react strongly)
- Traces of oxygen, water vapor, carbon monoxide
- White and blue clouds form over 5% of the surface.

Surface

- Clouds of reddish dust on the surface because of iron oxide
- No liquid water
- North polar cap made of water ice, about 2 kilometers (1.2 miles) thick
- South polar cap covered with carbon dioxide ice, about 8 meters (25 feet) thick
- Two large craters, Hellas and Argyre, made by impact of meteors
    - Both in the southern hemisphere
    - Hellas is 3 miles deep and 1,400 miles across.
- Tharsis
- Shield volcanoes in northern hemisphere
    - Show ancient huge lava flows
    - Four huge volcanoes reaching a height of 18 miles
    - Biggest, Olympus Mons, visible from earth as a dark spot
    - Syrtis Major a lower volcano, made of dark volcanic rock
- Network of canyons called Valles Marineris in northern hemisphere
- Large plain called Chryse Planitia
    - Possibly ancient flooding on this plain

Weather

- Wind storms whip up dust into dust storms.
    - Dust spreads all around the planet.
- At equator, high temperature 26 degrees Celsius (78.8 Fahrenheit) in summer
    - -146 degrees Celsius (-230.8) in winter
- Huge difference between temperature at poles and equator
- In winter, much of atmosphere freezes into polar caps.
- From surface, air is pink.

Core

Probably made of iron sulfide (a heavy combination of iron and sulfur)
Possibly partly liquid

Mantle

Made of silicate (minerals which are lighter than the materials in the core)
Lighter than the core

Crust

Crust ranges from 50 km (31 miles) to 125 km (77 miles) in thickness.
Soil made up of magnesium, sodium, potassium, chloride, traces of other chemicals

EXCERPTS ABOUT MARS

Up to 25 percent of Mars's entire atmosphere freezes out each season into the polar caps. . . . In winter the southern ice cap extends to 50 degrees south and is one to two meters thick around its central permanent area; in summer the cap remains as a small residual core. Because of the shortness of the southern summer, the southern cap retains some frozen carbon dioxide as well as frozen water. The north polar cap of Mars contains frozen water in addition to the carbon dioxide that makes up the South Polar cap. The north pole experiences six months of darkness each winter, and in summer and fall it is often obscured by dust storms. . . . The polar cap contains two types of layers: Light-toned, nearly uniformly bedded layers lie above darker-toned beds that form shelves and benches at the bottom. The older, darker beds appear to include a large fraction of sand, while the upper layers may be a mixture of ice and dust.[91]

A shield volcano is created by many flows of lava building up layer after layer over very long periods of time. The extreme height of the volcanoes of Mars shows how thick the crust must be: A thinner crust couldn't support the weight of the enormous mountains. The size of the volcanoes indicates that the activity that created them continued for an extremely long time. In addition to [the huge volcanoes in] the Tharsis area, there are many smaller volcanoes on Mars, most of which are located in the northern hemisphere.[92]

It is a cold, dry desert world. It hasn't rained in millions of years. In fact, pure liquid water can't even exist on the open surface. If you were to pour a glassful on the ground, it would just boil away until it was gone. An

91. Linda T. Elkins-Tanton, *Mars* (Chelsea House, 2006), pp. 91–92.
92. Ron Miller, *Mars* (Twenty-First Century Books, 2006), pp. 28–29.

ice cube would merely disappear gradually. This is beause the air pressure on Mars is so low.[93]

Mars has two moons, and their names are Phobos and Deimos. Because of their odd shape, some astronomers have compared them to potatoes. Both moons are made of rock and ice and are very small, as far as moons go. They are actually asteroids that strayed too close to the planet's gravitational field. Phobos is about 13 miles (21 km) across at its widest point. It orbits Mars once every seven hours and thirty-nine minutes. By contrast, our Moon takes about twenty-seven days to orbit Earth. Phobos's orbit is slowly shrinking. Astronomers estimate that in about 50 million years, Phobos will either crash into Mars or break into pieces from the force of the planet's gravity. Deimos is even smaller than Phobos. With a width of about 8 miles (13 km), this moon is one of the smallest bodies in the entire Solar System. Deimos completes one orbit every thirty hours and eighteen minutes.[94]

[T]he famous Martian dust storms . . . aren't just local events on Mars; large dust storms can occasionally completely engulf the planet in a haze of particles, completely obscuring the view of the surface. Early warnings of dust storms include yellow clouds. . . . Hellas Basin . . . is the big crater gouged out of the southern hemisphere of Mars by an asteroid hit in the distant past. . . . In the winter, Hellas is often completely covered in frost; in the summer, it's a place where dust storms often get started. . . . [O]bservers with larger telescopes will notice that Mars appears to sport grey-green blotches on its surface. These are the highlands of Mars, which are not actually green but merely look that way in contrast to the more orangish tint of the planet's plains and deserts.[95]

STEP TWO: **Write a draft of the present point-of-view section of the description**

Look back at the draft you wrote in Step One. Choose one part of the description and ask yourself: If I were standing in space or in the atmosphere, looking *at* Mars, what would this part of the planet look, sound, smell, feel, or taste like? Or ask yourself: If I were standing *on* Mars and looking around, or looking up, what would this part of Mars look, sound, smell, feel, or taste like?

93. Miller, p. 31.

94. George Capaccio, *Mars* (Marshall Cavendish Benchmark, 2010), p. 23.

95. John Scalzi, *The Rough Guide to the Universe* (Rough Guides, 2003), pp. 110–111.

Write two or three sentences describing your chosen part of Mars, using the present point of view.

If you have difficulty, ask your instructor for help.

STEP THREE: **Settle on a metaphor or simile**

Jot down at least one metaphor or simile that could help describe one of the following:

The dryness of the planet (no free water)

The bleak, bare surface of the planet (no vegetation, all rock and desert)

The contrast between the orange-red dusty surface of the planet and the white polar caps

The size/shape of the moons

If you have difficulty, ask your instructor for help.

STEP FOUR: **Complete the final draft**

Now you will combine the three elements of the description. Insert the present point-of-view sentences into your removed point-of-view description at the appropriate place; then insert your metaphor, simile, or figurative language.

If necessary, read back over the examples in the last three weeks to see the different ways in which writers make use of figurative language and mixed point of view.

Your finished draft should be more than 200 words but not more than 500 words in length.

If you have difficulty, ask your instructor for help. And when you are finished, show your composition to your instructor.

Week 15: Combining Chronological Narrative of a Scientific Discovery and Scientific Description

Day One: Original Narration Exercise

Focus: Summarizing a narrative by choosing the main events and listing them chronologically

STEP ONE: **Read**

Read the following excerpt from the adventure novel *Big Red* by Jim Kjelgaard. Danny, the novel's main character, works for a rich man named Mr. Haggin who owns a kennel of champion Irish Setters. Danny's favorite dog in the kennel is the show dog Big Red. Mr. Haggin won't allow Big Red out to hunt, because he's afraid the dog will be injured and no longer be able to win ribbons in dog shows.

In this excerpt, Big Red has escaped from the kennel and is on the trail of the legendary killer bear Old Majesty. Danny needs to catch Big Red and get him back home before Mr. Haggin notices that his prize dog is out in the wilderness.

> The red dog barked once, and flung himself across the clearing straight at the bear. Danny wanted to shriek at him not to do it, to come back because the bear would certainly kill him. But his tongue was a dry, twisted thing that clung to the roof of his mouth, and he could utter no sound. For one tense moment the bear stood his ground. Then he dropped to all fours, and with Red close behind him, disappeared in the forest.
>
> Danny probed the forest with his eyes, and strained his ears, but could neither see nor hear anything. He turned and ran, back down Stoney Lonesome and through the beech woods to the father's clearing. He flung himself inside the cabin, snatched up his gun and a handful of cartridges, and ran back. For five minutes he stood by the dead bull, watching and listening.

But the forest had swallowed both bear and dog.

Danny tried to stifle the panic that besieged him. It was no longer fear of Old Majesty, or of Mr. Haggin and anything he might do, but he was afraid for Red. When Old Majesty had drawn him far enough away he would certainly turn to kill him. Danny suppressed a sob and went forward to find their trail.

He found it, leading out of the glade straight toward the back reaches of the Wintapi. Running hard, the bear had bunched his four feet together and scuffed the leaves every place he struck. Danny ran, hating the sluggishness of his feet and the snail's pace at which they carried him. It was his best speed, but the dog and bear were travelling three times as fast. A mile from the glade he found where the bear had slowed to a trot, and a half mile beyond that where he had turned for the first time to face the pursuing dog.

A huge, knobby-limbed beech raised at the border of a bramble-thick patch of waste land, and the bear had whipped about with his back to the trunk. Danny's heart was leaden as he looked about for tell-tale mats of red hair or drops of blood. But all he saw was the plainly imprinted tale of how the red dog had come upon and charged the bear. Old Majesty had left his retreat by the beech tree, and with whipping front paws had tried to pin the red dog to the earth. Red had danced before him, keeping out of reach while he retreated. A hundred feet from the tree the bear, afraid to leave his rear exposed while a dog was upon him and a man might come, had gone back. Red had charged again, and again had danced away from the bear's furious lunges. Then the bear had left the tree.

"He smelt me comin'," Danny whispered to himself. "Red, you're sure playin' your cards right. If only I can stay close enough to keep him runnin', to keep him from ketchin' you. . ."

But tracking over the boulders was painfully slow work. Sweat stood out on Danny's forehead while, by a broken bramble, a bit of loosened shale, or an occasional paw print between the boulders, he worked out the direction that Old Majesty had taken. The sun reached its peak, and began slowly to sink toward its bed in the west. Danny clenched his hands, and wanted to run, but by doing so he would lose the trail. And, if he did that, Red would be forever lost too.

The first shades of twilight were darkening the forest when Danny finally crossed the boulders and was again among trees. He found the bear's trail in the scuffed leaves there, and with his rifle clutched tightly to him ran as fast as he could along it. Old Majesty had climbed straight up the long, sloping nose of a hump-backed ridge and had run along its top. Then he had dipped suddenly down into a stand of giant pines. Black night overtook Danny there. He bent over, painfully picking out each track and following it. When he could no longer do that, he got down on his hands and knees and tried to follow the trail by feeling out each track. But that was impossible.

"Keep your head, Danny," he counselled himself. He sat down with his back against a huge pine, straining his ears into the darkness for some bark or snarl, something that might tell him where the bear had gone. But there was only silence. A dozen times he started up to peer hopefully about for dawn. But the night was a thousand hours long. Not able to sleep, he sat against the tree looking into the night-shrouded maze of lost valleys and nameless canyons into which the bear had gone. Then, after an eternity, a gray shaft of light dropped through one of the pines to the needle-littered earth. Danny leaped to his feet. By bending very close to the earth he could see and follow the tracks. And, as daylight increased, he could run once more. He followed the trail down the mountain, and up the side of another one. Along its crest he went, down and up another mountain. And it was from the top of this that he heard a dog's bark.

Danny stopped, let his jaw drop open the better to listen. The bark was not repeated, but there had been no mistake about hearing it. Danny looked down into the wide, boulder-studded valley that stretched beneath him, and put his fingers into his mouth preparatory to whistling. But he stopped himself in time. If the bear and dog were down there, a whistle or sound would only warn Old Majesty that he was coming, and would send him off on another wild chase. Danny studied the valley carefully. The trees in it were only saplings and fire cherries, but the boulders were huge. The bear would make his stand against a boulder rather than one of the small trees. Danny scrutinized each boulder, and selected the one from which he thought the dog's bark had drifted.

But he had to go very carefully now, very slowly. A wrong move, a misstep, and everything would be ruined. He walked down the mountain. Once on the valley floor he dropped to his hands and knees and crawled, placing each hand and foot carefully, cautious that his clothing should brush against no branch or twig that might make a sound. A hundred feet from the boulder he had chosen, he peered over a small rock and saw Old Majesty.

Perched on a shelf of rock, the bear was five feet from the ground. Huge, monstrous, a presence rather than a beast, his great head was bent toward the ground. Danny saw Red, lying on the ground ten feet before the bear, raising his head suspiciously every time the bear moved, ready to charge or retreat. Danny's hands trembled when he levelled the rifle over the little rock. This was a heaven-sent chance.

Ross had told him that a show dog must be no less than perfect, and there was one chance in fifty of killing that huge bear with a single shot. He would come toppling from his perch with snapping jaws and slashing paws. Red, knowing that at last he was reinforced by the man for whom he had waited, would be upon the bear. Not long, just long enough to get a ripped foot or a slashed side before

Danny could send home the shot that would kill the bear. Just long enough to make him entirely useless to Mr. Haggin, to give Danny a chance of getting him. Danny sighted. Then he took his rifle down and crawled around the little rock.

He slithered over the ground, crawling forward with ready rifle held before him, and was twenty feet from the boulder when Old Majesty, all of whose attention had been riveted on the dog, looked up. The rank odor of the great bear filled Danny's nostrils, and for a moment he looked steadily into the eyes of his ancient enemy. Then Red was beside him, backing against Danny's knees, still looking at the bear. Danny's left hand reached down to grasp the dog's collar, his right brought the rifle up.

But Old Majesty slid off the back end of the boulder and was gone.[96]

STEP TWO: **Write summary sentences**

You will now summarize the passage in three or four sentences and write those sentences down on your own paper.

This is the last narration summary exercise in this year's workbook. In the last 11 weeks, you've practiced summarizing by noting down important events and then combining those events into three or four sentences. In this last exercise, try to streamline the process by combining the two steps. Write three or four sentences summarizing the main events in the story, and then show them to your instructor.

You may find it helpful to underline the most important events in the excerpt above, and then look only at those events as you write. You may also need to write five or more sentences and then edit them by cutting out unnecessary details and combining sentences.

If you have difficulty with this assignment, ask your instructor for help. When you're finished, show your work to your instructor.

Day Two: Outlining Exercise

Focus: Finding the central topic in each paragraph of a chronological narrative that includes a scientific description of an object or phenomenon

STEP ONE: **Read**

Read the following excerpt from *Changes in the Wind: Earth's Shifting Climate* by Margery and Howard Facklam. The first paragraphs take place during World War II, a time when the United States and Japan were at war.

---

96. Jim Kjelgaard, *Big Red* (Holiday House, 1945), pp. 21–26.

An "incendiary bomb" is a bomb intended to start a fire by exploding and spreading some sort of fast, hot-burning fuel all over the target area. In World War II, most incendiary bombs had the chemical phosphorus in them.

The "troposphere" is the lowest part of the Earth's atmosphere; that is, the section closest to the ground. It has a depth of anywhere between 7 and 20 kilometers (about 4.5 to 12.5 miles). Most of the phenomena we associate with day-to-day weather occur in the troposphere. The next layer up is called the "stratosphere." It runs up to 50–60 kilometers (about 31–38 miles) above the earth's surface.

— — —

> One hundred and eleven B-29 bombers flew in formation toward Japan at dawn. It was November 24, 1944, and their mission, with the code name San Antonio, was to bomb industrial sites near Tokyo. From a base in the South Seas, the planes droned through the sky at altitudes between 27,000 and 30,000 feet, intending to drop the bombs on a path from west to east. As they made a turn toward the east to approach Tokyo, the heavy aircraft were suddenly pushed ahead in 150-mile-an-hour winds. Neither the aircraft nor the released bombs could adjust to the wind drift. Most of the bombs missed their targets. . .
>
> At about the same time American bombers were reporting the strong high-altitude winds, some loggers in Montana found a huge balloon stuck in a tall pine tree. It was marked with the Japanese emblem of a rising sun. Bits and pieces of similar balloons were found in the western states, and speculation ran high that the balloons carried spies or deadly germs. But the biggest worry centered around where the balloons had come from. With what we then knew of winds, it seemed impossible that the balloons could have floated all the way from Japan. They must have been launched from off-shore submarines. 
>
> It turned out, of course, that the balloons had ridden the jet stream 5,000 miles to America. Designed to drop incendiary bombs and then self-destruct to destroy the instruments, the balloons failed only because the equipment froze in the jet stream's sub-zero temperatures.
>
> Like a tunnel of wind, the jet stream flows in an undulating series of loops at the outer edge of the troposphere, where it blends into the stratosphere. Wherever there are extreme temperature differences, the jet stream is fastest. When cold polar air penetrates deep into the warmer air of the south, the wintertime jet stream at the leading edge of such a cold air mass forms a ribbon 4 miles deep and 300 miles wide, traveling more than 300 miles an hour. In summer, when the temperature differences between air masses are less, the jet stream slows. . . .

The number of loops or waves in a jet stream varies. Meteorologists think that during the warm medieval years, it streamed across the Northern Hemisphere in four big loops, but during the Little Ice Age, the jet pattern moved south in five loops. Most of the time these loops move quickly in short periods of changing weather, but now and then they stall. Then we're in for long periods of the same kind of weather. That's what happened during the winter of 1976 and 1977, when the Northeast was held in the cold grip of blizzards and the West Coast had a long hot spell. [97]

STEP TWO: **Construct a one-level outline**

This week's passage combines two of the topics you've been studying: a chronological narrative, and a scientific description of a phenomenon (the jet stream).

As in previous weeks, you'll need to find a major point for each section. Because the sections alternate between chronological narrative and description, you'll have to use both of the methods you've studied. If the section seems to be chronological narrative, ask:

1. What is the main thing or person that this section is about? *Or* What is the major event in this section?
2. Why is that thing, person, or event important?

If the section seems to be primarily descriptive, ask:

What part or aspect of the jet stream does this section describe?

If you're not sure which method will work best, try both.

You may mix phrases and sentences if necessary. If you have difficulty, ask your instructor for help. And when you're finished, check your assignment with your instructor.

Day Three: Analyzing the Topos

Focus: Understanding the form of a chronological narrative that includes a scientific description of an object or phenomenon

The passage you outlined in your last writing session was a brief chronological narrative that made use of a scientific description of a phenomenon—a combination of two forms you have already learned. Today, you will examine two different ways of combining chronological narrative with scientific description.

97. Margery and Howard Facklam, *Changes in the Wind: Earth's Shifting Climate* (Harcourt Brace Jovanovich, 1986), pp. 5–6.

STEP ONE: **Chronological narrative of a past event as an introduction to scientific description**

In Week 4 of this course, you learned that a chronological narrative can serve as an introduction to a longer piece of writing. In the passage about the jet stream, the first two sections are a brief chronological narrative about a historical event; this serves as an introduction to a longer description and explanation of the jet stream. (You only have three paragraphs of this description, but the book itself has much more.)

A chronological narrative from history can be an excellent introduction to a scientific description. The story of the failed bombing mission and the strange discovery of Japanese balloons in Montana tells you what the jet stream can *do*; once you know this, the description of the jet stream itself makes much more sense.

Look again at this excerpt from Susan Casey's book *The Wave: In Pursuit of the Rogues, Freaks, and Giants of the Ocean*, which you saw for the first time in Week 4 of this course.

> *57.5° N, 12.7° W, 175 miles off the coast of Scotland*
> *February 8, 2000*
>
> The clock read midnight when the hundred-foot wave hit the ship, rising from the North Atlantic out of the darkness. Among the ocean's terrors a wave this size was the most feared and the least understood, more myth than reality—or so people had thought. This giant was certainly real. As the RRS *Discovery* plunged down into the wave's deep trough, it heeled twenty-eight degrees to port, rolled thirty degrees back to starboard, then recovered to face the incoming seas. . . . Captain Keith Avery steered his vessel directly into the onslaught, just as he had been doing for the past five days. . . . He stood barefoot at the helm, the only way he could maintain traction after a refrigerator toppled over, splashing out a slick of milk, juice, and broken glass (no time to clean it up—the waves just kept coming). . . . [The] waves suddenly grew even bigger and meaner and steeper. Avery heard a loud bang coming from *Discovery's* foredeck. He squinted in the dark to see that the fifty-man lifeboat had partially ripped from its two-inch-thick steel cleats and was pounding against the hull.[98]

After this chronological narrative of past events, Casey goes on to a scientific description of an object or phenomonon—the waves themselves ("The significant wave height, an average of the largest 33 percent of the waves, was sixty-one feet, with frequent spikes far beyond that. . .").

In both of these passages, a chronological narrative about past events is used as an attention-getting introduction to a scientific description of objects or phenomona.

98. Casey, pp. 3–4

STEP TWO: **Chronological narrative of scientific discovery combined with a scientific description**

In Weeks 4–7 of this course, you studied two kinds of chronological narratives: chronological narratives about a past event, and chronological narratives about scientific discoveries.

A chronological narrative about a past event can serve as an interesting introduction to a scientific description—but the introduction isn't completely *necessary.* You could understand both the description of the jet stream and the description of the wave perfectly well without the chronological narration that introduces each.

But a chronological narrative about a scientific discovery often *needs* a scientific description to round it out. Read again this chronological narrative about the scientific discoveries of Antoni van Leeuwenhoek, from Alma Payne Ralston's book *Discoverer of the Unseen World:*

> In considering various ways to test the new contrivance, he thought of the appearance of the fresh water in Berkelse Mere, the inland lake located "about two hours from Delft." Its water was always clear in winter. But during the summer it lost this clearness and became whitish in color with little green clouds floating through it. The country people believed the change in the water's appearance was caused by the dews that occurred at that time; for this reason they called it "honeydew."
>
> This was hearsay, Leeuwenhoek reasoned. He would have to see for himself. Accepting a belief as a fact, without being curious enough to test it, was just the kind of thing that had been going on for centuries. Here was a chance for him, one of the most curious amateurs of science, to satisfy his curiosity about the nature of the inland lake. In so doing, he might also make a contribution to science. And it would give him an opportunity to test the quality of his newly made microscope and the clearness of his glass pipettes.
>
> So he journeyed to Berkelse Mere, to the southeast of Delft. Here he scooped up a generous sample of the marshy water and put it into a container. It was too late to examine the water when he returned home that night. So he put the container in the office-laboratory where he did all of his work and study.
>
> The following night he assembled his simple equipment and prepared to observe the Berkelse Mere water by the light of a single candle. First he sucked a drop of water into a little glass pipette which he had glued onto the rod of his newest microscope. In reality the instrument was "a simple magnifying glass," and this is what he always called it. It consisted of two matched oblong sheets of metal, which encased a tiny bi-convex, or football-shaped, lens. The whole thing was smaller than a small oblong football ticket.
>
> Leeuwenhoek carefully lifted the microscope and pressed the minute lens close to one eye. He could not believe what he saw. There before him was a veritable swimming pool of earthly particles, green streaks, and little

"animalcules"! The streaks were spirally wound like serpents and "orderly arranged, after the manner of copper or tin worms, which distillers use to cool their liquors as they distill over." The amazing thing about these little figures was that they were only as thick as a strand of hair (the common form of green alga *Spirogyra*).

He saw other particles that had only the beginning of streaks. But all consisted of very small green globules joined together. Among these many odd-shaped particles were many little "animalcules." He did not know it, but undoubtedly at least some of these were Protozoa. Some were round in shape, others were elongated or oval.

Some of the creatures had two little legs near the head and two fins at the end of their bodies (probably rotifers). Others were elongated and moved very slowly (probably ciliates).

These "animalcules," as he referred to bacteria and Protozoa in all his observations, were of several colors, some being white and transparent, while others were green in the middle, banded by white (probably *Euglena viridis*); others sparkled with green scales, and still others were a kind of dove-gray. He wrote: "The motion of most of these animalcules in the water was so swift, and so various, upwards, downwards, and round about, that 'twas wonderful to see: and I judge that these little creatures were above a thousand times smaller [in volume, not in linear dimensions] than the smallest ones I have ever seen, upon the rind of cheese, in wheaten flour, mould and the like" (mites).[99]

Notice that the chronological narrative of scientific discovery leads seamlessly into the description of what Leeuwenhoek saw through his microscope: a scientific description of an object or phenomenon (the microscopic creatures in the water).

STEP THREE: **Examine the models**

Read the following three passages. In each one, a chronological narrative is combined with a scientific description of an object or phenomenon. In each passage, draw a line between the chronological narrative and the scientific description. Then, write in the margin beside the chronological narrative whether it is about "past events" or "scientific discovery."

In the spring of 1609, a friend of Galileo's told him about an optical device built in Holland. Magnifying lenses had been used in eyeglasses to improve eyesight since the late 13th century. However, the Dutch spyglass was the first device used for "seeing faraway things as though nearby." It had been created as a toy.

99. Ralston, pp. 16–19.

Galileo was intrigued. He began working on his own version of the telescope. To create his telescope, Galileo first had to learn how to grind and polish glass lenses, a complicated task. In about a month, however, he had built a telescope that made objects appear three or four times larger than their normal size.

Before long, Galileo had built a telescope that could magnify objects to eight or nine times their normal size. On August 21, he traveled to Venice to show off his invention to the Senate. He asked the senators to climb to the top of a tower and peer through his telescope. The senators were astonished to see boats approaching Venice that were more than two hours away. . . .

In the coming months, Galileo worked to create telescopes that were more and more powerful. In November 1609, he invented a telescope that was 15 times more powerful than the human eye. Within the next five months, he created a telescope twice as powerful as that one.

The telescope that Galileo created is known today as a refracting telescope. It was about five or six feet in length. In a refracting telescope, light enters the end of the telescope's tube and passes through a convex lens (one that is curved outward). The convex lens bends the light rays, directing them to a focal point. These light rays spread out when they hit a concave lens (one that is curved inward) at the opposite end of the tube. The rays covered more of the viewer's retina and appeared larger than normal.[100]

Peg knew she was sick, but she . . . tried to hide her illness from her mother. But Peg's temperature rapidly spiked to 102 degrees. Her neck, back, and legs began to ache; a weariness like nothing she'd ever felt came over her. . . . Peg and her parents thought she had the flu. The were wrong. The following morning, her doctor diagnosed her with poliomyelitis. Peg's life literally changed overnight. One day she could walk, run, and hold her own books. The next, she was paralyzed from the neck down, unable to move her arms or legs. Peg spent the next year of her life struggling to regain mobility. After months of intense physical therapy, she succeeded. Not every poliomyelitis victim was as fortunate. . . .

Today we know that polio is caused by a virus. A virus is a submicroscopic agent made up of a protective shell of proteins surrounding the virus's genetic material. Viruses are parasitic, meaning they cannot reproduce without a host body. A virus typically enters a host body through the nose or mouth, when the host inhales or ingests material contaminated with the virus.[101]

100. Robin Santos Doak, *Galileo: Astronomer and Physicist* (Compass Point Books, 2005), pp. 45–48.
101. Stephanie True Peters, *The Battle against Polio* (Benchmark Books, 2005), pp. 1–2.

(This next paragraph is intentionally difficult—a challenge! But even if you don't understand everything in it, you should still be able to carry out the instructions.)

> In the 1930s Alan Hodgkin of Cambridge University, also working on the nerves of frogs, showed that the outer membrane of an axon acts like an electric capacitor. . . . Hodgkin's research was interrupted by the Second World War, but in the late 1940s he teamed up with Andrew Huxley (brother of the novelist Aldous Huxley), and started working on the axons of squids. Most axons are microscopically thin, but squids also have two "giant axons," about a millimetre in diameter, big enough for electrodes to be inserted right into them. In a series of four papers published in 1952, Hodgkin and Huxley showed that the mechanism of the nerve impulse worked with positively-charged atoms ("ions") of sodium and potassium. When an axon is resting, it maintains a considerable excess of sodium ions outside it, and a similar excess of potassium ions inside. As an action potential sweeps along an axon, its outer membrane becomes "depolarised"—it suddenly lets the sodium ions flow through it into the axon, reversing the electrical charge. A split second later, potassium ions flow the other way, and the original electric charge is restored.[102]

Day Four: Practicing the Topos

Focus: Learning how to write a chronological narrative that includes a scientific description of an object or phenomenon

Today, you'll put together a composition that includes both a chronological narrative and a scientific description of an object or phenomenon.

Since you have already practiced putting together a chronological narrative of past events and a description (Week 11), today you'll put together a chronological narrative about a scientific discovery that includes a scientific description.

STEP ONE: **Write a rough draft of the description**

You'll begin today's assignment by writing a brief description of a deep-ocean vent.

First, turn to the Scientific Description chart in your Composition Notebook and read the "Procedure" and "Remember" points out loud.

Next, read the facts that follow, and study the pictures.

102. Rupert Lee, *The Eureka! Moment: 100 Key Scientific Discoveries of the 20th Century* (Routledge, 2002), pp. 88–89.

Finally, write a rough draft of your description. This description should contain at **least two** of the following three elements:

1. A section that describes, from a removed point of view, each part of an object or phenomenon and tells what it's made from.
2. A section that also describes at least one part of the object or phenomenon from a present, personal point of view, using at least three of the five senses (smell, taste, touch, hearing, sight).
3. A metaphor, simile, or some other use of figurative language that makes some part of the object or phenomenon more vivid and real to the reader.

Your description should be at least 150 and not more than 250 words.

FACTS ABOUT DEEP-OCEAN VENTS
Taken partly from *Ocean: An Illustrated Atlas* by Sylvia A. Earle and Linda K. Glover (National Geographic Society, 2009) and the *Encyclopedia of Marine Science* by C. Reid Nichols and Robert G. Williams (Facts on File, 2009).

Deep-ocean hydrothermal vents
A gap or crack between rock plates in the ocean floor
Volcanic activity nearby
Water goes into the gap, touches magma, and overheats.
Water shoots back out of the vents between 212 and 570 degrees Fahrenheit (100 to
300
degrees Celsius).
Water does not boil because it is under too much pressure.
Water then cools to about 73 degrees Fahrenheit (23 degrees Celsius).
Water is "milky," cloudy with minerals.
"Black smokers"
Deep-ocean hydrothermal vents which spew out black sulfides (minerals with sulfur in them)
Superheated water, hotter than 350 degrees Celsius (662 degrees Fahrenheit)
Spews out of mineral piles with holes at the top, like chimneys
"Chimneys" can be as tall as 60 meters (about 200 feet).
Giant shellfish
Giant mussels
Yellow shells
Live on bacteria that they filter out of the seawater
Giant clams
White shells, red flesh rich in oxygen
Each clam about a foot across
White crabs

Nibble on the tube worm stalks
Eat the giant mussels

Tube worms

Tube worms

White stalks waving from the ground, red plumes at top filled with blood (hemoglobin)
No mouths or digestive tracts
Live on the energy produced by bacteria that live inside them
Can grow as long as 2.4 meters (nearly 8 feet long)

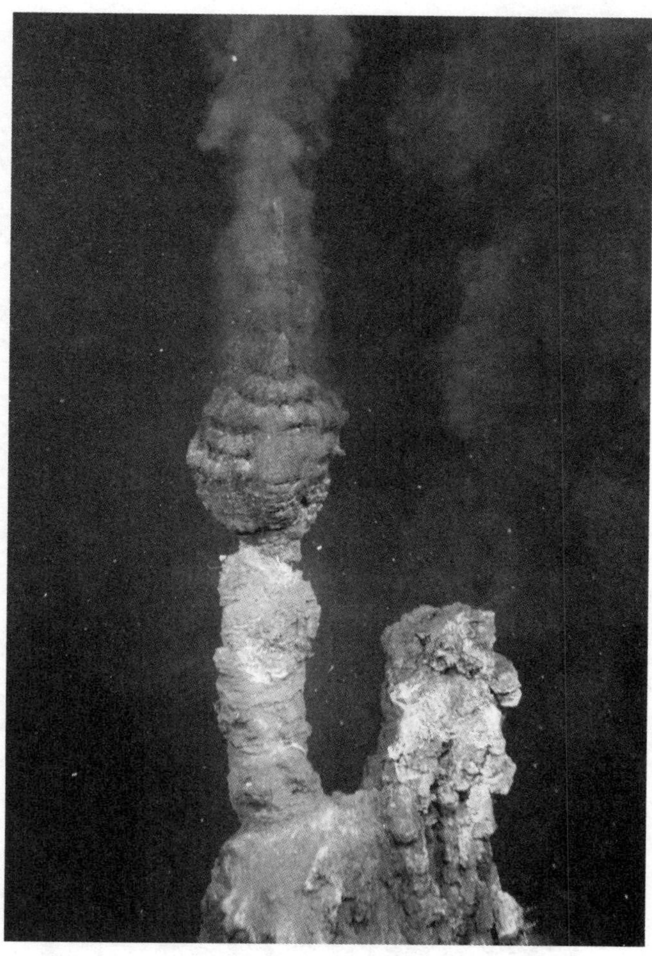

Black smoker called "The Brothers." Public domain photo from the National Oceanic and Atmospheric Administration.

Hydrothermal vents on the deep ocean floor. Public domain photo from the National Oceanic and Atmospheric Administration.

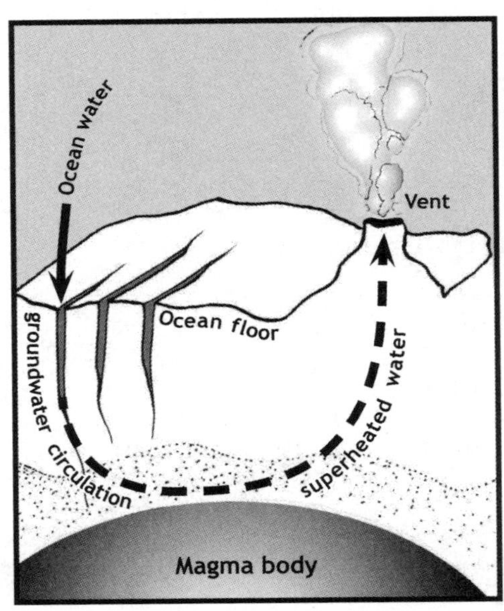

Structure of a hydrothermal vent.

Tube worms. Public domain photograph from the National Undersearch Research Program Collection.

If you have difficulty with this assignment, ask your instructor for help.

STEP TWO: **Write a rough draft of the chronological narrative**

Now that you know what a deep-ocean hydrothermal vent is, you'll go back and write the first part of your composition—the chronological narrative about the discovery of the vents.

Before you begin, turn to the Chronological Narrative of a Scientific Discovery chart in your Composition Notebook. Read the points under the "Procedure" and "Remember" columns out loud.

Next, look through the list of events covering the 1977 discovery of deep-ocean hydrothermal vents. Decide which main events and details you will include. (This is a brief list, so you may decide to include most of them.)

Finally, write your brief narrative. This should be at least 100 and no more than 300 words. Remember, you don't need to to include *every* element on the chart; you can choose, for example, to leave out the paragraph of background information.

EVENTS LEADING TO THE DISCOVERY
OF DEEP-OCEAN HYDROTHERMAL VENTS

Scientists predicted "hot spots" on the ocean floor

- Tectonic plates (plates in the Earth's crust) meet under the ocean.
- When plates shift, magma (liquid rock) often erupts.
- Scientists predicted that this would cause places on the ocean floor to heat up.
- These spots had never been seen before 1977.

The 1975 expedition

- Included French and American research scientists
- Called "FAMOUS" ("French-American Mid-Ocean Undersea Study")
- Included American scientist Robert Ballard
- Searched for hydrothermal vents in the Atlantic Ocean
- Submarine dived to the Mid-Atlantic Ridge.
    - Ridge: boundary between two tectonic plates
    - Located in the center of the Atlantic Ocean, running between the American and European/African continents
    - Between the plates is a gap where magma erupts onto the ocean floor.
- No hydrothermal vents were found.

1976 experiments

- Unmanned crafts ("diving saucers") were sent into the Galapagos Rift.
    - Rift: boundary between two tectonic plates near the Galapagos Islands
    - Volcanic activity common
    - When plates move, magma spills onto the ocean floor.
- Samples of water were brought back.
- Water had strange mineral content.

The 1977 expedition

Sponsored by the National Oceanic and Atmospheric Administration
Included French and American research scientists
Scientists used the *Alvin,* 25-foot-long submarine designed for deep ocean use.
Expedition led by scientist Robert Ballard

He wrote, "Suddenly, our floodlights revealed a swaying field of orange pink dandelions, their puffy heads pulsing with fine webs of filaments. . . . The lumped mounds of pillow lava were thick with jutting chalk white clam shells, some of them a foot in length." From *Explorations,* by Robert Ballard (Hyperion, 1996), p. 190.

Submarine dove into the Galapagos Rift.
Dove down to 2,500 meters
Discovered hot springs in the ocean floor: hydrothermal vents
Expedition included scientists John Corliss and John Edmond.

They wrote, "Shimmering water streams up past giant tube worms, never before seen by man. A crab scuttles over lava encrusted with limpets, while a pink fish basks in the warmth." From *Ocean: An Illustrated Atlas,* p. 158

They also called the vents "lush oases in a sunless desert . . . a phenomenon totally new to science." From *Ocean: An Illustrated Atlas,* p. 158

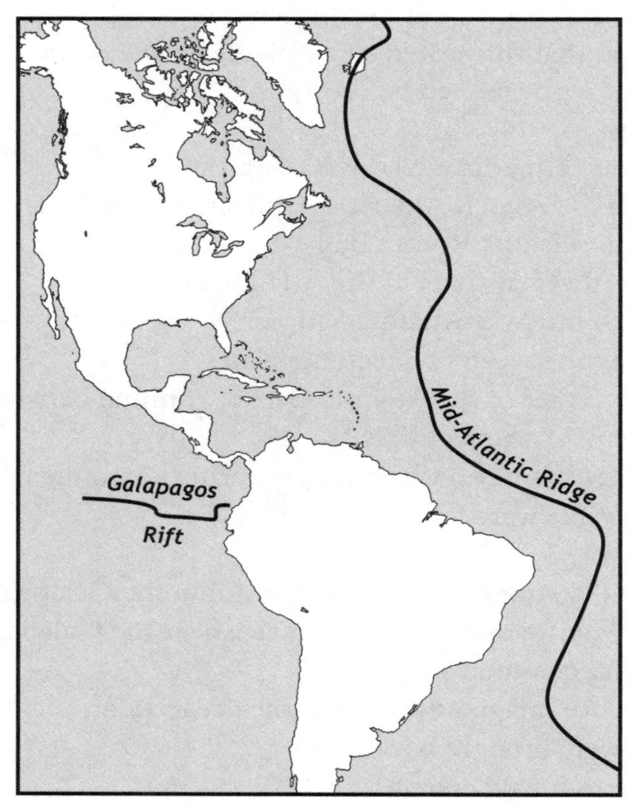

STEP THREE: **Finalize the composition**

Now read your entire composition out loud. Listen to each sentence. If any of your phrases or sentences sounds rough or awkward, try phrasing them in different ways until you find a combination of words that sounds smoother or easier to understand.

When you are satisfied with your composition, show it to your instructor.

Part III

SENTENCE SKILLS WEEKS 16–22

Overview of Weeks 16–22

In the last 12 weeks, you practiced three important basic skills: summarizing a story in three or four sentences (narration), finding the main idea in each paragraph of a written composition (outlining), and using descriptions and chronological narrations (topoi) to build compositions of your own.

All three of those skills have to do with *organization*—figuring out the structure of written work. In this third part of your course, you'll continue to practice organization: you'll keep working on your outlining, and you'll learn a few more topoi to use as composition building blocks.

But you won't need to do any more narrations. Summarizing a story is a basic writing skill that was preparing you for the more advanced skill of outlining. Now that you're able to find the main idea in a paragraph, you can give the narration practice a rest.

Instead, you'll add in another more advanced skill: examining the structure and organization of *sentences*. Outlining and topoi exercises teach you how to organize a whole composition, but each sentence should also be carefully organized. In this part of the course, you'll start to study structure and organization on the sentence level through exercises known as *copia*.

Copia

You should already have three labelled sections in the beginning of your Composition Notebook (Narrations, Outlines, and Topoi), followed by two blank sections and then a final section labelled Reference. Label the first remaining blank section "Copia."

Copia (a Latin word meaning "abundance") is the nickname of a famous Renaissance writing text called *Brevis de copia praeceptio* ("A Short Rule for Copiousness"), written by the Renaissance scholar and theologian Desiderius Erasmus and printed in 1512. In *Copia,* Erasmus teaches students how to use many different kinds of sentences ("abundant" ways of expression). He then took a single sentence, "Your letter pleased me greatly," and rephrased it 195 different ways, including:

Your epistle exhilarated me intensely.
At your words a delight of no ordinary kind came over me.
How exceedingly agreeable did we find your epistle!
Your brief note made me burst with joy.
Your by no means displeasing letter has arrived.[103]

In the copia exercises, you'll be rewriting, rephrasing, and rewording assigned sentences. This will teach you to use variety and will make you familiar with many different patterns of sentences.

Erasmus explained the importance of variety in this way:

> . . . [I]t will help in avoiding . . . the repetition of a word or phrase, an ugly and offensive fault. It often happens that we have to say the same thing several times. If in these circumstances we find ourselves destitute of verbal riches and hesitate, or keep singing out the same old phrase like a cuckoo, and are unable to clothe our thought in other colours or other forms, we shall look ridiculous . . . and we shall also bore our wretched audience to death.[104]

These exercises will help you avoid ever boring anyone to death.

Place all completed copia exercises in the fourth section of your notebook.

Outlines

You will continue to work on outlines. When you've finished these outlines, place them in the second section of your notebook.

Topoi

You will continue to learn new topoi. File the compositions you write as part of your topoi lessons under "Topoi" in the third section of your notebook, and continue to copy the patterns you're learning into the "Reference" section of your notebook.

Narrations

You won't be doing these any more, but you should keep them in your notebook so that you can admire them.

---

103. Desiderius Erasmus, *Copia: Foundations of the Abundant Style: De duplici copia verborum ac rerum Commentarii duo*, trans and ed. Betty I. Knott, in *Collected Works of Erasmus: Literary and Educational Writings 2*, ed. Craig R. Thompson, vol. 28 (University of Toronto Press, 1978), ch. 33.
104. Erasmus, p. 302.

Week 16: Description of a Person

Day One: Outlining Exercise

Focus: Finding the central topic in each paragraph of a character study

STEP ONE: **Read**

Read the following description of Queen Elizabeth I (1533–1603), from a biography written at the beginning of the twentieth century. Most of the passage is self-explanatory, but you may want to know that Zucchero is an alternate spelling of Zuccari; Federico Zuccari (1543–1609) was an Italian painter. William Camden (1551–1623) was the first historian to chronicle the reign of Queen Elizabeth. A "contemporary historian" is a historian who lived at the same time as the person or event the historian is writing about.

Queen Elizabeth was of majestic and graceful form, a little above the medium height, "neither too high nor too low," as she herself . . . remarked. She had hair of a colour between pale auburn and yellow, black eyes, which were "beautiful and lively," a fair, clear complexion, a Roman nose, a small mouth with thin, firmly set lips, and a forehead broad and high. Her face was striking and commanding rather than delicately beautiful, the countenance of one born to rule. She possessed many personal attractions and no one could be more charming and gracious upon occasion than this mighty Princess of the Royal House of Tudor, with that slow, sweet smile of hers and her quick, ever-ready wit.

Sir Francis Bacon says, "She was tall of stature, of comely limbs, and excellent feature in her countenance; majesty sat under the veil of sweetness, and her health was sound and prosperous."

There were a great many portraits painted of her both as Princess and as Queen. In her pictures, Elizabeth was fond of displaying her slender, delicate hands, of which she was very proud. One of the best known portraits of her is the so-called "Rainbow Picture" by Zucchero. In this her slim, tapering fingers are free from rings, but her costume and her coiffure are most elaborate. Her tightly-curled hair is bedecked with jewels and surmounted by a crown, and the stiffly starched ruff is conspicuous.

Indeed, the Queen's one extravagance consisted in a lavish manner of dressing. At the time of her death there were said to be three thousand gowns in her wardrobe, for she disliked to part with any of them, although she had worn some only once or twice. Before her accession to the throne, however, as her position was uncertain and her life often in danger, she assumed a manner of dressing, plain and simple in the extreme, as seemed fitting to her condition. . . . Upon becoming Queen, she allowed her taste for elaborate costumes and rich jewels full play, for she was always fond of arousing admiration in her subjects, and of outshining the ladies of her Court in splendour of apparel. No one before or since has excelled "Good Queen Bess," as she was affectionately called, in magnificence of attire and almost fantastic display of jewels.

. . . Elizabeth possessed remarkable mental endowments. Devoted from her earliest years to study, and particularly to history, she became the ablest and greatest woman England has ever had. Her understanding of the problems of European politics was noteworthy. In the Council Chamber she was distinguished for sound common sense, great shrewdness, and clear insight. Her proficiency in languages was extraordinary. She was an excellent Latin scholar and could converse in that language with rare facility. . . . She spoke and wrote French, Italian, Spanish and Flemish with the same ease as her native English. She also studied Greek extensively, and could converse in it. She learned very readily, and, when only twelve years old, had made considerable progress in the sciences, geography, mathematics and astronomy.

"She was of admirable beauty and well deserving a Crown, of a modest gravity, excellent wit, royal soul, happy memory, and indefatigably given to the study of learning; insomuch, as before she was seventeen years of age, she understood well the Latin, French and Italian tongues and had an indifferent knowledge of Greek. Neither did she neglect music so far as became a Princess, being able to sing sweetly and play handsomely on the lute," writes Camden, the contemporary historian of her reign.

Elizabeth was always fond of poetry and composed some sonnets and other verses, which are altogether worthy of mention. In addition, she translated some poems from the French, and Sallust's "De Bello Jugurthino" from the Latin; also a play of Euripides and two orations of Isocrates from Greek into Latin. Further, she wrote a comment[ary] on Plato, and translated a dialogue of Xenophon from Greek into English. In 1593, when she was sixty years old, Her Majesty found time, in the midst of her State duties, to translate from the Latin into smooth and very elegant English the five books of Boethius' "Consolations of Philosophy," and in 1598 the greater part of Horace's "De Arte Poetica," and a little treatise by Plutarch, called "De Curiositate." Almost the whole of these manuscripts are in the Queen's own clear and beautiful handwriting, which was so admired by her tutors.[105]

STEP TWO: **Construct a one-level outline**

You will notice that this passage is not divided into sections. Treat each paragraph as a separate section and find the main idea in each one.

Like the passages you've seen in the last few weeks, this passage is a description. When finding the main idea, you will probably want to ask "What part or aspect of Queen Elizabeth does this paragraph describe?" However, there are two paragraphs that will need a slightly different approach: the second and the sixth.

See if you can figure out how to word the main idea in each of those paragraphs on your own. If you need help, though, you may ask your instructor.

When you're finished, check your assignment with your instructor.

Day Two: Analyzing the Topos

Focus: Understanding the form of a description of a person

In the last few weeks, you've studied the forms of two types of description: description of a place, and scientific description of an object or phenomenon. The passage you outlined in the last writing session introduces you to a third type: description of a person.

STEP ONE: **Examine model passages**

When you think "description of a person," you probably think of appearance: hair and eye color, age, height and weight, nose, chin, etc. But a description of a person can include *many* details that aren't just about physical appearance.

Look back at your outline. Although you will have phrased many of the points differently, your outline probably sounds something like this:

I. Queen Elizabeth's appearance
II. Sir Francis Bacon's description
III. Portraits of Queen Elizabeth
IV. Queen Elizabeth's clothes

105. Gladys Edson Locke, *Queen Elizabeth: Various Scenes and Events in the Life of Her Majesty* (Sherman French & Co., 1913), pp. 1–4.

V. Elizabeth's intelligence
VI. Camden's description
VII. Elizabeth's writings

Each paragraph of the description deals with a different aspect of Queen Elizabeth. They could be categorized as this:

	Topic of paragraph	Aspect
I.	Queen Elizabeth's appearance	*Physical appearance*
II.	Sir Francis Bacon's description, VI. Camden's description	*What others thought of her*
III.	Portraits of Queen Elizabeth	*How she was portrayed*
IV.	Queen Elizabeth's clothes	*How she behaved*
V.	Elizabeth's intelligence, VII. Elizabeth's writings	*Her mind*

Here's another description of a person—this one a fictional person. You're probably familiar with him already.

> Oh! But he was a tight-fisted hand at the grindstone, Scrooge! a squeezing, wrenching, grasping, scraping, clutching, covetous, old sinner! Hard and sharp as flint, from which no steel had ever struck out generous fire; secret, and self-contained, and solitary as an oyster. The cold within him froze his old features, nipped his pointed nose, shrivelled his cheek, stiffened his gait; made his eyes red, his thin lips blue; and spoke out shrewdly in his grating voice. A frosty rime was on his head, and on his eyebrows, and his wiry chin. He carried his own low temperature always about with him; he iced his office in the dog-days; and didn't thaw it one degree at Christmas.
>
> External heat and cold had little influence on Scrooge. No warmth could warm, no wintry weather chill him. No wind that blew was bitterer than he, no falling snow was more intent upon its purpose, no pelting rain less open to entreaty. Foul weather didn't know where to have him. The heaviest rain, and snow, and hail, and sleet, could boast of the advantage over him in only one respect. They often "came down" handsomely, and Scrooge never did.
>
> Nobody ever stopped him in the street to say, with gladsome looks, "My dear Scrooge, how are you? When will you come to see me?" No beggars implored him to bestow a trifle, no children asked him what it was o'clock, no man or woman ever once in all his life inquired the way to such and such a place, of Scrooge. Even the blind men's dogs appeared to know him; and when they saw him coming on, would tug their owners into doorways and up courts; and then would wag their tails as though they said, "No eye at all is better than an evil eye, dark master!"[106]

106. Dickens, pp. 3–5.

Like the passage about Queen Elizabeth, this description tells us something about what Scrooge looks like—and much more.

Look at the first paragraph. This tells you that Scrooge is old, with a pointed nose, wrinkled skin, a stiff walk, red eyes, blue lips, and a thin wiry beard. Dickens also tells you how Scrooge *sounds:* he has a grating voice. But while Dickens is giving you these details about Scrooge's personal appearance, he is also describing Scrooge's strongest character quality. He is tight-fisted, squeezing, wrenching, grasping, scraping, clutching, covetous: all adjectives that tell you of his *miserliness.*

The next paragraph tells you about another character quality of Scrooge: he isn't affected by anything outside him. And the final paragraph, like the quotes from Francis Bacon and the historian Camden, tells you what *others* thought of Scrooge.

STEP TWO: **Write down the pattern of the topos**

Copy the following onto a blank sheet of paper in the Reference section of your Composition Notebook. You will be adding to this page, so leave plenty of room.

Description of a Person
Definition: A description of selected physical and non-physical aspects of a person

Procedure	Remember
1. Decide on which aspects will be included. They may include: Physical appearance Sound of voice What others think Portrayals and portraits Character qualities Challenges and difficulties Accomplishments Habits Behavior Expressions of face and body Mind/intellectual capabilities Talents and abilities Self-disciplines Religious beliefs Clothing, dress Economic status (wealth) Fame, notoriety, prestige Family traditions, tendencies	

STEP THREE: **Identify aspects in descriptions of persons**

Read through the following descriptions. There are spaces in the margins next to each aspect covered in the description. Write in the margins the aspect that those particular sentences of the description are covering; use the list above.

When you are finished, show your work to your instructor.

Unable to walk, unwilling to stand, Roosevelt made a virtue of immobility. Because he sat, the great figures of the world sat with him. No more did they pose strolling through formal gardens or striding down great halls. Instead, they posed with the President for formal portraits or, unbending, for informal chatty poses. ________________

Roosevelt's face changed expression with the quickness, the sureness, of a finished actor's. It was amused, solemn, sarcastic, interested, indignant. It was always strong and confident and it was never dull.[107] ________________

Cleopatra may be one of the most recognizable figures in history but we have little idea of what she actually looked like. Only her coin portraits—issued in her lifetime, and which she likely approved—can be accepted as authentic. . . . A capable, clear-eyed sovereign, she knew how to build a fleet, suppress an insurrection, control a currency, alleviate a famine. An eminent Roman general vouched for her grasp of military affairs. Even at a time when women rulers were no rarity she stood out, the sole female of the ancient world to rule alone and to play a role in Western affairs. She was incomparably richer than anyone else in the Mediterranean. And she enjoyed greater prestige than any other woman of her age as an excitable rival king was reminded when he called, during her stay at court, for her assassination. (In light of her stature, it could not be done.) Cleopatra descended from a long line of murderers and faithfully upheld the family tradition but was, for her time and place, remarkably well behaved.[108]

____

____

____

____

107. "America Loved the Roosevelts," in *Life* Magazine, Nov. 25, 1946 (Vol. 21, No. 22), p. 110.
108. Stacy Schiff, *Cleopatra: A Life* (Little, Brown and Company, 2010), pp. 1–2.

The next day, Monday, is Gandhi's "day of silence." He does not speak, but he listens. As he said once laughingly, it is the best opportunity to impose upon him all things one wants him to hear. He must hear without replying (though he does not forbid himself certain brief written answers). Precisely at 10 AM he arrives. His irregular chuckle announces him as he ascends the stairs; and I seat him in a big folding arm chair next to my table upon which I rest my elbows and from my swivel chair I lean towards him. Immediately he pulls his naked feet from his sandals, and, enveloped in his cloak, he folds his legs under him. He wears big bifocal glasses which allow him to see far and near. . . . The ears stand out. The forehead is wide and well built; it is deeply wrinkled when he speaks. . . . This first impression of frailty is deceiving; the man is solid. His big, thin hands which clutch his cloak over his arms are all bones, veins and . . . muscles.[109]

Day Three: Practicing the Topos

Focus: Learning how to write a description of a person

In your last writing session, you learned that a description of a person can include many aspects besides physical appearance. Today, you'll practice writing your own description, following this pattern.

STEP ONE: **Review the pattern of the topos**

Read the description of Beethoven below, from the classic reference *Grove's Dictionary of Music and Musicians.* Using the Description of a Person chart in your Composition Notebook, write the aspects covered by the description on the lines in the margin.

When you are finished, show your work to your instructor.

Those who saw him for the first time were often charmed by the eager cordiality of his address, and by the absence of the bearishness and gloom which were attributed to him by others. His face may have been ugly, but all admit that it

109. *Rolland's Journal*, quoted in *The Gandhi Reader: A Source Book of His Life and Writings,* by Gandhi and Homer Alexander Jack (Indiana University Press, 1956), pp. 385–386.

was remarkably expressive. "Every change of feeling," says the painter Klober, who painted him in 1818, "in his mind, showed itself at once unmistakably in his features." When lost in thought and abstracted his look would naturally be gloomy, and at such times it was useless to expect attention from him; but on recognising a friend his smile was peculiarly genial and winning. . . . His head was large, the forehead both high and broad, and the hair abundant. It was originally black, but in this last years of his life, though as thick as ever, became quite white, and formed a strong contrast to the red colour of his complexion. . . . His teeth were very white and regular, and good up to his death; in laughing he showed them much. When in pleasant frame of mind his voice was soft, but on occasion he could raise it, and in singing we read of him roaring. . . . His hands were much covered with hair, the fingers strong and short (he could barely span a tenth), and the tips broad, as if pressed out with long practising from early youth. He was very particular as to the mode of holding the hands and placing the fingers. . . . His attitude at the piano was perfectly quiet and dignified, with no approach to grimace, except to bend down a little towards the keys as his deafness increased. . . . Though so easily made angry, his pains as a teacher must have been great. "Unnaturally patient," says one pupil, "he would have a passage repeated a dozen times till it was to his mind"; "infinitely strict in the smallest detail," says another, "until the right rendering was obtained."[110]

STEP TWO: **Plan the description**

Like a description of a place or a chronological narrative, a description of a person can act as a building block in a larger composition. If you were writing a paper about the attack of the Spanish Armada, you might use portraits and the accounts of contemporary historians to describe Philip II of Spain, or the English admiral Sir Francis Drake; the descriptions would make your paper more interesting. If you were writing about the solar system, you might decide to describe Galileo or Copernicus; if you were writing about art or music, you might use a description of Handel or Picasso as a way to make your composition more vivid.

In future lessons, you'll practice using portraits and accounts to write descriptions of people from the past. Today, you'll begin to develop this skill by writing a description of a real person—someone you know in person. This description can be of you, one of your family

110. Sir George Grove, *Grove's Dictionary of Music and Musicians,* Vol. 1 (Macmillan & Co., 1904), pp. 224–225.

members, or an acquaintance. The purpose of this exercise is to help you become more aware of the different aspects that can be included in a vivid, well-written description.

Start to plan out your description by brainstorming. On a piece of scratch paper, jot down as many words, phrases, and short sentences as you can think of for each of the aspects listed in the Description of a Person chart.

You'll probably think of several words or phrases for some of the aspects, and none at all for others. Your brainstorming will let you know which aspects to concentrate on, and which to avoid. No description should try to cover *all* aspects of a person. (Notice that in the description of Beethoven, family tradition, religious beliefs, self-disciplines, and several other aspects aren't addressed at all.) However, your description *should* include physical appearance.

If you're unable to think of more than five or six words/phrases/sentences overall, you might want to consider describing a different person.

STEP THREE: **Write the description**

Now use your notes and write your description, following these directions:

1. Include at least five but no more than eight of the aspects listed on the Description of a Person chart.
2. The physical appearance of the character should be one of the aspects included.
3. The description should be at least 200 but not more than 600 words in length.
4. The description should be based in fact—but you have the freedom to exaggerate or invent *two* (no more!) aspects of the description.
5. You may not use any of the following words: *nice, good, bad, beautiful, lovely, attractive, handsome, pretty, ugly, sparkling, twinkling, soft, loud, famous, poor, rich, smart,* and *dumb.* These words are so common that they convey no specific image to the reader's mind.

If necessary, ask your instructor for help. When you are finished, check your work with your instructor.

Day Four: Copia Exercise

Focus: Using the thesaurus to improve writing

This week, you'll work on your first copia exercise. Over the next weeks, these exercises will make you familiar with many different forms and styles of expression.

STEP ONE: **Review thesaurus use**

Back in Week 3, you were introduced to thesaurus use. Remember, a thesaurus is a reference book that groups together words with similar but different shades of meaning.

If you are comfortable with using the thesaurus, you can go on to Step Two. Otherwise, review the following:

A thesaurus contains two types of lists.

The first half of the thesaurus contains words grouped by meaning and part of speech. These word groups all have numbers. For example, the list headed

630. Imagination

might contain:

1. **nouns** that name different sorts of imagination (fantasy, creative thought, inventiveness, illusion, wishful thinking, daydreaming) as well as names for people who imagine (poet, visionary, prophet, dreamer) and names for things that are imagined (pipe dream, castle in the sky, imagistic poetry);
2. **verbs** for the act of imagining (imagine, fancy, dream up, envision, idealize); and
3. **adjectives** that convey a quality of imagination (imaginary, fanciful, make-believe, ideal, otherworldly, enchanted, spellbound).

The second half of the thesaurus contains an alphabetical listing of thousands of vocabulary words. This is the part of the thesaurus that you'll go to first as you write.

When you worked on the description in your last writing session, you were told not to use the common (and almost meaningless) word *nice.* Suppose that *nice* was the first word that came to your mind when you were writing. To find a better word, you would turn to the second half of the thesaurus and look up *nice* in the *n* section.

Beneath the word *nice,* you would find a series of other adjectives with different shades of meaning, each followed by a number: for example,

attentive *530.15*
conscientious *974.15*
kind *938.13*
pleasant *863.6*
tasty *428.9*

Which of these comes closest to the meaning of *nice* that came to your mind as you wrote? Once you've decided (the person you're thinking of probably isn't "tasty," but "attentive" is much closer!), you would turn back to the group of words that matches the number.

If you chose "attentive," you would find that Section 530 contains words having to do with *attention.* There are 23 different subgroups under Section 530. The first four subgroups contain nouns; the next ten contain verbs; the six after that, adjectives; and the final three, adverbs and interjections. If you looked down to subgroup 15 of Section 530, you would find a series of adjectives closely related to the adjective *attentive:*

heedful, mindful, diligent, interested, concerned, fascinated
and many more.

STEP TWO: **Explore synonyms for basic noun, verb, and adjective forms**

Practice your thesaurus skills now, using the following two sentences from the descriptions studied this week. The first describes Elizabeth; the second, Cleopatra.

For each underlined noun, adjective, and verb, find four synonyms in your thesaurus. List those synonyms on the lines provided. Remember that you must provide noun synonyms for nouns, adjective synonyms for adjectives, and verb synonyms for verbs.

After you've found the synonyms, rewrite each sentence twice on your own paper, choosing from among the listed synonyms. Do not repeat any of the synonyms. When you've finished, read your sentences out loud and listen to how the sound and rhythm change with each new set of adjectives, nouns, and verbs.

When you're finished, show your work to your instructor.

Her face was striking and commanding rather than delicately beautiful, the countenance of one born to rule.

striking: __________ __________ __________ __________

commanding: __________ __________ __________ __________

beautiful: __________ __________ __________ __________

rule: __________ __________ __________ __________

A capable, clear-eyed sovereign, she knew how to build a fleet, suppress an insurrection, control a currency, alleviate a famine.

suppress: __________ __________ __________ __________

insurrection: __________ __________ __________ __________

alleviate: __________ __________ __________ __________

Week 17: Description of a Person

Day One: Outlining Exercise

Focus: Finding the central topic in each paragraph of a character study

STEP ONE: **Read**

Read the following description of Abraham Lincoln, written by one of his contemporaries: Isaac Newton Arnold (1815–1884), a congressman who was a strong supporter of Lincoln. Arnold introduced the 1862 bill that abolished slavery in the United States territories; he also drafted the original document that eventually became the Thirteenth Amendment to the Constitution.

– – –

Physically, he was a tall, spare man, six feet and four inches in height. He stooped, leaning forward as he walked. He was very athletic, with long, sinewy arms, large, bony hands, and of great physical power. Many anecdotes of his strength are given which show that it was equal to that of two or three ordinary men. He lifted with ease five or six hundred pounds. His legs and arms were disproportionately long, as compared with his body; and when he walked, he swung his arms to and fro more than most men. When seated, he did not seem much taller than ordinary men. In his movements, there was no grace, but an impression of awkward strength and vigor. He was naturally diffident, and even to the day of his death, when in crowds, and not speaking or acting, and conscious of being observed, he seemed to shrink with bashfulness. When he spoke, or listened, this appearance left him, and he indicated no self-consciousness. His forehead was high, his hair very dark, nearly black, and rather stiff and coarse; his eye-brows were heavy, his eyes dark-grey, very expressive and varied; now sparkling with humor and fun, and then deeply sad and melancholy; flashing with indignation at injustice or wrong, and then kind, genial, droll, dreamy;

always changing with his moods. His nose was large, clearly defined and well shaped; cheek-bones high and projecting, his mouth firm.

He was easily caricatured—but difficult to represent as he was in marble or on canvas. The best bust of him is that of Volk, which was modeled from life in May, 1860, while he was attending court at Chicago. Among the best portraits, in the judgment of his family and intimate friends, is that of Carpenter, in the picture of the Reading of the Proclamation of Emancipation before the Cabinet.

. . . Mentally, he had a perfect eye for truth. His mental vision was clear and accurate: he saw things as they were. . . . He ever sought the real, the true, and the right. He was exact, carefully accurate in all his statements. He analyzed well; he saw and presented what lawyers call the very *gist* of every question. . . . His reasoning powers were keen and logical, and moved forward to a demonstration with the precision of mathematics . . . he possessed not only a sound judgment, which brought him to correct conclusions, but that he was able to present questions so as to bring others to the same result.

His memory was strong, ready, and tenacious. His reading was limited in extent, but his memory was so ready, and so retentive, that in history, poetry, and general literature, no one ever remarked any deficiency. As an illustration of the power of his memory, I recollect to have once called at the White House, late in his Presidency, and introducing to him a Swede, and a Norwegian; he immediately repeated a poem of eight or ten verses, describing Scandinavian scenery and old Norse legends. In reply to the expression of their delight, he said, that he had read and admired the poem several years before, and it had entirely gone from him, but seeing them recalled it.

The two books which he read most were the Bible and Shakespeare. With these he was very familiar, reading and studying them habitually, and constantly. He had great fondness for poetry, and eloquence, and his taste and judgment in each was exquisite. . . . He read and recited from the Bible and Shakespeare, with great simplicity, but remarkable expression and effect. Often when going to and from the army, on the steamers and in his carriage, he took a copy of Shakespeare with him, and not unfrequently read aloud to his associates. After conversing upon public affairs, he would take up his Shakespeare, and addressing his companions, remark, "What do you say now to a scene from Macbeth, or Hamlet," and then he would read aloud, scene after scene, never seeming to tire of the enjoyment. On the last Sunday of his life, as he was coming up the Potomac, from his visit to City Point and Richmond, he read many extracts from Shakespeare. . . .

As a public speaker, without any attempt at oratorical display, I think he was the most effective of any man of his day. When he spoke, everybody listened.

It was always obvious, before he completed two sentences, that he had something to say, and it was sure to be something original, something different from anything any one had heard from others, or had read. He impressed the hearer at once, as an earnest, sincere man, who believed what he said. Today, there are more of the sayings of Lincoln, repeated by the people, more expressions, sentences, and extracts from his writings and speeches, familiar as "household words," than from those of any other American. Next to the Bible, and Shakespeare, there is no other source so prolific of these familiar phrases and expressions as his writings and speeches. . . .

Another source of his great intellectual power was the thorough, exhaustive investigation he gave to every subject. . . . Mr. Lincoln . . . required time thoroughly to investigate, before he came to his conclusions, and the movements of his mind were not rapid, but when he reached his conclusions he believed in them, and adhered to them with great firmness and tenacity. When called upon to decide quickly upon a new subject, or a new point, he often erred, and was ever ready to change when satisfied he was wrong.[111]

STEP TWO: **Construct a one-level outline**

Like last week's reading, this passage isn't divided into sections. Treat each paragraph as a separate section; each one addresses a different aspect of Abraham Lincoln.

When you're finished, check your work with your instructor.

Day Two: Analyzing the Topos

Focus: Understanding the form of a description of a person

In last week's lessons, you learned that a description of a person includes more than simply physical appearance; descriptions can also include personality, habits, behaviors, place in society, the perceptions of others, and more. Today, you'll begin to see how a description can be written to give either a positive or negative impression.

STEP ONE: **Examine model passages**

Before you go on, answer a quick question about the description of Lincoln from the last lesson. Just off the top of your head, do you think that the author admired Lincoln or despised him?

111. Isaac Newton Arnold, *The History of Abraham Lincoln and the Overthrow of Slavery* (Clarke & Co., 1866), pp. 674–680.

The author, Isaac Newton Arnold, admired Lincoln tremendously.

How do you know this? Arnold makes several direct statements about Lincoln that are highly complimentary; for example, that he was "an earnest, sincere man," that his "taste and judgment" in poetry and eloquence "was exquisite," that he had "sound judgment," and more. But Arnold shows his admiration for Lincoln indirectly, too.

Read again Arnold's lines describing Abraham Lincoln's height and his habit of hunching over:

> Physically, he was a tall, spare man, six feet and four inches in height. He stooped, leaning forward as he walked. He was very athletic, with long sinewy arms, large, bony hands, and of great physical power. His forehead was high, his hair very dark, nearly black, and rather stiff and coarse; his eye-brows were heavy, his eyes dark-grey, very expressive and varied; now sparkling with humor and fun, and then deeply sad and melancholy; flashing with indignation at injustice or wrong, and then kind, genial, droll, dreamy; always changing with his moods. His nose was large, clearly defined and well shaped; cheek-bones high and projecting, his mouth firm.

Now read a description of Lincoln from a book published, after the Civil War, by a southern writer who blamed Lincoln for the devastation caused by the war:

> Abraham Lincoln was six feet four inches high. He was thin in the chest, wiry, sinewy, raw-boned, and narrow across the shoulders. His legs were unnaturally long and out of proportion to his body. His forehead was high and narrow, his jaws long, his nose long, large and blunt at the tip, ruddy and turned awry toward the right. A few hairs here and there sprouted on his face. His chin projected far and sharp and turned up to meet a thick, material, downhanging lip. His cheeks were flabby, the loose skin in folds or wrinkles. His hair was brown, stiff and unkempt. His complexion very dark, his skin yellow, shriveled and leathery. His whole aspect was cadaverous and woe-struck. His ears were large and stood out at almost right angles from his head. He had no dignity of manner, and was extremely ungainly and awkward.[112]

Portraits of Lincoln tell us that both of these descriptions are more or less accurate—but they give very different impressions of Lincoln! Each one is *slanted,* or biased, in a different direction. The first description makes the reader inclined to like Lincoln; the second, to despise him.

Both writers choose their words very carefully. With your pencil, underline the word "athletic" in the first description (third sentence) and "thin in the chest" in the second description (second sentence). Both descriptions tell you that Lincoln was "sinewy," meaning that he didn't

---

112. George Edmonds, *Facts and Falsehoods Concerning the War on the South, 1861–1865* (A. R. Taylor & Co., 1904), pp. 34–35.

have much fat on him, so that his tendons showed. But the first writer is careful to tell you that he was strong and sinewy, while the second implies that he was frail.

Now look at the descriptions of Lincoln's forehead. In the first description, underline "high." In the second, underline "high and narrow." A high forehead can imply intelligence—but a high and narrow forehead means that Lincoln had a pointy head, implying less space for his brain.

The positive description tells us that Lincoln's hair was dark, black, stiff, and coarse. Underline those words. The negative description also adds the unflattering word "unkempt"; underline it now.

Underline "cheek bones high and projecting" in the first description and "cheeks were flabby, the loose skin in folds" in the second description. Both of those things are true. But which is the more flattering detail—and which one makes Lincoln sound hideous?

The flattering description talks about Lincoln's eyes but ignores his complexion. Underline "expressive and varied" in the first description. The unflattering description doesn't contradict this—instead, the writer doesn't mention Lincoln's eyes at all. Instead, the writer describes Lincoln's complexion as "yellow, shriveled and leathery." Underline those words.

Finally, underline the words in both descriptions that tell about Lincoln's physical behavior: "leaning forward as he walked" in the first description and "extremely ungainly and awkward" in the second. The first description is neutral, but along with all the good things in the first description, it adds to the positive impression of Lincoln. The second description uses two unflattering words, "ungainly" and "awkward," to describe this leaning forward.

Glance back at all the underlined words. Can you see how each writer carefully chooses his words to steer the reader towards an opinion of Abraham Lincoln?

STEP TWO: **Identify word choice in descriptions**

In the following descriptions, circle the words that seem "slanted" in one direction or another. In the margin of each description, write P for positive (the writer wants us to *like* the person being described) or N for negative (the writer wants to encourage *dislike*).

The books from which these quotes are taken are listed at the end of the lesson, so that you will not know the identity of the people described until the exercise is finished.

When you are finished, discuss your work with your instructor.

> This man is darkness. All you have to do is look at him. Lank hair flapping sideways on the forehead; cold malicious eyes full of hate; the strained pouting lips . . . a bitter closed tightness of expression and narrowness—above all narrowness.

> Large lustrous dark brown eyes, kindly eyes—honest, earnest eyes—which you saw at once were the windows of a great soul. Eyes that gleamed with a high unfaltering purpose, and a dauntless courage, and could serenely look impending disaster and death in the face.

> [He] was by nature a bold and free thinker . . . all his sympathies were warmly enlisted with the party of resistance.

He was a confirmed infidel, a howling atheist, and a lover of French revolutionary excess.

Her hair is of a rich chestnut tint. Her complexion is that of a delicate brunette, and this accords with the darkness of her eyes, hair, and majestic eyebrows.

Almost skeletal in appearance, dark eyes hooded in a sallow complexion, untrimmed moustache, sitting in a corner buried in a newspaper, occasionally taking a sip of tea, seldom joining in the banter of the group.

STEP THREE: **Add to the pattern of the topos**

Turn to the Description of a Person chart in your Composition Notebook. Add the bolded part below under the "Remember" column.

Description of a Person
Definition: A description of selected physical and non-physical aspects of a person

Procedure	Remember
1. Decide on which aspects will be included. They may include: Physical appearance Sound of voice What others think Portrayals and portraits Character qualities Challenges and difficulties Accomplishments Habits Behaviors Expressions of face and body Mind/intellectual capabilities Talents and abilities Self-disciplines Religious beliefs Clothing, dress Economic status (wealth) Fame, notoriety, prestige Family traditions, tendencies	**1. Descriptions can be "slanted" using appropriate adjectives.**

Footnotes for quotes in Step Two

This man is darkness . . .[113]
Large lustrous dark brown eyes . . .[114]
[He] was by nature a bold and free thinker . . .[115]
He was a confirmed infidel . . .[116]
Her hair is of a rich chestnut tint . . .[117]
Almost skeletal in appearance . . .[118]

Day Three: Practicing the Topos

Focus: Summarizing nonfiction by choosing the main events and listing them chronologically

Today, you'll practice rewriting two descriptions, changing the slant of each one.

STEP ONE: **Read the description**

Begin by reading carefully through the following description of the great scientist Isaac Newton, drawn partly from the writings of his admirer John Conduitt. John Conduitt married Isaac Newton's niece Catherine; Newton lived with the couple towards the end of his life.

Read with pencil in hand, and mark each word or phrase that seems to be slanted. The first one is done for you.

> He always lived in a very <u>handsome generous</u> manner . . . always hospitable, and upon proper occasions gave splendid entertainments. He was generous and charitable without bounds. . . . He had such a meekness and sweetness of temper, that a melancholy story would often draw tears from him. . . . He was blessed with a very happy and vigorous constitution; he was of a middle stature, and rather plump in his latter years; he had . . . a comely and gracious aspect, and a fine head of hair, as white as silver, without any baldness. To the time of his last illness he had the bloom and colour of a young man. . . He retained all his senses and faculties to the end of his

113. William E. Leuchtenburg, *The White House Looks South: Franklin D. Roosevelt, Harry S. Truman, Lyndon B. Johnson* (Louisiana State University Press, 2005), p. 125.
114. Franklin Lafayette Riley, *General Robert E. Lee after Appomattox* (New York: The Macmillan Company, 1922), p. 197.
115. John Torrey Morse, *Thomas Jefferson* (Houghton Mifflin, 1898), p. 15.
116. Contemporary critics of Jefferson, quoted by Francis G. Couvares in *Interpretations of American History: Through Reconstruction* (Simon & Schuster, 2000), p. 6.
117. Agnes Strickland, *Life of Mary, Queen of Scots*, vol. 1 (George Bell and Sons, 1888), p. 34.
118. Ian Kershaw, *Hitler: A Biography* (W. W. Norton, 2008), p. 55.

> life, strong, vigorous and lively. He continued writing and studying many hours every day till the period of his last illness.[119]

STEP TWO: **List the qualities described**

When you studied descriptions of places, you learned that a description of a place can serve a purpose. You can describe a castle in a way that shows the reader how spectacularly beautiful the building is—or you can describe its walls and moats and towers so that the reader will see how strong the castle is. The castle is the same—but the reader comes away with a different impression.

The same is true of descriptions of people.

Imagine that you're babysitting your favorite two-year-old cousin. This cousin is very persistent if she wants something. She's cute and smart, but if she wants a cookie, she'll ask for it over and over again (very sweetly) until you give up and hand her a cookie. If you were describing this aspect of your cousin, you might tell the story of the cookie and then say "She is so determined!" But someone who doesn't like children would tell the story and then say "She is so demanding!"

Being determined and being demanding are actually two sides of the same aspect of your cousin. She's persistent. Depending on the circumstances (and on who's around), persistence can be a good thing—or an annoying thing.

Many aspects of people can be viewed from two different angles. Someone who is hard-working can be diligent—or she can be driven. Someone who is easygoing can be peaceful—or he can be lazy.

To rewrite a description from the opposite point of view, you have to examine each aspect described by the writer and figure out what the flip side of each one is. Look at the chart below. Down the left-hand side are listed the different aspects (described in a positive way) of Isaac Newton. In the center column, you will need to write the positive way to look at that aspect. In the right-hand column, you will try to figure out what the negative side of that aspect is.

Look at the first entry in the chart. The description tells you that Isaac Newton lived in a "handsome generous" way, which is an old way of saying "very generous." Newton's hospitality, willingness to pay for "splendid entertainments," and his charitability are all examples of one aspect: his generosity.

What's the flip side of generosity? If you give away too much, spend too much on entertainment, and feed too many people who want to stay for the night, you'll go broke. If you were looking at Isaac Newton critically, you might say: "He's wasting money and overspending."

Work on finishing the chart now. A few of the other spaces in the columns are filled out to help you. If you have trouble thinking of the flip side of any of these qualities, try looking them up in the thesaurus.

This is a challenging assignment, so ask your instructor for help if necessary.

---

119. George Godfrey Cunningham, *Lives of Eminent and Illustrious Englishmen: From Alfred the Great,* Vol. 4 (A. Fullarton & Co., 1833), p. 402.

ISAAC NEWTON

DESCRIPTION	GOOD THING	BAD THING
handsomely generous, hospitable, gave entertainments, charitable	generosity	overspending wasting money
meek and sweet easily moved to tears		
happy and vigorous constitution strong, vigorous, lively		
comely and gracious aspect	handsome	too interested in looks
thick hair, white as silver	striking, attention-grabbing	theatrical, showy
bloom and colour		red-faced, flushed
retained his senses		
wrote and studied every day		

STEP THREE: **Write the description**

Now use your chart to rewrite the description, making all of Isaac Newton's good qualities sound like bad qualities. For example, instead of

He always lived in a very handsome generous manner . . . always hospitable, and upon proper occasions gave splendid entertainments. He was generous and charitable without bounds,

you might begin by writing,

He always lived in a wasteful, spendthrift fashion, allowing anyone who asked to come and stay, eat his food, and drink his wine. He lavished huge amounts of money on elaborate parties, and gave away money to any gambler or beggar who asked.

Feel free to use your imagination.

You'll probably feel like you're being very unkind to Isaac Newton. Don't worry; you're not actually writing a description of the real Isaac Newton. You're writing a reaction to John Conduitt's exaggerated description of a perfect old man. (You might be interested to know that at least one of Newton's friends described the scientist as rarely smiling, grave, and withdrawn).

Your finished composition should be at least 100 and not more than 250 words.

Check your work with your instructor when you're finished.

Day Four: Copia Exercise

Focus: Transforming nouns and adjectives

In the last few weeks, you've become familiar with using the thesaurus to find synonyms for nouns, adjectives (and adverbs), and verbs. Replacing a word with a synonym is the simplest way to change a sentence. When Erasmus rephrased his sentence "Your letter pleased me greatly," the first thing he did was replace "letter," "pleased," and "greatly" with synonyms, like this:

noun verb adverb
Your letter pleased me greatly.

noun verb adverb
Your epistle exhilarated me intensely.

You will continue to practice this kind of substitution, but now you'll begin to vary sentences by altering their grammatical structure.

STEP ONE: Understand how to transform nouns to adjectives and adjectives to nouns

Look carefully at these descriptive phrases, drawn from this week's descriptions.

adj adj noun
a bold and free thinker ______________________

(prep phrase)
noun prep noun
seldom joining in the banter of the group ______________________

(prep phrase)
adj adj noun prep noun
a bitter closed tightness of expression ______________________

In the first phrase, the adjectives "bold" and "free" both modify the noun "thinker." But both of those adjectives could be turned into nouns:

bold — boldness free — freedom

and made into a prepositional phrase following the noun "thinker." Write

a thinker of boldness and freedom

on the line to the right of the original phrase.

Here's your first rule for transforming sentences: Most descriptive adjectives can be turned into nouns and placed into a prepositional phrase that modifies the original noun.

This works in reverse as well. When a prepositional phrase modifies a noun, you can usually turn the noun of the phrase into a descriptive adjective. In the second phrase, the prepositional phrase "of the group" modifies the noun "banter." Write

the group banter

on the line to the right of the original phrase. In this case, you don't even have to change the form of the word, because "group" can be either an adjective or a noun.

Be sure that you say the sentence variations out loud when you do this; sometimes your variation will sound so awkward that you'll need to make other changes. Look at the third phrase. The prepositional phrase "of expression" modifies the noun "tightness," but if you were to change this to:

adj adj adj noun
a bitter closed expressive tightness

the phrase becomes very confusing! Instead, you could leave "expression" as a noun and change the noun "tightness" to an adjective:

adj adj adj noun
a bitter closed tight expression

You could then change the adjective "bitter" to a noun and put it in a prepositional phrase that modifies "expression." Write

a closed tight expression of bitterness

on the line to the right of the phrase.

STEP TWO: **Begin the Sentence Variety chart**

Write "Sentence Variety" on the top of a blank sheet of paper. Write the following principle and illustration on the first line:

descriptive adjectives ⟷ nouns   an eloquent man
a man of eloquence

You will be adding to this chart in future lessons. Place it in the Reference section of your Composition Notebook.

STEP THREE: **Practice sentence variety**

Complete the following exercise on the lines provided. Avoid awkward phrases! When you are finished, check your work with your instructor.

In the following phrases, identify the descriptive adjectives. Where possible, turn the descriptive adjectives into nouns and rewrite the phrases, using prepositional phrases where necessary.

his reasoning powers were keen and logical ______________________________

an earnest and sincere man ______________________________

In the following phrases, identify the nouns
which can be turned into descriptive adjectives. Rewrite the phrases, turning the nouns into adjectives; you may need to eliminate prepositions and other words.

in reply to the expression of their delight ______________________________

the party of resistance ______________________________

such a meekness and sweetness of temper ______________________________

this man is darkness ______________________________

The following phrase can be altered in two ways. Write them on the lines provided. If necessary, ask your instructor for help.

her hair is of a rich chestnut tint ______________________________

____

STEP FOUR: **Vary one of your own sentences**

From your own written work this week, choose a sentence that contains either descriptive adjectives that can be transformed into nouns, or a prepositional phrase that can be turned into a descriptive adjective. Write the transformed sentence on the lines below.

____

____

____

____

____

Week 18: Using a Metaphor to Organize a Character Description

Day One: Outlining Exercise

Focus: Finding the central topic in each paragraph of a biographical sketch

STEP ONE: **Read**

Read the following biographical sketch of the Flemish painter Jan Brueghel (pronounced BROY-gull), known for his detailed, exact landscapes and still life paintings. A biographical sketch is a combination of character description and chronological narrative; it gives chronological details of the subject's life, but also includes paragraphs that are organized around aspects of the subject's character, personality, appearance, and accomplishments.

"Subject" is also a grammatical term, but in this context, "subject" refers to the person the biographical sketch is about.

— — —

Jan Brueghel, the son of Pieter Brueghel, was born in Brussels in 1568. He belonged to a family of artists; his father and brother, known as Pieter Brueghel the Elder and Pieter Brueghel the Younger, were both painters, and his son Jan Brueghel the Younger would also become a painter. To distinguish him from his relatives, Jan Brueghel is often known as Velvet Brueghel because of his habit of wearing velvet clothing.

His father died when Jan was still too young to learn from him. When his mother died in 1578, the young Brueghel went to live with his grandmother, who taught him the first principles of art. When he was about twenty, Jan travelled to Italy to study and paint. After seven years, he returned to his home country and settled in Antwerp. His last master was Peter Goetkint [HOOT-kintd], by whom he was instructed in oil painting.

He began with painting fruit and flowers after nature, which he executed with incredible neatness; but when he went to Italy, he altered his subjects to landscapes, sea-ports, and markets, with a number of figures, wonderfully exact and correctly drawn, though of a small size. As well as landscapes, his Italian paintings also include scenes from the Bible, mythology, and history. He continued to paint flowers upon his return to Antwerp, and perhaps is best known for his detailed still life paintings of botanical subjects.

His touch is delicate, his figures are correct, and the carriages, which he was fond of introducing into his landscapes, are realistic. His flower paintings are similarly detailed, with careful attention to the exact color and construction of each bloom. Once, when commissioned during the winter to paint a series of spring flowers, Brueghel delayed beginning the work simply so that he could paint the flowers from life.

The great painter Rubens admired him so much that he asked him to insert the landscape scenery in several of his pictures; in return for this, Rubens often painted the figures in the pictures of Brueghel. One of their finest joint performances was the picture of Adam and Eve in Paradise. Brueghel also assisted, in a similar manner, the painters Steenwyck, Mompert, Rothenamer, and Van Balen.

In his painting *Vertumnus and Pomona,* based on a mythical story, the variety of flowers, fruits and trees is so great that the eye is bewildered; and though the proportions of the objects are small, to the observer they seem like nature itself—particularly a fig tree in a large garden pot, which appears wonderfully lifelike in the colouring of the stem, branches, and fruit. The figures themselves, Vertumnus and Pomona, were painted by Rubens. In the gallery of the archiepiscopal palace at Milan is a lovely desert landscape of Brueghel, in which Giovanni Battista Crespi painted the figure of St. Jerome; also in Milan is an oval picture of the Virgin, by Rubens, surrounded with a garland of flowers, by Brueghel. Alone, Brueghel painted the animals entering Noah's Ark, as well as *The Blind Leading the Blind,* in which a line of beggars staggers through a spectacular landscape. A smaller painting, *A Vase of Flowers*, shows a glass vase filled with both wildflowers and garden flowers, with the presence of short-lived moths and insects representing the temporary, transient nature of life.[120]

STEP TWO: **Construct a one-level outline**

Find the main idea in each paragraph of the biographical sketch. You will probably find it most useful to ask "What aspect of Jan Brueghel's life or character does this paragraph focus on?"

Try to word the main idea of each paragraph on your own; if you need help, though, you may ask your instructor. When you're finished, check your work with your instructor.

---

120. Freely adapted from Matthew Pilkington, *A General Dictionary of Painters*, rev. ed. (Thomas Tegg, 1840), pp. 80–81.

Day Two: Analyzing the Topos

Focus: Using a metaphor to organize a description

This week, you'll investigate one more way of organizing a description: using a *governing metaphor.*

When you learned how to write a description of a place, you studied the use of figurative language. Remember: Similes are comparisons that announce themselves by using "like" or "as," or by otherwise spelling out that figurative language is being used. The Iraqi writer Juman Kubba uses a simile when she describes her mother:

. . . *[S]he was like a tent and a shield that we all hid under and took shelter beneath.*[121]

Metaphors speak about one thing in terms of another, without using "like," "as," or other signals. Here is how Victor Hugo describes a group of aristocratic young ladies in *The Hunchback of Notre-Dame*:

. . . *these fair damsels, with their keen and envenomed tongues, twisted, glided, and writhed around* . . .[122]

He never says "They are like snakes!" Instead, he simply describes them in the same terms he would use for a snake.

STEP ONE: **Examine a model passage**

Look at the first paragraph of Charles Dickens's description of Scrooge in *A Christmas Carol*:

> Oh! But he was a tight-fisted hand at the grindstone, Scrooge! a squeezing, wrenching, grasping, scraping, clutching, covetous, old sinner! Hard and sharp as flint, from which no steel had ever struck out generous fire; secret, and self-contained, and solitary as an oyster. The cold within him froze his old features, nipped his pointed nose, shrivelled his cheek, stiffened his gait; made his eyes red, his thin lips blue; and spoke out shrewdly in his grating voice. A frosty rime was on his head, and on his eyebrows, and his wiry chin. He carried his own low temperature always about with him; he iced his office in the dog-days; and didn't thaw it one degree at Christmas. [123]

121. Juman Kubba, *The First Evidence: A Memoir of Life in Iraq under Saddam Hussein* (McFarland & Co., 2003), p. 172.
122. Victor Hugo, *The Hunchback of Notre-Dame* (Carey, Lea and Blanchard, 1834), p. 194.
123. Dickens, p. 3.

Dickens begins with two similes: Scrooge is "as hard and sharp as flint" and "secret, and self-contained, and solitary as an oyster."

But the rest of the description is a metaphor. When Dickens says that Scrooge is "cold within," he's describing Scrooge's character. "Cold" is an adjective which we often use for someone who has no love or compassion ("warmth") for others. When we say someone is "cold," we don't mean *physically* cold. A person with a cold personality still has a body temperature of 98.7 degrees.

So does Scrooge—but when Dickens writes this description, he uses *physical cold* as the governing metaphor. He doesn't say "Scrooge was as cold as an iceberg." Instead, he describes Scrooge's physical appearance and his actions *in terms of* physical cold.

Look carefully at how Dickens describes Scrooge's nose, cheeks, walk, eyes, and lips:

The cold within him froze his old features	*nipped his pointed nose*
	shrivelled his cheek
	stiffened his gait
	made his eyes red
	his thin lips blue

All of these phrases are *metaphorical.* Scrooge's nose, cheeks, eyes, and lips are a perfectly normal temperature, but Dickens speaks of them as though they were physically cold.

Take a few minutes now to investigate Dickens's method. Look up "cold" in your thesaurus. In the following chart, write synonyms for "cold" that mean *physically cold* in the first column. Write synonyms for cold that mean *uncaring, unresponsive* in the second column. (Some synonyms may appear in both columns.)

COLD (physically cold)	COLD (uncaring, unresponsive)
______________________	______________________
______________________	______________________
______________________	______________________
______________________	______________________
______________________	______________________
______________________	______________________

When you are finished, show your chart to your instructor.

Now look back at the description of Scrooge. Dickens wants to describe Scrooge's character as *cold (uncaring, unresponsive),* so he has imagined what *physical cold* would do to Scrooge's appearance. Then, he has described Scrooge's nose, cheeks, eyes, lips, and walk as though *physical cold* made them what they were.

In the same way, he has described Scrooge's white beard, eyebrows, and hair as though *physical cold* changed their color:

A frosty rime was on his head, and on his eyebrows, and his wiry chin.

He also writes of Scrooge's actions as if Scrooge carried actual freezing temperatures around with him.

He iced his office in the dog-days; and didn't thaw it one degree at Christmas.

By using a single metaphor (physical cold) to describe every aspect of Scrooge's appearance, character, and action, Dickens is able to organize his description and make it effective. Imagine if Dickens had written the description of Scrooge like this:

His nose was pointed, his cheeks were shrivelled, and he walked stiffly. His eyes were bloodshot, his lips were blue, and his voice was low and rough. His hair, eyebrows, and beard were white.

You still might be able to picture Scrooge in your mind, but this physical description wouldn't tell you anything about what Scrooge is like.

Of course, Dickens could have just added:

Scrooge was cold and distant

to his description of Scrooge's physical appearance. But good writers always try to do more than one thing at the same time. Instead of writing a physical description, and then writing a separate character description, Dickens makes his writing more effective, more powerful, and more memorable by using a metaphor to do both at the same time.

A metaphor doesn't have to take up a whole paragraph. In *Les Misérables,* the novelist Victor Hugo describes the bandit Gueulemer as if he were a gigantic stone and metal statue—just as huge, hard, and impossible to destroy—in just two lines:

> Gueulemer was a Hercules without a pedestal. . . . He was six feet high and had a marble chest, brazen biceps, cavernous lungs, a colossus's body, and a bird's skull.[124]

124. Victor Hugo, *Les Misérables* (Carleton, 1862), p. 94.

STEP TWO: **Add to the pattern of the topos**

Turn to the Description of a Person chart in your Composition Notebook. Add the bolded point below under the "Remember" column.

Description of a Person

Definition: A description of selected physical and non-physical aspects of a person

Procedure

1. Decide on which aspects will be included. They may include:
   - Physical appearance
   - Sound of voice
   - What others think
   - Portrayals and portraits
   - Character qualities
   - Challenges and difficulties
   - Accomplishments
   - Habits
   - Behaviors
   - Expressions of face and body
   - Mind/intellectual capabilities
   - Talents and abilities
   - Self-disciplines
   - Religious beliefs
   - Clothing, dress
   - Economic status (wealth)
   - Fame, notoriety, prestige
   - Family traditions, tendencies

Remember

1. Descriptions can be "slanted" using appropriate adjectives.
2. **An overall metaphor can be used to organize the description and give clues about character.**

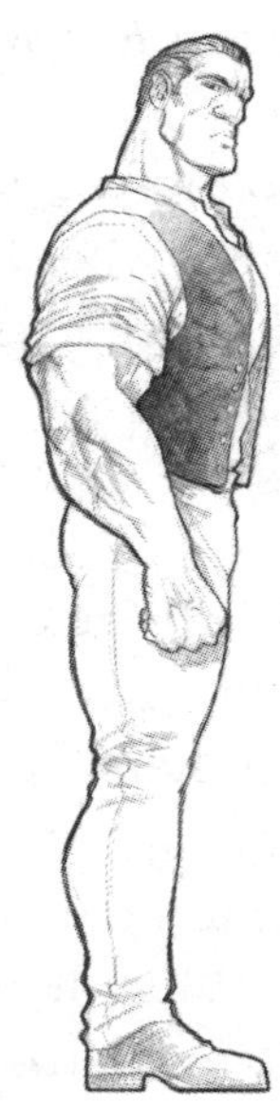

Gueulemer

Day Three: Practicing the Topos

Focus: Using a governing metaphor in a character description

In your last writing session, you saw how the novelist Charles Dickens used the metaphor of physical cold to organize his description of Scrooge's appearance, character, and action. Today, you'll work on using a governing metaphor in a character description.

STEP ONE: **Review the connection between character and description**

Read the following description of the eighteenth-century Frenchman Joseph Fouche, who served the dictator Napoleon Bonaparte as Minister of Police. This description was written by historian Alan Schom in his biography of Napoleon.

> Tall, thin, hollow chested, slightly stoop shouldered, with thin reddish-blond hair, a pale—indeed colorless—unhandsome face, as expressionless and dead as his watery gray eyes, his thin-drawn bloodless lips rarely emitting more than an occasional caustic sentence or order, completed by a cold, aloof, forbidding bearing. . . . When standing at an official reception in his dark, simple dress . . . he rarely moved, apart from his long bony hands. . . . Men and women would be arrested, interrogated, tortured, imprisoned, or executed on his personal orders, and he . . . felt nothing; he was simply doing his job.[125]

In this description, Alan Schom is describing both the character and the appearance of the Minister of Police. The minister is completely ruthless (without pity, without feeling, without mercy) and hard-hearted. He doesn't feel, he doesn't react; he doesn't even *move.*

In the second line of the description, circle *pale, colorless, expressionless.*

In the third line, circle *dead, bloodless.*

In the fourth line, circle *cold.*

Now think for a minute. What is pale, colorless, expressionless, bloodless, and cold?

A dead man.

A man who is as ruthless and merciless as the Minister of Police isn't *actually* dead, but he is dead to the sufferings of others; so Alan Schom uses the metaphor of a dead man to describe Joseph Fouche.

125. Alan Schom, *Napoleon Bonaparte* (HarperCollins, 1997), pp. 264–265.

STEP TWO: **Prepare to write the description**

Today, you'll write a description of the English king Henry VIII, as he was in his later years. The description should follow the same pattern as the descriptions of Scrooge and Joseph Fouche; it should tell the reader about Henry's physical appearance and character, and should also include a sentence or two about an action that Henry habitually performed (like Scrooge's "icing" his office, and Fouche standing motionless at official receptions).

Prepare to write the description by reading the following excerpts about Henry VIII and studying the portrait of him. Mark lightly with a pencil those aspects of Henry that you might want to include in your description. Be sure to glance at the aspects listed on your Description of a Person chart; you should include at least three of them in your description.

Pick and choose from the details in the excerpts; you shouldn't try to include all of them.

> Henry's skeleton, discovered in 1813, was six feet two inches in length. Henry was certainly of strong and muscular build; the Spanish ambassador reported in 1507 that "his limbs are of a gigantic size." . . . Several sources testify to Henry's fair skin, among them, the poet John Skelton, who called him "Adonis, of fresh color." His hair, strands of which still adhered to his skull in 1813, was auburn, and he wore it combed short and straight in the French fashion. . . . In visage, the . . . King resembled his handsome grandfather, Edward IV, with a broad face, small, close-set, penetrating eyes, and a small, sensual mouth; Henry, however, had a high-bridged nose. . . . Kings were expected to be masterful, proud, self-confident, and courageous, and Henry had all these qualities in abundance, along with a massive ego . . .[126]

> . . . Henry soon had "a beard which looks like gold." Queen Katherine, however, so disliked it that she "daily made him great instance, and desired him to put it off for her sake."[127]

> This monarch, from the natural habit of his body, increased by a devotion to the pleasures of the table, had now grown extremely unwieldy and corpulent; his temper, at all times headstrong, had become of late unusually

126. Alison Weir, *Henry VIII: The King and His Court* (Random House, 2002), p. 5.
127. Ibid., p. 214.

fierce; and the utmost care in those who attended him was frequently unsuccessful in preventing the most frightful paroxysms of resentment and fury.[128]

Beneath a robe of crimson velvet furred with ermine, the king wore a coat of raised gold, with a tabard shining with rubies, emeralds, great pearls, and diamonds.[129]

The old wound on his leg had re-opened and an abscess had formed, which would remain open and suppurating for the rest of his life. . . . From now on, he would have to wear a dressing and have the leg bound up. . . . As his frustration at his enforced inactivity grew, along with the pain he suffered, he would become increasingly subject to savage and unreasonable rages. He was nearly forty-five now, growing bald, and running to fat . . . more egotistical, more sanctimonious, and more sure of his own divinity, while still seeing himself as a paragon of courtly and athletic knighthood.[130]

The abscess on his leg was slowing him down, and there were days when he could hardly walk. . . . Worse still, it oozed pus continually, and had to be dressed daily, not a pleasant task for the person assigned to do it as the wound stank dreadfully. . . . [T]he King had become exceedingly fat; a new suit of armour, made for him at this time, measured 54" around the waist. He was . . . quick to burst out in temper, and given to bouts of black depression as the years advanced.[131]

His suspicion was aroused on the slightest pretext, and his temper was getting worse. Ill-health contributed not a little to this frame of mind. The ulcer on his leg caused him such agony that he sometimes went almost black in the face and speechless from pain. He was beginning to look grey and old, and was growing daily more corpulent and unwieldy.[132]

Henry acquired a passionate and lifelong devotion to music . . . when he was king his minstrels formed an indispensable part of his retinue, whether he went on progress through his kingdom, or crossed the seas on errands of peace or war. He became an expert performer on the lute, the organ and the harpsichord, and all the cares of State could not divert him

---

128. Patrick Fraser Tytler, *Life of King Henry the Eighth* (Oliver & Boyd, 1837), p. 450.
129. Ibid., p. 23.
130. Alison Weir, *The Six Wives of Henry VIII* (Grove Press, 1991), p. 302.
131. Ibid., p. 416.
132. Albert Frederick Pollard, *Henry VIII* (Longmans, 1919), p. 402.

> from practising on those instruments both day and night. He sent all over England in search of singing men and boys for the chapel royal. . . . Not only did he take delight in the practice of music by himself and others; he also studied its theory and wrote with the skill of an expert. Vocal and instrumental pieces of his own composition, preserved among the manuscripts at the British Museum, rank among the best productions of the time; and one of his anthems, "O Lorde, the Maker of all thyng," is of the highest order of merit, and still remains a favourite in English cathedrals.[133]

STEP THREE: **Plan the governing metaphor**

You'll write your description of Henry VIII using the governing metaphor of a *wounded lion*. Nowhere in your description will you use the word "lion" (just as Victor Hugo never came out and said "These damsels are snakes"). Instead, as you write about Henry VIII, you'll use some of the same verbs, nouns, and adjectives that you would use to write about a lion.

Take some time now to brainstorm these words. On a piece of scratch paper, jot down the following:

VERBS	NOUNS	ADJECTIVES
prowl	mane	dangerous

Under these headings, write down as many lion-related words as you can think of. You've been given a starter word in each category. For verbs, think about what lions do; for nouns, think not only about the parts of a lion, but about other names for lions ("predator," for example). For adjectives, think of any words that would describe a lion.

Reading the entry about "lion" in an encyclopedia or online source will give you plenty of ideas. You may also find it helpful to look up the word "lion" in your thesaurus. In what word groups does the word "lion" appear? Turn to those word groups and read through them for ideas.

Once you've thought of a few words in each category, use your thesaurus to look up additional words. If you look up "dangerous," for example, you might find two subgroups listed, "perilous" and "unreliable." "Perilous" is a much better word for a lion than "unreliable," so you would turn to that subgroup. Along with "perilous," you would find "menacing" and "threatening," both of which you could use in your description.

Try to find eight to ten words to list in each category. If you have difficulty, ask your instructor for help.

STEP FOUR: **Use the governing metaphor to write the description**

Now write your description, following these directions:

133. Pollard, pp. 24–25.

1. It should be at least 50 words long and no more than 150.
2. Aim to use at least four or five of the words from your list.
3. Cover at least three of the aspects in your Description of a Person chart.
4. Use at least one adverb.

You can use your imagination in describing Henry and his actions. Remember that not every single part of the description needs to fit into the metaphor. Schom tells us that Fouche has reddish-blond hair, which doesn't fit his "dead man" metaphor; Dickens says that Scrooge is hard, tight-fisted, and secretive, none of which have anything to do with cold. The metaphor should guide you in writing *much,* but not all, of your description; you can write about Henry VIII as if he were a lion and still add that he liked music, without trying to make it sound as if lions like music.

Here is a starting line for you, in case you're stuck: "In his later years, King Henry VIII was still majestic and commanding, with an auburn mane and kingly manner."

If you need help, ask your instructor. When you're finished, show your description to your instructor.

Day Four: Copia Exercise

Focus: Transforming active and passive verbs

STEP ONE: **Review**

In the following sentence, identify the descriptive adjectives. Turn the descriptive adjectives into nouns and rewrite the phrases. Hint: you will need to change the verb "be" to "have."

Kings were expected to be masterful, proud, self-confident, and courageous.

____

In the following phrase, identify the nouns which can be turned into descriptive adjectives. Rewrite the phrase, turning the nouns into adjectives and eliminating the prepositional phrase.

errands of peace or war _______________________

Check your work with your instructor.

STEP TWO: **Understand how to transform passive verbs into active verbs**

Look carefully at these sentences, drawn from this week's descriptions.

> The figures themselves were painted by Rubens.
> His suspicion was aroused on the slightest pretext.

Underline the subject of each sentence once and the complete verb (main verb plus helping verbs) twice.

You should have underlined:

figures were painted
suspicion was aroused

Both of these verbs are in the passive voice, which means that the subject *receives* the action of the verb. The figures didn't paint anyone; someone else painted the figures. Write "p" over the verb "were painted" in the first sentence. The suspicion doesn't arouse anything; other things arouse the subject. Write "p" over the verb "was aroused" in the second sentence.

In a sentence with a verb in the active voice, the subject *does* the action of the verb. Most sentences can be rewritten so that the voice changes from passive to active. Read the next two sentences out loud:

subject passive verb prepositional phrase
The figures were painted by Rubens.

subject active verb direct object
Rubens painted the figures.

The first sentence is the original, with the verb in the passive voice. A verb in the passive voice often needs a prepositional phrase following it. Since the subject isn't doing the action, the prepositional phrase can tell you more about who is actually *causing* the action of the verb.

When you rewrite a passive verb to make it active, the object of the prepositional phrase can become the subject. The subject, which is receiving the action of the verb anyway, then becomes the direct object.

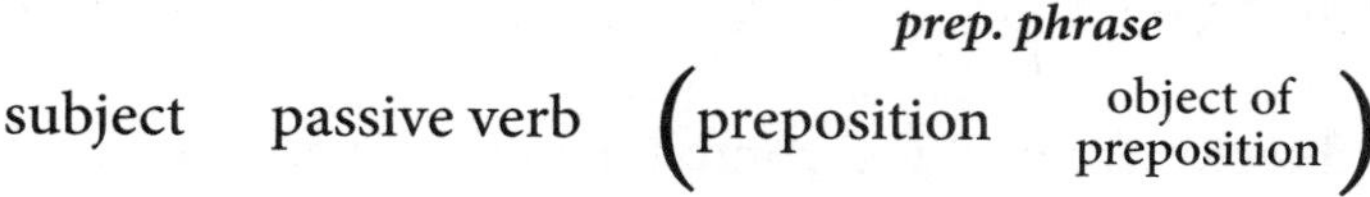

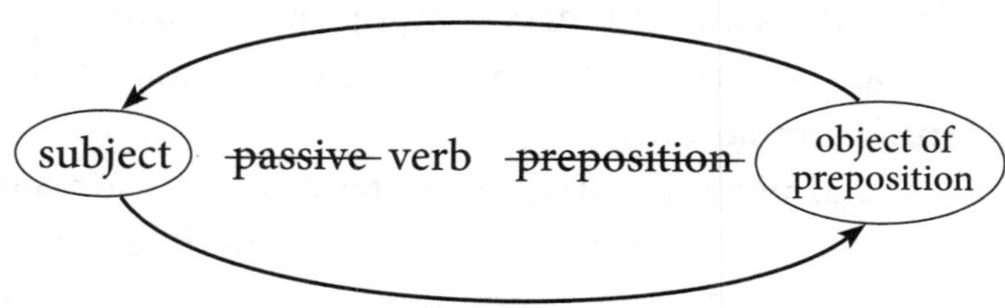

subject (*old o.p.*) active verb direct object (*old subject*)

Now read the next three sentences out loud.

subject passive verb prepositional phrase
His suspicion was aroused on the slightest pretext.

subject active verb direct object
The slightest pretext aroused his suspicion.

subject active verb direct object prepositional phrase
The courtiers aroused his suspicion with the slightest action.

In the second and third sentences, the passive voice has been changed to active voice. But in the second sentence, it isn't completely clear *who* is arousing suspicion. "Pretexts" can't really arouse anything—a pretext is an excuse, a reason for doing something that isn't the *true* reason. So if you rewrite this sentence, you have to invent a new subject for it.

Writers often use the passive voice when they want to avoid giving the responsibility for causing the verb to any one subject. Sometimes this is a good idea; the third sentence puts all the blame on the courtiers, but the truth about Henry VIII was that *everyone* and *everything* made him suspicious. In this sentence, the passive voice allows the writer to be more accurate.

STEP THREE: **Add to the Sentence Variety chart**

Add the following principle and illustration to the Sentence Variety chart you started in Week 17:

passive verb ←——→ active verb The kingdom was ruled by its king.
The king ruled his kingdom.

STEP FOUR: **Practice sentence variety**

In the following sentences, underline the subject once and the complete passive verb (main verb plus any helping verbs) twice. Circle any prepositional phrases that tell you more about who or what caused the action of the verb.

On your own paper, rewrite each sentence, making the passive verbs active, making the subjects into direct objects, and providing a subject—either from the prepositional phrases in the sentences, or from your imagination.

When you're finished, read both the original sentences and your sentences out loud. Sometimes, the revised sentence will sound better—and sometimes the original will be much clearer than the rewritten sentence! Place a checkmark by any of your sentences that sound like improvements on the original.

Show your completed work to your instructor.

She was almost petrified with fear.

Hodgkin's research was interrupted by the Second World War.

He had even found an old, rotten English sailboat in a shed, and was fascinated by it.

The youngest of them was called Dullhead, and was sneered and jeered at and snubbed on every possible opportunity.

The ill-fated *Star* was caught and ground to pieces as if she were no stronger than a child's cardboard toy.

If the food in the cells is pollen paste, it was placed there by a bee.

Week 19: Biographical Sketch

Day One: Outlining Exercise

Focus: Finding the central topic in each paragraph of a biographical sketch

STEP ONE: **Read**

Read the following biographical sketch of the nineteenth-century writer Edgar Allan Poe. Remember: a biographical sketch is a combination of character description and chronological narrative.

Few men of genius have ever lived a sadder or more unfortunate life than Edgar Allan Poe. That he was a man of brilliant genius is now apparent to everyone, but during his lifetime he often had a hard struggle to get his tales and poems printed at all, and there were times when he lived in actual want.

The poet's own temperament and bringing-up were, perhaps, responsible for some of his troubles. He was the son of David Poe, a Marylander of Irish extraction, and Elizabeth Arnold, a young English actress. It was on one of his parents' acting tours that Poe was born in Boston, February 19, 1809. When the boy was still very young both parents died and left their three children alone and penniless in Richmond, Virginia. Edgar was a brilliant and beautiful child and he so attracted a wealthy Scotch merchant named Allan, that the latter finally adopted the boy and gave him his own name.

He was taken to England by his new parents and placed at school under the Rev. Dr. Bransby, whom Poe has described in his tale of "William Wilson."

He was a remarkably bright and clever boy and, his master says, "would have been a very good boy had he not been spoilt by his parents." These school days seem to have been among the pleasantest of the poet's life, but he was recalled to America after a few years and placed in an academy at Richmond. Here he not only distinguished himself by his aptitude for languages, especially for French, but also for his athletic feats. He excelled at leaping, rowing, swimming and in all other sports that boys love. . . .

In 1826, Poe entered the University of Virginia. But, though he was a successful and even a distinguished student, his career here was brief. He contracted debts of which Mr. Allan did not approve and which he refused to pay. A stormy scene took place, and the upshot was that Poe left home to make his way alone. Little is known of his career for the next year or so. Apparently he tried his hand at literature, chiefly poetry, but with ill-success. In 1829, Mrs. Allan, for whom he had much affection, died, and, finding home still less pleasant, Poe again published a little volume of poems. As they attracted no attention, however, he induced Mr. Allan to send him to [college at] West Point. He remained here from July until the following March, when he was expelled for disobedience.

From this time on he turned to literature as his profession. Mr. Allan was now married again and Poe had only himself to depend upon. For some time life was a struggle, but in 1833 he received a hundred dollar prize offered by a magazine for the best story and in this way he won some literary friends and eventually was made editor of the *Southern Literary Messenger*. . . . From this time on Poe's life was a continual struggle with adverse circumstances, although his best work was done in these years. In 1837 he went to New York, where he wrote for various papers, but the next year we find him in Philadelphia, writing and editing *Graham's Magazine*. He was a very brilliant and successful editor, but the fruits of his labors went to others, and the weird tales which he wrote for this paper brought him little except fame. Still, this period was the happiest of his life, for his reputation as a story writer was spreading even to Europe and he had a pleasant little home in the city.

It was shortly after this that his wife [Virginia Clemm, whom he had married in 1835 when she was only 14 and Poe was 27] met with an accident which rendered her an invalid for the rest of her life. The anxiety caused by this misfortune, together with fresh business troubles, so preyed upon Poe's delicate nervous organization that he began to resort to the stimulants that eventually clouded his intellect and wrecked his life. He became straitened for money and could no longer give his wife the comforts she needed, a fact which increased his despair.

At this juncture an opportunity opened for Poe in New York, and in 1845 he moved to Fordham, a suburb of the city. Here he wrote "The Raven" for the *Evening Mirror*, and it at once brought him more fame than all his other writings put together. Little money came with it, however. The paper of which Poe had acquired control failed for want of funds, and for a time the family had not enough for the necessities of life.

> Friends, however, came to their aid, but a still heavier blow was to fall on the unhappy poet. In 1846 his wife died and thereafter Poe was never fully himself again. . . . His life was a wreck and he died miserably in Baltimore three years later.[134]

STEP TWO: **Construct a one-level outline**

Even though this biographical sketch moves forward chronologically, it is still a descriptive piece. If you ask the chronological narration question, "What is the main thing or person that this paragraph is about?" the answer is always going to be "Poe." Instead, ask the description question, "What aspect of Poe's life does this paragraph describe?"

When you're finished, check your assignment with your instructor.

Day Two: Analyzing the Topos

Focus: Understanding the form of a biographical sketch

Both this week and last week, you outlined a biographical sketch. Remember: a biographical sketch combines elements of both character description and chronological narrative. It gives chronological details of the subject's life, but also includes paragraphs that are organized around aspects of the subject's character, personality, appearance, and accomplishments.

You'll need two colored pencils for this lesson. (The instructions say "green" and "red," but any two colors will work.)

STEP ONE: **Examine model passages**

Read the following brief biographical sketch of the poet John Milton. ("Pamphleteering" means that Milton helped support the cause of Oliver Cromwell, who helped drive Charles I off the throne of England, by writing short essays which were printed on flyers and distributed to the public.)

> John Milton, the famous English poet, was born at London in 1608. The early part of his life was spent in study and travel; he commenced to write about 1640, and took an active part by pamphleteering in the civil war. An ardent Cromwellian, he was arrested on the return of Charles II, but was released in two months. He now spent his time up to his death, in 1674, in writing.

---

134. *Standard Classics, With Biographical Sketches and Helpful Notes* (Educational Publishing Company, 1910), pp. 274–276.

> His principal poems are "Paradise Lost," a fairy play called "Comus," and "Allegro and Penseroso." The best critics of every country regard "Paradise Lost" as one of the most sublime productions of human genius, though it only brought the author one hundred and fifty dollars.[135]

This biographical sketch only has two parts! In the first paragraph, the writer lists chronologically some of the important events in John Milton's life. In the second paragraph, he describes John Milton's most famous writings.

In the left-hand margin beside the first paragraph, write "Chronological life events" with your green pencil. In the margin beside the second paragraph, write "Greatest accomplishments" with your red pencil.

This is a very simple form of a biographical sketch: a summary of life events, followed by a survey of the subject's accomplishments. You can see how the sketch combines elements from two forms you've already studied. The list of life events is a condensed chronological narrative; the paragraph about greatest accomplishments describes an aspect of John Milton's character and personality. The green pencil represents the techniques taken from your Chronological Narrative of Past Events chart; the red pencil represents aspects taken from the Description of a Person chart.

Here is another version of a simple biographical sketch, written about a very different subject.

> Sargon of Akkad (reigned c. 2340–2284 BC) [was k]ing and founder of the Akkadian Dynasty. Sargon became the subject of a whole variety of cuneiform texts where he is generally portrayed as an exemplary ruler. He was described as destined by the gods (especially Ishtar) to conquer the "four corners of the universe" and presiding over peace and prosperity. Some of these accounts also credit him with a mysterious birth (by a priestess) and a miraculous Moses-like rescue from abandonment in a basket in the river. He was said to have journeyed very far and to have settled disputes in Anatolia. Much of this is fictional. . .
>
> It appears that Sargon began his career as a courtier of King Ur-Zababa in Kish. His rise to power was triggered by his victory over Lugalzagesi of Uruk. He then gained control over all the other Sumerian cities but based himself at Akkad, presumably a new [city]. He always called himself "king of Akkad." During his long reign, he claims to have led various campaigns abroad: He subdued Elam to the east and moved westward, conquering Mari and other cities in Upper Mesopotamia and southern Anatolia.[136]

Like the sketch of John Milton, this combines elements of description and chronological narrative. The first paragraph tells you what others said about Sargon, and about his fame and

135. Reuben Parsons, *A Biographical Dictionary: For the Use of Colleges, Schools and Families* (Sadlier & Co., 1872), p. 180.
136. Gwendolyn Leick, *Historical Dictionary of Mesopotamia* (Scarecrow Press, 2003), p. 102.

notoriety. With your red pencil (Description of a Person), write "What others think/Fame, notoriety" in the margin beside the first paragraph.

The second paragraph lists Sargon's conquests (which is about all we known about him) in chronological order. With your green pencil (Chronological Narrative of Past Events), write "Chronological conquests" in the margin beside the second paragraph.

Look at a slightly more complicated biographical sketch, this one of the Canadian medical pioneer Maude Elizabeth Abbott (1869–1940).

> Maude Elizabeth Abbott spent her life both making and preserving medical history. After her mother died, her father, Jeremiah Babin, immigrated to the United States and left his two small daughters to be raised by their maternal grandmother, who had their name legally changed to Abbott. Maude had an intense yearning for education throughout her life.
>
> After high school, she entered the McGill Faculty of Arts [in Montreal, Quebec]—or rather, the Donelda Department for Women, since the sexes were segregated; she graduated valedictorian and received the Lord Stanley Gold Medal. She and others petitioned for admission to the McGill Medical School, but were denied. Instead Abbott attended the University of Bishop's College Medical School where she received her M.D. with honors in 1894.
>
> During most of her years in high education, Abbott and other women were taught separately from men and suffered from the intense prejudice of both male students and faculty. . . . Especially in the field of medicine, women practitioners were stigmatized as unfeminine, immodest, and physically and emotionally incapable.
>
> Abbot went to Edinburgh for postgraduate training (1894–1897) and returned to Montreal to begin private medical practice. She received a part-time appointment in the Royal Victoria Hospital and was soon engaged in research on heart murmurs that resulted in a significant paper. When this paper was read (by a male colleague) at the Medico-Chirurgical Society, Abbott was proposed and accepted as the society's first woman member.
>
> Working under a governor's fellowship for research, Abbott became a world authority on congenital heart disease; William Osler, one of Canada's most distinguished physicians, asked her to contribute the chapter on congenital heart diseases for the medical textbook he was preparing. . . . Due to her status as an authority in pathology and heart disease, Abbott was sought after by medical institutions around the world. Most she turned down, since she was held in Canada by . . . the care of her invalid sister Alice. . . .
>
> However in 1923 she was persuaded to accept a two-year "loan" to the Woman's Medical College of Pennsylvania as professor of pathology and bacteriology. She returned to McGill and the post of assistant professor, where she remained until her forced retirement at age 65.

> During her career, Abbott published more than one hundred papers and books, edited the *Canadian Medical Association Journal,* and was internationally acclaimed for her work in both heart disease and the history of medicine.[137]

This biographical sketch, like the others, contains chronological events in the subject's life, but it also uses more elements from the Description of a Person format than the previous two.

With your green pencil, write "Chronological events" next to the second paragraph, the fourth paragraph, and the sixth paragraph. Together these three paragraphs tell, in chronological order, the most important events in Abbott's life as a physician.

With your red pencil, write "Introduction" next to the first sentence in the first paragraph. Like many descriptions, this paragraph begins with an introductory statement that sums up the subject.

This paragraph also covers two other aspects of description—Abbott's family and her mind/intellectual capabilities (her intense yearning for education). With your red pencil, write "Family" and "Mind" next to the first paragraph.

The third paragraph talks about the difficulties Abbott faced in her education—another aspect of description. With your red pencil, write "Challenges and Difficulties" next to the third paragraph.

In the fifth paragraph, you learn about Abbott's talents and abilities; write "Talents and abilities" in red next to the fifth paragraph. And in the final paragraph, the sketch sums up Abbott's accomplishments. Write "Accomplishments" in red next to the final paragraph.

Notice that whatever else is included (or left out), a biographical sketch *always* includes a chronological summary of important life events.

STEP TWO: **Write down the pattern of the topos**

Copy the following onto a blank sheet of paper in the Reference section of your Composition Notebook.

Biographical Sketch

Definition: A chronological summary of the important events in a person's life combined with description of aspects of the person

Procedure	Remember
1. Decide on the life events to list in the chronological summary.	
2. Choose aspects from the Description of a Person chart to include.	

137. Marilyn Bailey Ogilvie and Joy Dorothy Harvey, *The Biographical Dictionary of Women in Science: Pioneering Lives from Ancient Times to the Mid-20th Century, Vol. 1, A-K* (Routledge, 2000), p. 2.

Day Three: Practicing the Topos

Focus: Learning how to write a biographical sketch

Today, you'll write your own brief biographical sketch. This can be as short as 125 words (about the length of the Milton biography) or as long as 400 words (the Abbott biography). It should contain a chronological list of important life events as well as at least one paragraph describing an aspect found on the Description of a Person chart.

STEP ONE: **Choose important life events**

Read down this list of important events in the life of the frontiersman Daniel Boone. With your pencil, lightly mark the events that you might want to include in your chronological narrative of life events. You should include at least four but not more than eight events.

Remember, as in your other chronological narrative assignments, that you can pick and choose as long as your final narrative makes sense. However, you should include Boone's birth and death.

You may find it helpful, as you're selecting events, to focus on one of four themes:

Boone as a soldier
Boone as a hunter/explorer
Boone as a family man
Boone and the Native American tribes

1734	Born in Berks County, Pennsylvania; at this time Pennsylvania was still a British colony
1746	Given his first rifle
1755–1756	Fought on the side of the British during the French and Indian War (1754–1763) (French and Indian War was fought between Great Britain and France, in North America, over possession of North American territory; the Native Americans were allied with the French)
1756	Married his neighbor Rebecca Bryan and settled in North Carolina, on the Yadkin river
1759	Fought against the Cherokee during the "Cherokee Uprising" (Cherokee Uprising was a struggle between the British colonists in North America and the Cherokee tribes)
	Forced to leave North Carolina by the Cherokee; moved with his family to Virginia
1762	Moved back to North Carolina; started to explore farther westward because of the number of people settling nearby.

1767 First went out of colonial territory into what is now Kentucky, during a hunting trip

1769 Set out on a two-year expedition into Kentucky; captured by the Shawnees, who then set him free and told him to leave Kentucky

1773 Daniel Boone took his family and 50 settlers to establish a colony in Kentucky; his son James and another young man were killed by the Shawnee and their allies, and the colony was abandoned.

1774 Fought with other colonists against the Shawnee and forced them to give up their claim to Kentucky. A new settlement in Kentucky was now planned.

1775 To prepare for a new settlement, Daniel Boone set out to blaze a new trail into Kentucky; with 30 others, he began to mark out the Wilderness Road, through the Cumberland Gap in the Appalachian Mountains, into what is now Kentucky He founded Boonesborough, Kentucky, on the Kentucky River. In September, he brought his family to Boonesborough.

1775–1782 Fought in the American Revolutionary War

1776 Boone's daughter Jemima and two other girls were captured by a Native American war party; Boone and others followed and captured the girls back.

1777 The British allied themselves with the Shawnee; in an attack on Boonesborough in April, Boone was shot in the leg.

1778 On an expedition to get salt for Boonesborough in February, Boone was captured by Shawnee warriors who were allies of the British. They took him back to their town of Chillicothe and adopted him to replace a warrior who had been killed. He escaped on June 16 and returned to Boonesborough.

1780 Boone became a lieutenant colonel in the local militia.

1781 Boone was elected to the General Assembly.

1782 Boone was elected sheriff.

1782 Fought the Battle of Blue Licks, one of the last of the American Revolution; his son Israel was killed during the battle.

1784 The stories of his adventures were published.

1799 Moved out of the current United States into the frontier country; settled in what is now Missouri

1820 Died in Missouri at the age of 85

STEP TWO: **Choose aspects to include**

The quotes below are taken from several different biographies of Daniel Boone. They give you more information about three different aspects that might appear in a description of Boone. You will need to include at least one of these aspects in your biographical sketch, using your own words. (You may include more than one, as long as your composition is 400 words or shorter.)

Read through these and make a tentative decision about which aspect you'll include in your composition.

You can choose where to place the descriptive paragraph or paragraphs in the composition, but there should be some connection between the events and the description. If you decide to describe habits and behavior, the paragraph should come just after an event in which Boone has been hunting, trapping, or exploring.

If you describe Boone's education, the paragraph should come early in the sketch, before the events in Boone's adult life.

A description of Boone's appearance doesn't really connect to any particular event; it shouldn't interrupt the narrative, though, so you should place it at the beginning or end.

HABITS AND BEHAVIORS

> Hunting and trapping were the constant thought of his life.[138]

> Hunting seemed to be the only business of his life; and he was never so happy as when at night he came home laden with game. He was an untiring wanderer.[139]

> "Too much crowded—too much crowded—I want more elbow-room."—Boone on his way to Missouri.[140]

> The rapid growth of the country soon made game scarce in Boone's neighborhood. Not only did the ever-widening area of cleared fields destroy the cover, but there were, of course, more hunters than before. Thus . . . [Boone] was compelled to take extended trips in his search for less-frequented places. It was not long before he had explored all the mountains and valleys within easy reach, and become familiar with the views from every peak in the region, many of them five and six thousand feet in height. As early as 1764–65 Boone was in the habit of taking with him, upon these trips near home, his little son James, then seven or eight years of age. . . . Frequently they would spend several days together in the woods during the autumn and early winter.[141]

APPEARANCE

> The stature and general appearance of this wanderer of the western forests, approached the gigantic. His chest was broad and prominent; his muscular powers displayed themselves in every limb; his countenance gave indication of his great courage, enterprise, and perseverance; and when he

138. Francis Lister Hawks, *The Adventures of Daniel Boone, The Kentucky Rifleman* (D. Appleton, 1850), p. 130.
139. Hawks, p. 18.
140. Hawks, p. 5.
141. Reuben Gold Thwaites, *Daniel Boone* (D. Appleton, 1902), p. 62.

spoke, the very motion of his lips brought the impression, that whatever he uttered could not be otherwise than strictly true.[142]

A description of Boone given . . . by one who knew him . . . provides yet another impression of him in late middle age. "His large head, full chest, square shoulders, and stout form are still impressed upon my mind. He was (I think) about five feet ten inches in height, and his weight say 175. He was solid in mind as well as in body, never frivolous . . . but was always quiet, meditative, and impressive, unpretentious, kind, and friendly in his manner." This is an appealing portrait of Boone. . . . It diverges in some points from the testimony of his son Nathan, who put his father's height at five eight, adding that "his hair was moderately black, eyes blue, and he had fair skin."[143]

1820 portrait of Daniel Boone by Chester Harding, the only one painted from life.

Forget the coonskin cap; he never wore one. Daniel Boone thought coonskin caps uncouth, heavy, and uncomfortable. He always wore a beaver felt hat to protect him from sun and rain. The coonskin-topped Boone is the image from Hollywood and television.[144]

A long hunting-shirt, of coarse cloth or of dressed deerskins, sometimes with an ornamental collar, was his principal garment; drawers and leggings of like material were worn; the feet were encased in moccasins of deerskin—soft and pliant, but cold in winter, even when stuffed with deer's hair or dry leaves, and so spongy as to be no protection against wet feet, which made every hunter an early victim to rheumatism. Hanging from the belt, which girt the hunting-shirt, were the powder-horn, bulletpouch . . . and tomahawk; while the breast of the shirt served as a generous pocket for food when the hunter . . . was upon the trail. For head-covering, the favorite was a soft cap of coonskin, with the bushy tail dangling behind; but Boone himself despised this gear, and always wore a hat.[145]

---

142. Hawks, p. 133.
143. Robert Morgan, *Boone: A Biography* (Algonquin, 2007), p. 380.
144. Morgan, p. xiii.
145. Thwaites, pp. 28–29.

EDUCATION

Thus freed from school, he now returned more ardently than ever to his favorite pursuit. His dog and rifle were his constant companions, and day after day he started from home, only to roam through the forests.[146]

He left school a perfectly ignorant lad. Some say that he afterward learned to write, and produce as an evidence, a little narrative of his wanderings in Kentucky, supposed to be written by himself. I believe, however, that to the day of his death, he could not write his name. The narrative spoken of, was, I think, dictated in some degree by him, and written by another.[147]

On the banks of the Schuylkill [River], Daniel Boone found all his education, such as it was.[148]

The education of Daniel Boone is a much disputed matter. He insisted to his children that he never had a day of formal education. His older brother Samuel's wife, Sarah Day, is said to have taught him the basics of the three Rs, but a glance at any of his letters reveals that he never completely mastered spelling and grammar. . . . In many ways, nature became his sole teacher, experience and observation his guides.[149]

146. Hawks, p. 18.
147. Hawks, p. 141.
148. Hawks, p. 21.
149. Michael A. Lofaro, *Daniel Boone: An American Life* (University Press of Kentucky, 2003) p. 5.

STEP THREE: **Write the sketch**

Now write your sketch, using the information from the last two steps and following these directions:

1. The sketch should begin with an introductory sentence that gives an overview of who Daniel Boone was and why he was important. Here are three introductory sentences from biographical sketches you've studied; you can model your introduction after these if necessary.
   Maude Elizabeth Abbott spent her life both making and preserving medical history.
   Sargon of Akkad (reigned c. 2340–2284) was king and founder of the Akkadian Dynasty.
   Few men of genius have ever lived a sadder or more unfortunate life than Edgar Allan Poe.
2. The chronological narrative should include at least four but not more than eight events from the chronological list.
3. You must also describe at least one aspect of Daniel Boone.
4. The paragraph(s) of description should be placed near a related event.
5. The sketch should be at least 125 but not more than 400 words in length.
6. Do not use the exact words of the source material—use your thesaurus! Remember that you can also rephrase by transforming descriptive adjectives to nouns (and vice versa), and by turning passive verbs into active verbs.

When you are finished, check your work with your instructor.

Day Four: Copia Exercise

Focus: Transforming active and passive verbs

STEP ONE: **Review**

In the following sentence, turn the appropriate descriptive adjectives into nouns and rewrite the sentence.

He was a brilliant and successful editor.

____

____

In the following sentence, turn the appropriate noun into a descriptive adjective and rewrite the sentence.

Poe published a little volume of poems.

____

____

In the following sentences, transform the passive verbs into active verbs. Remember: you will need to provide a subject (you may find one in a prepositional phrase following the verb), and the current subject will become an object.

He was taken to England by his new parents.

____

He was made the editor of the *Southern Literary Messenger.*

____

Check your work with your instructor.

STEP TWO: **Understand how to transform active verbs into passive verbs**

Last week, you practiced turning passive verbs into active verbs. You can also transform sentences by turning active verbs into passive verbs.

Look carefully at these sentences:

Sargon subdued Elam to the east.

Some of these accounts also credit him with a mysterious birth.

Underline the subject of each sentence once and the complete verb (main verb plus helping verbs) twice. Write DO over each direct object.

____

You should have marked the following words:

DO
<u>Sargon</u> <u>subdued</u> Elam

DO
some credit him

If you underlined "accounts" as the subject of the second sentence, remember that the subject of a sentence cannot be in a prepositional phrase. "Accounts" is the object of the preposition "of."

In both of these sentences, the verbs are in the active voice, which means that the subject *does* the action of the verb. The action of the verb is then received by the direct object.

Sentences with active verbs and direct objects can usually be rewritten so that the verb becomes passive and the direct object becomes the subject. Read the next two sentences out loud:

subject active verb DO
Sargon subdued Elam to the east.

subject passive verb prepositional phrase
Elam, to the east, was subdued by Sargon.

The first sentence is the original, with the verb in the active voice. In the second sentence, I have done the reverse of what you learned to do last week.

The direct object "Elam," which was receiving the action of the active verb "subdued," becomes the subject. It is still receiving the action of the verb, because the helping verb "was" makes the verb into a passive verb. The subject moves to the end of the sentence and becomes the object of the preposition (which I added) in a prepositional phrase that shows who causes the action to happen.

subject active verb direct object

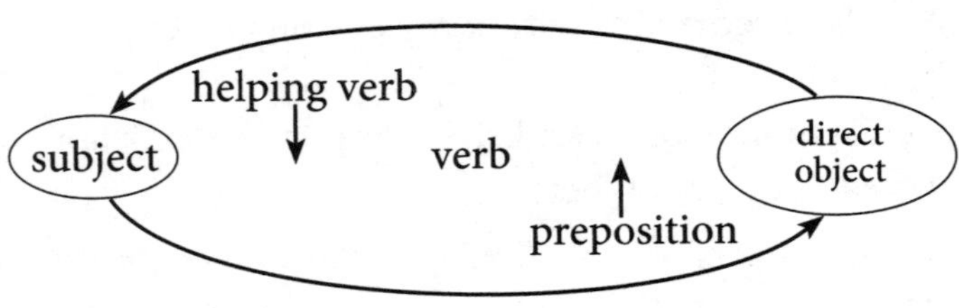

prep. phrase

subject *(old d.o.)* passive verb (preposition object of preposition)

Why would you decide to do this? The original sentence comes from a paragraph about Sargon. But if you were writing a paragraph about Elam, it would seem more natural for Elam to be the subject of the sentence. Read the next two sets of sentences out loud and listen for the difference.

> Elam was constantly under attack. Its soldiers fought off many assaults, but then Elam was subdued by Sargon.

> Elam was constantly under attack. Its soldiers fought off many assaults, but then Sargon subdued Elam.

The passive verb in the first set of sentences keeps the focus on Elam instead of switching it to Sargon.

Now read the next two sentences out loud.

subject / active verb / DO

Some of these accounts also credit him with a mysterious birth.

subject / passive verb / prepositional phrases

He is credited with a mysterious birth by some of these accounts.

You would make this change if you wanted to keep the focus on Sargon rather than shifting it over to the accounts that talk about him. (Notice that the object pronoun "him" has to become the subject pronoun "he" when it moves from being the object of the preposition to the subject of the sentence.)

Passive verbs can be the sign of a sloppy writer. If you're working on a science essay, it's much easier to write "Oxygen was first recognized as an element over 200 years ago" than to go to the trouble to find out *who* discovered it (and when) so that you can write "Carl Scheele first identified oxygen in 1771." But using a passive verb often helps you keep an essay focused. So whenever you use a passive verb, you should be sure that you know exactly why you've decided to go with the passive instead of the active voice.

STEP THREE: **Practice sentence variety**

In the following sentences, underline the subject once and the complete active verb (main verb plus any helping verbs) twice. Write DO above each direct object.

On your own paper, rewrite each sentence, making the active verbs passive, transforming direct objects into subjects, and moving the subjects into prepositional phrases. Make any other necessary changes (such as using an object pronoun instead of a subject pronoun).

When you're finished, read both the original sentences and your sentences out loud. Sometimes, the revised sentence will sound better—and sometimes the original will be much clearer than the rewritten sentence. Place a checkmark by any of your sentences that sound like improvements on the original.

Show your completed work to your instructor.

The king wore a coat of raised gold.

His Italian paintings also include scenes from the Bible.

Cleopatra enjoyed greater prestige than any other woman of her age.

Pare covered the wounds with a salve composed of egg yolk, turpentine, and oil of roses.

The cold within him froze his old features, nipped his pointed nose, shrivelled his cheek, stiffened his gait.

STEP FOUR: Vary one of your own sentences

From your own written work this week, choose a sentence that contains an active verb and a direct object. Transform this sentence by making the active verb passive. Write the transformed sentence on the lines below.

____

____

____

____

____

Week 20: Biographical Sketch

Day One: Outlining Exercise

Focus: Finding the central topic in each paragraph of a biographical sketch

STEP ONE: **Read**

Read the following short account of the life and work of the ancient mathematician Archimedes (pronounced ark-eh-MEED-ease). If you haven't read before about the Punic Wars, you should know that the three Punic Wars were fought between Rome and the North African city of Carthage between 264 and 146 BC. Both the Romans and the Carthaginians wanted to control the city of Syracuse, on the island of Sicily (which fell right between the two powers). A *quinquereme* (third paragraph) was a heavy warship.

There are only five paragraphs in this passage, but there is a lot of detail in each paragraph. In Step Two, you'll be given some help outlining it.

— — —

If the ordinary person were asked to say off-hand what he knew of Archimedes, he would probably, at the most, be able to quote one or other of the well-known stories about him: how, after discovering the solution of some problem in the bath, he was so overjoyed that he ran naked to his house, shouting *Eureka, eureka!* (or, as we might say, "I've got it, I've got it"); or how he said "Give me a place to stand on and I will move the earth"; or again how he was killed, at the capture of Syracuse in the Second Punic War, by a Roman soldier who resented being told to get away from a diagram drawn on the ground which he was studying. . . .

Archimedes perished in the Roman sack of the city of Syracuse in 212 BC, and, as he was then an old man (perhaps 75 years old), he must have been born about 287 BC. He was the son of Phidias, an astronomer, and was a friend and kinsman of King Hieron of Syracuse and his son Gelon. He spent some time at Alexandria studying with the successors of Euclid (Euclid who flourished about 300 BC was then no longer living). It was . . . probably in Egypt that he invented the water-screw known by his name, the immediate purpose being the drawing of water for irrigating fields. After his return to Syracuse he lived a life entirely devoted to mathematical research. . . .

During the siege of Syracuse Archimedes contrived all sorts of engines against the Roman besiegers. There were catapults so ingeniously constructed as to be equally serviceable at long or short range, and machines for discharging showers of missiles through holes made in the walls. Other machines consisted of long movable poles projecting beyond the walls; some of these dropped heavy weights upon the enemy's ships and on the constructions which they called *sambuca,* from their resemblance to a musical instrument of that name, and which consisted of a protected ladder with one end resting on two quinqueremes lashed together side by side as base, and capable of being raised by a windlass; others were fitted with an iron hand or a beak like that of a crane, which grappled the prows of ships, then lifted them into the air and let them fall again.

Marcellus is said to have derided his own engineers with the words, "Shall we not make an end of fighting with this geometrical monster? He uses our ships like cups to ladle water from the sea, drives our siege-engines away, and, by the multitude of missiles that he hurls at us all at once, outdoes the hundred-handed giants of mythology!" But the exhortation had no effect. The Romans were in such abject terror that, "if they did but see a piece of rope or wood projecting above the wall they would cry 'there it is,' declaring that Archimedes was setting some engine in motion against them, and would turn their backs and run away. So Marcellus desisted from all fighting and assault, putting all his hope in a long siege."

Archimedes died, as he had lived, absorbed in mathematical contemplation. The accounts of the circumstances of his death differ in some details. Plutarch gives more than one version in the following passage: "Marcellus was most of all afflicted at the death of Archimedes, for, as fate would have it, he was intent on working out some problem with a diagram, and, his mind and his eyes being alike fixed on his investigation, he never noticed the incursion of the Romans nor the capture of the city. And when a soldier came up to him suddenly and bade him follow to Marcellus, he refused to do so until he had worked out his problem to a demonstration; whereat the soldier was so enraged that he drew his sword and slew him. Others say that the Roman ran up to him with a drawn sword, threatening to kill him; and, when Archimedes saw him, he begged him earnestly to wait a little while in order that he might not leave his problem incomplete and unsolved, but the other took no notice and killed him. Again, there is a third account to the effect that, as he was carrying to Marcellus some of his mathematical instruments, sundials, spheres, and angles adjusted to the apparent size of the sun to the sight, some soldiers met him and, being under the impression that he carried gold in the vessel, killed him." The most picturesque version of the story is that which represents him as saying to a Roman soldier who came too close, "Stand away, fellow, from my diagram," whereat the man was so enraged that he killed him.[150]

STEP TWO: **Construct a one-level outline**

This passage is a biographical sketch of Archimedes. Like the other biographical sketches you've studied, it mixes aspects of description with a narrative of important events in Archimedes's life.

Use the following hints to construct your outline.

Paragraph 1. The main idea here is an aspect of description. You last saw this aspect in the biographical sketch of Sargon.

Paragraph 2. This paragraph does *not* cover an aspect.

Paragraph 3. Archimedes created a lot of them.

Paragraph 4. The focus in this paragraph shifts away from Archimedes to something else.

Paragraph 5. You're on your own.

When you're finished, check your work with your instructor.

Day Two: Analyzing the Topos

Focus: Understanding the form of a biographical sketch

This week, you'll study one last way to construct a biographical sketch.

If you glance back at the biographical sketch of Archimedes, you'll see that his inventions are mentioned more than any other aspect or part of his life. In fact, the chronological narrative of his life only takes up three sentences of the whole composition! This is a particular form of biographical sketch: a sketch where the focus is on what the subject is most known for (his work, profession, and achievements).

You'll need your green and red colored pencils again for this lesson, as well as a regular pencil.

STEP ONE: **Examine model passages**

Read the following paragraphs about the Persian scholar Omar Khayyám. Khayyám wrote a very famous book of poems, now known as *The Rubáiyat of Omar Khayyám.* But he was also an accomplished mathematician, although this work is not as well known.

---

150. Thomas Heath, *Archimedes* (Macmillan, 1920), pp. 1–3.

This passage has mathematical terms in it that will probably be unfamiliar to you. But you don't need to know what a third-degree equation or binomial coefficient is in order to read about Khayyám's accomplishments.

> Omar Khayyám was born at Nishapur, Iran, around 1048. Early in his life, he developed interests in science and math—particularly algebra. Unlike many scientists of his time, he did not accept the patronage of a king; instead, he lived a quiet life searching for knowledge and traveling to great centers of learning, exchanging views with other scholars.
>
> He made an attempt to classify most algebraic equations, including the third-degree equations, and in fact, offered solutions for a number of them. His book *Maqalat fi al-Jahr wa al-Muqabila (Articles on Algebra and Comparatives)* is a masterpiece that marked a major advancement in the development of algebra. Omar Khayyám was the first to find the binomial theorem and to determine binomial coefficients.
>
> In geometry, he studied the generalities of the ancient Greek mathematician Euclid and contributed to the theory of parallel lines. At the request of a king, he produced a remarkably accurate solar calendar (*Al-Tarikh-al-Jalali*), which had an error of only one day in 3770 years, thus making it superior to the Gregorian calendar, which had an error of one day in 3330 years.
>
> His other accomplishments include the development of methods for the accurate determination of specific gravity. In metaphysics, he wrote three books, and he also became a renowned astronomer and a physician. In the West, however, he is best known for his enchanting book of poetry, *Rubáiyat* (quatrains), translated into English by Edward Fitzgerald.[151]

This sketch has two elements: an introductory paragraph with basic information about Khayyám's life (where and when he was born, what his life was like), and then three more paragraphs describing all of the things Khayyám discovered in mathematics and science.

There are very few life events in this sketch—because we don't *know* very much about Khayyám's life. A biographical sketch focusing almost completely on the subject's work is a good choice if you're writing about an ancient or little-known subject. Often, you'll find that you just don't have enough information to construct a full chronological narrative, or to cover more than one or two aspects of a description. We don't know what Khayyám did every day; we don't know anything about his family, his appearance, his habits, or his behavior.

But we do have the work he left behind—and that's what we can use to write a sketch about him.

Even if you *do* know quite a lot about someone's life, you can still write a biographical sketch that focuses on the subject's work. Read the following sketch of Noah Webster. As

151. Masoud Kheirabadi, *Islam* (Chelsea House Publishers, 2004), p. 105.

you read, use your regular pencil to lightly underline every sentence that discusses Webster's *writings*.

A *philologist* is someone who studies the historical development of languages and how they have changed over time.

> Noah Webster, the famous philologist, was born in Hartford, Connecticut, in 1758. He entered Yale, but his studies were interrupted by the outbreak of the War of Independence, and for a time he served in his father's company of militia. After graduating, he became a teacher, but devoting his leisure hours to the study of law, he was admitted to the Bar in 1781.
>
> At this time he compiled several text-books, including a spelling book, which met with such great success that, though he received a royalty of less than one cent per copy, the proceeds were sufficient to support himself and his family during the twenty years spent in the preparation of his dictionary. His speller is still in use, and over 62,000,000 copies have been published.
>
> Webster published a number of political pamphlets, and in 1786 he delivered a course of lectures which were published under the title *Dissertations on the English Language.* In 1788, he established in New York the *American Magazine*, but it lived only twelve months, and the next year he settled in Hartford as a lawyer. However, four years later, he moved to New York and established a daily paper, the *Minerva,* a title that was afterwards changed to *Commercial Advertiser.* In 1794, he published a pamphlet on *The Revolution in France*, and he was the author of a history of pestilences and a number of other works.
>
> In 1807, he began work on his *American Dictionary of the English Language.* Many years were devoted to this labor, and in 1824 he went to Europe to consult literary authorities and books not to be found in this country. In the library of the University at Cambridge, England, the dictionary was at last finished, and Webster returned to America with the manuscript in 1825. Three years later was published the first edition of the dictionary, which contained 12,000 words and 40,000 definitions not to be found in any similar work.
>
> Webster's character was that of a man both genial and frank. He was deeply religious—a systematic student of the Bible, and during the last thirty-five years of his life a member of an Orthodox Congregational church. He died in New Haven, Connecticut, in 1843.[152]

We know plenty of facts about Noah Webster's life. Any encyclopedia can tell you that Webster's family was descended from William Bradford, leader of Plymouth Plantation; that he was 16 when he went to Yale; that he married a wealthy woman; that he was involved in politics,

152. Louis Albert Banks, *The Story of the Hall of Fame* (The Christian Herald, 1902), pp. 389–390.

opposed slavery, helped found Amherst College, and had eight children. But none of those life events appear in this sketch, because the sketch is about Webster's writings, and particularly those writings that had to do with language.

If you underlined the sentences dealing with Webster's writing career, you should have ended up underlining every single sentence in the second, third, and fourth paragraphs. All the other aspects of Webster's life mentioned, as well as the chronological narrative, are in the first and last paragraphs only.

Using your green pencil to represent the chronological narrative of Webster's life, underline all three sentences in the first paragraph, and the very last sentence of the last paragraph. These four sentences cover the important life events in the biographical sketch.

Using your red pencil, underline the first two sentences of the last paragraph. These descriptive sentences tell you about two aspects of Webster: his character and his religious beliefs.

Now go back to your red pencil. In the three central paragraphs, circle each date. You should find six dates. Notice that Webster's work, the focus of this whole part of the sketch, is covered in chronological order. This is an excellent way to organize paragraphs that talk about the subject's work: write about each major achievement in chronological order.

Finally, look back one last time at the sketch about Omar Khayyám. Since we don't know what order Khayyám made his discoveries in, the writer organizes this part of the sketch another way. Using your regular pencil, write "Algebra" next to the second paragraph. Write "Geometry and Calendar" next to the third paragraph. Write "Other" next to the fourth paragraph. These paragraphs are organized around the different types of work Khayyám did.

STEP TWO: **Add to the pattern of the topos**

Turn to the Biographical Sketch chart in your Composition Notebook. Add the bolded points below under the "Remember" column.

Biographical Sketch

Definition: A chronological summary of the important events in a person's life combined with description of aspects of the person

Procedure	Remember
1. Decide on the life events to list in the chronological summary.	**1. The main focus can be on the subject's work/accomplishments**
2. Choose aspects from the Description of a Person chart to include.	**a. Listed chronologically** **b. Listed by subject/topic**

Day Three: Practicing the Topos

Focus: Learning how to write a biographical sketch

Today, you'll write a biographical sketch of Shakespeare, organizing most of the composition around his accomplishments.

Shakespeare is a good subject for this kind of sketch, because we don't actually know a huge amount about his life. We know the dates for some of the biggest events, but we don't know what he was doing for at least seven years of his career; we don't know exactly when many of the plays were written or acted; and we don't even know what he looked like. (The most famous portrait of Shakespeare was made after he died, so the engraver might not have ever seen Shakespeare in person.)

But we do have his works—many of them. So your sketch will focus on these.

Shakespeare's portrait on the First Folio, 1623

STEP ONE: **Draft the chronological narrative**

This biographical sketch should begin with a paragraph giving a basic chronological narrative of Shakespeare's life. This should be followed by at least three paragraphs discussing Shakespeare's works.

You can either put all of the chronological narrative in the first paragraph or divide it into two parts (like the Webster sketch does). If you divide it, the first paragraph would cover Shakespeare's life through 1599, when his company began acting at the Globe and his plays really moved to the center of his life. Then you would stop, write your paragraphs about his work, and then write a final paragraph about the last years of Shakespeare's life, when he went back to Stratford and then finally died.

Pattern 1
Chronological narrative, birth to death
Paragraphs about work

Pattern 2
Chronological narrative, birth to 1599
Paragraphs about work
Chronological narrative, 1613–1616

Using the following list of events, write a rough draft of your chronological narrative now. Try to use your own wording. The chronological narrative can be as short as 50 words or as long as 150.

If you have trouble, ask your instructor for help. If not, you can continue on to Step Two without showing your work.

Basic life events

April, 1564	Born at Stratford-upon-Avon
1571	Began school at the Free School in Stratford
1577	Left school and became a butcher's apprentice
1582	Married Anne Hathaway
1583	Daughter Susanna born
1585	Twins Hamnet and Judith born
	Convicted of poaching deer, left Stratford for London
1585–1592	Worked in the theatre, became part owner of a theatre company called Lord Chamberlain's Men
1596	Son Hamnet died
1599	The Globe Theatre built in London; Shakespeare's company acted there
1602	Bought 100 acres of land in Stratford plus a cottage
1613	Globe Theatre burned down, Shakespeare retired to Stratford
1616	Shakespeare died, April 23

STEP TWO: **Draft the paragraphs about work**

Now, you'll work on writing the paragraphs about Shakespeare's work.

Below, you'll see three separate pieces of information. The first is a chronological list of Shakespeare's major works. The second is a list of Shakespeare's plays, divided by type (comedy, tragedy, history). The third is part of an essay telling more about each play. (It would be a boring sketch if you just listed the plays; you should be able to give a little more detail, but I'm assuming that you haven't yet *read* all 36 plays.)

As you read through this information, keep two things in mind.

First, there are two ways to organize these paragraphs. You can write one paragraph about the tragedies, one about the comedies, and one about the histories—the method followed in the biographical sketch of Omar Khayyám. Definitions of each type of play are provided; you would want to use some of this information.

Or you can put the plays in chronological order and and write about each one—the method followed in the Noah Webster sketch. If you follow this second method, you may want to know that Shakespeare's plays are traditionally divided into three periods: 1590–1594 (early or first), 1595–1600 (middle or second), and 1601–1609 (late or third). The essay below tells a little more about these periods.

You don't need to put in the dates for every single play, but try to use at least three dates. You may use either commas or parentheses to set off the dates.

Pattern 1	*Pattern 2*
The histories	First period works (1590–1594)
The comedies	Second period works (1595–1600)
The tragedies	Third period works (1601–1609)

Second, don't try to list all of the plays! An essay with a long list of titles is boring and hard to read. Pick at least six but not more than eight or ten plays to mention, and make sure that you say something specific about each one. If you are already familiar with some of Shakespeare's work, use your background knowledge as well as the information in the essay.

If you have trouble, ask your instructor for help. If not, you can continue on to Step Three without showing your work.

Major works, chronological

(note that it is impossible to know exactly what year many of the plays were written)

1592	Wrote and produced *Henry VI, Part 1*
Early 1590s	Wrote *Richard III, Henry VI, Part 2,* and *Henry VI, Part 3* Probably also wrote *Titus Andronicus, The Comedy of Errors, The Taming of the Shrew,* and *The Two Gentlemen of Verona*
Mid-1590s	Wrote and produced *A Midsummer Night's Dream, The Merchant of Venice, Much Ado about Nothing, As You Like It, Twelfth Night*
Late 1590s	Wrote and produced *Henry IV, Part 1, Henry IV, Part 2,* and *Henry V;* also probably *Romeo and Juliet* and *Julius Caesar*
1598	Produced Ben Jonson's play, *Every Man in His Humour*
1599	Shakespeare's company began to act at the Globe. *Julius Caesar* one of the first plays performed at the Globe.
Early 1600s	Wrote and produced *Measure for Measure, Troilus and Cressida,* and *All's Well That Ends Well;* also *Hamlet, Othello, King Lear, Macbeth, Antony and Cleopatra, Coriolanus*
1604	*Othello* performed for King James I at the royal court
1609	*Shakespeare's Sonnets* first published
1623	The *First Folio* published, containing 36 comedies, histories, and tragedies of Shakespeare; first collection of Shakespeare's printed plays

Shakespeare's plays by type

Comedy: *Twelfth Night, Much Ado about Nothing, The Tempest, A Midsummer Night's Dream, All's Well That Ends Well, The Merchant of Venice, As You Like It, The Comedy of Errors, Winter's Tale, Cymbeline, Love's Labour's Lost, Two Gentlemen of Verona, The Merry Wives of Windsor, Measure for Measure, The Taming of the Shrew*

"A Shakespearean comedy is a story of love ending with a ringing of marriage bells. Not only the hero and the heroine in love, but all are in love, and so in the end there is not one marrriage but a number of marriages."[153]

153. N. Jayapalan, *History of English Literature* (Atlantic Publishers, 2001), p. 74.

". . . what defines a Shakespearean comedy is a light touch, a happy ending, and a wedding. . . . To Shakespeare, comedy meant that foolish humans were able to triumph over adversity."[154]

Tragedy: *Hamlet, King Lear, Macbeth, Othello, Julius Caesar, Antony and Cleopatra, Coriolanus, Romeo and Juliet, Titus Andronicus*

"Shakespearean tragedy is . . . the story of one person, the hero, or at most of two, the hero and heroine. . . . The story leads up and includes the death of the hero. . . [Tragedy is] a tale of suffering and calamity, [ending with] death."[155]

History: *Richard II, Richard III, King John, Henry IV, Part 1, Henry IV, Part 2, Henry V, Henry VI, Part 1, Henry VI, Part 2, Henry VI, Part 3*

A historical play is a retelling of historical events, combined with the playwright's own imagination.

Descriptions of the plays and of the three periods of Shakespeare's development
The following summary of the most important of Shakespeare's plays is condensed from Benjamin Griffith Brawley's *A Short History of the English Drama.*

> The first period of Shakespeare's dramatic development (1590–1594) was essentially one of apprenticeship and imitation. The young artist was improving himself in versification. While the period placed most emphasis on comedy it also made a strong beginning in tragedy and history.
>
> Thoroughly typical is *Love's Labour's Lost* (1591). This play makes unusual use of rhyme, a mark of the dramatist's earlier years. The rather artificial plot is of a king and three of his lords who forswear the company of ladies for three years in order to devote themselves to study.
>
> *The Comedy of Errors* (1591) depends for its merit primarily upon its rapid action and its use of mistaken identity.
>
> The three plays of *Henry VI* are concerned with the historical events of the close of the Hundred Years' War and of the Wars of the Roses.
>
> *Richard III* (1593), is based on the life of Richard, Duke of Gloucester, who killed his two nephews and committed other crimes to gain his crown. Richard's soliloquy, "Now is the winter of our discontent," and Richard's call, "A horse! a horse! my kingdom for a horse!" are best known.
>
> *Richard II* (1594) shows advance in the subtle art of characterization. This is best seen in the interpretation of Richard himself. Toward the end of the play, Richard rises in dignity; and the scenes of his death are in the vein of genuine tragedy.

154. Cork Milner, *The Everything Shakespeare Book* (Adams Media, 2008), p. 11.
155. Jayapalan, p. 69.

Word-play and a highly lyrical character combine to give *Romeo and Juliet* an early date among Shakespeare's plays. It has been customary to give 1592 as the date of a first version, and 1597 as that of a revision. The brilliant poetry,and the strong development of character in the course of the play make *Romeo and Juliet* one of the most appealing dramas ever given to the world.

In the plays of his second period (1595–1600), Shakespeare shows that he has become full master of his art. He devotes himself mainly to comedy. All traces of apprenticeship and imitation disappear from his work.

A Midsummer Night's Dream (1595) holds together three plots: (1) the complicated loves of two men and two women, (2) the quarrel and reconciliation of the king and queen of fairies, and (3) the play within a play of Bottom and his companions.

The Merchant of Venice (1595) is distinguished by its skilful weaving together of three entirely unrelated threads of plot.

The Taming of the Shrew (1596) seems to have been built on an earlier play of unknown authorship, *The Taming of a Shrew.* The main story is that of a wilful and ungovernable young woman who is subdued by a husband who assumes a temper even more wilful and ungovernable than hers. It is by no means certain that Shakespeare wrote the whole of the play.

The first part of *Henry IV* (1597) deals with the revolt of the Percies, in which Hotspur is the brilliant figure until he is killed by Prince Henry. The second leads to the death of Henry IV and the final elevation of the Prince as king. The supreme creation of the plays is Falstaff, one of the greatest comic figures in all literature.

Henry V (1598) is Shakespeare's last effort in the field of history, and in it Shakespeare portrays the ideal English king.

In *Much Ado about Nothing* (1599), the leading woman of the play is the great wit Beatrice. This lady is most famous for her combats with Benedick, a young lord of Padua.

As You Like It (1599) is a careful weaving together of serious and comic elements. Rosalind is one of Shakespeare's most charming women and Touchstone is the wittiest of all the dramatist's fools.

Twelfth Night (1600) might well claim to be the finest of all Shakespeare's comedies. The plot was drawn from a variety of sources and few situations in the play are essentially new. Never were the high comedy of romance and the low comedy of ordinary English life more perfectly blended.

In the third period of his dramatic activity (1601–1609), Shakespeare rose to his greatest heights as a literary artist.

The story of *All's Well that Ends Well* (1602) is a strange one of a noble-minded young woman who falls in love with a man hardly worthy of her, who is insulted by this man, who places herself in a dangerous and compromising situation in order to win his loyalty, and who at length wins him, having satisfied even the hard conditions that he placed on her.

Measure for Measure (1603) is a vivid satire on the evils of society. The atmosphere is gloomy throughout.

Hamlet (1602, second version 1604) is a world masterpiece. In such things as the motive of revenge, the use of the ghost, the play within a play, and madness as a dramatic motive, Shakespeare was simply employing old material; but there is nothing trite about his finished product. By its magnificent phrase and rich poetry and its deep insight into human passion, the play continues to attract and baffle.

In *King Lear* (1605), the drama is the tragedy of old age. Lear is deceived by his older daughters, Goneril and Regan; it is only after days of suffering and a terrible night of storm that he finds out the true quality of Cordelia, his youngest daughter, who loved him too much to humor his whims and deceive him.

Macbeth (1606) is commonly given a place with *Hamlet, Othello,* and *King Lear* as one of Shakespeare's greatest productions. It is much the shortest of the tragedies. While Lady Macbeth to some extent influences her husband, Macbeth is the architect of his own fate. The tragedy is not so much in the number of people killed as in the downfall of a noble man.[156]

STEP THREE: **Finish the sketch**

Now put your composition together. Read through it out loud, listening for any awkward sentences. Then read it again, looking for mistakes in spelling, punctuation, and capitalization. If you used any passive verbs, ask yourself whether an active verb would be better.

When you are content with your work, show it to your instructor.

Day Four: Copia Exercise

Focus: Indirect objects and prepositional phrases

STEP ONE: **Review**

In the following sentence, turn the appropriate descriptive adjective into a noun and rewrite the sentence.

156. Condensed from Benjamin Griffith Brawley, *A Short History of the English Drama* (Harcourt, Brace & Co., 1921), pp. 61–81.

Webster published a number of political pamphlets.

____

In the following sentence, turn the appropriate noun into a descriptive adjective and rewrite the sentence.

He did not accept the patronage of a king.

____

In the following sentence, transform the passive verb into an active verb and rewrite the sentence.

His studies were interrupted by the outbreak of the War of Independence.

____

In the following sentence, transform the active verb into a passive verb and rewrite the sentence.

Archimedes contrived all sorts of engines against the Romans.

____

STEP TWO: Understand how to transform indirect objects into prepositional phrases

When you learned how to make a passive verb into an active verb, you also learned how to take the subject of a sentence and transform it into the object of a preposition. So, when the sentence

Regan deceives King Lear

becomes

King Lear is deceived by **Regan**

the subject, Regan, becomes the object of the preposition "by."

There is another part of speech that can be transformed into the object of a preposition: the indirect object. This is a simple transformation, but you can use it to bring some variety to your sentences.

An indirect object is a word that is indirectly affected by an action verb. In the sentence

S V IO DO

Annie Sullivan gave Helen a doll.

"doll" is the direct object; it receives the action of the verb "gave" (meaning that the doll itself was the thing given). "Helen" is the indirect object. Helen didn't get given. No one picked her up and handed her over. But the action of giving the doll *did* affect Helen; she ended up with a new doll.

Indirect objects can be taken out of their place (between the verb and the direct object), and paired up with a preposition to express the same meaning:

S V DO PREP OP

Annie Sullivan gave a doll to Helen.

In this transformed sentence, the indirect object has become the object of the preposition "to."

STEP THREE: **Add to the Sentence Variety chart**

Write the following principle and illustration on the next line of your Sentence Variety chart:

indirect object → object of the preposition		The mother gave the baby a bottle. The mother gave a bottle to the baby.

STEP FOUR: **Practice sentence variety**

In the following sentences, transform each indirect object into an object of a preposition and rewrite the sentence on the line below.

His mother gave him a fine rich cake.

____

Mary, get me a silk thread and a chunk of fire.

____

They offered him gold and silver.

____

Jane showed Michael a little pebbly hollow.

____

WEEK 21: SEQUENCE: NATURAL PROCESS

Day One: Outlining Exercise

Focus: Finding the central topic in each paragraph of a sequence of events

STEP ONE: **Read**

Read the following passage.

— — —

You could say that salmon live to reproduce. Born in freshwater such as streams, lakes, and rivers, salmon migrate to the salt water of oceans, where they spend most of their lives. When it is time for them to spawn (or reproduce), salmon make the difficult journey back to their freshwater birthplaces. Soon after this challenging trip and the exhausting process of mating, they die off.

Science still hasn't fully figured out how exactly salmon find their way back home. These journeys sometimes last thousands of miles. Some scientists say that salmon use smell. Other scientists have theorized that the brain of a salmon can respond to the Earth's magnetic field. But the truth is that no one knows for sure how salmon find their way home.

As the time for the journey back to their birthplaces grows close, salmon stop feeding and change color and shape. The male salmon grows dog-like teeth and a hump on its back, and its mouth becomes more curved. Both male and female salmon change to a darker color, which makes it easier to blend into the darker water of freshwater lakes and rivers. This makes the fish less visible to those who like to eat salmon, like bears and humans.

The trip home is long and tiring. Chinook and sockeye salmon that were born in Idaho and have migrated to the Pacific Ocean now have to travel more than 900 miles and climb more than 7,000 feet to make it back to the rivers where they were born. Swimming home, salmon lose a lot of energy fighting river currents, rocks, and downed trees. The energy loss changes the fish's body. If you catch a salmon on its way back to its birthplace, you'll see that the flesh is much paler and mushier than the pink flesh of salmon in saltwater. Only the toughest salmon finish the journey and find a mate.

Salmon that have reached the waters where they were born collect in calm, cool places with clean gravel bottoms. The female uses her tail to scoop out gravel from the bottom of the river, creating a depression called a mating bed. The mating bed can be quite large — as large as six feet wide and ten feet long. Meanwhile, the male patrols the area to keep away intruders like smaller fish.

Once the mating bed is ready, the male and female salmon line up next to each other. The female releases eggs while the male releases milt (the reproductive fluid that fertilizes the eggs). The eggs settle into the depression of the gravel bed. Now, the female covers the area with fresh gravel from another part of the river, protecting the new eggs so they have a chance to mature. The mating pair will do this again in several gravel beds.

Then, exhausted by the journey back home and the process of mating, most salmon that have spawned die within a week or two. Only a very small minority of salmon—all females who lived in the Atlantic Ocean—live to mate again.

As for the eggs, they take several months to hatch. When the hatchlings emerge, they feed themselves from little sacs on their bellies that contain a kind of yolk. As the young fish grow, they develop vertical stripes on their bodies, which help hide them from predators. In several years, these baby salmon will change into adolescents, ready to begin their migration to saltwater. Their exteriors mutate once again, becoming a silvery color that helps them blend into the ocean more easily.

Once they reach the oceans, these young salmon will spend anywhere between one to five years in the salt water. Then, when the time to mate arrives, they too will seek home, heading upriver to their birthplaces. Out of every thousand eggs laid by spawning salmon, only one will make it back to the very same spot, years later, to start the process again.

STEP TWO: **Construct a one-level outline**

This passage walks you through the spawning cycle of salmon. Each paragraph explains a different part of the cycle. The exception is the first paragraph; like an introduction to a description, the first paragraph gives an overview of the entire process.

Construct your one-level outline now. If you have difficulty, ask your instructor for help. When you are finished, show your outline to your instructor.

Day Two: Analyzing the Topos

Focus: Understanding the form of a sequence describing a natural process

The passage you read for the last exercise is an example of a *sequence,* a form you haven't seen before.

A sequence has something in common with a chronological narrative of past events; both list a series of events in the order that they happened. A chronological narrative tells you about events that happened *once.* The Rosetta Stone was only found once; Leeuwenhoek only discovered microscopic creatures for the first time once; Genghis Khan's men only pursued Muhammad Shah to his final hiding place one time.

But a sequence lists events that happen over and over and over again. In science, a sequence can describe the steps in a natural process—like the birth of a star, the transformation of peat into coal, or the germination of a seed. In history, a sequence can describe the way that a past process worked—the way a seventeenth-century mill ground grain into flour, or how a navigator on a sailing ship read the sky and set his course. Or a sequence can tell *how* to do something in the future: do a magic trick, train a dog, roast a chicken.

STEP ONE: **Examine model passages**

Your outline of the sequence about salmon probably looked something like this:

I. Salmon spawning ______________________
II. How salmon find their way ______________________
III. Changes before the journey
IV. The journey itself
V. Getting ready to mate
VI. The spawning itself
VII. After the spawning
VIII. The salmon grow.
IX. The process begins again.

____

Like the first sentence in a description, the first paragraph sums up the whole process of salmon spawning. With your pencil, write on the first line to the right "Introduction/ summary."

The second paragraph tells you what scientists know and don't know about the process. On the second line, write "Scientific background."

The next six paragraphs each describe one step in the process, moving chronologically from the beginning to the end. Turn your paper sideways, and write "Step-by-step process" on the lines.

The final paragraph tells you when the process will happen again. Remember, a sequence describes a series of steps that repeats itself over and over. On the final line, write "The cycle repeats."

Read the following description carefully, looking for the same elements.

> Honey is a sticky fluid collected from flowers by several kinds of insects, particularly the honey bee; and the common honey bee from the earliest period has been kept by people in hives for the advantage and enjoyment which its honey and wax gives. It is found wild in North America in great numbers, storing its honey in hollow trees and other suitable locations, but is not native to this country, having been introduced in North America by European colonists.
>
> In the spring of the year the colony consists of a queen and workers, with no drones present. During the winter the bees remain quiet, and the queen lays no eggs, so that there are no developing bees in the hive. The supply of honey is also low, for they have eaten honey all winter, and none has been collected and placed in the cells.
>
> As soon as the days are warm enough the bees begin to fly from the hive in search of the earliest spring flowers. From these flowers they collect the nectar, which is transformed into honey, and pollen, which they carry to the hive on the pollen-baskets on the third pair of legs. The nectar is taken by the bee into its mouth, and then passes to an enlargement of the alimentary canal known as the honey-stomach, where it is acted upon by certain juices secreted by the bee. The true stomach lies just behind the honey-stomach; and if the bee needs food for its own immediate use it passes on through the opening between the two stomachs.
>
> On its arrival in the hive the bee places its head in one of the cells of the comb and deposits there the nectar which it has carried in. By this time the nectar has been partly transformed into honey, and the process is completed by the bees by fanning the cells to evaporate the excess of moisture which still remains. When a cell has been filled with the thick honey the workers cover it with a thin sheet of wax unless it is to be eaten at once.
>
> The pollen is also deposited in cells, but is rarely mixed with honey. The little pellets which the bees carry in are packed tightly into cells until the cell is nearly full. If a cell of pollen is dug out of the comb, one can often see the layers made by the different pellets.

> This collecting of nectar and pollen continues throughout the summer whenever there are flowers in bloom, and ceases only with the death of the last flowers in the autumn.[157]

You should have recognized three of the same elements in this sequence.

The first paragraph is an introduction and summary: what honey is, where it comes from, and where bees live. Write "Introduction/Summary" in the margin next to the first paragraph.

The next four paragraphs progress, step by step, through the honey-making process. Write "Step-by-step process" in the margin next to those paragraphs.

The last paragraph tells you that the process repeats itself "whenever there are flowers in bloom." Write "The cycle repeats" in the margin next to the final paragraph.

This sequence doesn't tell you what scientists think about bees, but it contains the other three elements.

Like descriptions and chronological narratives, sequences can stand on their own or form a small part of a longer composition. If a sequence stands on its own, it should have at least three of the elements listed above. But a sequence that's part of a larger essay can have just one element: the step-by-step process. The following simple sequence appears in a much longer chapter about growth and decay in nature:

> For example, imagine a single-celled organism (such as a bacterium or an amoeba) which reproduces by cell division. Imagine also that the organism is sitting on a very large supply of nutrients and reproducing as fast as it can. At first, there is only one cell. This cell divides and then there are two cells; these two cells divide and then there are four cells; the four cells divide and there are eight cells; and so on.[158]

The step-by-step process of cell division is the only element in that sequence. Write "Step-by-step process" in the margin next to the paragraph.

A short sequence can also have just two elements, like the following:

> The ancient Norse people believed that a rainbow was the "bridge of the gods," connecting heaven to Earth. Many other cultures have regarded rainbows as a symbol of peace and hope.
>
> Rainbows form when beams of sunlight break through a shower of rain. Each raindrop acts as a miniature prism, bending and slicing the white light of the sun up into the colours of the spectrum—ranging from violet to deep red.[159]

---

157. Rudolph John Bodmer, *The Book of Wonders* (Bureau of Industrial Education, 1916), p. 528.
158. Gregory Neil Derry, *What Science Is and How It Works* (Princeton University Press, 1999), p. 290.
159. *1000 Wonders of Nature* (Reader's Digest Association, 1994), p. 374.

Next to the first paragraph, write "Introduction/summary." Next to the second, write "Step-by-step process."

STEP TWO: **Write down the pattern of the topos**

Copy the following onto a blank sheet of paper in the Reference section of your Composition Notebook.

Sequence: Natural Process

Definition: A step-by-step description of a cycle that occurs in nature

Procedure	Remember
1. Describe the natural process chronologically, step by step. 2. Decide which other elements to include: a. Introduction/summary b. Scientific background c. Repetition of the process	

Day Three: Practicing the Topos

Focus: Learning how to write a sequence describing a natural process

Today, you'll work on constructing the core element of a sequence: the step-by-step process.

STEP ONE: **Plan the step-by-step process**

Using the following paragraphs of information, list all of the events, in the order in which they occur, that happen to a star as it begins to age and then dies. Not all of the steps are listed in each paragraph, and some of the paragraphs overlap. You'll have to work out the order in which the steps occur.

Try to use phrases and very brief sentences rather than complete detailed sentences on your list. If you copy down complete sentences from the paragraphs, you'll make it much harder to use your own words rather than the words of the source material when you actually write your paragraphs.

When you are finished with your list, check it with your instructor before continuing on.

> . . . [A]ll stars that use hydrogen for their energy source are grouped together because of that one common characteristic. These are

hydrogen-burning stars and hydrogen-burners are called *main sequence stars*. Our Sun is a main sequence star because it is using hydrogen as its source of fuel. . . . As a star consumes its supply of hydrogen, a core composed of heavier elements [like helium] forms. . . . Several changes occur within the star. First, it shrinks and gets hotter. . . . At these high temperatures, with much of the hydrogen converted to helium, the star is beginning to grow hungry for a new energy source. The energy provided by hydrogen is dwindling but the star is not hot enough to cause helium to fuse. Helium fusion takes a temperature greater than 20 million degrees. The star is not hot enough so the helium is not providing any energy. It's just sitting there in the core of this hungry star. . . . The star begins its collapse toward oblivion . . . . Now, gravity is crushing the helium core, raising its temperature and density. Eventually . . . the core reaches 20 million degrees.[160]

The helium-enriched core of the aging star shrinks . . . more and more energy dumps into the outer layers of the star, increasing its temperature—and its pressure. So while the core shrinks, the outer layers of the star expand dramatically, cooling as they do. As this happens, the star becomes more luminous (because it's larger) and cooler. . . . The resulting star is called a red giant . . . about 100 times larger than the Sun, with a core that is less than 1 percent of the size of the star. . . . A red giant continues on its unstable career . . . outwardly expanding and inwardly shrinking. At some point, however, the shrinking of the core raises its temperature sufficiently to ignite the helium that has been patiently accumulating there.[161]

As the bloated star attains its red giant status, the core temperature—which has been steadily increasing as the core contracts—hits the minimum to start helium burning. . . . When part of the degenerate core ignites, the heat generated by the fusion spreads rapidly through the core. The rest of the core quickly ignites. . . . This out-of-control process in the core is called the helium flash. The whole process of helium core ignition in the helium flash takes place in a very short time—perhaps only a few minutes! We will never see this helium flash in a star, for the action takes place deep in the core. . . . [After the initial flash,] [t]he star quietly burns helium in the core and hydrogen in a layer around the core.[162]

[W]hen the helium fuel is all burned, the fires go out . . . the core of the star is essentially dead. . . . [Meanwhile,] outer core layers . . . [continue

160. Gerry A. Good, *Observing Variable Stars* (Springer, 2003), pp. 10–11.
161. Christopher Gordon De Pree and Alan Axelrod, *The Complete Idiot's Guide to Astronomy* (Alpha, 2001), p. 165.
162. Michael Zeilik, *Astronomy: The Evolving Universe* (Cambridge University Press, 2002), pp. 342–343.

> to] burn helium and hydrogen at an intense pace and the outermost part of the star continues to expand . . . [T]he outer envelope of the star move[s] progressively farther from the core of the star. . . . [This] forms a new highly unusual stellar structure called a planetary nebula. This nebula has a small, dense, core made of the spent carbon ash with a shell of material still burning helium into carbon. A span of relatively empty space about the size of Earth's solar system surrounds the core, succeeded outward by a glowing ring consisting of the ejected outer layers of the former giant star. . . . The planetary nebula stage marks the death . . . of the star. When stars die, however, they do not go away. . . As the dead stars fade from view they go through two more stages, the white dwarf and the black dwarf stages.[163]

> White dwarfs are faint old stars. . . . Most of them are about the same size as the Earth, but they are 300,000 times its mass. . . . At the white dwarf stage of their lives, the nuclear furnaces inside these stars have stopped burning. They are dimming down, and at some point they will stop contraction. This happens when the electrons in the atoms of gas that remain in their cores push against the contraction and the star enters a state of equilibrium—no more contraction, no more energy source. What is left is a stellar mass so dense that a small spoonful of the star's material would weigh 10 tons![164]

> Black dwarf: the theoretical celestial object that remains after a white dwarf has used up all of its fuel and cooled off completely to a solid mass of extremely dense, cold carbon. A white dwarf will eventually become a black dwarf unless it has a companion star from which it can take sufficient mass to . . . collapse into a neutron star or black hole. No black dwarf has ever been observed. Because the estimated cooling time for a white dwarf is in the trillions of years, it is unlikely that there are many, if any, black dwarfs in our universe. . .[165]

STEP TWO: **Divide the list into paragraphs**

In Step Three, you'll write a step-by-step sequence that tells how a hydrogen-burning star dies. This sequence should be organized into paragraphs: one paragraph for each stage in the star's death. Looking at your list, draw lines between the events to separate them into stages. Jot down the name of the stage beside each set of events.

---

163. Timothy Kusky, *Encyclopedia of Earth and Space Science, Vol. 1* (Facts on File, 2010), p. 704.
164. Carolyn Collins Petersen and John C. Brandt, *Hubble Vision: Further Adventures with the Hubble Space Telescope* (Cambridge University Press, 1995), p. 115.
165. *The American Heritage Science Dictionary* (Houghton Mifflin, 2005), p. 76.

Hint: the first stage is *not* "red giant." You'll have to make up your own name for the first stage.

When you are finished, check your work with your instructor.

STEP THREE: **Write the sequence**

Using your list and referring back to the source material for details, write five (or six) paragraphs about the death of a star. Each stage should be described in a separate paragraph.

Don't use the exact words of the source material; use your thesaurus to find synonyms and rephrase where possible.

Give at least one descriptive detail about the star in each stage (color, temperature, size, mass, etc.).

When you are finished, check your work with your instructor.

Day Four: Copia Exercise

Focus: Transforming infinitives into participles

STEP ONE: **Review**

Rewrite the following sentences according to the instructions. Check your work with your instructor.

Turn the appropriate descriptive adjective into a noun.

Water droplets in the atmosphere act like prisms.

____

Turn the appropriate two nouns into descriptive adjectives.

Rainbows form when beams of sunlight break through a shower of rain.

____

Transform the passive verb into an active verb.

The common honey bee from the earliest period has been kept by people.

Transform the active verb into a passive verb.

From these flowers, the bees collect the nectar and honey.

____

Transform the indirect object into the object of a preposition.

Twenty thousand bees can bring the hive a pound of nectar.

____

STEP TWO: Understand how to transform infinitives into participles

Read the following two sentences out loud.

The star begins **to grow** hungry for a new energy source.

The star begins **growing** hungry for a new energy source.

In the first sentence, the main verb *begins* is followed by an *infinitive.* An infinitive is a verb form that starts with *to.* Write *inf.* over the bolded "to grow" in the first sentence.

In the second sentence, the main verb is followed by a *participle.* A participle is a verb form that ends with *ing.* Write *part.* over the bolded "growing" in the second sentence.

When a main verb is followed by an infinitive, you can often change that infinitive to a participle. In the next two sentences, underline the main verb twice. Write *inf.* over the infinitive and *part.* over the participle.

The outermost part of the star continues to expand.

The outermost part of the star continues expanding.

In both sentences, you should have underlined the main verb "continues." "To expand" is the infinitive; "expanding" is the participle.

When you change an infinitive to a participle, you might have to make other changes to the sentence. The changes might be minor, like inserting punctuation:

The male salmon patrols the area to keep away intruders.

The male salmon patrols the area, keeping away intruders.

Or you might need to rearrange the words in the sentence so that it's easier to understand. Read the next three sentences out loud:

The darker color makes it easier to blend into the water.
(The darker color makes it easier blending into the water.)
The darker color makes blending into the water easier.

Not every infinitive can be changed into a participle. Read the next two sentences out loud.

Only a few salmon live to mate again.
Only a few salmon live mating again.

Always read your transformed sentences out loud to make sure that they still make sense!

STEP THREE: **Add to the Sentence Variety chart**

Write the following principle and illustration on the next line of your Sentence Variety chart:

infinitives ⟷ participles	The truth needs saying. The truth needs to be said.

STEP FOUR: **Practice sentence variety**

In the following sentences, transform each infinitive into a participle and rewrite the sentence on the line below. The last sentence will require you to make another change as well; be careful!

Check your finished work with your instructor.

When a red giant starts to expand, its core temperature is still low.

____

The core contracts until the helium begins to ignite.

____

The hydrogen shell continues to burn as the core contracts.

____

WEEK 22: SEQUENCE: NATURAL PROCESS

Day One: Outlining Exercise and Topos Review

Focus: Finding the central topic in each paragraph of a sequence of events; reviewing the form of a sequence

STEP ONE: **Read**

Read the following passage about severe weather. Some of the terms and abbreviations may be unfamiliar, so review them before you read:

Condensation point: the temperature at which water in the air will turn liquid
Latent heat: heat released or absorbed during a change of state (such as condensation, melting, or boiling).
Tropopause: the boundary between the troposphere (the lowest layer of the Earth's atmosphere) and the stratosphere (the second layer of the atmosphere).
Supercooled: when a liquid is chilled past its usual freezing point but remains liquid (usually because it has been chilled so quickly).
-40° C (-40° F): Celsius and Fahrenheit are two different temperature scales, but this isn't a mistake; -40° is the point at which the two scales meet.
m/s: meters per second.
ft/s: feet per second.

— — —

Thunderstorms can happen almost anywhere, but are the most frequent over land in low and mid-latitudes during the hottest months of the year. A thunderstorm goes through a number of stages, from developing to mature and then decline, but normally lasts no more than half an hour.

When the lower atmosphere is humid and unstable, conditions are ripe for a thunderstorm. The warm moist air at the surface starts to rise and, when it reaches the condensation point, clouds start to form. As the water vapor in the

air condenses out into clouds, it releases latent heat, making the clouds rise still further. In severe storms, the rising air, an updraft, reaches heights of over 12 kilometers (7 miles) and travels at speeds of 10 m/s (33 ft/s).

When it reaches the tropopause in the low levels of the upper atmosphere, the moisture-laden air stops rising and is spread out by the force of the jet stream to form the familiar anvil-shaped cloud—cumulonimbus. The cloud's rapid ascent means that the supercooled water droplets inside are swept up to high levels where, even though their temperature may fall to -40° C (-40° F), they may remain in a liquid form for some time or coalesce with ice crystals and snowflakes in the upper reaches of the cloud.

A thunderstorm reaches its mature and most devastating phase when it starts to rain or snow. When the water droplets or ice crystals in the cloud become large enough and heavy enough to succumb to gravity, they fall to the ground as rain or snow. They create a downdraft of cool air as they fall, which counteracts the warm rising updraft. This happens because, when the falling water droplets and ice crystals reach warmer levels of the atmosphere nearer the ground, the ice starts to melt and absorbs some of the heat. This cooling process reinforces the downdraft (causing heavier rainfall) but stops the unstable updrafts of warm air, which initially set the storm off.

At this stage, the storm goes into decline. However, the downdrafts sometimes undercut nearby warm air, thereby triggering off another updraft and setting the next storm into action. This is why storms rumble across the countryside one after the other in a haphazard manner, each following slightly different tracks.[166]

STEP TWO: **Review the pattern of the topos**

Before you try to outline this passage, look back over the elements that are often present in a sequence:

Introduction/summary
Scientific background
Step-by-step process
Repetition of the process

---

166. William James Burroughs, *The Climate Revealed* (Cambridge University Press, 1999), p. 126.

A sequence often has so much detail in each paragraph that it's hard to locate the most important point. Knowing what each paragraph is doing can help you with your outline.

Decide which element of the sequence each paragraph belongs to, and jot the answer down in the margins of the passage. Before you go on to the next step, check your work with your instructor.

STEP THREE: **Construct a one-level outline**

Now that you know what each paragraph is doing, outlining the passage should be easier.

Start with the first paragraph. You can't just outline this by writing:

I. Introduction/summary

because that doesn't say anything about the *content* of the passage. Ask yourself "What is this paragraph introducing me to?" The answer could become your first major point.

As you outline the next three paragraphs, ask yourself "Which stage of the process does this paragraph describe?"

Then ask yourself "In that stage of the process, what is the first, or most important, or biggest thing that happens?"

See if you can figure out how to approach the last paragraph.

If you're still confused, you can ask your instructor for help. When you are finished, show your work to your instructor.

Day Two: Practicing the Topos, Part One

Focus: Learning how to write a sequence describing a natural process

Over the next two days you'll write about the life of the octopus. You will be putting together a full sequence with all four elements. Today you'll work on your step-by-step process; tomorrow, you'll add the other three elements—and one other thing.

The plural of *octopus* can be either *octopi* or *octopuses*. Both are used.

STEP ONE: **Plan the step-by-step process**

Follow the same instructions as last week: use the following paragraphs of information and list all of the events, in the order in which they occur, that happen in an octopus's life. As before, try to use phrases and very brief sentences rather than complete detailed sentences.

When you are finished with your list, check it with your instructor before continuing on.

Like a chicken's egg, what we call an octopus egg is a complete package, with cushioning material, a yolk for nutrition, and a shell for protection. . . . Octopus eggs are typically oval or teardrop shaped, and most are tiny, the size of a grain of rice.[167]

Once the eggs are laid, the female guards them diligently, not leaving the nest until they hatch. She defends the nest against intruders, all the while blowing water out of her funnel to keep the water circulating around them. The eggs of the common octopus take approximately seven weeks to hatch, and when they do, a miniature version of the parent emerges. (There is no "larval" stage at which the neonates [newborns] are different in any other way from the adults but size.) A newborn common octopus is about the size of a flea, and it can change color. Some species are born larger and immediately drop to the bottom, but the tiny babies of [the most common octopus] join the vast legions of plankton, drifting at the mercy of the current and susceptible to the predation of any animal larger than they are.[168]

When hatched, the baby is fully formed, a miniature version of its parents with all eight legs, a bulblike head, and a tiny but sharp mouth. Its life at this stage is poorly understood, but biologists have found baby octopuses in the open ocean, well above the seafloor. Soon, however, the small octopuses settle to the seafloor, where they inhabit rocky crevices, reefs, or sandy bottoms similar to adult habitats.[169]

The young octopus fresh from the egg is of about the size of a large flea. . . At this early stage of its existence the young octopus seeks and enjoys the light which it will, later in life, carefully shun. It manifests no desire to hide itself in crevices and recesses, as the adult does, but swims freely about in the water, often close to the surface, propelling itself backward by a series of little jerks. . .[170]

[T]hey are solitary creatures. They live their lives alone, concentrating on housing and feeding. Because of their soft-bodied vulnerability, octopuses protect themselves by occupying a crevice, a cave, or . . . a pottery jar or pot . . . the octopus occupies a particular nest for a long time and ventures forth only to hunt for food, or in the case of the males, to look for a mate.[171]

---

167. Jennifer A. Mather, Roland C. Anderson, and James B. Wood, *Octopus: The Ocean's Intelligent Invertebrate* (Timber Press, 2010), p. 28.
168. Richard Ellis, *Monsters of the Sea* (Knopf, 1994), p. 298.
169. Ron Hirschi, *Octopuses* (Carolrhoda Books, 2000), p. 37.
170. Henry Lee, *Aquarium Notes: The Octopus* (Chapman and Hall, 1875), p. 66.
171. Ellis, p. 299.

However, exactly how males find females is not known for sure. They may simply encounter or bump into them by chance or may locate them by "smell" or chemosensory means. . . . After mating, females often take several months to "bulk up" and find a suitable den in which to lay their eggs. The female typically blocks up the entrance to her small den with rocks. . . . The female does not eat while . . . guarding the eggs. Because octopuses have no fat, she lives off protein metabolism, usually shrinking to about half her starting weight, during the brooding process, and dies shortly after the eggs hatch. Studies on brooding females have determined that if the female is eaten or taken away from her clutch of eggs, they will all die before hatching, victims of egg predators such as sea stars.[172]

A male and female meet to mate and then the female octopus lays her eggs in capsules and attaches them to a rock or den with a string-like substance. The female then guards her eggs until they hatch. She washes them with water to prevent fungus and to shoo away fish that want to eat the eggs. One female octopus lays thousands of eggs. It takes one to three months for babies to appear. The mother never leaves the eggs. . . After her eggs have hatched, it is the end of her life cycle and she dies. Once the baby octopi have hatched, not many survive. Left on their own, many are eaten by predators.[173]

Mating and reproducing in octopuses takes place at the end of their lives, which is the case for most cephalopods. The parents provide no care for the young once the eggs hatch. The males' life work is completed once they mate, and they usually die shortly after. Females die just after their eggs hatch. . . . Even the largest octopus species has a life span of three to four years at most, and for the smallest species it's six months or less. Some deep-water octopuses may live longer, but everything is slower in the cold depths. Octopuses don't really die young; they die after a full life (unless they get eaten). Their complete life spans just happen to be a lot shorter than ours.[174]

Before they die, the males may crawl out of the water onto the beach. As their organs, especially the brain, start to deteriorate, they begin to behave abnormally, appearing to crawl aroud aimlessly. During this senescent [aging] period, their state is quite a bit like that of humans with Alzheimer's disease. They stop eating and lose weight. They often develop white sores on their bodies. They leave the shelter and protection of their

---

172. Mark W. Denny and Steven Dean Gaines, *Encyclopedia of Tidepools and Rocky Shores* (University of California Press, 2007), p. 417.
173. Katie Kubesh, Kimm Bellotto, and Niki McNeil, *Predators of the Deep* (In the Hands of a Child, 2007), pp. 14–15.
174. Mather et al., p. 137.

> dens and do not camouflage themselves to hide from predators. They are especially vulnerable at this time to being eaten by large, relatively slow predators such as . . . sharks or killer whales.[175]

STEP TWO: **Divide the list into paragraphs**

Before you write your sequence, you'll need to organize your information into paragraphs: one paragraph for each major stage of an octopus's life.

The stages are:

embryo/egg
hatchling/young
mature
reproducing
old age

Looking at your list, draw lines between the events to separate them into stages. Jot down the name of the stage beside each set of events.

When you are finished, check your work with your instructor.

STEP THREE: **Write the step-by-step process**

Using your list and referring back to the source material for details, write six paragraphs about the life cycle of an octopus. Each stage should be described in a separate paragraph. Don't use the exact words of the source material: use your thesaurus to find synonyms, and rephrase where possible.

Give at least one descriptive detail about the octopus in each stage (behavior, habits, appearance).

Day Three: Practicing the Topos, Part Two

Focus: Learning how to write a sequence describing a natural process

You've finished the core element of your sequence, but a fully developed sequence of natural events has three other elements. Today, you'll finish your composition by adding these elements, plus a brief description of what the mature octopus looks like.

175. Denny and Gaines, p. 417.

STEP ONE: **Write the introduction**

Go back now and read the first paragraphs of the salmon essay (p. 279), the honey essay (p. 282), and the passage on thunderstorms (p. 291). All three of these sequences have an introductory paragraph that tells you what the subject of the sequence is. Each paragraph also draws you into the composition by telling you something interesting about that subject.

Using the information below, write a similar introductory paragraph that has two to five sentences. This paragraph could use one of two themes:

The octopus is a very intelligent creature OR

People have always been fascinated and frightened by the octopus.

If you have trouble getting started, you can use one of the sentences above as your first sentence.

Remember not to use the exact words of your source material.

> At aquariums, workers have to keep a close eye on the octopus. The octopus is a smart curious creature. . . . Even the largest octopus can squeeze through a narrow opening in the top of an aquarium. Once it escapes, an octopus can live a long time on land before the lack of water suffocates it. Jacques Cousteau once reported that a friend's pet octopus escaped from its aquarium and was found in the library paging through the books.[176]

> Jacques Cousteau, the French naturalist, filmed an octopus in a water-filled glass tank on a table, on the deck of his yacht, the *Calypso*. The octopus climbed out of the tank, slithered to the corner of the table, felt with its tentacles for a table leg that it could not see, slid down the table leg, dragged itself across the deck and dropped to the safety of the sea below . . . the animal faced a problem, saw an opportunity, formulated an escape stragey and a plan, executed the plan at great risk to life, and succeeded.[177]

> And there lies in wait the awful Octopus, a monster of insatiable voracity, of untameable ferocity, and of consummate craft; of sleepless vigilance, shrouded amidst the forest of sea-weed, and from the touch of whose terrible arms no living thing escapes. It attains to an enormous size in those seas, the arms being sometimes five feet in length, and as thick at the base as a man's wrist. No bather would have a chance if he once got within the grasp of such a monster, nor could a canoe resist the strength of its pull.[178]

---

176. Kubesh et al., p. 15.
177. Derek K. Hitchins, *Systems Engineering: A 21st Century Systems Methodology* (John Wiley, 2007), p. 461.
178. John Timbs, *Eccentricities of the Animal Creation* (Seeley, Jackson and Halliday, 1869), p. 283.

> Fabulous stories are related of the habits of [the octopus] and of its tremendous strength. We are told of how it attacks and upsets small boats, or of how one may silently reach into a boat with its long snaky tentacles and drag a sailor overboard to its death. Of course, these stories are untrue, for the octopus is timid in nature.[179]

This passage, from a 1922 news article, repeats myths about a "giant octopus." This probably never happened. But you could use it to show how people used to think about the octopus.

> Fishermen off the island of Jersey described recently their fight with a huge octopus, which seized the mast of the boat with one tentacle, nearly overturning the craft, while a second tentacle caught a fisherman and almost dragged him overboard. Jellylike and slimy as this creature seems to be, its tentacles are so tough as to resist slashing knives. Only blows between the eyes with sharp boathooks slew the monster. . . . The monster devilfish has eight grasping tentacles, each with double rows of suckers, radiating from the mouth, which is armed with a large, horny beak, used for tearing the prey held in the tentaces. The animal propels itself by ejecting water through a mouthlike funnel.[180]

STEP TWO: **Write the paragraph about scientific knowledge**

Go back now and read the second paragraph of the salmon essay (page 279). This paragraph tells you something about the current state of scientific knowledge. You'll write a similar paragraph now about the octopus, after reading the passages below.

Your paragraph should be two to five sentences in length. It should say two things:

People have known about the octopus for a long, long time.

Not enough actual scientific study has been done.

If you have trouble getting started, you can use the two sentences above. After each sentence, give an example or detail.

When you're finished, show your paragraph to your instructor.

> More than 2200 years ago . . . [the philosopher and natural scientist] Aristotle . . . recorded observations of the habits and reproduction of the octopus. . . . Alexander the Great, who, in his youth, was under his tuition for ten years, gave him . . . a large sum of money and a staff of assistants. According to Pliny the latter were sent to various parts of Asia and Greece under orders to collect animals of all kinds, and . . ."to watch their habits so closely that nothing relating to them should remain unknown." Aristotle thus accumulated a multitude of notes and observations, many of which . . . were marvellously

179. John Franklin Daniel, *Animal Life of Malaysia* (Bobbs-Merrill, 1908), p. 168.

180. Robert E. Martin, "Sailors' Battle with Huge Octopus Revives Tales of Dread Sea Monsters." In *Popular Science,* December 1922, p. 37.

> accurate. . . . [The octopus] has, therefore, been long known to naturalists. The ancient Egyptians [represented] it in their hieroglyphics; the Greeks and Romans were well acquainted with it, and since the time of Homer many of the ancient poets and authors have mentioned it in their work.[181]
>
> Unfortunately, octopus research is lagging behind studies of many other sea animals. Studies of fish such as sharks, swordfish, salmon, and many other commercially valuable species usually get the most research money. . . . People still have much to learn about octopuses.[182]
>
> Most of our knowledge . . . comes from studies of just two species, *O. vulgaris* and *Enteroctopus dofleini* . . . due to both their fisheries value and their proximity to major centres of scientific research in the northern hemisphere. At this stage, knowledge of the vast majority of . . . octopus species . . . is considered rudimentary or nonexistent. This is despite reference to octopus . . . dating back more than 2300 years.[183]

STEP THREE: **Write about the repetition**

You already have enough source material to write your final paragraph, about the repetition of the whole process.

Three of the sequences you've read have finished with this sort of paragraph. Those paragraphs have told you:

When the thunderstorm is over, more thunderstorms continue to form.

Bees keep on collecting nectar all summer.

Young salmon start the process all over again.

Your paragraph should tell the reader, in one to three sentences, that once the Octopus eggs have hatched, the whole cycle will begin again.

If you have trouble getting started, ask your instructor for a prompt. When you're finished, show your composition to your instructor.

STEP FOUR: **Add a brief physical description**

Now you'll write a brief description—three to six sentences—of the adult octopus. You'll put this description into your sequence in one of two places:

181. Henry Lee, p. xiv.
182. Hirschi, p 44.
183. R. N. Gibson, R. J. A. Atkinson, and J. D. M. Gordon, *Oceanography and Marine Biology* (CRC Press, 2008), p 107.

1. Right after the paragraph about the mature octopus.
2. Between the scientific knowledge paragraph and the beginning of the step-by-step process.

You can decide where the paragraph sounds most natural.

To describe an octopus, use the model for a scientific description of an object or phenomenon. You can take a minute to review that chart in the Reference section of your Composition Notebook.

When you write this description, use the removed impersonal point of view.

Use any details from the source material you've already seen, plus the paragraphs and photos below:

> The octopus has eight arms, joined at their bases by a web and surrounding a beaked mouth. These arms can be regrown if they are lost in a fight. . . . [T]heir bodies are short and rounded instead of streamlined. The two large eyes are located at the top of the body sack. . . . The common octopus, *O. vulgaris* . . . may exceptionally reach a span of 10 feet (3 meters) but is usually much smaller.[184]

> The octopus has three hearts that pump blue blood. It has a huge pouch-shaped head that holds all its internal organs and a mouth. It has no ears and can't hear, but it has two highly developed eyes that can swivel to see in all directions. It has eight powerful tentacles, or arms. . . . Inside the mouth is a sharp parrotlike beak. The beak is used to bite prey and inject it with paralyzing, flesh-dissolving saliva before tearing it to pieces . . . Because it has neither bones nor shell, the octopus can compress itself to about a thirtieth of its width and squeeze through narrow openings. . . . By contracting skin cells filled with pigment, an octopus can completely change both its color and texture to match its background in only half a second. It will also turn white with fear or red with rage.[185]

Credit: Cigdem Sean Cooper/ Shutterstock.com

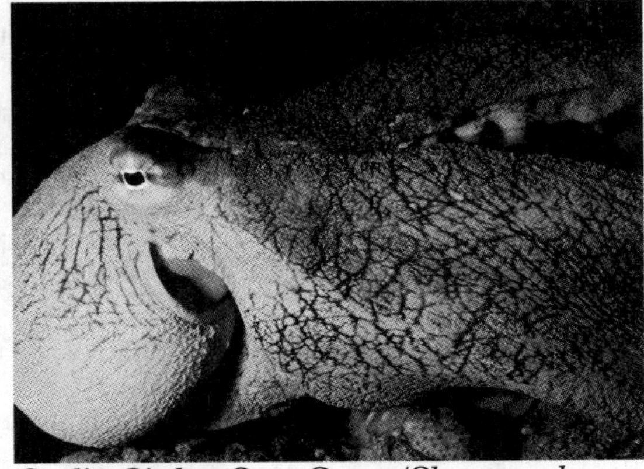

Credit: Cigdem Sean Cooper/Shutterstock.com

---

184. Maurice Burton and Robert Burton, *The International Wildlife Encyclopedia*, Vol. 1 (BCP Publications, 1969), p. 1779.
185. Dan Greenburg, *Attack of the Giant Octopus* (Spotlight, 2009), pp. 58–59.

STEP FIVE: **Put the composition together**

Now put your composition together in the following order:

Introduction
Scientific knowledge
(Description)
Step-by-step process
(Or description here)
Repetition

Read it out loud, checking for grammatical errors and awkward sentences.
When you are finished, show your composition to your instructor.

Day Four: Copia Exercise

Focus: Review transforming sentences

Today, you'll review what you've already learned about transforming sentences. Take a few minutes now to read down your Sentence Variety chart.

STEP ONE: **Read**

Read the following excerpt, adapted from the accounts of a nineteenth-century naturalist. As you read, underline any phrases that can be easily transformed, using the principles you've already learned. ("Easily" means that the transformation doesn't sound incredibly awkward and stilted.)

You may find this helpful:

There are two adjectives which can become nouns.

There is one active verb that can become passive, and one passive verb that can become active.

There is one infinitive that can be turned into a participle.

> Professor Beale, a distinguished naturalist, was searching for shells on a North Pacific island when he found a small octopus, creeping with its eight tentacles over some rocks towards the sea. Curious to find out how strong the animal was, the professor tried to stop its progress by pulling on one of its tentacles. Finally, with a huge effort and a jerk, he separated the octopus from the rock. The moment the arms came free, the octopus flew directly at the naturalist

> and fixed with the same strength on his bare arm. When the creature was finally pried away, its powerful suckers had drawn blood wherever they attached.[186]

If you cannot find the five phrases to be transformed, ask your instructor.

STEP TWO: **Transform sentences**

Rewrite the excerpt on your own paper, transforming each marked sentence. When you are finished, show your work to your instructor.

186. Freely adapted from *Appleton's Journal*, Vol. 11 (D. Appleton & Co., 1874), p. 146.

Part IV

BEGINNING LITERARY CRITICISM: PROSE WRITING ABOUT STORIES WEEKS 23–26

Overview of Weeks 23–26

You should have one last blank section left in your notebook. Label it "Literary Criticism."

Up until now, you've been writing brief compositions in history and science and practicing your outlining. But the next four weeks will introduce a different kind of writing. You'll learn how to write *about* stories and poems.

The process of actually *writing* stories and poems is "creative writing." But when you write about your *opinion* of a story or poem, that's "literary criticism." Basic literary criticism is a type of writing that you'll be asked to do in high school and college—even if you're not an English major. Even engineering students and mathematicians have to know how to write a basic piece of literary criticism.

When you do literary criticism, you start out by looking at how stories are put together: what makes them gripping or boring, how the plots unfold, how the writer convinces you to care about the characters, why some stories are satisfying and others aren't.

In the next four weeks, you'll begin to build some of the very basic skills needed for more advanced literary criticism.

Week 23: Hero/Villain, Protagonist/Antagonist

Day One: Read

Focus: Reading

The first step in doing literary criticism is to read the story. *All* you have to do today is read the story. You should go to a comfortable place and read it for enjoyment. Don't criticize it; don't have an opinion about it; don't be thinking about what you might have to write in the next lessons. Just read.

STEP ONE: **Understand the background**

The first story you'll read for this unit is "Rikki-Tikki-Tavi" by Rudyard Kipling. The story is found in Appendix III.

Rudyard Kipling was born in 1865. His parents were English, but Kipling was born in Bombay, India. At that time, much of India was controlled by the British Empire. The British government sent colonists from England to live in India, and the Indian government was controlled by British officials and the British army. Many writers at Kipling's time wrote about English families who lived in India. (You may have read *A Little Princess* by Frances Hodgson Burnett. Sara Crewe's father is an Englishman living in India who sends his daughter back to England to school.)

Kipling died in 1936, at the age of 70. He wrote *The Jungle Book, Kim, Captains Courageous,* many other short stories, and poems.

STEP TWO: **Read**

Read and enjoy.

Eat a cookie while you're reading.

Day Two: Think

Focus: Hero and villain, protagonist and antagonist, conflict

Today, you'll examine how this story works; tomorrow, you'll write about the story.

It's always easier to write about a piece of literature if you've talked about it first. Putting your ideas into spoken words is a little easier than putting your ideas directly down on paper.

In Steps Two–Four below, you'll see lines and definitions. In each of these steps, your instructor will carry on a dialogue with you. At the end of each dialogue, you'll write a brief observation on the lines. These observations will help you construct your brief essay tomorrow.

STEP ONE: **Identify the characters**

On a piece of scratch paper, list all of the characters in the story—even the minor ones—in two columns.

There is a very basic division in this story: it has two different kinds of characters. What are they? Identify them, and write this at the top of each column.

When you're finished, you should have a short column and a long column. Check your work with your instructor.

STEP TWO: **Identify the protagonist**

hero/heroine: a central character with admirable qualities
protagonist: the character who wants to get, become, or accomplish something

____

____

____

____

STEP THREE: **Identify the antagonist**

antagonist: the character, force, or circumstance that opposes the protagonist
villain: an antagonist with evil motives

____

____

____

____

____

STEP FOUR: **Identify the conflict**

conflict: the clash between protagonist and antagonist

____

____

____

____

____

STEP FIVE: **Begin the Literary Terms chart**

On the top of a blank piece of paper, write "Literary Terms." Underneath, write the terms learned in this lesson, along with the definitions provided. Place the chart in the Reference section of your notebook.

Day Three: Write

Focus: Writing about the story

Today, you'll write your first (short) essay of literary criticism.

This essay will have two parts: a brief summary of the story and three paragraphs discussing the protagonist, antagonist, and conflict.

STEP ONE: **Write the summary**

Begin by writing a narrative summary of the story on your scratch paper, just as if you were writing one of the narrations you practiced earlier in the year. This summary should be at least three but not more than eight sentences long.

If you have trouble, ask your instructor for help. When you are finished, check your summary with your instructor.

STEP TWO: **Write the analysis**

Now answer the following questions in two short paragraphs:

First paragraph:

1. Who is the protagonist? What does he want? Why?
   Hint: try not to use the word "protagonist" in your paragraph.
2. Who is the antagonist? What does he/they want? Why?
   Hint: don't use the word "antagonist"!

Second paragraph:

3. How do these wants result in conflict? In what scenes does this conflict most clearly appear?

When you are finished, show your work to your instructor.

STEP THREE: **Assemble the essay**

Compare the analysis with the narrative summary. They are similar—but while a narrative summary tells you what happened, an analysis tells you *why*. Your narrative summary *might* have mentioned what the cobras wanted, or what Rikki-tikki-tavi wanted, but it could still be a perfectly good narrative summary if you didn't mention either.

Look carefully at the beginning of the narrative summary. There is information in this first sentence (or maybe the first two sentences) that does not appear in your analysis. What is this information? Take that sentence(s) and make it the first line of your first paragraph. This sentence "sets the scene" for your analysis by telling the reader who the characters are.

When you are finished, read your essay out loud. If any sentences sound awkward, correct them. Show your final essay to your instructor.

Day Four: Literary Language

Focus: Synecdoche

In previous lessons, you've studied two major kinds of figurative language: metaphors and similes. Remember, a simile compares two things *explicitly* by using "like" or "as," or otherwise spelling out for you that figurative language is being used:

like ruddy smears upon the palpable brown air

A metaphor doesn't announce itself by using the words "like" or "as," or by saying that one thing "seems like" or "resembles" another. Instead, the writer simply speaks about one thing in terms of another:

the houses opposite were mere phantoms

Today you'll learn about a particular kind of metaphor called *synecdoche* (pronounced sih-NEK-du-kee).

STEP ONE: **Understand synecdoche**

Read the following passage from "Rikki-Tikki-Tavi" out loud:

> Without waiting for breakfast, Rikki-tikki ran to the thornbush where Darzee was singing a song of triumph at the top of his voice. The news of Nag's death was all over the garden, for the sweeper had thrown the body on the rubbish-heap.
>
> "Oh, you stupid tuft of feathers!" said Rikki-tikki angrily. "Is this the time to sing?"

When Rikki becomes angry with the bird Darzee, what does he call him? Underline the phrase "stupid tuft of feathers."

Synecdoche is a particular kind of metaphor in which a writer uses *part* of a thing to represent the *whole*. The bird Darzee *has* tufts of feathers, but when Rikki uses one part of Darzee as a name for the whole bird, he is using synecdoche.

You have probably heard synecdoche many times without knowing it. When a sea captain in a book or movie calls "All hands on deck!" he is using synecdoche. What he really means is "All sailors on deck!" But the sailors have hands, and their hands are the most important part of them—so he calls for their *hands* (the part) when he really wants *the whole sailor.* If a hero in a story shouts "Beware my blade!" what he really means is "Watch out for my sword!" or "Watch out for my skill with the sword!" "Blade" is just one *part* of the *whole* sword.

Wise sayings and proverbs often use synecdoche. In the Old Testament proverb "A lying tongue hates its victims," "lying tongue" is one body part of a person who tells lies. Using "lying tongue" in place of the whole person highlights one particular characteristic of that person. In the Danish proverb "A hearth of your own is worth gold," "hearth" stands for "your own home"—a hearth (fireplace) is just one part of that home.

STEP TWO: **Add to the Literary Terms chart**

On your Literary Terms chart, write the following three definitions:

simile: a comparison that uses "like," "as," or similar words
metaphor: a comparison that speaks of one thing in terms of another
synecdoche: a kind of metaphor that uses a part to represent the whole

STEP THREE: **Identify synecdoche**

In the following sentences, underline the words or phrases that use synecdoche. On the line next to each sentence, write the name of the whole that the word or phrase refers to. The first is done for you.

In came Mrs. Fezziwig, one vast substantial smile. In came the three Misses Fezziwig, beaming and lovable.
—Charles Dickens, *A Christmas Carol* ______Mrs. Fezziwig herself______

The uncle sat down with his niece and went over the individual qualities of the many suitors who sought her hand.
—Miguel de Cervantes, *Don Quixote* ____________________

Some men never enter a church door til they die.
—English proverb ____________________

The White House claimed that President Nixon was "under great strain."
—W. Dale Nelson, *Who Speaks for the President?* ____________________

The third fleet, equipped by the Goths in the ports of Bosphorus, consisted of five hundred sails.
—Edward Gibbon, *The Decline and Fall of the Roman Empire* ____________________

There were eager ears, understanding ears, stubborn ears, and ignorant ears which failed to make sense of what he was saying.
—Ronald Blythe, *Talking to the Neighbours* ____________________

New faces greet me at the door.
—*Scribners Monthly,* Vol. 22 ____________________

All around him, he saw small farmers suffering: too many mouths to feed and never enough bread.
—David Laskin, *The Long Way Home* ____________________

Week 24: Hero/Villain Protagonist/Antagonist

Day One: Read

Focus: Reading

STEP ONE: **Understand the background**

This week, you'll read the short story "The Necklace" by Guy de Maupassant (pronounced *ghee duh moh pah SAWHN*). The story is found in Appendix III.

Guy de Maupassant and Rudyard Kipling lived at the same time; de Maupassant was born in 1850, so he was 15 years older than Kipling. He died in 1893, at the early age of 42.

Maupassant (his full name was Henri René Albert Guy de Maupassant) was a French writer, famous for his short stories. "The Necklace," one of his best-known stories, is set in Paris.

The French names in the story might not be familiar to you. The pronunciations are below. Try saying them out loud a few times before you read.

Georges Ramponneau	*Zhorzh RAM pon no*
M. and Mme. Loisel	*MUH syuh* and *MAH dahm Lwazel*
Mathilde	*ma TEEL duh*
Mme. Forestier	*MAH dahm for ES tee ay*
Seine	*Sen*
coupés	*COOP ay*
Rue des Martyrs	*roo deh MAH tear*
Palais Royal	*pah lay roy AHL*
francs	*fhraw*
Champs Élysées	*SHAHN zay lee zay*
Jeanne	*Zhahn*

STEP TWO: **Read**

Read and enjoy.

Day Two: Think

Focus: Hero and villain, protagonist and antagonist, conflict

Today, you'll examine how this story works; tomorrow, you'll write about the story.

In Steps Two–Four your instructor will carry on a dialogue with you. At the end of each dialogue, you'll write a brief observation on the lines. These observations will help you construct your brief essay tomorrow.

STEP ONE: **Identify the characters**

There are only three characters in this story who have names and speeches. List them on a piece of scratch paper.

STEP TWO: **Identify the protagonist**

____

____

____

____

STEP THREE: **Identify the antagonist**

____

____

____

____

STEP FOUR: **Identify the conflict**

____

____

____

____

Day Three: Write

Focus: Writing about the story

Like last week's essay, this assignment will have two parts: a brief summary of the story and three paragraphs discussing the protagonist, antagonist, and conflict.

STEP ONE: **Write the summary**

Begin by writing a brief narrative summary of the story on your scratch paper. This summary should be four to eight sentences long. You don't need to talk about the characters' wants and plans because you'll cover this in the second part of the essay; focus on what actually *happens* in the story (this will help you keep the story short).

If you have trouble, ask your instructor for help. When you are finished, check your summary with your instructor.

STEP TWO: **Write the analysis**

Now write about the following topics in three short paragraphs. You may draw on the notes you made in the last writing session.

First Paragraph

Describe what Madame Loisel, the protagonist, wants. At the end of the paragraph, tell briefly how the necklace fits into these wants.

Second Paragraph

Describe what Madame Loisel, the antagonist, wants. Begin your paragraph by mentioning the loss of the necklace. End the paragraph by describing the actions that Madame Loisel, the antagonist, takes.

Third Paragraph

Describe the outcome of the conflict between Madame Loisel's two sides. This paragraph can be as short as one sentence, but you can also choose to make it longer.

When are you are finished, show your analysis to your instructor.

STEP THREE: **Assemble the essay**

Compare the analysis with the narrative summary. Notice that the two pieces of writing do *not* overlap nearly as much as the narrative summary and analysis from last week. This is because a narrative summary describes actions (external, outside the character), and an analysis describes wants and desires (internal, inside the character's head). The real conflict in this story is internal, inside Madame Loisel herself, so the narrative summary does not tell you everything you need to know about the conflict.

Make your narrative summary the first paragraph of your essay. You should now have a four-paragraph essay. Read the essay out loud. Eliminate any unnecessary repetition. If any sentences sound awkward, correct them.

Show your final essay to your instructor.

Day Four: Literary Language

Focus: Inversion/surprise

STEP ONE: **Understand inversion**

The first time you read "The Necklace," you were probably surprised by the last two sentences. Like Madame Loisel, you believe through most of the story that the diamond necklace is real. Like Madame Loisel, you don't find out the truth until the very end.

This is called *inversion*, and a story that uses inversion is often called a *surprise story*.

When you read a story, you often have information that the main characters don't. For example, in "Rikki-Tikki-Tavi," you discovered something about Nag that Rikki doesn't know:

> . . . though Rikki-tikki had never met a live cobra before, his mother had fed him on dead ones, and he knew that all a grown mongoose's business in life was to fight and eat snakes. Nag knew that too and, at the bottom of his cold heart, he was afraid.

Because you know that Nag is afraid, it isn't really a surprise to you when Rikki is able to kill him.

But in "The Necklace," neither you *nor* Madame Loisel know that the necklace is fake. You spend the whole story believing that she is doing something necessary and noble in replacing the necklace with real diamonds. In the last two sentences, both you and Madame Loisel find out how pointless her ten years of struggle have been. Your whole opinion of her actions changes—or *inverts.*

When a writer uses inversion, he or she withholds information until the end. When you receive this information, your point of view suddenly changes. To invert something is to turn it inside out or upside down; inversion causes you to turn your initial opinion of the story completely around because you have received new information.

In "The Necklace," the inversion is very sudden and unexpected. But sometimes inversion can be more gradual, as you and the character slowly discover together that your original point of view was wrong.

The American short story writer O. Henry[187] was a master of inversion. Some of his stories have sudden inversions, but others are more gradual. "The Ransom of Red Chief" is a surprise story in which the inversion takes place over the whole course of the story.

Take some time now to read "The Ransom of Red Chief" in Appendix III. After you have finished, read Step Two below.

You'll notice that the narrator uses a number of unusual words that you may not be familiar with. This is part of his character (and he doesn't always use them correctly either). You don't need to know the meaning of all of the words to enjoy the story. Mark words that you don't know lightly with a pencil and keep reading. When you've finished, you can look up any words that have made the story unclear to you.

STEP TWO: **Understand the surprise story**

The inversion in this surprise story takes place in several steps. The first comes almost as soon as Sam and Bill kidnap their victim. Instead of being frightened, the boy starts having "the time of his life."

The second inversion comes when Bill, instead of frightening the boy, becomes so frightened that "from that moment" his "spirit was broken."

The third inversion comes when the boy's father asks for the ransom—instead of paying it.

And the fourth and final inversion comes when Bill and Sam decide to pay the ransom just to get rid of Red Chief.

By the time Bill and Sam hand over the money and run, the kidnapping story has been completely inverted. They are the captives—not the the captors! But you're not suddenly surprised, because O. Henry has been leading you up to this moment all along.

187. "O. Henry" is a pen name (the invented name a writer uses for his work). His real name was William Sydney Porter.

STEP THREE: **Add to the Literary Terms chart**

On your Literary Terms chart, write the following two definitions:

> inversion (plot): an unexpected revelation that reverses the meaning or action of the story
> surprise story: a story that uses inversion to change the reader's point of view

("Plot" is inserted in parentheses because "inversion" can also be used as a grammatical term.)

WEEK 25: SUPPORTING CHARACTERS

Day One: Read

Focus: Reading

In the last two weeks, you've practiced answering basic literary analysis questions about complete short stories—stories that have a beginning, a middle, and an end.

But you can also use these same questions to write about *part* of a book. Often, you'll find it useful to be able to write about a book you haven't finished yet. Books that are long or difficult may take weeks (or more) to read from beginning to end. Writing about each section or chapter as you finish it can help you remember what you've read. And if you need to write a long and detailed paper about a long book, your short essays can be the rough material you draw from. Using short essays as "notes" for a longer essay is much less intimidating than creating a long essay from scratch.

You may also find it interesting to see how your point of view about particular characters changes from the time you first encounter them, until the end of the book.

STEP ONE: **Understand the background**

This week, you'll read a single chapter—Chapter III—from *Anne of Green Gables* by Lucy Maud Montgomery. The chapter is in Appendix III.

Lucy Maud Montgomery (1874–1942) was Canadian and wrote many of her stories and novels about Prince Edward Island, the smallest province in Canada. *Anne of Green Gables* was the first novel about the orphan Anne Shirley. Set in the late 1800s, it told how Anne Shirley came from the orphanage (called the "orphan asylum") to live with the childless Marilla Cuthbert and her brother Matthew. Montgomery later wrote seven more novels about Anne and her family.

In Chapter I of *Anne of Green Gables*, Marilla and Matthew ask their friend Mrs. Spencer to go to the orphan asylum in Nova Scotia, about two hundred miles away, and pick out a boy who can come and help them on the farm. At this time, it was common for couples to give a home to orphans in exchange for work; the orphans weren't formally adopted, but in better homes, they became part of the family. (In worse situations, they were treated like unpaid servants.)

The boy is supposed to arrive on the train from Nova Scotia. But when Matthew arrives at the station, he finds that Mrs. Spencer has misunderstood their request. Instead of a boy, the orphan asylum has sent a little girl. Chapter II describes her as a "child of about eleven, garbed in a very short, very tight, very ugly dress of yellowish-gray wincey. She wore a faded brown sailor hat and beneath the hat, extending down her back, were two braids of very thick, decidedly red hair. Her face was small, white and thin, also much freckled; her mouth was large and so were her eyes, which looked green in some lights and moods and gray in others."

Matthew knows that Marilla won't be happy about this, but he can't leave the little girl alone in the train station, so he brings her home for the night. On the way, her imagination and cheerful conversation win him over.

In Chapter III, the two arrive back at Green Gables, where Marilla Cuthbert is waiting for Matthew to bring home a boy.

STEP TWO: **Read**

Read and enjoy.

Day Two: Think

Focus: Shifting protagonists and antagonists; supporting character

Today, you'll examine how this story works; tomorrow, you'll write about the story.

In Steps One–Three your instructor will carry on a dialogue with you. At the end of each dialogue, you'll write a brief observation on the lines. These observations will help you construct your brief essay tomorrow.

STEP ONE: **Identify the first protagonist-antagonist pair**

____

____

STEP TWO: Identify the second protagonist-antagonist pair

STEP THREE: Identify the supporting character

supporting character: a character who helps, supports, or hinders the protagonist or antagonist

STEP FOUR: Add to the Literary Terms chart

Write the definition of "supporting character" on your Literary Terms chart, using the same format as your other definitions.

Day Three: Write

Focus: Writing about the chapter

By now, you should be familiar with the structure of the essay you'll be writing: first, a brief summary of the chapter; then, several paragraphs discussing the protagonist, antagonist, and conflict. Today, you'll also add a paragraph about the supporting character.

STEP ONE: **Write the summary**

Begin by writing a brief narrative summary of the chapter on your scratch paper. This summary should be three to six sentences long. You don't need to talk about the characters' wants because you'll cover this in the second part of the essay; focus on what actually *happens* in the chapter. You will need to include some of the information given about Chapters I and II of the book.

Remember that chapter titles go in quotation marks but that book titles are italicized (or underlined).

When you are finished, check your summary with your instructor.

STEP TWO: **Write the analysis**

Now write about the following topics in three short paragraphs. Each paragraph must be at least two sentences long but can be as long as five or six sentences. You may draw on the notes you made in the last writing session.

First Paragraph

Discuss what Anne, as the protagonist, wants; then describe what opposes her.

Second Paragraph

Discuss what Marilla, as the protagonist, wants; then describe what opposes her.

Third Paragraph

Discuss how Matthew, as a supporting character, supports or hinders at least one of the other characters.

When you are finished, show your analysis to your instructor.

STEP THREE: **Assemble the essay and provide transitions**

Make your narrative summary the first paragraph of your essay. You should now have a four-paragraph essay. Eliminate any unnecessary repetition.

The paragraphs all make sense individually, but they probably don't seem to flow into each other. The narrative summary isn't related to the three paragraphs, and although the three paragraphs all make sense, the reader might wonder: Why is the writer telling me this?

In order to make a literary essay readable, you may need to provide transitions. For example, imagine that the first two paragraphs in your essay are:

NOTE: DO NOT READ THE FOLLOWING UNLESS YOU HAVE FINISHED YOUR OWN SUMMARY AND ANALYSIS!

> Anne Shirley comes to Green Gables by mistake. When she arrives, she finds out that Marilla Cuthbert wants a boy instead. Anne is crushed, but Marilla insists that she only wants a boy—even though Matthew changes his mind and suggests that Anne stay.
>
> Anne desperately wants to stay at Green Gables, but Marilla insists that they need to have a boy instead. She tells Anne that there is no place for a girl at Green Gables.

Individually, those paragraphs are fine. But you need to explain to the reader why you're going back, in the second paragraph, to talk some more about Anne. After all, the reader probably figured out from the first paragraph that Anne wants to stay at Green Gables.

To do this, you need to provide a *transition.* Your transition should explain to the reader that you're getting ready to examine the author's use of literary techniques.

At the beginning of your second paragraph, insert a sentence that expresses one the following:

> In *Anne of Green Gables,* Lucy Maud Montgomery tells more than one story.
>
> "Marilla Cuthbert Is Surprised" tells us about two protagonists and a supporting character.

You may use one of these sentences, but try to rephrase and use synonyms so that you do not repeat the *exact* words. You may also write a sentence of your own.

Now read your essay out loud. If any sentences sound awkward, correct them.

When you are finished, show your essay to your instructor.

Day Four: Using Direct Quotes

Focus: Using direct quotes to support conclusions

Today, you will examine the use of direct quotes in a literary essay and will then go back to add quotes to yesterday's composition.

STEP ONE: Understand the use of direct quotes in a literary essay

Read the following excerpts from essays about *Tom Sawyer, The Once and Future King,* and *Ozma of Oz* by L. Frank Baum.

> Tom's struggle with the adult world is brought out in his relationship with Aunt Polly, who has to play the dual role of a loving mother and a strict father, and she expresses her dilemma: "Every time I let him off, my conscience does hurt me so, and every time I hit him my old heart most breaks."[188]

> Merlin teaches Wart the important lessons of life he will need when he is king: how to use his imagination and how to use his intellect to outwit the strong who "will try to conquer you." Other lessons are "Always look before you leap," "Love is a powerful thing," and "Get an education" by learning to read.[189]

> The book starts with Dorothy Gale of Kansas on a boat, then being washed overboard and clinging to a chicken-coop, whose only other occupant is a hen named, by Dorothy, Billina. Unexpectedly, the hen can talk, and when Dorothy says, "I thought hens could only cluck and cackle," the hen replies, "I've clucked and cackled all my life, and never spoken a word before this morning, that I can remember. But when you asked a question, a minute ago, it seemed the most natural thing in the world to answer you. So I spoke, and I seem to keep on speaking, just as you and other human beings do. Strange, isn't it?" Thus, at the beginning of the book, the question of the defining quality of language—humans have language, and hens generally don't—is put before us.[190]

---

188. K. Balachandran, *Critical Essays on American Literature* (Sarup & Sons, 2005), p. 172.
189. Kevin J. Harty, *Cinema Arthuriana* (McFarland & Co., 2002), p. 119.
190. Ronald Chrisley and Sander Begeer, *Artificial Intelligence: Critical Concepts,* Vol. 1 (Routledge, 2000), p. 148.

In each one of these paragraphs, the writer makes a statement about the book:

> "Aunt Polly has to be both loving mother and strict father."
>
> "Merlin teaches Wart the lessons he will need to be king."
>
> "The difference between animals and humans is the ability to talk."

But instead of just making the statement, the writer gives you *proof* for it—by quoting directly from the book itself.

From now on, whenever you write a literary essay, you should include at least one direct quote from the book. Direct quotes tell the reader that you're not just making up the points in your essay; they're actually based on something *in* the literature itself.

For example, the third paragraph of your literary analysis of *Anne of Green Gables* might have sounded something like this:

> Matthew is on Anne's side. He wants her to stay, and he thinks that he and Marilla could be good for Anne.

Compare that paragraph with *this* one:

> Matthew is on Anne's side. He wants her to stay; he tells Marilla, "It's kind of a pity to send her back when she's so set on staying here." He also thinks that he and Marilla could be good for Anne. When Marilla says, "What good would she be to us?" Matthew answers, "We might be some good to her."

The second paragraph is not only more interesting, but sounds more authoritative (as though the writer really knows what he's talking about).

STEP TWO: Review the rules for using direct quotes

A direct quote can be either a quote from the story itself ("And to bed, when she had put her dishes away, went Marilla, frowning most resolutely") or a speech made by one of the characters ("Oh, she can talk fast enough. I saw that at once").

The rules for using direct quotes are similar to the rules for using dialogue—but not exactly the same. Read through the following rules now. Don't worry about memorizing these rules. Just refer back to them as you use direct quotes in your own work, and the correct form will soon become familiar to you.

1. Use quotation marks to surround an exact quote.
   "To bed went Matthew."

2. If the exact quote contains dialogue, use double quotation marks around the exact quote and single quotation marks around the dialogue.
   " 'There wasn't any boy,' said Matthew wretchedly. 'There was only her.' "

3. A direct quote should never just sit in the middle of a paragraph as an independent sentence, with no tag. (In quotations, the "dialogue tag" is called an "attribution tag.") Don't write
   Matthew wanted Anne to stay. "Well now, she's a real interesting little thing," persisted Matthew.

Instead, write,
   Matthew wanted Anne to stay. When Marilla said that Anne should go back to the asylum, Matthew said, "Well now, she's a real interesting little thing."

4. If an attribution tag ("the author writes" or "Anne said") comes before a direct quote, use a comma after the tag:
   The author tells us, "Anne looked around her wistfully."

UNLESS the direct quote is preceded by "that":
   The author tells us that "Anne looked around her wistfully."

5. If there is no attribution tag, just put direct quotes around the quote but do not use a comma; the quote can simply become part of your sentence.
   When Anne was alone in the room she "looked around her wistfully."

6. The punctuation at the end of the speech itself goes *inside* the closing quotation mark. Exceptions: exclamation points and question marks go inside the closing quote if they are part of the original quote, but outside of the closing quotation mark if not.
   When Anne looked around, she saw walls that were "painfully bare and staring"!
   The braided rug was one that "Anne had never seen before."

(In the original story, "painfully bare and staring" has no exclamation point after it.)

STEP THREE: **Add direct quotes to your essay**

Now go back to the essay you assembled in the last writing session. Add at least one direct quote to each of the three literary analysis paragraphs. These direct quotes should not be more than 12–15 words each but should be at least 4–6 words.

When you are finished, check the punctuation of your quotes against the rules above. Once you have proofread your essay, show it to your instructor.

Week 26: Idea Stories

Day One: Read

Focus: Reading

STEP ONE: **Understand the background**

Today's story, "The Bowmen," was written by the Welsh author Arthur Machen (1863–1947). Machen was best known as a writer of suspense and fantasy.

You're probably familiar with the word *fantasy,* but you might not know that "fantasy" is a formal *genre label.* "Genre" means "category." It is the name we use for a particular type or form of literature; works that use similar forms, or have similar purposes, belong in the same genre. *Mystery* is a genre, because mysteries have the same form (a puzzle is solved by the end of the book). *Comedy* is a genre, because although funny stories may have very different forms, they all have the same purpose—to make you laugh.

Fantasy takes place in a world that doesn't exist. The writer Orson Scott Card defined fantasy as "all stories that take place in a setting contrary to known reality."[191] A world where a ring can make you invisible is a fantastical world. So is a world where animals talk, people fly, magical spells work, and swords are drawn from stone.

"The Bowmen" is a fantasy story set in a very real time: World War I. World War I was particularly devastating for Britain (of which Wales is a part); almost a million British soldiers were killed in the war. Machen wrote the story in 1914, near the beginning of the war.

There is some British slang in the story that you may not completely understand, but that won't affect your understanding of the story. However, you might want to be familiar with the following terms:

191. Orson Scott Card, *How to Write Science Fiction and Fantasy* (Writers Digest Books, 2001), p. 17.

Allied. World War I was fought between two groups of countries, the Allied Powers (Britain, France, and the Russian Empire) and the Central Powers (the German Empire, the Austro-Hungarian Empire, the Ottoman Empire, and the Kingdom of Bulgaria).

The Retreat of the Eighty Thousand. The British troops were forced to retreat from the French border at the Battle of Mons, on August 23, 1914 (just a month before this story was published).

The Censorship. The British government read the letters sent home by soldiers and crossed out any sentences (or whole paragraphs) that seemed to give away information about the war.

Sedan. Machen uses this term to mean "absolute defeat." In 1870, the French were forced to surrender to the Germans at Sedan, France. This led to the ultimate defeat of France in the Franco-Prussian War. All of Machen's readers in 1914 would have known about Sedan.

Sidney Street. In 1911, London police had a famous shootout on Sidney Street with a group of robbers.

Bisley. The British National Rifle Association used to meet at a field called Bisley Common to practice their shooting.

Agincourt. At the Battle of Agincourt in 1415, an outnumbered English army led by Henry V defeated a much larger French force.

Salient. A salient is a place in a battlefield where the territory held by one army juts into the territory of the other army, like a peninsula. The salient is surrounded by enemy forces on three sides.

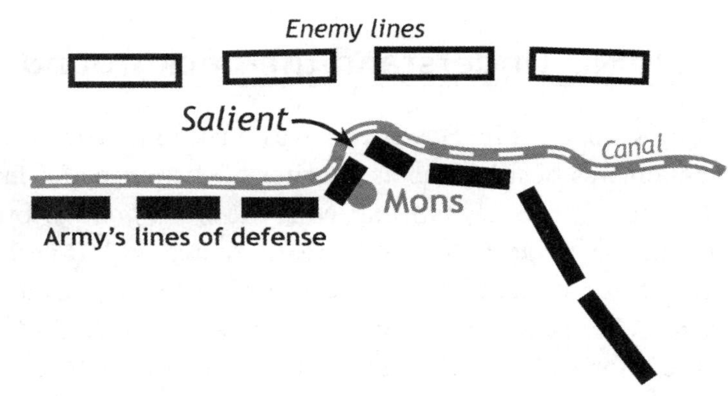

STEP TWO: **Read**

Read and enjoy. The story is in Appendix III.

Day Two: Think

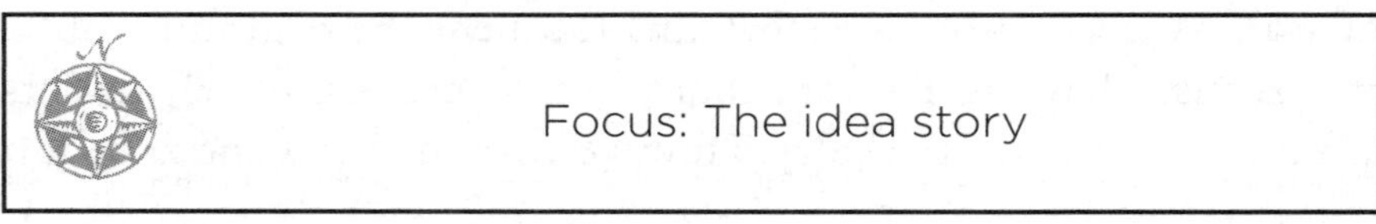

Today, you'll examine how this story works; tomorrow, you'll write about the story.

In Steps One and Two, your instructor will carry on a dialogue with you; you will complete the final step on your own. At the end of each step, write a brief observation on the lines provided.

Note that *St.* is the correct abbreviation for the word "saint." You may write either *Saint George* or *St. George*.

STEP ONE: **Identify the protagonist and antagonist**

STEP TWO: **Identify the idea in the story**

idea story: a story that solves a problem, explores a what-if, or answers a question

"The Bowmen" describes **what** would happen **if** . . .

STEP THREE: **Learn about the story's effect**

An idea story can have a powerful effect on readers. Take a few minutes now and read the following excerpts about the reaction of British readers to "The Bowmen."

> Even though the author vigorously claimed that the tale of "The Bowmen" was entirely fictional . . . this did not prevent the story from spreading as gospel truth all over the country, preached in sermons and reinforced by rumours from the front. To Machen's astonishment, independent witnesses stepped forward corroborating the apparition, but exchanging St. George for angels. . . . [A] stream of newspaper reports, pamphlets, and books in 1915 . . . immortalised the Angels of Mons.[192]

> The . . . Battle of Mons began on August 23, and the British . . . in spite of great heroics . . . were inevitably forced to retreat. The casualties might have been greater, had the troops not been experienced veterans. Meanwhile, back in England, the . . . writer Arthur Machen wrote . . . [a] fictional tale for the *Evening News* in which the retreating troops were assisted by a host of bowmen, the ghosts of Agincourt. Within weeks, rumour had transmogrified Machen's bowmen into the Angels of Mons, who had supposedly hovered overhead just at the point when the Germans were about to launch their final attack, causing them to fall back in fear and amazement. Machen himself was amazed at this turn of events, but the angel story was unstoppable, taking on the status of a legend, and those soldiers lucky enough to return home obligingly reported similar tales of supernatural happenings on the battlefield. There's a painting of the angelic event, by one Marcel Gillis, in the Mons Hotel de Ville.[193]

Now read Arthur Machen's own account of how his story was turned into legend.

> It was in *The Weekly Dispatch* that I saw the awful account of the retreat from Mons. I no longer recollect the details; but I have not forgotten the impression that was then made on my mind. I seemed to see a furnace of torment and death and agony and terror seven times heated, and in the midst of the burning was the British Army. . . . And in the meantime the plot of "The Bowmen" occurred to me. . . . Such as it was, "The Bowmen" appeared in *The Evening News* of September 29th, 1914.

---

192. Stefan Goebel, *The Great War and Medieval Memory: War, Remembrance, and Medievalism in Britain and Germany, 1914–1940* (Cambridge University Press, 2007), p. 247.

193. Martin Dunford and Phil Lee, *Belgium & Luxembourg* (Rough Guides, 2002), p. 290.

. . . Having written my story, having groaned and growled over it and printed it, I certainly never thought to hear another word of it. . . . But in a few days from its publication the editor of [another newspaper] wrote to me. He wanted to know whether the story had any foundation in fact. I told him that it had no foundation in fact of any kind or sort; I forget whether I added that it had no foundation in rumour but I should think not, since to the best of my belief there were no rumours of heavenly interposition in existence at that time. Certainly I had heard of none. Soon afterwards the editor of [the journal] *Light* wrote asking a like question, and I made him a like reply. It seemed to me that I had stifled any "Bowmen" mythos in the hour of its birth.

A month or two later, I received several requests from editors of parish magazines to reprint the story. I—or, rather, my editor—readily gave permission; and then, after another month or two, the conductor of one of these magazines wrote to me, saying that the February issue containing the story had been sold out, while there was still a great demand for it. Would I allow them to reprint "The Bowmen" as a pamphlet, and would I write a short preface giving the exact authorities for the story? I replied that they might reprint in pamphlet form with all my heart, but that I could not give my authorities, since I had none, the tale being pure invention. The priest wrote again, suggesting—to my amazement—that I must be mistaken, that the main "facts" of "The Bowmen" must be true . . . It seemed that my light fiction had been accepted by the congregation of this particular church as the solidest of facts; and it was then that it began to dawn on me that if I had failed in the art of letters, I had succeeded, unwittingly, in the art of deceit. This happened, I should think, some time in April, and the snowball of rumour that was then set rolling has been rolling ever since, growing bigger and bigger, till it is now swollen to a monstrous size.

It was at about this period that variants of my tale began to be told as authentic histories. At first, these tales betrayed their relation to their original. In several of them the vegetarian restaurant appeared, and St. George was the chief character. In one case an officer—name and address missing—said that there was a portrait of St. George in a certain London restaurant, and that a figure, just like the portrait, appeared to him on the battlefield, and was invoked by him, with the happiest results. . . . Other versions of the story appeared in which a cloud interposed between the

> attacking Germans and the defending British. In some examples the cloud served to conceal our men from the advancing enemy; in others, it disclosed shining shapes which frightened the horses of the pursuing German cavalry.[194]

Finish today's work by making a few notes on the lines below about the story's effect. Write two or three sentences describing how "The Bowmen" affected the English public, and then one or two sentences describing Arthur Machen's reaction. Try to use a few of Machen's own words (in quotes) in your answer.

When you are finished, show your work to your instructor.

194. Arthur Machen, *The Angels of Mons: The Bowmen and Other Legends of the War* (G. P. Putnam's Sons, 1915), pp. 3–12.

Day Three: Write

Focus: Writing about an idea story

Today's essay, like the others you've written, will include a summary and a paragraph or two about the protagonists and antagonists. It will also include two new elements: a brief look at the story's main idea, and a description of the story's effect on its readers.

STEP ONE: **Write the summary**

Begin by writing a brief narrative summary of the story. This summary should be three to five sentences in length. You may find it useful to use some or all of the sentences you wrote in Day Two, Step Two.

In the first sentence, mention both the name of the story and the author.

When you are finished, check your work with your instructor.

STEP TWO: **Write about the idea**

In Day Two, you learned that "The Bowmen" is an idea story. Instead of writing about the protagonist, antagonist, and conflict, you'll use the central paragraphs of your essay to discuss the main idea of the story.

"The Bowmen" describes what would happen if St. George came to help the English. This central part of your essay should tell *why* St. George appeared when he was summoned. The story hints at two reasons. The first has to do with the motto on the plate; the second, with the character qualities of the English and German armies (you've already written briefly about this in Step One of the last lesson, so you may want to make use of those sentences).

Try to write a paragraph of four to six sentences describing why St. George appeared, covering both of these reasons. If you have trouble, ask your instructor for help.

When you are finished, check your work with your instructor.

STEP THREE: **Write about the story's effect**

Now conclude your essay with the paragraph you wrote in Step Three of yesterday's lesson. You should now have a three-paragraph essay.

Read your entire essay out loud. Eliminate any unnecessary repetition. Check your punctuation and spelling. If any sentences sound awkward, correct them.

When you are finished, show your entire essay to your instructor.

Day Four: Reviewing Terms and Forms

Focus: Summarizing a narrative by choosing the main events and listing them chronologically

In this last lesson of the unit, you'll review the literary terms you've used and construct a basic chart to guide you through future essays.

STEP ONE: **Add to the Literary Terms chart**

Write the following definitions on your Literary Terms chart, using the same format as your other definitions.

genre: a particular type or form of literature; works that use similar forms or have similar purposes

fantasy: a genre in which stories are set in a world that doesn't exist

Now choose three colored pencils. Use one colored pencil to represent "character," the second to represent "structure," and the third to represent "language."

With the first colored pencil, underline the definitions of *hero/heroine, protagonist, antagonist, villain,* and *supporting character.* All of these definitions have to do with the characters in stories.

With the second colored pencil, underline the definitions of *conflict, inversion, surprise story, fantasy,* and *genre.* All of these definitions have to do with the ways stories are put together, or structured.

With the third pencil, underline the definitions of *simile, metaphor,* and *synecdoche.* All of these definitions have to do with how words are used within the story.

STEP TWO: **Construct the Essay Chart**

In the last four weeks, you've practiced four different ways to write a literary essay. There are many other ways to write an essay, but following the methods you've been practicing will help you start to write about literature on your own.

Copy the following chart onto your own paper and put it in the Reference section of the Composition Notebook. When you need to write about a novel or story, you can follow the steps on this chart to get you started.

1. Write a basic narrative summary

2. Who is the protagonist? What does he or she want?
   Write several sentences answering these questions.

3. Who or what is keeping the protagonist from getting what he or she wants? What does the antagonist want? Write several sentences answering these questions.

IF
ANSWERS ARE INTERESTING
(CHARACTERS HAVE
REAL STRUGGLES),
then ask

4. What scenes show the conflict between protagonist and antagonist? Write several sentences describing these scenes.

5. Is the protagonist a hero? If so, how do you know? Is the antagonist a villain? If so, how do you know?

6. Is there a supporting character? If so, does he or she help or hinder?

IF
ANSWERS ARE BORING
(CHARACTERS HAVE
SIMPLE WANTS),
then ask

4. Does the story solve a problem, explore a what-if, or answer a question? If so,
   4a. What is the problem? OR
   4b. What is the "what if"? OR
   4c. What is the question?

Part V

RESEARCH WEEKS 27–31

Overview of Weeks 27–31

You now know how to construct a basic outline; how to put together chronological narrations, descriptions, biographical sketches, sequences, and basic literary essays (the topoi); and how to alter sentences with basic transformations of nouns, adjectives, and verbs. Now that you're moving towards the end of this course, you'll review and add to the skills you've learned in the first 26 weeks.

Your focus will be on two skills in particular. First, you've learned how to do a one-level outline, but now you'll begin to work on constructing two-level outlines (a skill you'll continue to develop in the next level of this course). Second, you'll continue to practice the topoi, but you'll now add footnotes and citations to your compositions.

Week 27: Two-Level Outlining

Day One: Introduction to Two-Level Outlining

Focus: Understanding the function of the second level of an outline

STEP ONE: **Understand the two-level outline**

Take a second look now at a passage you first read in Week 2 of this course.

> Five hundred years ago, 60 million bison—or buffalo, as they are more often called—roamed the grasslands of North America. They meant life itself to plains nations like the Blackfoot of what is now southern Alberta. The Blackfoot moved slowly across the land, following the herds and carrying with them everything they had. They hunted deer and antelope, they grew tobacco, and they gathered wild turnip and onion. But for centuries it was the buffalo that provided for the Blackfoot people. Buffalo hides made their tipis and their clothing. Buffalo sinews were their thread. Buffalo bones made clubs and spoons and needles. They even used dried buffalo dung as fuel for their campfires. To the Blackfoot, buffalo meat was "real" meat and nothing else tasted so good. They trusted the buffalo to keep them strong.
>
> The Blackfoot had always gone on foot, using dogs to help carry their goods, for there were no horses in North America until Spanish colonists brought them in the 1500s. Soon after that, plains people captured animals that had gone wild, or stole them in raids. They traded the horses northward and early in the 1700s,

> horses came to the northern plains. Suddenly the Blackfoot were a nation on horseback. How exciting it was, learning to ride a half-wild mustang and galloping off to the horizon![195]

In Week 2, you used this passage to study one-level outlines. Today, you'll use it to see how a two-level outline is constructed.

In a two-level outline, the main Roman-numeral points still sum up the central idea of the paragraph. However, you'll now add *subpoints* under each main point. These subpoints are each given a capital letter:

I. Main point
 A. First subpoint
 B. Second subpoint
 C. Third subpoint
II. Main point
 A. First subpoint
 B. Second subpoint

Each of the subpoints should provide a specific piece of information from the paragraph that relates *directly* to the main idea.

The best way to find subpoints is to first find your main point, and then ask yourself: What additional information does the paragraph give me about each of the people, things, or ideas in the main point?

Let's see how this works for the passage above. For the first paragraph, the main point you chose back in Week 2 might have sounded something like this:

I. The Blackfoot people used buffalo for food, clothing, and many other purposes.

There are two major people, things, or ideas in that point: the Blackfoot people, and the buffalo. In order to find your subpoints, ask two questions: What other important thing does the paragraph tell me about buffalo? And what other important thing does the paragraph tell me about the Blackfoot's *use* of the buffalo?

The answers to those questions are: The paragraph tells you how many buffalo there were—60 million. And it also tells you that the Blackfoot used the buffalo to keep them strong.

The two-level outline of the paragraph might read like this:

I. The Blackfoot people used buffalo for food, clothing, and other purposes.
 A. There were 60 million buffalo in North America.
 B. The Blackfoot relied on the buffalo to keep them strong.

195. Janet Lunn and Christopher Moore, *The Story of Canada* (Key Porter Books, 1992), p. 313.

Often, beginners will try to to use the capital-letter subpoints to give specific details about the paragraph:

I. The Blackfoot people used buffalo for food, clothing, and other purposes.
  A. They hunted deer and antelope too.
  B. They made clothing from buffalo.
  C. They ate buffalo meat.
  D. They made clubs and spoons and needles from buffalo bones.

These are actually details about exactly *how* the Blackfoot used the buffalo to keep themselves strong. Details like this would only appear in a three-level outline, which you won't practice until a later level of this course.

I. The Blackfoot people used buffalo for food, clothing, and other purposes.
  A. There were 60 million buffalo in North America.
  B. The Blackfoot relied on the buffalo to keep them strong.
    1. They made clothing from buffalo.
    2. They ate buffalo meat.
    3. They made clubs and spoons and needles from buffalo bones.

Try to remember this (you'll get plenty of practice in the next few lessons): Each capital-letter subpoint should make an independent statement relating directly to something in the main Roman-numeral point. So you'll need to leave out unnecessary detail.

A two-level outline of the second paragraph might begin with the main point "The Blackfoot tribe learned to use horses in the 1700s." In that case, the subpoints should answer the questions "What is the most important additional information that this paragraph gives me about the Blackfoot? What is the most important additional information that it gives me about the horses?"

An acceptable outline might look like this:

II. The Blackfoot tribe learned to use horses in the 1700s.
  A. They had always gone on foot before.
  B. The horses were brought to North America by Spanish colonists.

STEP TWO: **Practice the two-level outline**

Read the following paragraph, taken from a history of East Asia, describing life in China after the Mongols invaded and seized power.

> Life in China under the Mongols was much like life in China under earlier alien rulers. Once order was restored, people did their best to get on with their lives. Some suffered real hardship. Many farmers had their lands

> expropriated;[196] others were forced into slavery or serfdom, perhaps transported to a distant city, never to see their family again. Yet people still spoke Chinese, followed Chinese customary practices in arranging their children's marriages or dividing their family property, made offerings at local temples, celebrated New Year and other customary festivals. . . . Teachers still taught students the classics; scholars continued to write books; and books continued to be printed.[197]

You will now construct a two-level outline of this paragraph. Begin by finding the main point and writing it down, using the Roman numeral I. When you are finished, check your work with your instructor. If you have difficulty, ask your instructor for help.

Once you have found the main point of the paragraph, your instructor will help you find your subpoints.

Day Two: Outlining Exercise

Focus: Finding the central topics and subtopics in each paragraph of a chronological narrative in history

STEP ONE: **Read**

Read the following excerpt about the beginning months of World War I, from *The World War* by Albert E. McKinley et al.

> As soon as the German leaders had determined upon war, their military machine was set in motion. The plan was first to attack France and crush her armies before the slow-moving Russians could get a force together; and then, after the defeat of France, to turn to the east and subdue Russia. The success of the plan was dependent upon the swift overthrow of France; and this in turn hinged upon the question as to whether German armies could invade France before the French were ready. Speed was the essential thing, and in order to gain speed Germany committed one of the greatest crimes in modern history.

196. Expropriated: taken possession of by the government, taken away from private owners for public or government use. (From the Latin *proprietas,* ownership, and *ex*, from, out of.)

197. Patricia Buckley Ebrey, Anne Walthall, and James B. Palais, *Pre-Modern East Asia to 1800: A Cultural, Social, and Political History* (Houghton Mifflin, 2006), p. 198.

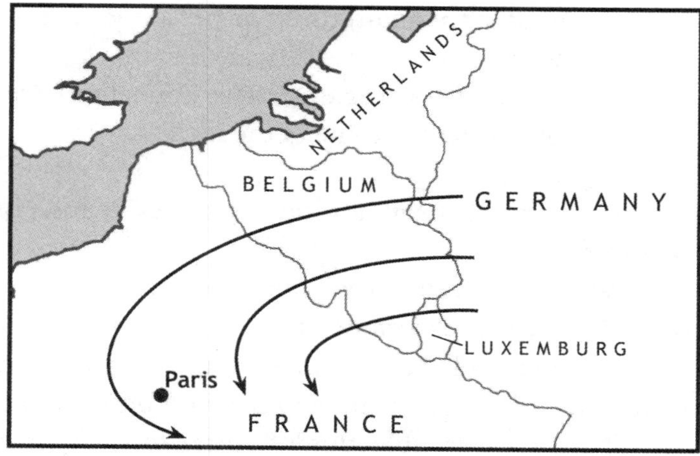

From the nearest point on the German boundary to Paris is only one hundred and seventy miles. But no rapid invasion of France could be made in this direction for two reasons: first, because of the very strong forts which protected the French frontier; and second, on account of the nature of the land, which presents to the east a series of five easily defended ridges, each of which would have to be stormed by an invader. A German attack directly across the French frontier could move but slowly past these natural and military obstacles; and the French nation would have ample time to mobilize its forces.

Consequently the German military leaders determined to attack France from the northeast. Here a comparatively level plain stretched from Germany through Belgium and France up to Paris itself. Many good roads and railways traversed the land. Few natural barriers existed to aid the defenders, and France, trusting to the neutrality of Belgium, had no strong fortifications on her northeastern frontier.

One obstacle to German invasion existed; it was what the German Chancellor once called "a scrap of paper"—a promise to respect the neutrality of Belgium, which Prussia, France, and England had agreed to by formal treaties. Similar treaties guaranteed the neutrality of Luxemburg, a small country east of Belgium. Upon these promises France had depended for the protection of her northeastern border; for the German Empire had accepted all the rights and all the duties of the treaties made by Prussia. But now, under the plea of necessity which "knows no law," the German rulers determined to break their promises, violate the neutrality of Belgium and Luxemburg, and crush France before an aroused and alarmed world could interfere.[198]

STEP TWO: **Construct a one-level outline**

Begin by finding the main idea in each of the four paragraphs.

This excerpt is a chronological narrative about a past event. When you practiced making one-level outlines earlier in this course, you learned that you can ask the following questions about a chronological narrative:

---

198. Albert E. McKinley, Charles A. Coulomb, and Armand J. Gerson, *The World War: A School History of the Great War* (American Book Co., 1919), pp. 77–78.

1. What is the main thing or person that this section is about? *Or* Is the section about an idea?
2. Why is that thing or person important? *Or* What did that thing or person do/what was done to it? *Or* What is the idea?

Sometimes, chronological narratives include descriptions. For a paragraph of description, you should ask:

What part of the place does this paragraph focus on? *Or* What aspect or part of the whole does this section describe?

As you look for the main idea in each paragraph, try to identify whether the paragraph is primarily a chronological narrative or a description. Then, ask the appropriate questions.

If you have trouble, don't hesitate to ask your instructor for help. And when you are finished, check your main points with your instructor before going on.

STEP THREE: **Construct a two-level outline**

Now go back and try to find two subpoints in each paragraph. Remember: the subpoints should make independent statements that relate *directly* to the main point.

Below, you will see questions and hints that will help you find the subpoints in each paragraph. Use these and construct your own two-level outline on your own paper.

When you are finished, check your work with your instructor.

I. Germany planned to invade France
  A. This point has to do with the timing of the invasion
  B. This point has to do with the pace of the invasion
II. The French frontier OR The frontier of France nearest Germany
  A. The first important characteristic of the French frontier
  B. The second important characteristic of the French frontier
III. The northeast of France OR The northeastern frontier of France
  A. The first important thing that the northeast frontier lacked
  B. The second important thing that the northeast frontier lacked
IV. The neutrality of Belgium and Luxemburg OR The decision to ignore neutrality of Belgium and Luxemburg
  A. This point has to do with France's relationship to the neutrality
  B. This point has to do with Germany's relationship to the neutrality

Day Three: Outlining Exercise

Focus: Finding the central topics and subtopics in each paragraph of a chronological narrative in science

STEP ONE: **Read**

Read the following excerpt about changing views of the solar system, from *Earth's Changing Environment.*

For centuries, Earth was simply "the world"—the only one known. Even most believers in a spherical Earth thought it to be a one-of-a kind object in the center of a spherical universe. The Sun, Moon, planets, and stars were generally thought to be of a very different nature from Earth. In fact, in the 4th century BC Aristotle proposed that they were made of a heavenly fifth element ("quintessence"), in addition to his supposed earthly elements of earth, water, air, and fire. The Sun and Moon, plus Mercury, Venus, Mars, Jupiter, and Saturn (all easily visible to the naked eye), were seen to gradually change position relative to the stars. This earned them the name planets, which meant "wanderers."

Most thinkers, including Aristotle, believed that Earth was motionless in the center of the universe. This is called the geocentric (Earth-centered) theory, and it was developed in greater detail by Ptolemy of Alexandria in around AD 150. Almost all astronomers accepted the theory for the next 1,400 years. In this view, Earth was certainly not a planet, because it was obviously not a wandering light in the sky.

In the 16th century AD Nicholas Copernicus of Poland proposed that Earth rotates on an axis through the North and South poles once a day—actually once a "sidereal" day, which is measured using the distant stars as a reference frame instead of the Sun. Earth's sidereal day is 23 hours, 56 minutes, and 4 seconds, which is a few minutes shorter than its "solar" day. Copernicus also said that Earth orbits, or revolves around, the Sun once a sidereal year (which is 365.256 days). He believed that the Moon orbits Earth, but that the other wanderers (the planets, not including the Sun) revolve around the Sun like Earth does. In this, Earth is a planet, because it, too, is a wanderer—around the Sun.

Copernicus' heliocentric (Sun-centered) theory was slow to be accepted. However, Johannes Kepler of Germany assumed this basic view in developing his three laws of planetary motion in the early 17th century. One of these laws states that a planet's orbit, or path around the Sun, is an ellipse, with the Sun not at the exact center but at one of two points called foci. Earth's orbit turns out to be more nearly a circle than the orbits of most of the other planets. Earth's distance from the Sun varies by only a small percentage, from about 91.4 million miles (147.1 million kilometers) in early January to some 94.5 million miles (152.1 million kilometers) in early July.[199]

STEP TWO: **Construct a one-level outline**

Begin by finding the main idea in each of the four paragraphs.

This passage is a chronological narrative, because it explains in chronological order the ideas that different scientists have had about the relationship between the Earth and the rest of the universe. You'll probably find it most useful to ask this version of the two questions you've been using:

1. What is the central idea in this passage?
2. Who held that idea?

Try those two questions now.

When you've finished your one-level outline, check your work with your instructor. If you have trouble finding the main idea, ask your instructor for help.

STEP THREE: **Construct a two-level outline**

Now go back and try to find two or three subpoints in each paragraph. Remember: the subpoints should make independent statements that relate *directly* to the main point.

Below, you will see hints that will help you find the subpoints in each paragraph. Use these and construct your own two-level outline on your own paper.

When you are finished, check your work with your instructor.

I.
   A. Where it was
   B. What others were like
   C. What others did

II.
   A. What it did at the center
   B. Who developed this
   C. Who accepted it

199. Compton's Learning Company, *Earth's Changing Environment* (Chicago: Encyclopedia Britannica, 2008), p. 91.

III.

A. What it does
B. What it and others do

IV.

A. What shape it is
B. How Earth's is a little different

Day Four: Outlining Exercise

Focus: Finding the central topics and subtopics in each paragraph of a description

STEP ONE: **Read**

The following passage is excerpted from a longer descriptive piece about three giant tree species that grow in California: the Monterey cypress, the common redwood, and the giant redwood.

— — — —

The most famous giants are the "big trees" of the Mariposa valley, technically known as the giant redwoods *(Sequoia gigantea)*. They stand in groups, and as single trees scattered along the valley, the scanty survivors of a race almost extinct. They are so large that to form any clear idea of their size is difficult. One fallen monster, hollow for a long distance from the ground, permits a horseman to ride in and go forward for one hundred and forty feet and then to ride out of a knot hole. The trees . . . vary from thirty to thirty-six feet in diameter and are from four hundred to four hundred fifty feet in height.

One of these old giants was cut, many years ago, by boring holes through it with a pump auger, the holes just touching each other, until the entire wood was cut away. Even then it refused to fall, so exactly erect had it grown, and some two days more were required to get it down. This was accomplished by driving wedges into one side by means of heavy logs used as battering rams, until it toppled over. A house has been built on the stump. A section twenty feet in diameter has been sawed off and exhibited in many places.

These "big trees" are survivors from a past era. . . . All the older trees are hollow, the central wood having decayed out to a great height. They have branches only near the top, and the foliage is scanty, so making the tree appear much like a tall shaft. The wood of these "big trees" is coarse and rather weak. Even if it were not right and wise to preserve the few still growing as monuments of the past, little use could be made of the wood as timber. The bark is thick

and hard, though somewhat fibrous, varying from twelve to fifteen inches in thickness, and probably one reason why these trees have survived is its protection.

The common redwood alone possesses value for timber. This is so valuable as to threaten its early extinction as a forest tree. The lumber is cut and sawed into lengths for logs in the usual way, and the wood is adapted to all uses in the construction of frame buildings. The trees are so large that the logs are usually split with wedges into quarters, and then these are sawed into lumber for inside finishing in the manner known as "quarter sawing," which makes the edge of the grain show in every board. The color is a deep red, much like cherry, only not quite so dark, and the wood works easily and smoothly, so making fine finishings.[200]

STEP TWO: **Understand how to construct a two-level outline**

You have been practicing two-level outlining by first constructing a one-level outline and then adding subpoints to each main point. That's a good way to practice two-level outlining for the first time, because it breaks the task down into smaller, manageable parts. Most often, though, you'll find it easier to find the main point and subpoints of each paragraph at the same time.

As you begin, remember that this passage is a *description*. When you outline a description, you can usually find the main topic of each paragraph by asking two questions:

1. What is the most important thing in this paragraph?
2. What aspect or part of the whole does this paragraph describe?

Look at the first paragraph of your reading now. The first sentence tells you what the paragraph is about; the most important thing in the paragraph is the species giant redwood, the *Sequoia gigantea*. So you would start to construct your outline by writing down:

I. Giant redwoods

Now you need to figure out what aspect or part of the species *Sequoia gigantea* is being described.

You can identify this aspect or part, and start to find your subpoints at the same time, by underlining each phrase that tells you something about giant redwoods, like this:

200. L. R. F. Griffin, "Study of Giant Trees." In *The School Journal,* Vol. LX, Jan.-June 1900, pp. 550–551.

> The most famous giants are the "big trees" of the Mariposa valley, technically known as the giant redwoods *(Sequoia gigantea)*. They stand in groups, and as single trees scattered along the valley, the scanty survivors of a race almost extinct. They are so large that to form any clear idea of their size is difficult. One fallen monster, hollow for a long distance from the ground, permits a horseman to ride in and go forward for one hundred and forty feet and then to ride out of a knot hole. The trees . . . vary from thirty to thirty-six feet in diameter and are from four hundred to four hundred fifty feet in height.

The paragraph tells you seven things about the giant redwoods:

They are the most famous of the giant trees.
They grow in the Mariposa valley.
They grow in groups and as single trees.
They are survivors of an almost extinct race.
They are very large.
They are 30–36 feet around.
They are 400–450 feet high.

(Notice that you wouldn't include the information about the fallen redwood tree that's large enough for a rider on horseback to ride through; that is a specific detail about *one* tree, not a piece of information about the whole species, "giant redwoods.")

The underlined phrases tell you where and how giant redwoods grow, what their reputation (fame) is like, what they're descended from, and what size they are. In other words, this is an *overall description of giant redwoods.* When you studied descriptions in Part II, you learned that a scientific description (like a description of a natural object) often begins with an introductory paragraph that gives a basic definition and overview of the object or phenomenon under study (page 153). This paragraph gives an overall survey of giant redwoods. So you would want to finish your main point by changing it to:

I. About giant redwoods OR Introduction to giant redwoods

Your list of underlined phrases helped you to identify the main point in the passage; now, you can turn those phrases into subpoints.

In the list below, the phrases have been grouped together by subject. The first three subjects have been listed for you; try to summarize the fourth subject in your own words. Write your answer in the blank before continuing on.

PHRASES	*SUBJECT*
They are the most famous of the giant trees.	*The fame of the trees*
They grow in the Mariposa valley. *They grow in groups and as single trees.*	*Where and how they grow*
They are survivors of an almost extinct race.	*Survivors of their race*
They are very large. *They are 30–36 feet around.* *They are 400–450 feet high.*	______________________

What did you write for the fourth subject?

Your answer should have been either *Their size* or *How big they are.*

Listing the phrases helps you to find the main point for each paragraph; it also helps you to figure out what subpoints are in the paragraph. A finished two-level outline for the first paragraph might look like this:

I. About the giant redwoods
  A. The fame of the trees
  B. Where and how they grow
  C. Survivors of their race
  D. Their size

You will not do three-level outlines until the end of the next level of this course, but (for your reference) here is what a three-level outline would look like.

I. About the giant redwoods
  A. The fame of the trees
  B. Where and how they grow
    1. In the Mariposa valley
    2. Some in groups
    3. Some as single trees
  C. Survivors of their race
  D. Their size
    1. One fallen tree
    2. 30–36 feet wide
    3. 400–450 feet high

STEP THREE: **Construct a two-level outline**

Now work on a two-level outline of each remaining paragraph by following the method described in Step Two. For each paragraph:

1. Find the most important thing in the paragraph.
2. Underline each phrase in the paragraph that tells you something important about it.
3. Finish your main point by answering the question "What aspect or part is being described?"
4. Group the important phrases together by subject. Each subject should give you a subpoint.

In the worksheet below, at least one of these steps has been completed for each paragraph. Using these hints, finish the remaining steps and construct your two-level outline.

When you are finished, check your work with your instructor. And if you have difficulty, ask your instructor for help.

WORKSHEET

One of these old giants was cut, many years ago, by boring holes through it with a pump auger, the holes just touching each other, until the entire wood was cut away. Even then it refused to fall, so exactly erect had it grown, and some two days more were required to get it down. This was accomplished by driving wedges into one side by means of heavy logs used as battering rams, until it toppled over. A house has been built on the stump. A section twenty feet in diameter has been sawed off and exhibited in many places.

PHRASES *SUBJECT*

II.

A.

B.

C.

D.

These "big trees" are survivors from a past era. . . . All the older trees are hollow, the central wood having decayed out to a great height. They have branches only near the top, and the foliage is scanty, so making the tree appear much like a tall shaft. The wood of these "big trees" is coarse and rather weak. Even if it were not right and wise to preserve the few still growing as monuments of the past, little use could be made of the wood as timber. The bark is thick and hard, though somewhat fibrous, varying from twelve to fifteen inches in thickness, and probably one reason why these trees have survived is its protection.

PHRASES *SUBJECT*

III.

A. Trees are hollow
B. Branches only near the top
B. Coarse and weak
C. Thick hard bark

The common redwood alone possesses value for timber. This is so valuable as to threaten its early extinction as a forest tree. The lumber is cut and sawed into lengths for logs in the usual way, and the wood is adapted to all uses in the construction of frame buildings. The trees are so large that the logs are usually split with wedges into quarters, and then these are sawed into lumber for inside finishing in the manner known as "quarter sawing," which makes the edge of the grain show in every board. The color is a deep red, much like cherry, only not quite so dark, and the wood works easily and smoothly, so making fine finishings.

PHRASES *SUBJECT*

IV. The wood of the common redwood

A.

B.

C.

D.

Week 28: Documentation

Day One: Outlining Exercise

Focus: Finding the central topics and selected subtopics in a chronological narrative that includes descriptions of character and place

STEP ONE: **Read**

The following passage comes from Jacob Abbott's classic biography *History of King Charles the First of England*. Charles I was born in 1600. His father, James VI of Scotland, was the closest living relative to Queen Elizabeth I of England; so when Elizabeth died in 1603, James became James VI of Scotland and James I of England at the same time.

Charles's mother was Anne of Denmark, and he had an older brother (Henry, the heir to the Scottish and eventually English throne) and an older sister, also named Elizabeth.

Charles I would become King of England in 1625. During his reign, a great civil war was fought in England. In 1649, Charles I became the only king of England to be executed for treason.

— — —

> Young Charles was very weak and feeble in his infancy. It was feared that he would not live many hours. The rite of baptism was immediately performed, as it was, in those days, considered essential to the salvation of a child dying in infancy that it should be baptized before it died. Notwithstanding the fears that were at first felt, Charles lingered along for some days, and gradually began to acquire a little strength. His feebleness was a cause of great anxiety and concern to those around him; but the degree of interest felt in the little sufferer's fate was very much less than it would have been if he had been the oldest son. He had a brother, Prince Henry, who was older than he, and, consequently, heir to his father's crown. It was not probable, therefore, that Charles would ever be king; and the importance of everything connected with his birth and his welfare was very much diminished on that account.

It was only about two years after Charles's birth that Queen Elizabeth died, and King James succeeded to the English throne. A messenger came with all speed to Scotland to announce the fact. He rode night and day. He arrived at the King's palace in the night. He gained admission to the king's chamber, and, kneeling at his bedside, proclaimed him King of England. James immediately prepared to bid his Scotch subjects farewell, and to proceed to England to take possession of his new realm. Queen Anne was to follow him in a week or two, and the other children, Henry and Elizabeth; but Charles was too feeble to go. . . .

One of the chief residences of the English monarchs is Windsor Castle, above London, on the Thames, on the southern shore. It is on an eminence overlooking the river and the delightful valley through which the river here meanders. . . . It has been for a long time the chief country residence of the British kings. It is very spacious, containing within its walls many courts and quadrangles, with various buildings surrounding them, some ancient and some modern.

Here King James held his court after his arrival in England, and in about a year he sent for the little Charles to join him. The child traveled very slowly, and by very easy stages, his nurses and attendants watching over him with great solicitude all the way. . . . Little Charles was four years old when he reached Windsor Castle. They celebrated his arrival with great rejoicings. . . .

Soon after this, when he was perhaps five or six years of age, a gentleman was appointed to take the charge of his education. His health gradually improved, though he still continued helpless and feeble. It was a long time before he could walk, on account of some malformation of his limbs. He learned to talk, too, very late and very slowly. Besides the general feebleness of his constitution, which kept him back in all these things, there was an impediment in his speech, which affected him very much in childhood, and which, in fact, never entirely disappeared. As soon, however, as he commenced his studies under his new tutor, he made much greater progress than had been expected. It was soon observed that the feebleness which had attached to him pertained more to the body than to the mind. He advanced with considerable rapidity in his learning. His progress was, in fact, in some degree, promoted by his bodily infirmities, which kept him from playing with the other boys of the court, and led him to like to be still, and to retire from scenes of sport and pleasure which he could not share.

The same cause operated to make him not agreeable as a companion, and he was not a favorite among those around him. They called him *Baby* Charley. His temper seemed to be in some sense soured by the feeling of his inferiority, and by the jealousy he would naturally experience in finding himself, the son of a king, so outstripped in athletic sports by those whom he regarded as his inferiors in rank and station. . . .

When he was about twelve years of age, too, his brother Henry died. This circumstance made an entire change in all his prospects of life. The eyes of the whole kingdom, and, in fact, of all Europe, were now upon him as the future sovereign of England. . . . When he was sixteen years of age, he was made Prince of Wales, and certain revenues were appropriated to support a court for him, that he might be surrounded with external circumstances and insignia of rank and power, corresponding with his prospective greatness.

In the mean time his health and strength rapidly improved, and with the improvement came a taste for manly and athletic sports, and the attainment of excellence in them. He became very famous for his skill in all the exploits and performances of the young men of those days, such as shooting, riding, vaulting, and tilting at tournaments. From being a weak, sickly, and almost helpless child, he became, at twenty, an active, athletic young man, full of life and spirit, and ready for any romantic[201] enterprise.[202]

STEP TWO: Identify the form of each paragraph

This passage combines three different forms that you've studied in previous weeks: a chronological narrative of past events, a place description, and a description of a person.

Go back now and write, in the margin next to each paragraph, a label that identifies each paragraph's form. Use the labels "narrative," "place," and "person." When you're finished, check your answers with your instructor.

STEP THREE: Construct a one-level outline

Construct a one-level outline on your own paper, using the questions suggested below to identify the main topic of each paragraph. When you're finished, check your answers with your instructor.

I. What part of Charles I's life is discussed?
II. What was the most important thing that happened?
III. What is described?
IV. What was the most important thing that happened?
V. What part of Charles I's life is discussed?
VI. What aspect of Charles I is described?
VII. What was the most important thing that happened?
VIII. What was the most important thing that happened?

201. In the nineteenth century, this word often meant "adventurous, chivalrous, daring, swashbuckling." The writer uses *romantic* in this old sense; he does not mean "having to do with love."

202. Jacob Abbott, *History of King Charles the First of England* (Henry Altemus Company, 1900), pp. 11–18.

STEP FOUR: **Construct a two-level outline of selected paragraphs**

Now expand the first four points on your outline by adding subpoints. Use the hints below. When you're finished, check your answers with your instructor.

I.
    A. This happened first
    B. This happened second
    C. This is how people felt about it
II.
    A. This happened first
    B. This happened second
    C. This happened third
III.
    A. The first aspect discussed
    B. The second aspect discussed
    C. The third aspect discussed
IV.
    A. This happened first
    B. This happened second
    C. This happened third

Day Two: Documentation

Focus: Citing source material properly

In the next few lessons, you'll work on developing your own chronological narration that includes a place and character description—all forms you've practiced already, and now need to review. But this time, you'll work on finding your own information: taking notes from sources and using it as you write.

Before you do this, you'll need to spend some time learning how to use those sources properly.

If you look back over previous weeks, you'll see that every excerpt—long or short—is followed by a superscript number that refers you to a footnote at the bottom of the page. At the back of this book, you'll see a "Works Cited" section, which lists every single book excerpted in this curriculum.

You should use notes and a Works Cited page whenever you quote from another writer—or use ideas and information that belong only to them. Today, you'll learn the proper form for notes and Works Cited pages.

STEP ONE: **Understand footnotes**

This book makes use of footnotes. Every quote is followed by a superscript number that comes *after* the closing quotation marks.

> "When you use someone else's words or ideas in your research paper, you *must* give credit."[203]

The superscript number leads to the footnote. Footnotes should be written like this:

> Author's name, *Title of Book* (Publisher, date of publication), p. #.

If there are two authors, list them like this:

> Author name and author name, *Title of Book* (Publisher, date of publication), p. #.

If your quote comes from more than one page of the book you're quoting, use "pp." to mean "page**s**" and put a hyphen between the page numbers.

> Author's name, *Title of Book* (Publisher, date of publication), pp. #-#.

Sometimes a book has been revised and put out in a new edition. If the book is a second (or third, or fourth, etc.) edition, put that information right after the title.

> Author's name, *Title of Book,* number of edition (Publisher, date of publication), p. #.

You can find all the information you need on the copyright page of the book (usually the second or third page in the book). On the following copyright page, look down until you see "Library of Congress Cataloging-in-Publication Data." This will always give you the author, title, edition (all in the second line of the data), and the date (on the next to last line). Underline each piece of information now. Then look back up the page to the top and find the name of the publisher. Underline it now.

203. Laurie Rozakis, *Schaum's Quick Guide to Writing Great Research Papers,* 2nd ed. (McGraw-Hill, 2007), p. 117.

> **The McGraw·Hill Companies**
>
> Copyright © 2007, 1999 by The McGraw-Hill Companies, Inc. All rights reserved. Printed in the United States of America. Except as permitted under the United States Copyright Acto of 1976, no part of this publication may be reproduced or distributed in any form or by any means, or stored in a data base or retrieval system, without the prior written permission of the publisher.
>
> 1 2 3 4 5 6 7 8 9 0 DOC/DOC 0 1 3 2 1 0 9 8 7
>
> ISBN 978-0-07-148848-8
> MHID 0-07-148848-0
>
> This book was set in Stone Serif by International Typesetting and Composition.
>
> McGraw-Hill books are available at special quantity discounts for use as premiums and sales promotions, or for use in corporate training programs. For more information, please write to the Director of Special Sales, McGraw-Hill Professional, Two Penn Plaza, New York, NY 10121-2298. Or contact your local bookstore.
>
> This publication is designed to provide accurate and authoritative information in regard to the subject matter covered. It is sold with the understanding that neither the author nor the publisher is engaged in rendering legal, accounting, or other professional service. If legal advice or other expert assistance is required, the services of a competent professional person should be sought.
>
> —From a Declaration of Principles jointly adopted by a Committee of the American Bar Association and a Committee of Publishers.
>
> **Library of Congress Cataloging-in-Publication Data**
>
> Rozakis, Laurie.
> Schaum's quick guide to writing great research papers / Laurie Rozakis.—2nd ed.
> p. cm.
> Includes bibliographical references and indexes.
> ISBN-13: 978-0-07-148848-8
> ISBN-10: 0-07-148848-0
> 1. Report writing. 2. Research. I. Title. II. Title: Quick guide to writing great research papers.
> LB1047.3.R69 2007
> 808'.02—dc22 2006103423

If you're using a regular word processing program, footnotes are easy to insert; there's a specific command on one of your menus that will automatically put the footnotes in and adjust the rest of the text on the page. The only thing you'll have to do is make sure that the text in the footnote is smaller than the text in your paper (usually about 2 points—in this book, the font is 11 point for the text and 9 point for the footnotes).

STEP TWO: **Understand endnotes and in-text citations**

If you're using a plain text program or handwriting your papers, footnotes can be much harder to place. There are two other acceptable ways to document quotes.

The first is endnotes:

"Otherwise, you're stealing their work."[1]

An endnote is written exactly like a footnote, except that the note is placed at the end of the paper instead of down at the bottom of the page where the quote occurs. The endnotes are usually headed like this:

ENDNOTES

[1] Laurie Rozakis, *Schaum's Quick Guide to Writing Great Research Papers,* 2nd ed. (McGraw-Hill, 2007), p. 117.

For a short paper, the endnotes can be placed on the last page. For a longer paper, you would want to have an entirely separate page headed ENDNOTES.

The second alternative is an in-text citation. With an in-text citation, you write the last name of the author, the date of the book, and the page number in parentheses after the closing quotation mark, but before the period.

"Learn how to avoid literary theft by documenting your sources correctly" (Rozakis, 2007, p. 117).

All of the other publication information about the book goes on the Works Cited page (which you'll find out about in a minute).

While you can use any of these three methods, I like footnotes the best. Endnotes force the reader to flip to the end of the paper to see where your quote came from (and when you flip, you lose your place). In-text citations clog up your writing and distract the reader.

STEP THREE: **Understand the Works Cited page**

The Works Cited page should be a separate page at the end of your paper. On it, you should list, in alphabetical order by last name of author, all of the books that you've quoted from (even if there's only one). The Works Cited page looks like this:

WORKS CITED

Rozakis, Laurie. *Schaum's Quick Guide to Writing Great Research Papers,* 2nd ed. New York: McGraw-Hill, 2007.

You'll see that there are three major differences between the way you list a book on the Works Cited page, and the way you list it in a footnote or endnote.

First, when you list a book on the Works Cited page, you list it alphabetically by the last name of the author. In the Works Cited section of this book, you'll see:

Riley, Franklin Lafayette. *General Robert E. Lee after Appomattox*. New York: The Macmillan Company, 1922.

Rogers, Julia Ellen. *Trees That Every Child Should Know: Easy Tree Studies for All Seasons of the Year.* New York: Doubleday, 1909.

Rozakis, Laurie. *Schaum's Quick Guide to Writing Great Research Papers,* 2nd ed. New York: McGraw-Hill, 2007.

Scalzi, John. *The Rough Guide to the Universe.* London: Rough Guides, 2003.

Schiff, Stacy. *Cleopatra: A Life.* New York: Little, Brown and Company, 2010.

Schom, Alan. *Napoleon Bonaparte.* New York: HarperCollins, 1997.

As you can see, "Rozakis" comes alphabetically between Rogers and Scalzi. This is in case the reader suddenly thinks "Wait, wasn't there a quote from a book by Laurie Rozakis? What was the book? How can I find it?" All the reader has to do is go to the Works Cited page and find "Rozakis" to get answers.

Second, you'll see that the publisher gets an additional identification: by city, not just by name. I'm not sure that I can think of a good reason why. Possibly, in the days before the internet, it was difficult to locate a publisher unless you knew what city's Yellow Pages to look in? Whatever the reason, the form has stuck.

If the publisher is in a huge and very well known city—New York, Los Angeles, London, Chicago—you just need to list the city. But for other cities, you should list both the city and the state, like this:

Bauer, Susan Wise. *Writing with Skill, Level 1.* Charles City, Va.: Peace Hill Press, 2012.

When you write a citation, you shouldn't use the postal code abbreviation for the state (VA). Instead, you should use the following standard abbreviations (and yes, these are silly and pointless rules):

Ala.	Alaska	Ariz.	Ark.	Calif.	Colo.
Conn.	Del.	Fla.	Ga.	Hawaii	Idaho
Ill.	Ind.	Iowa	Kan.	Ky.	La.
Maine	Md.	Mass.	Mich.	Minn.	Miss.
Mo.	Mont.	Neb.	Nev.	N.H.	N.J.
N.M.	N.Y.	N.C.	N.D.	Ohio	Okla.
Ore.	Pa.	R.I.	S.C.	S.D.	Tenn.
Texas	Utah	Vt.	Va.	Wash.	W. Va
Wis.	Wyo.				

Sometimes the publisher provides an address in the first few pages of the book. But if you can't find it, the simplest way to find the city is to use WorldCat, the largest online library reference tool.

To use WorldCat, go to http://www.worldcat.org. Type the title of the book and the author's last name into the search box. If you were to type *Schaum's Quick Guide to Writing Great Research Papers Rozakis* into the box and hit "Search," here's what would come up:

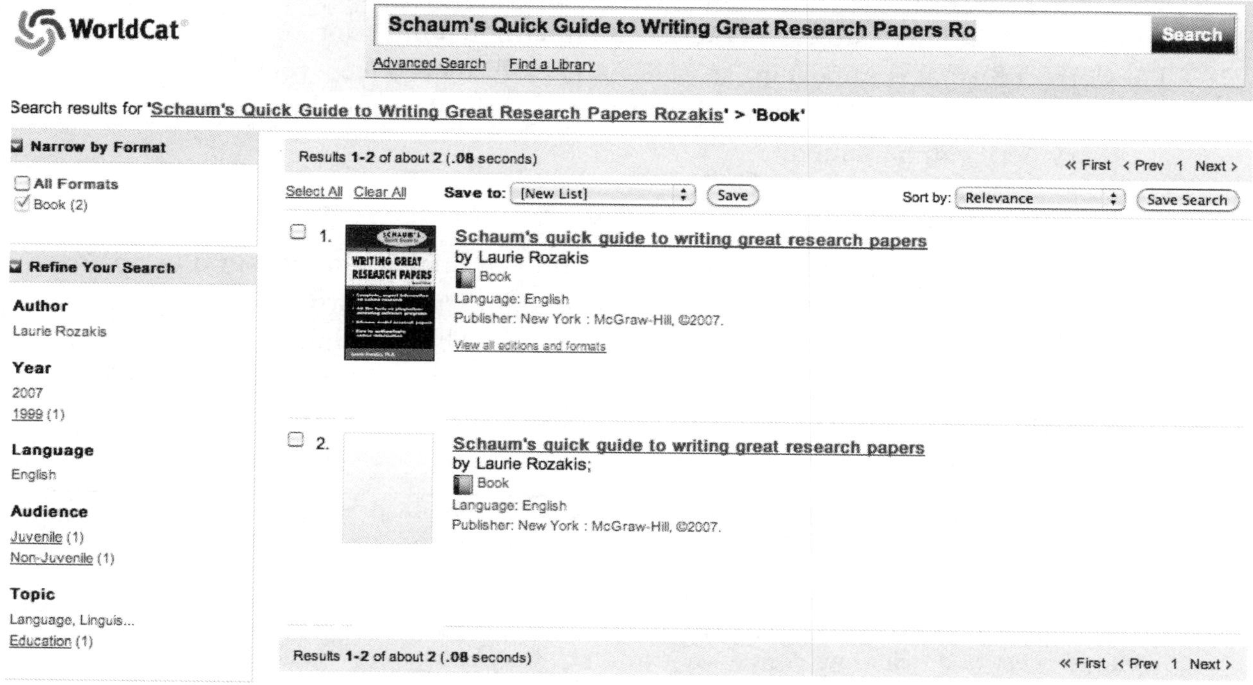

All the information you need for your Works Cited page is right there: title, author, publisher, date, and city (New York).

To sum up, here's how Works Cited entries should be formatted:

WORKS CITED

Author last name, author first name. *Title.* Publisher city: publisher, publisher date.

STEP FOUR: **Practice documentation**

Using your word processing program, type the following paragraph and footnote each quote properly, using the page images and copyright pages provided. Attach a properly formatted Works Cited page, doing whatever additional research is necessary. Not all of the copyright pages below are in the exact same format—see if you can find the information you need.

If you are not using a word processing program, you may use endnote format instead. When you are finished, check your work with your instructor.

> Most ideas are not completely original; we "use ideas from other people all the time" and "weave them into our working and academic lives."[1] But we should also give credit to the authors whose words we use. After all, they came up with the ideas first—and spent plenty of blood, sweat, and tears doing so. And don't forget that "failure to properly credit your sources could get you in big trouble, whether it's an intentional omission or not."[2] The correct format is important as well. As Dick Francis once wrote, in a novel on a completely different subject: "If you get the form of things right . . . every peril can be tamed."[3]

SOURCE A (Superscript 1)
This excerpt is from a book by Colin Noville. The World Cat information is found on the next page. Be sure to use the right page number! And notice that there are two cities noted for the publisher. That's because the book was published in both the United Kingdom and the United States. If you live in North America, you should use the second city listed—the one that's in the USA. Your book has probably come from that publisher, not the one overseas.

It can be argued that all imitative learning is plagiarism. We use ideas from other people all the time, weave them into our working and academic lives, gradually taking ownership of them until we eventually forget who influenced us in the first place; referencing becomes difficult, if not impossible, in some situations (see Angélil-Carter 2000; Pennycook 1996; Lensmire and Beals 1994). However, plagiarism, in an academic context, refers to a deliberate decision not to acknowledge the **work** of others in

WHAT ELSE IS TO COME? 5

assignments – or deliberately ignoring an obligation to do this. But more later on plagiarism (see Chapter 4).

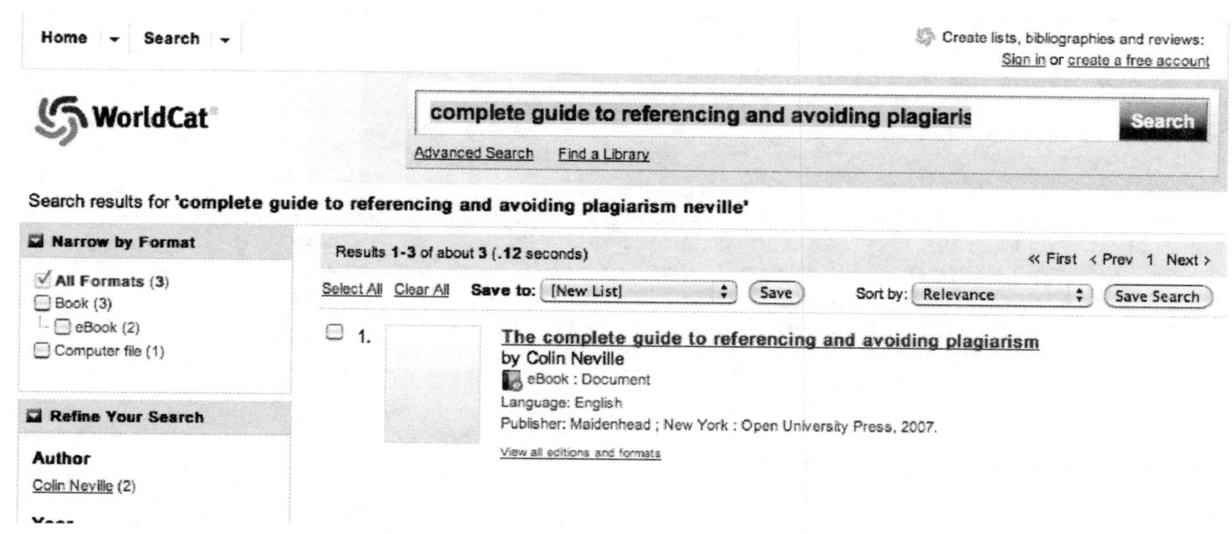

SOURCE B (Superscript 2)

»»» CHAPTER 9: Step 9: Compile a Complete Reference List »»» 141

There are a number of other style guides available; each field prefers a specific style, and many have developed their own guidelines (flip ahead to Additional Resources: Style & Format Guides to see a larger list of style guides). Thus, you should always double check with your professor to see what style she wants you to use.

The reference list: More than an afterthought!

Even though the reference list falls at the end of your paper, make no mistake – it's extremely important! Any errors you make could result in an author being denied credit for her work. Incorrect citations might make it difficult or impossible for your peers to do their own research on the topic. Failure to properly credit your sources could get you in big trouble, whether it's an intentional omission or not.

13 Lucky Steps to Writing a Research Paper

by Kelly Garbato, © 2005

ISBN: 0-9767249-0-1

Published by: Peedee Publishing, a subsidiary of Hot Dog!, LLC

7111 West 151st Street
Suite 113
Overland Park, Kansas 66223
www.peedeepublishing.com

Cover Design and Artwork by Kelly Garbato, © 2005

SOURCE C (Superscript 3)

Page 193

Thomas braked to a halt outside her house in Eaton Square and opened the car door for us to disembark. On the pavement I thanked the princess for the journey. Politeness conquered all. With the faintest gleam of amusement she said she would no doubt see me at Ascot, and as on ordinary days held out her hand for a formal shake, accepting the sketch of a bow.

"I don't believe it," Danielle said.

"If you get the form of things right," the princess said to her sweetly, "every peril can be tamed."

THE BERKLEY PUBLISHING GROUP
Published by the Penguin Group
Penguin Group (USA) Inc.
375 Hudson Street, New York, New York 10014, USA
Penguin Group (Canada), 10 Alcorn Avenue, Toronto, Ontario M4V 3B2, Canada
(a division of Pearson Penguin Canada Inc.)
Penguin Books Ltd., 80 Strand, London WC2R 0RL, England
Penguin Group Ireland, 25 St. Stephen's Green, Dublin 2, Ireland (a division of Penguin Books Ltd.)
Penguin Group (Australia), 250 Camberwell Road, Camberwell, Victoria 3124, Australia
(a division of Pearson Australia Group Pty. Ltd.)
Penguin Books India Pvt. Ltd., 11 Community Centre, Panchsheel Park, New Delhi—110 017, India
Penguin Group (NZ), Cnr. Airborne and Rosedale Roads, Albany, Auckland 1310, New Zealand
(a division of Pearson New Zealand Ltd.)
Penguin Books (South Africa) (Pty.) Ltd., 24 Sturdee Avenue, Rosebank, Johannesburg 2196, South Africa

Penguin Books Ltd., Registered Offices: 80 Strand, London WC2R 0RL, England

This is a work of fiction. Names, characters, places, and incidents either are the product of the author's imagination or are used fictitiously, and any resemblance to actual persons, living or dead, business establishments, events, or locales is entirely coincidental.

BREAK IN

A Berkley Book / published by arrangement with G. P. Putnam's Sons

Copyright © 1986 by Dick Francis.

Day Three: Avoiding Plagiarism

Focus: Understanding common knowledge and proper documentation

In the last lesson, you learned proper documentation for direct quotes. But that's not the only time that you should use footnotes. Whenever you use someone else's words and ideas—even if you change the words around or use your own phrasing—you should add a footnote that gives credit to the original author.

However, if the words and ideas you're using are "common knowledge," you don't need to footnote. It's not always easy to tell the difference, so you'll spend today learning more about this principle.

STEP ONE: **Understand the definition of plagiarism**

If you use someone else's words or ideas without giving them credit, you are *plagiarizing.* (The word comes from the Latin noun *plagiarius*, or "kidnapper"—you're "kidnapping" someone else's work and pretending that it is your own.)

The simplest form of plagiarism is copying someone else's exact words. Imagine that you were collecting information to write your own chronological narration about Charles I of England and came across this passage in Jacob Abbott's biography:

> The executioner, who wore a mask that he might not be known, began to adjust the hair of the prisoner by putting it up under his cap, when the king, supposing that he was going to strike, hastily told him to wait for the sign. The executioner said that he would. The king spent a few minutes in prayer, and then stretched out his hands, which was the sign which he had arranged to give. The axe descended.[204]

(Look down at the footnote and notice something important: the *second* time you quote from a book, you don't need to write all the same information in the footnote. You can just write the last name of the author and the page number of the quote.)

If you used this information in your own chronological narration, you would *not* want to write:

> Charles I ascended the scaffold for his execution. He spent a few minutes in prayer, and then stretched out his hands. The executioner swung the axe and beheaded him.

The second sentence of your paragraph would use the exact same words as the third sentence of Jacob Abbott's paragraph. Using Abbott's words without acknowledging him would be plagiarism. Instead, you would want to write

> Charles I ascended the scaffold for his execution. He "spent a few minutes in prayer, and then stretched out his hands."[1] The executioner swung the axe and beheaded him.
>
> [1] Jacob Abbott, *History of King Charles the First of England* (Henry Altemus Company, 1900), p. 282.

204. Abbott, p. 282.

To avoid plagiarism, you have to put quotation marks around the words that are taken directly from Abbott's biography and also provide a footnote.

But plagiarism can also happen if you use someone's ideas without giving them credit—even if you change the words.

Here's an example. In 2006, a major publisher in New York, called Little, Brown & Co., published a novel called *How Opal Mehta Got Kissed, Got Wild, and Got a Life*. The novel was written by a first-year college student named Kaavya Viswanathan. She got a lot of attention for writing a novel at such a young age—but before long, a number of readers started to point out that the ideas and scenes in Viswanathan's book were very, very close to ideas and scenes in novels by four other writers. Here are some examples of the similarities:

Viswanathan's book	Other books
"He had too-long shaggy brown hair that fell into his eyes, which were always half shut. His mouth was always curled into a half smile, like he knew about some big joke that was about to be played on you." (p. 48)	"He's got dusty reddish dreads that a girl could never run her hands through. His eyes are always half-shut. His lips are usually curled in a semi-smile, like he's in on a big joke that's being played on you but you don't know it yet." (Megan McCafferty, *Sloppy Firsts* [Random House, 2001], p. 23)
"Five department stores, and 170 specialty shops later, I was sick of listening to her hum along to Alicia Keys . . ." (p. 51)	"Finally, four major department stores and 170 specialty shops later, we were done." (McCafferty, p. 237)
"Poster reads, 'If from drink you get your thrill, take precaution—write your will.' " (p. 118)	"Warning reads, 'If from speed you get your thrill / take precaution—make your will.' " (Salman Rushdie, *Haroun and the Sea of Stories* [Granta Books, 1991], p. 35)

Viswanathan's book	Other books
"And I'll tell everyone that in eighth grade you used to wear a 'My Little Pony' sweatshirt to school every day," I continued. Priscilla gasped. "I didn't!" she said, her face purpling again. "You did! I even have pictures," I said. "And I'll make it public that you named your dog Pythagoras . . ." Priscilla opened her mouth and gave a few soundless gulps . . . "Okay, fine!" she said in complete consternation. "Fine! I promise I'll do whatever you want. I'll talk to the club manager. Just please don't mention the sweatshirt. Please." (p. 282)	"And we'll tell everyone you got your Donna Karan coat from a discount warehouse shop." Jemima gasps. "I didn't!" she says, colour suffusing her cheeks. "You did! I saw the carrier bag," I chime in. "And we'll make it public that your pearls are cultured, not real . . ." Jemima claps a hand over her mouth . . . "OK!" says Jemima, practically in tears. "OK! I promise I'll forget all about it. I promise! Just please don't mention the discount warehouse shop. Please." (Sophie Kinsella, *Can You Keep a Secret?* [Random House, 2005], p. 350)
"The whole time, Frederic (I wondered if anyone dared call him Freddie) kept picking up long strands of my hair and making sad faces. 'It must go,' he said. 'It must all go.' And it went. Not all of it, because after four inches vanished, I started making panicked, whimpering sounds that touched even Frederic's heart . . ." (p. 57)	"Meanwhile, Paulo was picking up chunks of my hair and making this face and going, all sadly, 'It must go. It must all go.' And it went. All of it. Well, almost all of it. I still have some like bangs and a little fringe in back." (Meg Cabot, *The Princess Diaries* [HarperCollins, 2001], p. 128)
"Every inch of me had been cut, filed, steamed, exfoliated, polished, painted, or moisturized. I didn't look a thing like Opal Mehta. Opal Mehta didn't own five pairs of shoes so expensive they could have been traded in for a small sailboat. She didn't wear makeup or Manolo Blahniks or Chanel sunglasses or Habitual jeans. . . . She never owned enough cashmere to make her concerned for the future of the Kazakhstani mountain goat population. I was turning into someone else." (p. 59)	"There isn't a single inch of me that hasn't been pinched, cut, filed, painted, sloughed, blown dry, or moisturized. . . . Because I don't look a thing like Mia Thermopolis. Mia Thermopolis never had fingernails. Mia Thermopolis never had blond highlights. Mia Thermopolis never wore makeup or Gucci shoes or Chanel skirts. . . . I don't even know who I am anymore. It certainly isn't Mia Thermopolis. *She's turning me into someone else.*" (Cabot, p. 12)

If just *one* of these similarities had been in Viswanathan's book, someone might have pointed it out—but most readers would have assumed that it was just coincidence. But because there were so *many* scenes borrowed from other writers (these are only a few), Viswanathan's publisher admitted that plagiarism had taken place and withdrew the book from publication.

As you can see, plagiarism can happen when entire ideas are taken from another writer—even if some, or even most, of the words have been changed.

So another way to write that paragraph about Charles I's execution might be like this:

> Charles I ascended the scaffold for his execution. He prayed for a few moments, and then he extended his hands in a sign.[1] The executioner swung the axe and beheaded him.
>
> ---
>
> [1] Jacob Abbott, *History of King Charles the First of England* (Henry Altemus Company, 1900), p. 282.

In this version, Jacob Abbott's words "spent a few minutes in prayer, and then stretched out his hands" have been rephrased as "He prayed for a few moments, and then extended his hands in a sign." But because the idea of Charles's praying and then stretching out his hands originally came from Abbott, the footnote is still necessary.

So do you have to use footnotes for every single idea in your next chronological narration?

No. You don't have to use a footnote for ideas, or facts, or details, or any other information that is considered "common knowledge."

STEP TWO: **Understand the concept of "common knowledge"**

If a piece of information is widely known by a large group of people, it is called "common knowledge." You don't have to footnote common knowledge.

Here's an example: Jacob Abbott's biography of Charles I begins with this paragraph:

> King Charles the First was born in Scotland. It may perhaps surprise the reader than an English king should be born in Scotland.[205]

You could begin your own chronological narrative with:

> Charles I was born in Scotland.

without having to footnote. Hundreds of historians know that Charles I was born in Scotland. Every biography of Charles I points out that Charles was born in Scotland. You could have discovered this without ever picking up Jacob Abbott's book. That is common knowledge.

Figuring out what is common knowledge and what isn't can be tricky. Generally, the following are considered to be common knowledge:

---

205. Abbott, p. 13.

Historical dates	"Charles I was born in 1600."
Historical facts	"Columbus claimed the New World for Spain."
Widely accepted scientific facts	"Lava erupts out of volcanoes."
Geographical facts	"Mount Everest is 29,029 feet above sea level."
Genealogical facts	"Charles I was the father of Charles II."
Definitions	"Honey is made out of nectar."
Proverbs and sayings	"A penny saved is a penny earned."
Well-known theories and ideas	"Snow happens when water in the atmosphere condenses and freezes."
Anything that can be learned through the senses	"Cyanide smells like almonds." "During a solar eclipse, the moon blocks the sun."

Here's one more example—a paragraph from my own book *The History of the Medieval World*, about the Frankish king Clovis.

> He settled on the old Roman town Lutetia Parisiorum, the Seine, and began to reinforce its walls. He issued a set of Latin laws for his domain, the Pactus Legis Salicae; the laws were very specific in forbidding the old Germanic traditions of blood revenge, instead substituting fines and penalties for clan-based revenge killings.[1]
>
> [1] Roger Collins, *Early Medieval Europe, 300–1000*, 2nd ed. (St. Martin's Press, 1999), p. 36.

I didn't footnote the first sentence because it's simply a historical fact. In the second sentence, the *existence* of the Latin laws is also a simple historical fact as well. But it was in Roger Collins's book that I first found the idea that Clovis's fines and penalties were intended to completely get rid of blood revenge. Just looking at the laws themselves, I would not have come up with that explanation. So I gave Roger Collins credit in a footnote.

If you aren't sure whether or not to insert a footnote, use one! As you read and write more, you will develop a better sense of what is and isn't common knowledge.

STEP THREE: **Practice!**

Mark each sentence CK (for "common knowledge") or NF (for "needs footnote"). When you're finished, check your answers with your instructor. Don't worry if you have trouble deciding; even scholars often disagree over whether or not a particular piece of information should be documented. Your instructor will explain the answers if necessary.

1. ________ To show his supremacy over the kings he had vanquished, Zheng took the title First Sovereign Qin Emperor, or Qin Shi Huangdi.

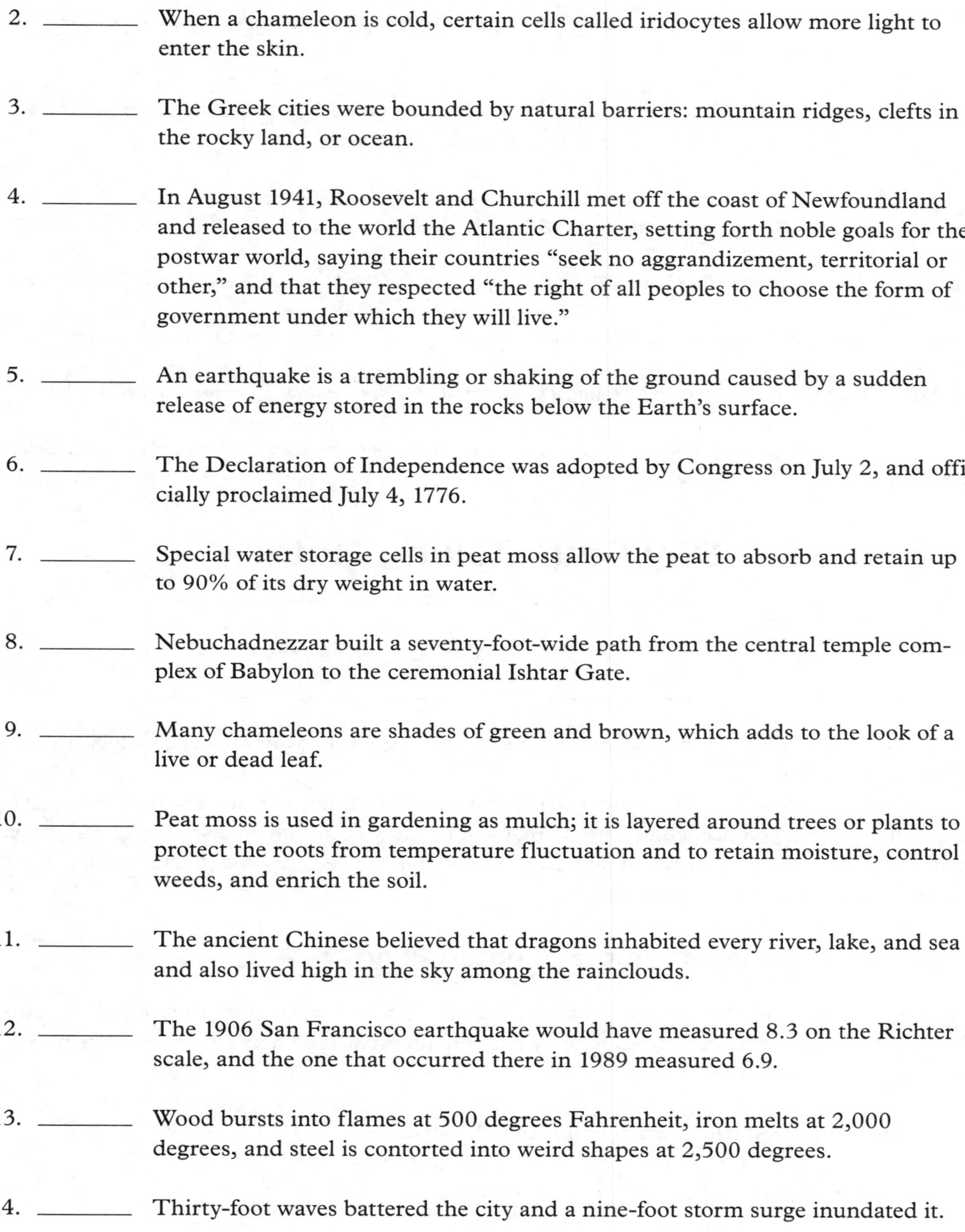

2. ________ When a chameleon is cold, certain cells called iridocytes allow more light to enter the skin.

3. ________ The Greek cities were bounded by natural barriers: mountain ridges, clefts in the rocky land, or ocean.

4. ________ In August 1941, Roosevelt and Churchill met off the coast of Newfoundland and released to the world the Atlantic Charter, setting forth noble goals for the postwar world, saying their countries "seek no aggrandizement, territorial or other," and that they respected "the right of all peoples to choose the form of government under which they will live."

5. ________ An earthquake is a trembling or shaking of the ground caused by a sudden release of energy stored in the rocks below the Earth's surface.

6. ________ The Declaration of Independence was adopted by Congress on July 2, and officially proclaimed July 4, 1776.

7. ________ Special water storage cells in peat moss allow the peat to absorb and retain up to 90% of its dry weight in water.

8. ________ Nebuchadnezzar built a seventy-foot-wide path from the central temple complex of Babylon to the ceremonial Ishtar Gate.

9. ________ Many chameleons are shades of green and brown, which adds to the look of a live or dead leaf.

10. ________ Peat moss is used in gardening as mulch; it is layered around trees or plants to protect the roots from temperature fluctuation and to retain moisture, control weeds, and enrich the soil.

11. ________ The ancient Chinese believed that dragons inhabited every river, lake, and sea and also lived high in the sky among the rainclouds.

12. ________ The 1906 San Francisco earthquake would have measured 8.3 on the Richter scale, and the one that occurred there in 1989 measured 6.9.

13. ________ Wood bursts into flames at 500 degrees Fahrenheit, iron melts at 2,000 degrees, and steel is contorted into weird shapes at 2,500 degrees.

14. ________ Thirty-foot waves battered the city and a nine-foot storm surge inundated it.

15. ________ The First Emperor built an impressive tomb guarded by thousands of life-size terra-cotta warriors.

16. ________ A magnitude 8 earthquake releases as much energy as detonating 6 million tons, or 6 billion kilograms, of trinitrotoluene, TNT.

Quotes 1, 11, and 15 from Arthur Cotterell, *Ancient China* (Penguin, 2005), pp. 16–17.
Quotes 2, 7, 9, and 10 from Sandra Alters and Brian Alters, *Biology: Understanding Life* (John Wiley & Sons, 2006), pp. 707 and 641.
Quotes 3 and 8 from Susan Wise Bauer, *The History of the Ancient World* (W. W. Norton, 2007), pp. 371 and 447.
Quotes 4 and 6, from Howard Zinn, *A People's History of the United States* (HarperCollins, 2010), pp. 412 and 77.
Quotes 5, 12, and 16 from Kenneth R. Lang, *The Cambridge Guide to the Solar System* (Cambridge University Press, 2003), p. 122.
Quotes 13 and 14 from Philip L. Fradkin, *The Great Earthquake and Firestorms of 1906* (University of California Press, 2005), pp. 16 and 19.

Day Four: Taking Notes

Focus: Collecting information

There's one more skill that you need to practice before you write your own chronological narrative: taking notes.

When you first learned how to write narratives, descriptions, and sequences, I gave you all of the information you needed in a list so that you could concentrate on learning how to write, rather than on collecting facts and details. But now that you've had some practice, you can begin to collect information for yourself.

STEP ONE: **Examine a sample of note-taking**

Think all the way back to the first chronological narrative you wrote this year—about Alexander the Great. You were instructed to use a list of main events and details to write your narrative. That list included:

Taught by Aristotle from ages 13–16
Most famous philosopher in the world at this time
Gave Alexander lifelong thirst for knowledge
Interested in medicine, philosophy, history

Those details were taken from several different histories. Here are excerpts from three of the sources that tell us about Alexander and Aristotle. The first two are biographies of Alexander; the third is a history of philosophy that talks about Aristotle.

> Aristotle was a **famous philosopher,** of course, but he was also an **authority on constitutional law, politics, poetry and rhetoric, astronomy and optics, metaphysics, medicine, zoology, and botany.** These last two disciplines he pioneered, in fact; a tireless observer and experimenter, he was the father of the scientific method as it still exists today. He was also the father of logic and was thus as qualified to teach Alexander how to think as what to think.[206]

> One can only imagine Alexander's exhilaration while sitting at the feet of a scholar whose wide interests matched his own boundless curiosity. A physician's son, **Aristotle was trained in medicine and evidently passed these skills on to** his most famous pupil. Later in life Alexander was known to tend to his soldiers' wounds, prescibe cures for friends, and advise doctors. Aristotle also seems to have lectured on zoology and botany . . . and **Alexander maintained a lifelong interest in these subjects.** [207]

> Aristotle, born 384 BC at Stagira (or Stageiros) in Thrace, and son of the physician Nicomachus, became in his eighteenth year (367) a pupil of Plato, and remained such for twenty years. After Plato's death (347) he repaired with Xenocrates to the court of Hermias, the ruler of Atarneus and Assos in Mysia. He remained there nearly three years, at the expiration of which time he went to Mitylene and afterward (343) to the court of Philip, king of Macedonia, where he lived more than seven years, until the death of that monarch. **He was the most influential tutor of Alexander from the thirteenth to the sixteenth years of the life of the latter** (343–340).[208]

When I read these paragraphs, I took notes on the details about Aristotle's tutoring of Alexander the Great and used those notes to make the list in your lesson.

You'll notice that I left out most of the information in the paragraphs. When you take notes, you must stay focused on *one particular topic or idea* and only write down the information that's directly related to that topic or idea. Otherwise, you'll end up simply copying most of your source. When I took notes on these paragraphs, I kept in mind that I only wanted details about *when and what Aristotle taught Alexander.* I ignored everything else.

---

206. Laura Foreman, *Alexander the Conqueror: The Epic Story of the Warrior King* (Da Capo, 2004), p. 43.
207. John Maxwell O'Brien, *Alexander the Great: The Invisible Enemy* (Routledge, 1994), p. 19.
208. Friedrich Ueberweg, George S. Morris, Henry B. Smith, Philip Schaff, Noah Porter, and Vincenzo Botta. *A History of Philosophy: From Thales to the Present Time* (C. Scribner & Company, 1872), p. 137.

Here's what my notes looked like:

Foreman, Laura. *Alexander the Conqueror: The Epic Story of the Warrior King*. Cambridge, Mass.: Da Capo, 2004.

"authority on constitutional law, politics, poetry and rhetoric" and other scientific fields (43)

"father of the scientific method" (43)

O'Brien, John Maxwell. *Alexander the Great: The Invisible Enemy.* New York: Routledge, 1994.

"trained in medicine and evidently passed these skills on" to Alexander (19)

"Alexander maintained a lifelong interest in these subjects" (19)

Ueberweg, Friedrich, George S. Morris, Henry B. Smith, Philip Schaff, Noah Porter, and Vincenzo Botta. *A History of Philosophy: From Thales to the Present Time*. New York: C. Scribner & Company, 1872.

"most influential tutor of Alexander from the thirteenth to the sixteenth years" of Alexander's life (137)

I looked at these notes when making the list for your lesson.

Notice that I didn't footnote any of this information. That's because I only used historical facts and was careful not to use the exact words of any of my sources.

STEP TWO: **Learn proper form for taking notes**

When you take notes, you should follow four simple rules.

1. Always write down the full bibliographical information of your source (author, full title, city of publisher, publisher, date) as if you were entering it on a Works Cited page.
2. Always quote directly and use quotation marks around the exact words of your source. You can combine this with brief paraphrases that sum up information you're not going to quote directly (as I did above for the Laura Foreman book).
3. Always write the page number of quotes right next to the words themselves.
4. If you are reading a book or resource online, *never* copy and paste words into your notes. Type them out yourself (this will force you to pick only the most important information).

This will help you write more efficiently—if you don't write down the full bibliographical information and page number *as you go*, you will end up having to go back and find it later—and you may have trouble locating the book or the page.

Most important, though, these rules will help you avoid plagiarism. If you write down the *exact words* that the source uses and then look at your notes as you write, you'll be able to avoid accidentally using another person's words without giving them credit.

There are two acceptable ways to take notes. Traditionally, students have been taught to take notes on 3x5 cards and then arrange the cards in order when they start to write. You can still use 3x5 cards for your notes. Use a different card for each quote, write the full bibliographical information about the source on the *first* card, and then just write the author's last name at the top of each remaining card.

However, now that most students use word processors, using 3x5 cards isn't necessary; typing your notes can be much more efficient than handwriting them. I took my notes above by creating a document in my word processor. I typed the full information for each book before I started to take notes on it. Then I made a list of important quotes (with page numbers!) under each book's title.

STEP THREE: **Practice taking notes**

Take notes on the following source, using proper form as illustrated above. You can choose to use either 3x5 cards or a word processing document.

All of your notes should be focused on one subject: the major events in Julius Caesar's life between January 49 BC and his death. You should list at least seven but no more than ten events.

Here are a couple of hints to help you keep your list of events to a manageable length. First, only list *Caesar's* actions or actions that *directly* affected him. Second, if a paragraph tells you that Caesar fought in three or four different places, or did three or four different things, don't write a sentence for each. For example, at the top of page xiv, you will see this paragraph:

> During the next twelve months, by a series of rapid military movements, Caesar secured Sicily, the great granary of the republic, conquered the senatorial forces in Spain, and finally, at Pharsalia, achieved a decisive victory over Pompey and his entire army.

The major event in this paragraph is that Caesar was victorious—in three different places. So you could write:

> Caesar conquered Sicily, the "senatorial forces in Spain," and Pompey. (xiv)

You can use this as one of your events.

If you have trouble, ask your instructor for help. When you're finished, show your notes to your instructor. Then hold on to them; you'll use them again next week.

The date of this book isn't on the copyright page, but it was published in 1901. Use the first listed city as the city of publication. And notice that "With Notes, Dictionary, and a Map of Gaul" is a subtitle. Even though a semicolon is used on the copyright page, when you write a book title you should insert a colon between the title and subtitle.

CAESAR'S COMMENTARIES

ON THE

GALLIC WAR;

WITH

NOTES, DICTIONARY, AND A MAP OF GAUL.

BY

ALBERT HARKNESS, LL. D.,

PROFESSOR IN BROWN UNIVERSITY.

REVISED EDITION, ILLUSTRATED.

NEW YORK :: CINCINNATI :: CHICAGO:

AMERICAN BOOK COMPANY

struction seemed inevitably to await Caesar and his cause; but the genius of the great commander rose with the magnitude of the occasion. Roman valor and discipline, inspired and guided by that genius, triumphed over all obstacles, and wrested victory from the hands of the enemy. A few days later, the despatches of Caesar announced to the Roman senate the fall of Alesia and the triumph of the Roman arms.

Another year of warfare followed, and the conquest of Gaul was complete. Eight years of heroic daring and bloody strife had added a mighty realm to the Roman dominions.

But already the question of the recall of Caesar was discussed in the senate, and a few months later, at the instance of Pompey, who had become his bitter rival, a decree was passed requiring him, under penalty of being declared a traitor to his country, to resign the governorship of both Gauls and disband his army. The news of this action reached Caesar at Ravenna, on the 10th of January, 49 B. C. Scarcely a day elapsed before his decision was made. With a single legion he crossed the Rubicon, the southern boundary of his province, and advanced into Italy. The prestige of his name gathered numerous recruits to his standard; town after town threw open its gates to the conqueror, and in sixty days after the edict of the senate declaring him a traitor to his country, the proscribed outlaw entered the capital the undisputed master of Italy. A bloodless victory and a triumphal march from the Rubicon to Rome, had accomplished one of the most remarkable revolutions recorded in the annals of the world.

The senatorial party, panic-stricken, had fled from the city in anticipation of the reënactment of the bloody scenes of proscription which had marked the triumphs of Marius and Sulla. But the magnanimity of Caesar disappointed both friends and foes. The frantic passion of the aristocracy, in their impotence and exile breathing out threats of proscription, contrasted strangely with the calm moderation of the victor in all the plenitude of his power.

During the next twelve months, by a series of rapid military movements, Caesar secured Sicily, the great granary of the republic, conquered the senatorial forces in Spain, and finally, at Pharsalia, achieved a decisive victory over Pompey and his entire army.

The remaining four years of Caesar's life were divided between military campaigns abroad and political reforms at home. We hear of him successively in Egypt, placing the disputed crown upon the head of Cleopatra; in Pontus, crushing the power of Pharnaces, and reporting his victory in those memorable words, "*Veni, vidi, vici;*" in Numidia, winning the signal victory of Thapsus; and finally in Spain, annihilating, in the desperate and bloody conflict at Munda, the last army which upheld the banner of Pompey. These varied military movements left him but little time for his contemplated work in the capital; yet the civil and political reforms which he actually accomplished, to say nothing of the magnificent schemes which he conceived, excite our wonder and admiration. With the comprehensive views of the true statesman, with marvellous power to arrange and organize, and with a keen perception of all the conditions of success, he entered with zeal upon the great work of reconstructing the Roman state. He corrected abuses, enriched the public treasury, reformed the calendar, equalized the public burdens, and strove in every way, as the head of a great nation, to give unity and symmetry to the new empire. But while he was yet in the midst of his wonderful career, with gigantic plans yet unaccomplished, designing men were plotting his ruin and his death. He had been loaded with titles and honors, and had been declared dictator for life; but his greatness had excited the envy of the nobles, while his insatiable ambition had awakened the fears of the people. He was suspected of aiming at the sceptre and the crown, and he paid the penalty with his life. He was assassinated in the senate house, on the 15th of March, 44 B. C.

Such was the tragic death of this remarkable man. He had achieved success in almost every field in which he had been called upon to act. He was a great commander, an eloquent orator, an accomplished writer, and a consummate statesman. Some of the finest literary works of the age were the productions of his genius. They related to a variety of subjects, and embraced both prose and poetry. The Commentaries on the Gallic and the Civil War have been commended and admired in all ages. They will amply repay patient and careful study.

Week 29: Writing from Notes: Chronological Narrative of a Past Event, Description of a Person, Description of a Place

Day One: Practicing the Topos, Part One: Taking Notes

Focus: Collecting information

You started off last week by outlining a a chronological narrative about Charles I of England that included a personal description and a description of a place. This week, you'll write a chronological narrative about Julius Caesar that follows the same pattern.

Like the narrative about Charles I, your finished composition will have eight paragraphs. Six of those paragraphs will be chronological narrative, one will be a paragraph describing Caesar, and one will be a paragraph describing the city of Ravenna as it appeared during Caesar's stay there. The chronological narrative will begin with Caesar at Ravenna, the news he got there, and his decision to cross the Rubicon. It will end with his death.

You'll use footnotes (or endnotes) as you write, and you will need to include a Works Cited page at the end. For each part of the paper—chronological narrative, personal description, place description—you should take notes from at least two different sources. You've already taken notes on one source that you can use for the chronological narrative. Five more sources are provided below. (Just for your information: page images are only provided for books that are old enough to be out of copyright, or "in the public domain." Books that are still protected by copyright are quoted instead.)

You'll spend today taking notes for your paper. When you are finished, show your notes to your instructor.

STEP ONE: **Take notes for the chronological narrative**

Remember to focus on Caesar and his actions, rather than on others. Do not list more than ten statements.

Source #1

This first excerpt is from a classic history text published by the Delphian Society, an organization that was formed in 1910 to help educate women. The book was a group effort, so the Society itself is considered the author. In your Works Cited page, list the author as "Delphian Society" (not "Society, Delphian"!).

480 THE WORLD'S PROGRESS.

In 49 B. C. Caesar had completed his Gallic campaign. The senate feared one who had made his name such a terror in the North, and asked him to disband his soldiers before returning to Rome. However, Caesar desired the consulship for the next year, and felt that without his army he would be no better off than any private Roman citizen. However, he agreed to disband his soldiers if Pompey would do likewise. This Pompey refused to do. Thereupon the senate unwisely notified Caesar that he must dismiss his army by a certain date or be declared a public enemy. Caesar was satisfied that without his army he would be helpless in Rome, and, marching rapidly, crossed the Rubicon, the stream north of Rome, over which no army had been allowed to come. Upon learning of his approach, Pompey gathered together what forces he could and moved south. Contrary to the fears of the Romans, Caesar brought order instead of turmoil to the city. No massacres, proscriptions or riots marked his entrance to the capital. Having established himself there, he moved to meet Pompey, for there was now civil war in Italy and one of two leaders had to prove himself master of the situation. Caesar brought a well trained body of soldiers, whereas Pompey had hurriedly gathered his forces together. As might have been foreseen, Pompey was defeated. Fleeing to Egypt, he was treacherously slain. This left Julius Caesar in control of the Roman world.

Having re-established the Ptolemies upon the throne of the Pharaohs, Caesar returned to Rome. There he proclaimed a holiday of fifteen days. He celebrated four triumphs: one for Gaul, one for Egypt, one for Pontus, and one for Africa. His rule in Rome was brief. He gathered into his own hands the important offices of the government, and instituted reforms that lived long after his time. First of all, he believed that Rome should be the capital of a great empire, not simply the recipient of advantages conferred by this wide area. Accordingly, the rights of citizenship were extended to the Gauls, Spaniards, and other provincials. Again, districts in the provinces were open to settlers from Italy. Instead of leaving provincial taxes to be longer farmed out, each town was made responsible for its share.

The senate lost its aristocratic nature when Caesar increased

THE STORY OF ROME. 481

its membership from 600 to 900 and brought into it men from various parts of Italy and the provinces. Economic conditions were bettered by the requirement of free laborers as well as slaves on estates, and many idle men of Rome were given employment on public works now undertaken. Moreover, imprisonment for debt was abolished.

Caesar made the fatal mistake, however, of setting aside the prejudices of men regarding the *forms* of government. There were those who failed to see that the days of the republic were in reality passed, and they resented Caesar's indifference to republican forms and appearances. These men found in Brutus a worthy although perhaps a misguided leader, who vainly hoped to restore the old republic by removing the great statesman of the age. A conspiracy was formed and in 44 B. C. the mighty Caesar fell in the senate house, a victim to the mistaken conceptions of eighty senators. Time was to show their attempt a failure, and to demonstrate that the sacrifice of Caesar could not stem the tide of natural forces.

The Delphian Course.
by Delphian Society.
Book
Language: English
Publisher: Chicago : The Society ©1913.

STEP TWO: Take notes for the personal description

Again, remember to focus on Caesar, not on others. You should have no more than 14 total statements between the two sources.

Source #2
This text was published in 1902. Remember to use the first city listed as the publisher's city.

ANCIENT HISTORY

TO THE DEATH OF CHARLEMAGNE

BY

WILLIS MASON WEST

ALLYN AND BACON
Boston and Chicago

450. Caesar's Character. — Caesar has been called the one original genius in Roman history. His gracious courtesy and unrivaled charm won all hearts, so that it is said his enemies dreaded personal interviews, lest they be drawn to his side. Toward his friends he never wearied in forbearance and love. In the civil war young Curio, a dashing but reckless lieutenant, lost two legions and undid much good work — to Caesar's great peril. Curio refused to survive his blunder, and found death on the field; but Caesar, with no word of reproachful criticism, refers to the disaster only to excuse it kindly by reference to Curio's youth and to "his faith in his good fortune from his former success."

In work, no man ever excelled Caesar in quick perception of means, fertility of resource, dash in execution, or tireless activity. His opponent Cicero said of him: "He had genius, understanding, memory, taste, reflection, industry, exactness." Numerous anecdotes are told of the many activities he could carry on at one time, and of his dictating six or more letters to as many scribes at once. Says a modern critic, "He was great as a captain, statesman, lawgiver, jurist, orator, poet, historian, grammarian, mathematician, architect."

No doubt "Caesar was ambitious." He was not a philanthropic enthusiast merely, but a broad-minded, intellectual genius, with a strong man's delight in ruling well. He saw clearly what was to do, and knew perfectly his own supreme ability to do it. Caesar and Alexander are the two great captains whose conquests have done most for civilization. But Caesar, master in war as he was, always preferred statesmanship, and was perfectly free from Alexander's boyish liking for mere fighting. Beside the Greek, the Roman had less of poetic idealism and more of practical sagacity. And yet the two had much in common, and both tower, mighty giants, above vulgar conquerors, like a Napoleon, moved by lower ambitions.

Source #3

Goldsworthy, Adrian Keith. *Caesar: Life of a Colossus.* New Haven, Conn.: Yale University Press, 2006, p. 3 (first paragraph) and p. 61 (second paragraph).

> Caesar was not a moral man; indeed, in many respects he seems amoral. It does seem to have been true that his nature was kind, generous, and inclined to forget grudges and turn enemies into friends, but he was also willing to be utterly ruthless. . . . He was extremely proud, even vain, especially of his appearance. It is hard to avoid the conclusion that from a young age Caesar was absolutely convinced of his own superiority. Much of this self-esteem was justified, for he was brighter and more capable than the overwhelming majority of other senators. . . .
>
> A number of portrait images of Caesar survive as busts or on coins. . . They show the great general or the dictator, his features stern and strong, his face lined and—at least in the few more realistic portraits—his hair thinning. These images radiate power, experience and monumental self-confidence, and at least hint at the force of personality of the man. . . . According to [the Roman historian] Suetonius, Caesar "is said to have been tall, with fair skin, slender limbs, a face that was just a little too full, and very dark, piercing eyes."

STEP THREE: **Take notes for the place description**

You shouldn't include more than ten statements between the two sources. You can include a sentence or two about the islands around Ravenna, since these islands affected Ravenna itself.

Source #4

Don't forget to add "Vol. 2" after the title when you write down the information about this book.

SKETCHES AND STUDIES

IN

SOUTHERN EUROPE

BY

JOHN ADDINGTON SYMONDS

AUTHOR OF "STUDIES OF THE GREEK POETS" ETC.

IN TWO VOLUMES

Vol. II.

NEW YORK
HARPER & BROTHERS, FRANKLIN SQUARE
1880

110 *Sketches and Studies in Southern Europe.*

RAVENNA.

The Emperor Augustus chose Ravenna for one of his two naval stations, and in course of time a new city arose by the seashore, which received the name of Portus Classis. Between this harbor and the mother city a third town sprang up, and was called Cæsarea. Time and neglect, the ravages of war, and the encroaching powers of Nature, have destroyed these settlements, and nothing now remains of the three cities but Ravenna. It would seem that in classical times Ravenna stood, like modern Venice, in the centre of a huge lagoon, the fresh waters of the Ronco and the Po mixing with the salt waves of the Adriatic round its very walls. The houses of the city were built on piles; canals instead of streets formed the means of communication, and these were always filled with water artificially conducted from the southern estuary of the Po. Round Ravenna extended a vast morass, for the most part under shallow water, but rising at intervals into low islands like the Lido or Murano or Torcello which surround Venice. These islands were celebrated for their fertility: the vines and fig-trees and pomegranates, springing from a fat and fruitful soil, watered with constant moisture, and fostered by a mild sea-wind and liberal sunshine, yielded crops that for luxuriance and quality surpassed the harvests of any orchards on the mainland. All the conditions of life in old Ravenna seem to have resembled those of modern Venice; the people went about in gondolas, and in the early morning barges laden with fresh fruit or meat and vegetables flocked from all quarters to the city

Source #5
This book has a very long title! When you cite it, just use *A Journey in Carniola, Italy, and France in the Years 1817, 1818,* Vol. 2. The publisher and city should be listed as Edinburgh: Archibald Constable and Co.

A

JOURNEY

IN

CARNIOLA, ITALY, AND FRANCE,

IN

THE YEARS 1817, 1818,

CONTAINING

REMARKS RELATING TO LANGUAGE, GEOGRAPHY, HISTORY, ANTIQUITIES, NATURAL HISTORY, SCIENCE, PAINTING, SCULPTURE, ARCHITECTURE, AGRICULTURE, THE MECHANICAL ARTS AND MANUFACTURES.

BY W. A. CADELL, ESQ. F. R. S. LOND. & ED.

WITH ENGRAVINGS.

IN TWO VOLUMES.

VOL. II.

EDINBURGH:

PRINTED FOR ARCHIBALD CONSTABLE AND CO. EDINBURGH; AND HURST, ROBINSON, AND CO. CHEAPSIDE, LONDON.

1820.

on Dante were delivered also in Bologna, Pisa, and Venice. *

Scarcity of Water in Ancient Ravenna.—In ancient Ravenna there was a great scarcity of fresh water. Martial says that a water cistern was of greater value at Ravenna, and produced a better rent than a vineyard; † the city being then intersected with canals, into which the sea flowed, as Venice is at this day.

Strabo's Description.—Strabo, who lived in the reign of Tiberius, describes Ravenna in the fifth book of his Geography in the following terms: "The largest city in the marshes is Ravenna, entirely built of wood, and intersected by canals through which the water flows, and the passage from one part of the town to the other is by bridges and

boats. It receives a considerable portion of sea-water at the flow of the tide, so that by the tide and by the rivers the mud is entirely carried off, and the unhealthy state of the atmosphere is prevented. And the place is so healthy that the Roman emperors fixed upon it for the training of gladiators. It is very remarkable and uncommon that the atmosphere is not unhealthy at Ravenna in a marsh. The same is observed at Alexandria in Egypt, where the inundation of the river in summer destroys the noxious effects of the marshes by covering them with water. The state of the vines at Ravenna deserves to be mentioned as wonderful; the marsh causes their rapid growth, and they bear much fruit; but the vines die at the end of four or five years."

Asparagus.—Pliny celebrates the cultivated asparagus of Ravenna. * At Rome, and in other parts of Italy at this day, wild asparagus collected in the fields is used at table in the month of March; they have also cultivated asparagus in the gardens. The wild asparagus is mentioned by Juvenal. †

Ancient Columns.—Many ancient monolithic columns of Levant marble still adorn the churches of

Day Two: Practicing the Topos, Part Two: The Chronological Narrative

Focus: Writing a chronological narrative
of a past event

In previous lessons, whenever you've been assigned a chronological narrative, you've also been given a list of events in chronological order. This week, you'll put together your own list of events before you write.

STEP ONE: **Arrange notes in chronological order**

You took notes about Caesar's actions from two books, *The Delphian Course* and *Caesar's Commentaries on the Gallic War.* In this step, you'll put the notes from both books together into one chronological list, cutting out unnecessary repetition.

Here's an example. From *Caesar's Commentaries,* you might have written down the following three events:

> Caesar found out about the senate's decree "at Ravenna, on the 10th of January, 49 BC." (xiii)
> Caesar "crossed the Rubicon . . . and advanced into Italy." (xiii)
> As he marched through Italy, "town after town threw open its gates" to him. (xiii)

From *The Delphian Course,* you might have written down:

> Caesar "completed his Gallic campaign" in 49 BC. (480)
> The senate was afraid of Caesar and "asked him to disband his soldiers." (480)
> Caesar refused and "crossed the Rubicon, the stream north of Rome." (480)

Putting those two lists together so that all of the events are in order would look like this:

> Caesar "completed his Gallic campaign" in 49 BC. (480)
> The senate was afraid of Caesar and "asked him to disband his soldiers." (480)
> Caesar found out about the senate's decree "at Ravenna, on the 10th of January, 49 BC." (xiii)
> Caesar refused and "crossed the Rubicon, the stream north of Rome." (480)
> ~~Caesar "crossed the Rubicon~~ . . . ~~and advanced into Italy." (xiii)~~
> As he marched through Italy, "town after town threw open its gates" to him. (xiii)

After putting the events in order, you would delete any notes that repeat the same information (like the crossed-out note above). If a note repeats *some* information but also provides new facts, you may leave it. For example, in the following:

> In 44 BC, Caesar was assassinated because of "the mistaken conceptions of eighty senators." (481)
> He was "assassinated in the senate house, on the 15th of March, 44 BC." (xiv)

the two notes repeat that Caesar was assassinated in 44 BC, but the first note tells you *who* and the second tells you *where* and *when*.

If you're using a word processor, create a new document and cut and paste information from both lists of events into it. If you're using note cards, simply arrange the cards in order and set aside the ones that have repeated information.

Notice that in the list above it's very obvious which notes are from *Caesar's Commentaries* (the page numbers are all in Roman numerals) and which ones are from *The Delphian Course* (they all come from page 480 or 481). But if the two sources had similar page numbers, you'd want to add a source or author name to each note to keep you from mixing them up by accident:

> Caesar refused and "crossed the Rubicon, the stream north of Rome." (Delphian Society, 480)
> As he marched through Italy, "town after town threw open its gates" to him. (Harkness, xiii)

Your last instruction: if it isn't completely clear what events happened first, just make an intelligent guess.

If you have trouble, ask your instructor for help.

STEP TWO: Divide notes into main points

Look one more time at that list of details about Alexander the Great back on pages 52–54.

Taught by Aristotle from ages 13–16
Most famous philosopher in the world at this time
Gave Alexander lifelong thirst for knowledge
Interested in medicine, philosophy, history
Father assassinated in 336 BC
Assassin was bodyguard, Pausanias
Pausanias then killed by rest of bodyguard
Succeeded his father to the throne
Twenty years old
Had all of his rivals to the throne murdered
Greek cities rebelled, had to reconquer them

Now that you've had some experience in outlining, you should recognize this format. It's a two-level outline, without the numbers and letters.

I. **Taught by Aristotle from ages 13–16**
   A. Most famous philosopher in the world at this time
   B. Gave Alexander lifelong thirst for knowledge
   C. Interested in medicine, philosophy, history

So right from the beginning of this course, you've been using an outline to write your compositions.

Before you can write your chronological narrative about Caesar, you need to make yourself an outline. You're going to do this by dividing your list of events up into five groups and giving each group a phrase or sentence that explains what it's about.

Here's an example. Imagine that these are the first eight notes that you have on your list.

Caesar "completed his Gallic campaign" in 49 BC. (480)
The senate was afraid of Caesar and "asked him to disband his soldiers." (480)
The senate told Caesar "to resign the governorship of both Gauls and disband his army." (xiii)
Caesar found out about the senate's decree "at Ravenna, on the 10th of January, 49 BC." (xiii)
Caesar refused and "crossed the Rubicon, the stream north of Rome." (480)
As he marched through Italy, "town after town threw open its gates" to him. (xiii)
Caesar reached the capital "sixty days after the edict of the senate." (xiii)
Caesar entered Rome and "brought order instead of turmoil to the city." (480)

The first four events are all leading up to the senate's decree, so you can group them all together and describe them like this:

I. The senate's decree to Caesar
   Caesar "completed his Gallic campaign" in 49 BC. (480)
   The senate was afraid of Caesar and "asked him to disband his soldiers." (480)
   The senate told Caesar "to resign the governorship of both Gauls and disband his army." (xiii)
   Caesar found out about the senate's decree "at Ravenna, on the 10th of January, 49 BC." (xiii)

These events will be the basis for the first paragraph of your chronological narrative. (The events at the beginning of your list may not be identical, but you can still use "The senate's decree to Caesar" as your first point.)

Now look at the next four events. What title or description would you give them?

After you've settled on a title or description, divide the remaining events into three more groups. Give each group a title or description. If you're using a word processor, give the titles Roman numerals and type them into your document, using the same format as above:

II. Title for second group of notes
    event
    event
    event
III. Title for third group of notes
    event
    event
    event

and so on. If you're using note cards, write each title on a separate note card and place it in front of the group of cards that it describes.

If you have trouble dividing the events into groups or giving them titles and descriptions, your instructor will help you.

When you're finished, you should have five groups of events. Show your work to your instructor before going on.

STEP THREE: **Write the chronological narrative**

Take a minute to review the Chronological Narrative of a Past Event chart in the Reference section of your notebook.

Using the outline you have created, write a five-paragraph chronological narrative about Julius Caesar. Write one paragraph for each main point. Your narrative should be at least 200 words but not longer than 400.

Do not use the exact words of your sources unless you use quotation marks and a footnote (or endnote). If you describe something that is common knowledge (like a historical event) in your own words, you do not need to provide a footnote. But if you use an idea that is not common knowledge, be sure to use a footnote even if you put the idea into your own words. If you're not sure, provide a footnote (better safe than plagiarizing!).

Be sure to quote directly from each source at least once.

Review these examples before you write.

Source material:

In 44 BC, Caesar was assassinated because of "the mistaken conceptions of eighty senators." (481)

Common knowledge, no footnote needed:

Caesar was assassinated by the senators of Rome in 44 BC.

Needs a footnote because it uses the exact words of the source:

"In 44 BC, the mighty Caesar fell."[1]

---

1. Delphian Society, *The Delphian Course* (The Society, 1913), p. 481.

Needs a footnote because it is the writer's specific idea that the senators made a mistake:

Caesar was assassinated in 44 BC because of "the mistaken conceptions of eight senators."[1]

---

1. Delphian Society, *The Delphian Course* (The Society, 1913), p. 481.

When you are finished, show your composition to your instructor.

Day Three: Practicing the Topos, Part Three: The Personal Description

Focus: Writing a description of a person

The passage about Charles I that you outlined at the beginning of last week was a chronological narrative that also included a description of a place (Windsor Castle) and a person (Charles I as a young man). Now that you've put together a basic chronological narrative, you'll add these elements to make a complete composition.

Today, you'll use your notes on Caesar's character and person to write a description of him.

STEP ONE: Review the elements of a personal description

Before you begin to write, go back and read through the Description of a Person chart in the Reference section of your notebook.

This should remind you that a description of a person can include much more than simple physical appearance. Glance back now at the notes you took on Willis Mason West's *Ancient History to the Death of Charlemagne* and Adrian Keith Goldsworthy's *Caesar: Life of a Colossus.* On a scratch piece of paper, jot down the aspects found in the Description of a Person chart that your notes also include.

For example, if you wrote

Caesar had "gracious courtesy and unrivaled charm" that attracted even his enemies. (381)

in your notes on *Ancient History to the Death of Charlemagne*, you would jot down

Character qualities
What others think

on your scratch paper.

You could also use "behaviors" or even "expressions of face and body" to classify that particular quote. Don't worry too much about which exact aspect is the "right" one; the goal here is to make sure that you cover several different aspects in your description.

When you're finished, you should have at least three or four aspects written down. If you have fewer than three, go back to the souce material and look for quotes that illustrate at least one more aspect of Caesar.

If you have trouble, ask your instructor for help.

STEP TWO: **Plan the personal description**

Look again at your Description of a Person chart. Notice that there are two suggestions in the "Remember" column. Before you go on, turn back to Weeks 17 and 18 in your text. Read the instructions for Days Two and Three in each week.

As you write your description of Caesar, you will slant it in either a positive or negative direction. (You'll review using a governing metaphor in a later lesson.)

Choose three or four nouns, adjectives, or verbs used in your notes, and look them up in your thesaurus. Make a list of possible synonyms, both positive and negative. For example, if you took the following note:

> Caesar had "gracious courtesy and unrivaled charm" that attracted even his enemies. (381)

you might decide to look up "gracious." You would find the synonyms:

> *gallant, chivalrous, mannerly, polished; suave, smug, glib, oily-tongued, ingratiating.*

If you wanted to slant your description positively, you could then write

> Caesar had a gallant courtesy and "unrivaled charm."[1]

[1]Willis Mason West, *Ancient History to the Death of Charlemagne* (Allyn and Bacon, 1902), p. 381.

If you chose to slant the description in a negative direction, you could write instead,

> Caesar had a smug, oily-tongued courtesy.

Since the original description was positive, you would probably want to leave off the direct quote from the source.

Aim to have at least three slanted words in your description, along with at least two direct quotes (you'll have to choose these carefully so that they go with the slant you've decided to use).

Once you've listed the synonyms you might make use of, you'll be ready to move on to the third step.

If you have trouble, ask your instructor for help.

STEP THREE: **Write the personal description**

Now use your notes and your list of synonyms to write a description of Caesar. Follow these guidelines:

1. Your description should be at least 50 and not more than 100 words long.
2. The description should be clearly slanted in a positive (admiring) or negative (critical) direction.
3. You should include at least one direct and one indirect quote.
4. The description should cover at least three different aspects of Caesar.

When you are finished, show your work to your instructor.

Day Four: Practicing the Topos, Part Four: The Place Description

Focus: Writing a description of a place

The final element of this week's composition is a description of the city of Ravenna, where Caesar heard about the senate's decree. After you write this description, you'll assemble the full composition, give it a title, and attach a Works Cited page.

STEP ONE: **Review the elements of a place description**

Turn to the Description of a Place chart in the Reference section of your Composition Notebook and read through it. If you don't remember some of the elements on the chart, go back in your text to the following lessons and read through the instructions:

Purpose: Week 8, Day Three

Space and distance words: Week 8, Day Four

Point of view: Week 9, Days Three and Four

Metaphors and similes: Week 10, Days Three and Four

When you are finished with your review, glance back over the notes you took on ancient Ravenna. On the lines below, jot down possible answers:

What purpose will this description serve? ______________________________

____

What point of view will I use? ______________________________

Which three space and distance words will be most useful? ______________________________

____

What metaphor or simile could I use? ______________________________

____

If you can answer these questions without help, go ahead. If you need help, your instructor can give you options to choose from.

STEP TWO: Write the place description

Using your notes, and making reference to the answers you wrote down above, write your description now. Follow these guidelines:

1. Your description should be at least 40 and not more than 90 words long.
2. The purpose of the description should be clear from the adjectives and nouns you use.
3. You should include at least one direct quote.
4. Your point of view should be consistent throughout.
5. The description should include one metaphor or simile.
6. The description should make use of at least two space and distance words.

STEP THREE: Assemble and title the composition

First, insert your place description into your chronological narrative.

The place description should be its own paragraph, and should come right after the paragraph where you mention Ravenna. If you didn't mention Ravenna in your chronological narrative, you'll need to go back and insert the fact that Caesar was at Ravenna after his Gallic campaign/when he heard of the senate's decree. You may also need to write a transitional sentence at the beginning of your place description, relating Caesar's experiences to the description. For example, if you've decided to show that Ravenna was a boring, backwater place to be, you might want to start your paragraph with a sentence like:

> Caesar was anxious to get to Rome, but instead he was forced to wait in Ravenna.

Second, insert your personal description into your chronological narrative.

You can choose where to put the personal description, as long as it doesn't break the flow of the narrative. For example, if you have three paragraphs describing, in order, Caesar's crossing the Rubicon, going through Italy, and then arriving in Rome, you wouldn't want to put the description of Caesar in between any of those paragraphs. That would be like forcing Caesar to stop marching towards Rome in order to give an interview. The most natural place for the description is probably near the end of the composition, either right before or right after the paragraphs describing Caesar's achievements. You may need to provide a transitional sentence or phrase such as "At this time in his life, Caesar was . . ."

Third, title your composition with one of the following:

Julius Caesar's Rise to Power in Rome
Julius Caesar Becomes Dictator
Julius Caesar Takes Control of Rome

Your title should be centered at the top of your first page.

When you are completely finished, make sure that your paper is double-spaced and that the footnotes are in the proper place. (Student papers done on a word processor should always be double-spaced.) If your paper is more than one page long, insert a page number at the bottom left or bottom center of each page.

If you have trouble with this assignment, ask your instructor for help. When you are finished, show your work to your instructor.

STEP FOUR: **Attach the Works Cited page**

You only have one page left to add.

Center the title "Works Cited" at the top of a new page. Beneath this title, aligned with the left-hand margin, list all of the sources you cited in your composition. Use the proper format:

> Author last name, Author first name. *Title.* City of publication: Publisher, date.

Single-space each entry, but double-space *between* each entry. This Works Cited page will be the last page of your composition. (It does not need to have a page number.)

Ask your instructor to check your Works Cited page when you are finished.

Week 30: Writing from Notes: Sequence: Natural Process, Scientific Description

Day One: Outlining Exercise

Focus: Finding the central topics and selected subtopics in each paragraph of a sequence of events

STEP ONE: **Read**

Read the following passage about how the human body controls and uses the act of breathing.

— — —

Delivering oxygen to each cell requires the cooperative efforts of the lungs, heart, trachea (windpipe), and bronchi, the airways that connect the trachea to the lungs.

Before reaching the lungs, air is inhaled through the nose or mouth, where larger impurities are filtered out. Oxygen then moves through the bronchial tree: the trachea, which is about as wide across as your thumb, somewhat smaller pipes called bronchi, and then a branching system of ever-smaller tubes that lead finally to the alveoli (a network of hundreds of millions of microscopic air sacs).

Surrounding these air sacs are millions of tiny blood vessels called capillaries. Oxygen passes through the wall of the alveoli and enters the bloodstream. In exchange, carbon dioxide leaves the blood, enters the alveoli, and is exhaled through the lungs. The oxygen-rich blood then travels to the heart for distribution throughout the body. . . .

The air you breathe is not pure. It is filled with dust, dirt, smoke, and other substances and microorganisms that we cannot see. Your lungs have an elaborate system for filtering out these impurities before they reach and damage the delicate air sacs, the alveoli. The lining of the bronchial tree contains glands

> that make mucus, a thick liquid that traps particles. In addition, the tubes of the bronchial tree are lined with tiny hairs called cilia that beat upward toward the mouth. The bronchial tubes are thus well-equipped to carry mucus (and any particles that have been caught) up to the mouth and nose to be coughed or sneezed out. The last line of defense is the white blood cells of the immune system, stationed in the lining of the bronchial tree and the alveoli where they can engulf particles or kill germs.[209]

STEP TWO: Identify the form of each paragraph

This passage is a sequence describing a natural process. When you studied the form of sequences, you learned that the following elements are often present:

Introduction/summary
Scientific background
Step-by-step process
Repetition of the process

In this particular passage, there is no scientific background or repetition. Instead, the passage describes two *different* (but related) step-by-step processes.

Mark each paragraph as introduction, first process, or second process. When you are finished, check your work with your instructor before going on.

STEP THREE: Construct a one-level outline

The last time you outlined a sequence of natural events, you asked yourself the following questions:

What is this paragraph introducing me to?
Which stage of the process does this paragraph describe?
In this stage of the process, what is the first, or most important, or biggest thing that happens?

Ask yourself the appropriate question about each paragraph of your reading in order to find the main point. If you have trouble, ask your instructor for help. When you are finished, check your work with your instructor.

STEP FOUR: Construct a two-level outline

Now go back and try to find the subpoints in paragraphs 2 and 3.

In a sequence, the subpoints in each paragraph should outline the major *steps* in the step-by-step process. The subpoints should not give descriptive details *about* those steps; instead, the subpoints should *name* those steps in order.

---

209. Anthony L. Komaroff, *The Harvard Medical School Family Health Guide* (Simon & Schuster, 1999), p. 493.

You should find two subpoints in the second paragraph, and three in the third paragraph. When you are finished, check your work with your instructor.

Day Two: Practicing the Topos, Part One: Taking Notes

Focus: Collecting information

Today, you will take notes for a descriptive sequence of your own. Remember that you should write the information for each source, properly formatted, at the top of the page where you're taking notes (or, if you use 3x5 cards, on the first card). Also remember to use quotation marks to surround the exact words of the source. Always put the page number in parentheses after each quote (even if you think you'll remember it).

If necessary, read the instructions for Week 28, Day Four to remind yourself of the proper form.

STEP ONE: **Review the elements of a sequence and a scientific description**

Before you begin to take notes, turn to the Sequence: Natural Process chart in the Reference section of your notebook and read through it. Then turn back to Week 22, Day Two, and read the instructions about constructing a sequence of natural events.

Next, turn to the Scientific Description chart in the Reference section of your notebook and review the elements of a scientific description. Finally, turn back to Week 12, Day Three, and read the instructions about writing a scientific description.

STEP TWO: **Make a preliminary plan**

In the next lesson, you'll write a descriptive sequence that includes a scientific description. Since you are combining two forms, you will not need to include every element of both.

Your sequence should explain the process of digestion. This sequence should have an introduction, a step-by-step explanation of the process, and a conclusion that discusses the repetition of the process. You should also include a brief scientific description of one or more digestive organs. This scientific description should describe each part of the organ(s), should take a particular point of view, and should include figurative language (a simple simile is fine).

Before you begin to take notes, read through both of the sources provided to get an overview of digestion. Then, decide which organ(s) you will describe as part of your composition. (This will keep you from taking unnecessary notes; if you're not going to describe an organ, you don't need to write down all of the details about it.)

STEP THREE: **Take notes**

Take notes on the following two sources, using proper form. You can choose to use either 3x5 cards or a word processing document.

You will see two different kinds of information in these sources: the different steps of digestion, and descriptions of the organs and what they do. When you are simply listing the steps of digestion, you do not need to quote directly. These steps fall under the heading of "widely accepted scientific facts." Scientific facts are generally considered to be common knowledge.

However, if you're using the same words that the source uses to describe an organ or a part of the process, you should use a direct quote.

For example, your notes on page 318 of *Real Things in Nature* might look like this:

> Food goes from the gullet to the stomach and is dissolved by gastric juice. (318)
> Food turns into "a soft mass, like very thick soup." (318)

It is a widely accepted scientific fact that food goes from gullet to stomach, and that gastric juices then dissolve it. But the particular description of the dissolved food as a "soft mass" and the simile "like very thick soup" belong to Edward Holden; you should use quotation marks to set this off.

Do not take more than 15 notes on either source!

When you are finished with your notes, show them to your instructor.

You may list the title simply as *Real Things in Nature* (it isn't necessary to list the entire subtitle).

REAL THINGS IN NATURE

A READING BOOK OF SCIENCE
FOR AMERICAN BOYS AND GIRLS.

BY
EDWARD S. HOLDEN, Sc.D., LL.D.,
LIBRARIAN OF THE UNITED STATES MILITARY ACADEMY, WEST POINT.

New York:
THE MACMILLAN COMPANY
LONDON: MACMILLAN & CO. LTD.
1910

318 THE HUMAN BODY.

in many cases. For instance, if your arm is badly burned and loses its power, your blood will bring the food necessary to make it well and strong again.

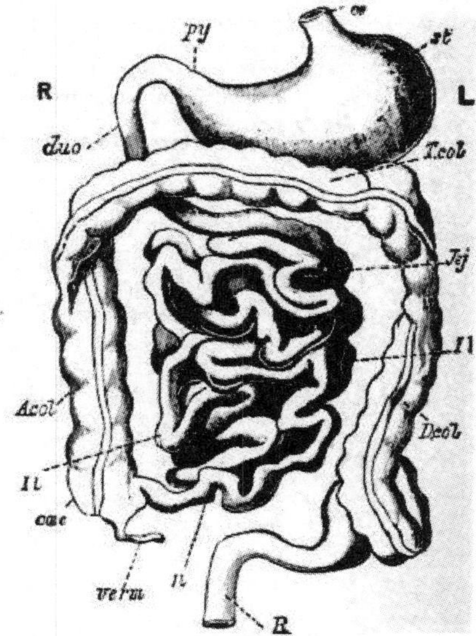

FIG. 298. The stomach, the large intestine, the small intestine (seen from the front): *st* is the stomach; *Il*, the small intestine; *A col, T col, D col*, the large intestine; *verm* is the appendix.

Food taken into the mouth is chewed and then swallowed. It goes through the gullet into the stomach. There it is dissolved by the *gastric-juice* and made into a soft mass, like very thick soup,

FOOD AND HOW IT IS USED. 319

called *chyme*. This is mixed with *bile* from the liver, and with other fluids, and passes into the small intestine where it is turned into a cream-like liquid called *chyle*.

Now at last the food is ready to be taken into the blood. The undigested and useless parts are passed along the bowels and finally ejected.

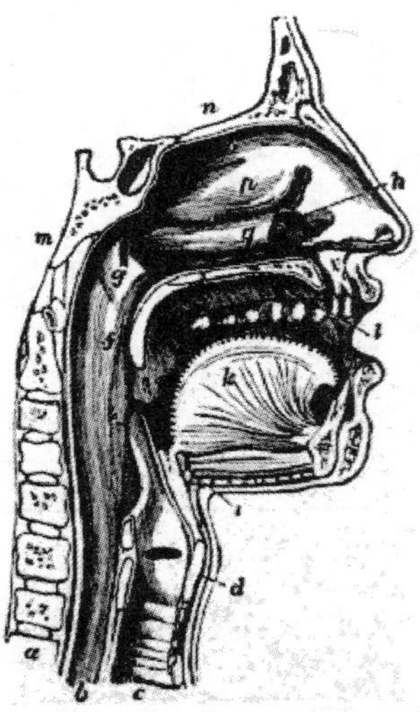

FIG. 299. The throat sliced down the middle: *b* is the gullet; *l*, the roof of the mouth; *c*, the windpipe; *k*, the tongue; *e* is a little lid which shuts down over the windpipe when you swallow so that food cannot go down "the wrong way." Put your fingers on the Adam's apple of the throat, outside, and pretend to swallow. You can feel how the little lid closes the windpipe.

320 THE HUMAN BODY.

Digestion in the Mouth.—If the food is well chewed there is a good supply of *saliva* (spittle) in the mouth. The mouth and gullet are lined with a soft red skin called the *mucous membrane*. (You can see part of it by standing in front of a mirror with your mouth wide open). The *saliva* moistens the food and gets it ready to be swallowed. You could not swallow a cracker—which would be mere dust—unless it were first moistened.

The smell of food, or even the thought of it, makes the *saliva* flow. "It makes your mouth water," we say.

Food Passes Down the Gullet Slowly.—It does not fall down as a brick falls down a chimney. The gullet is a small tube full of rings of muscle which seize the bits of food and move them along from ring to ring. Horses drink with their heads lower than their stomachs by this means. The water they drink is made to flow up-hill.

Gastric Juice.—The moment food enters the stomach gastric juice trickles out, somewhat as sweat on the skin, and begins to digest the food.

A Canadian hunter was accidentally shot so that the bullet left a hole from his abdomen into the stomach. His doctor was able to see exactly how digestion went on by experiments made through this wound.

After a time, sometimes one hour, sometimes as much as four hours, the *chyme* of the stomach begins to move into the small intestine. Usually the stomach is entirely emptied about three or four hours after a meal.

DIGESTION IN THE SMALL INTESTINE.. 321

Digestion in the Stomach.

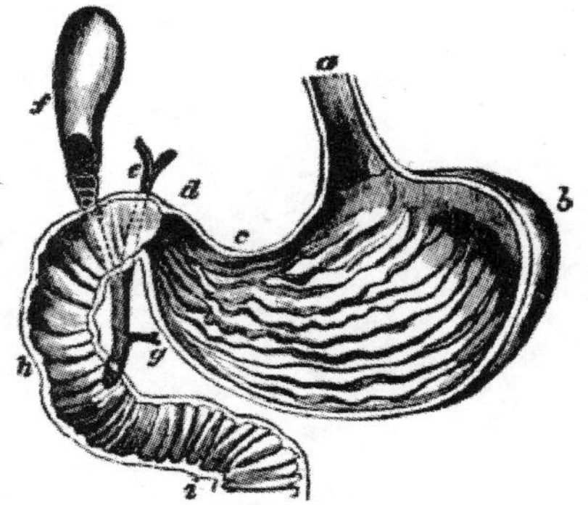

Fig. 300. The stomach sliced in two so as to show: *a*, the lower end of the gullet; *d*, the opening into the small intestine; *e*, the tube through which *bile* comes from the liver. The stomach is large enough to hold about four pints. Its walls are stout and muscular. Inside it is covered with a ***mucous membrane*** full of thousands of small glands that give out ***gastric juice***.

Digestion in the Small Intestine.—The small intestine is coiled up in folds which, if extended, would be about 20 feet long. (See Fig. 298.) It takes up the ***chyme*** and passes it along by its rings of muscle. At the same time the ***chyme*** is changed into ***chyle***—which is very nutritious and looks like cream. As the ***chyle*** passes along it is absorbed, sucked up, by thousands of small tubes. From some of these tubes the ***chyle*** goes into the blood at once. Other tubes take part of it, mix it with ***lymph*** and pour it into a large blood-vessel, ready for use in making new blood.

21

When you use the following, just list the title as *The Class Book of Nature*. The author's full name is John Frost. Hartford, the city of publication, is in Connecticut.

THE

CLASS BOOK OF NATURE;

COMPRISING LESSONS ON

THE UNIVERSE,

THE THREE KINGDOMS OF NATURE,

AND

THE FORM AND STRUCTURE

OF

THE HUMAN BODY.

WITH QUESTIONS AND NUMEROUS ENGRAVINGS.

EDITED BY J. FROST.

FOURTH EDITION.

HARTFORD.

BELKNAP AND HAMERSLEY.

1839.

DIGESTIVE ORGANS. 219

LESSON VIII.

THE ORGANS OF DIGESTION.

As there is a constant waste going on in our bodies, it is needful that it should be regularly supplied with nourishment. For this purpose, we take food, and have a stomach and various other parts, fitted for changing it into a proper form for repairing our system.

The changes which our food undergoes to prepare it, constitute what is called *digestion;* and the actual laying down of new matter by the different vessels is called the process of *nutrition.*

The stomach is a hollow bag, placed just below the breast bone, and lying partly across the body. It is large enough in a grown man to hold about three pints of fluid, and is joined to the mouth by a tube, or passage, called the *gullet.* The opening into this is seen lying quite at the back of the throat, and it receives the food after it has been crushed by the teeth, or *masticated,* and mixed with saliva. In this pulpy state it is passed into the stomach by the gullet pressing it downwards.

After the food has remained in the stomach for a time, it begins to contract and pushes it through an opening into the *intestines.*

The intestines form one continued canal, or tube, about five or six yards long, lying in a wonderfully small space, and most curiously folded one upon another.

On page 220, "eminences" means "bumps" or "elevations"; the villi are like tiny fingers.

220 DIGESTIVE ORGANS.

They have several coats or linings, the inner one being red, full of plaits, and covered with little eminences, termed *villi*, which give it a *velvety* appearance. These *villi* are the beginnings of the vessels which convey away the nourishing juice.

The outer coat of the intestines is smooth and shining, and always moistened by a watery fluid to keep it soft, and to allow the parts to move easily over each other.

Between these two coats is another, called the muscular coat. It is this which enables the intestines to push forward their contents, and which gives to them a constant motion, something like that of a worm when crawling, and hence called, vermicular, or *peristaltic*.

The following image is of page 223:

The food which we eat to supply the waste in our bodies, is first submitted to the action of the teeth. These, by their hardness and sharpness, break it into small fragments, whilst the glands give out saliva in abundance.

By these means the food is made into a soft pulp, and in this state it passes into the stomach. When it is received there, the vessels of that part throw out a fluid called the *gastric* juice. This is a very powerful solvent, and by mixing with the food, brings it into a half fluid state, when it is called *chyme*, and is of a grayish colour.

This change being finished, the lower opening of the stomach, which had remained fast closed, whilst it was going on, opens and permits the *chyme* to pass into the small *intestines*. Here it is made still more fluid, by the addition of various juices, and becomes of a milky whiteness, and now it is called *chyle*. In this state it meets with the *bile*, which is supposed to have the property of separating the *nutritious* from the useless parts.

The reader has learnt that the inner surface of the small intestines is lined by *villi*, which are the mouths of *lacteals*. These are now actively at work, taking up the milky part of the chyle, and carrying it to a number of glands, where it undergoes some farther change.

From these it is carried forwards, till all the *lacteals* are at last collected into one large duct, which conveys the stream of chyle, now fitted for mixing with the blood, along the spine, up as high as the neck; here it opens into one of the great veins, and after passing through the heart and lungs, becomes perfectly mixed, and ready for *nutrition*.

These are the changes undergone by our food before it becomes blood, and they come under the general term, *digestion*.

Day Three: Practicing the Topos, Part Two: Write

Focus: Writing a descriptive sequence combined with a scientific description

Today you will use your notes to write a descriptive sequence of digestion, combined with a scientific description of at least one of the organs used for digestion.

STEP ONE: **Write the description**

Start by writing your description.

Go through your notes and mark with a highlighter (or underline) the notes that describe particular organs. Then, use those notes and the illustrations in the source texts to write a description, following these guidelines:

1. The description must focus on one particular digestive organ.
2. The description must be at least two sentences and 40 words in length.

3. The description should have a consistent point of view.
4. The description should tell what at least two parts of the organ look like and what they do.
5. At least one metaphor or simile should be used.

You may use a direct quote, but this is not a requirement. Remember to footnote the exact words or ideas of the source material, but not generally accepted scientific facts.

If you have trouble with your description, ask your instructor for help. When you're finished, show your description to your instructor.

STEP TWO: **Write the sequence**

Now you'll use the same strategy you used for your Julius Caesar paper to arrange your notes and write your sequence.

Go back to your notes and rearrange them so that all of the events involved in digestion are listed in order. If you're using a word processor, create a new document and cut and paste information from both lists of events into it. If you're using note cards, simply arrange the cards in order and set aside the ones that have repeated information. You can cut the notes that simply give description, since your description is already written.

Be sure not to lose track of which notes go with which source.

Once you've arranged all of your events in order, go back and divide them into groups. Each group of events should cover a different stage of digestion.

Give each group a Roman numeral and a title or description.

Then write your composition. Write one paragraph for each main point. Do not use the exact words of your sources unless you use quotation marks and a footnote. If you describe a scientific fact in your own words, you do not need to provide a footnote. If you're not sure, use a footnote.

Your completed sequence should be at least 150 words in length. Use at least one direct quote.

If you have trouble with any of these steps, ask your instructor for help. If not, you can wait to show your composition to your instructor until it is assembled in the next step.

STEP THREE: **Assemble the composition**

Now insert your description into your sequence at the most appropriate place—probably where the organ is first mentioned.

Attach a Works Cited page where you list the bibliographical information for the book or books you cited in your paper.

Give your paper a title, centered on the first page. (Nothing fancy—"Human Digestion" is fine.)

Make sure that your paper is double-spaced. If it is more than one page in length, not including the Works Cited page, give the pages numbers. If there is only one page, you do not need to give it the number "1."

When you are finished, show your work to your instructor.

Day Four: Copia Exercise

Focus: Main verbs and infinitives

STEP ONE: **Review**

Take a few minutes now to read down your Sentence Variety chart. When you are finished, rewrite the following sentences (freely adapted from Edward Holden's *Real Things in Nature*). Each sentence contains a phrase or clause that can be easily transformed, using the principles you've already learned.

If you have difficulty, ask your instructor for help. When you are finished, check your work with your instructor.

Underneath the skin is a layer of fat, and under the fat are the muscles.

____

____

The outer layer of our skin is dead and is continually being worn away.

____

____

The science of physiology teaches us the uses of all the parts of the body.

____

____

The muscles of our body make it possible for us to move, to walk, and to stand erect.

____

____

STEP TWO: **Understand how to transform main verbs into infinitives**

In the last copia exercise that you did (back in Week 22), you learned that a main verb can be followed by an infinitive (a verb form that starts with "to"). You also learned that an infinitive can be changed to a participle, and vice versa.

infinitive
The star begins to grow hungry for a new energy source.

participle
The star begins growing hungry for a new energy source.

With your pencil, underline the word "begins" twice (in both sentences). This is the main verb of the sentence.

A main verb can be followed by an infinitive (or participle) that completes its meaning. But you can also transform a main verb *into* an infinitive or participle. Read the following two sentences out loud, listening the differences in sound.

We breathe whether we think about it or not.

We continue to breathe whether we think about it or not.

With your pencil, underline the word "breathe" in the first sentence twice. Write "main verb" above it. In the second sentence, underline "continue" twice. Write "main verb" above it. Then underline "to breathe" once and write "inf." above it.

In the second sentence, the main verb has been changed to an infinitive. But since that leaves the sentence without a main verb, a *new* main verb has to be provided.

This changes the meaning of the sentence a little bit. If I had decided to use other main verbs, the meaning of the sentence would change yet again.

We remember to breathe whether we think about it or not.
We don't forget to breathe whether we think about it or not.
We need to breathe whether we think about it or not.

You can also add adjectives and nouns, if necessary, to help connect the main verb to the infinitive.

adj.
We are able to breathe whether we think about it or not.

noun
We have the ability to breathe whether we think about it or not.

When you change the main verb to an infinitive, you have the opportunity to add another level or shade of meaning to your sentence.

STEP THREE: **Add to the Sentence Variety chart**

Write the following principle and illustrations on the next line of your Sentence Variety chart.

main verb ⟷ infinitive	I usually plan ahead. I usually need to plan ahead. I usually manage to plan ahead.

STEP FOUR: **Practice sentence variety**

In the following sentences, transform each main verb into an infinitive. Rewrite each sentence twice, providing a new main verb each time.

Chyme moves from the stomach into the small intestine.

____

____

____

____

Babies learn to use their mucles as they grow.

____

____

____

____

You should understand how your body works.

Week 31: Writing from Notes: Biographical Sketch, Description of a Person

Day One: Outlining Exercise

Focus: Finding the central topics and selected subtopics in each paragraph of a biographical sketch

STEP ONE: **Read**

Read the following biographical sketch of physicist Marie Curie, born in 1867. Marie Curie won two Nobel prizes, one in physics in 1903 and the second in chemistry in 1911; she was the first person to win two Nobel prizes.

Piezoelectricity is an electrical charge that is produced when pressure is put on certain kinds of crystals (such as quartz and tourmaline). "Ecole Superieure de Physique et de Chimie" is French for "College of Physics and Chemistry."

— — —

Curie was born in Warsaw, the fifth and last child in the family. Her multilingual father taught physics and mathematics at a high school; her mother ran a small boarding school for girls in their home.

Warsaw was under Russian rule when Curie was at school, so the students had their lessons in Russian. Curie won a gold medal for her achievements in secondary school but overworked during her last school year and was sent to stay with relatives in the country for a few months to recover.

Curie and her older sister Bronya decided to study medicine in Paris, where women were admitted. They planned to work to save money for Bronya's education; once she was qualified and earning, she would send for Curie to start her university education. Curie became a resident governess in the village of Szczuki and ran a literacy class for the village children. By 1885, the sisters had saved enough money for Bronya to begin her studies in Paris. Five years later, Curie joined her there. Her sister was to marry Casimir, a fellow medical student; Marie could live with them. By July 1893 she took her first physics examination and was at the top of her group. In 1894, using a government scholarship from Poland, she studied for a degree in mathematics, which she achieved with distinction. . . .

In 1894 she was introduced to Pierre Curie, a physicist who with his brother Jacques had worked on piezoelectricity. Pierre's parents lived at Sceaux, on the outskirts of Paris. Marie and Pierre Curie were married on 26 July 1895 and went off for a bicycling honeymoon. Pierre Curie was a lecturer at the Ecole Superieure de Physique et de Chimie in Paris. Marie Curie was allowed a room in the same building as she needed space for her experiments on the magnetic properties of tempered steels; she was aided by a grant from the Society for the Advancement of National Industry, and her results were published in 1897. On 12 September that year their first daughter, Irene, was born. . . .

Pierre Curie was appointed as a professor at the Sorbonne in 1904, with Marie in charge of his laboratory. She taught part time at Sevres until their second daughter, Eve, was born in December 1904. Pierre had published twenty-one papers between 1898 and 1904, some coauthored (five with Marie), but after that he did no more experimental work, as he fell too ill; yet he continued with his teaching responsibilities. After the family had returned from a holiday in the countryside, on 19 April 1906, Pierre Curie fell in front of a pair of horses and his skull was crushed. Marie Curie stepped into her husband's position as professor. . . . She gave her first lecture at the Sorbonne on 5 November 1906, the first woman to lecture there in physics.[210]

STEP TWO: **Construct a one-level outline**

When outlining a biographical sketch, the most useful question you can ask yourself is "What aspect of the person's life or character does this paragraph focus on?" In Week 18, you asked yourself this question while outlining a biographical sketch of the painter Jan Brueghel; in Week 19, you asked the same question for a biographical sketch of Edgar Allan Poe.

That question will work very well for the first two paragraphs of the sketch. For the last three paragraphs, however, you may need to take a slightly different approach.

Each one of these paragraphs progresses chronologically through events in Marie Curie's life. Each paragraph also covers a certain span of time. One way for you to sum up each paragraph would be: List the period of time that the paragraph covers. For example, the third paragraph could be given the title:

210. Catharine M. C. Haines, *International Women in Science: A Biographical Dictionary to 1950* (ABC-CLIO, 2001), pp. 76–77.

III. Curie's life between secondary school and 1894

That's not a very exciting main point, but it's a very accurate summing up of the main purpose of the paragraph.

But you could also sum up the paragraph by going back to a question you've used for many other outlines: What is the most important thing that happens to Marie Curie in this paragraph?

She begins her university education. The paragraph tells you everything that leads up to Curie's university entrance, but the whole point of those details is that Curie finally made it to the university and began to study physics and mathematics.

Now do a one-level outline of this passage. For paragraphs three through five, provide two main points—one that sums up the period of time, and one that tells the most important thing that happens in the paragraph. Write the outline like this:

III. Curie's life between secondary school and 1894 OR
Curie begins her university education

(You can use those main points for III.)

If you have difficulty, ask your instructor for help. When you're finished, show your work to your instructor.

STEP THREE: **Construct a two-level outline**

Now go back and add subpoints to your outline for points III, IV, and V only.

In a biographical sketch that progresses chronologically, the subpoints are likely to be the most important events in each paragraph. Try to list ONLY the events that are *directly related* to the main points that tell the most important thing that happens in the paragraph. So, for the third paragraph, ONLY include those events that are directly related to Curie's beginning her university education. (That means that Bronya's education and marriage shouldn't be subpoints. Those events are indirectly related to Curie's own education, so those would appear in a more detailed outline.)

Try to use only four subpoints for III, three subpoints for IV, and three subpoints for V.

Day Two: Practicing the Topos, Part One: Taking Notes

Focus: Collecting information

Today, you will take notes for a biographical sketch of the French queen Marie Antoinette. Remember that you should write the information for each source, properly formatted, at the top of the page where you're taking notes (or, if you use 3x5 cards, on the first card). Also remember to use quotation marks to surround the exact words of the source. Always put the page number in parentheses after each quote (even if you think you'll remember it).

STEP ONE: **Review the elements of a biographical sketch and description of a person**

Before you begin to take notes, turn to the Biographical Sketch chart in the Reference section of your notebook and read through it. Then turn back to Week 19, Day Two, and Week 20, Day Two and read the instructions in both of those lessons.

Next, turn to the Description of a Person chart in the Reference section of your notebook and review the elements of a personal description. Finally, turn back to Week 16, Day Two; Week 17, Day Two; and Week 18, Day Two. Read the instructions about writing descriptions in all three of those lessons.

Remember—your biographical sketch will include selected aspects from the Description of a Person chart.

STEP TWO: **Make a preliminary plan**

In the next two lessons, you'll take notes and write a biographical sketch that includes selected aspects from the Description of a Person chart.

You will have three major choices to make as you take notes and write. Here's a summary of your choices:

1. What will the focus be?
   First option: A chronological listing of major life events
   Second option: A brief summary of life events, followed by a survey of the subject's accomplishments and achievements
2. What aspects from the Description of a Person chart will you include?
3. Which of the following strategies will you use? (You have to pick one.)
   First option: Slant your description (and sketch) in either a positive or negative

direction by using appropriate adjectives, nouns, and verbs

Second option: Choose an overall metaphor to give clues about the character of your subject.

Before you begin to take notes, read through all of the sources provided on pp. 422–429 to get an overview of the subject of Marie Antoinette. Then, make a tentative decision about each of these choices. (You may change your mind later, but this will help focus your note-taking so that you don't write down too many unnecessary details.)

STEP THREE: **Take initial notes from an encyclopedia**

In the next two steps, you will take notes on the following sources, using proper form. You can choose to use either 3x5 cards or a word processing document.

The first source is an article from the *Chambers's Encyclopedia*, a well-respected British encyclopedia. When you're writing about a new subject, an encyclopedia is often the best place to start. Encyclopedia entries give you a succinct summary of the most important facts about your subject, and this will give you some idea of the topics that your composition should cover.

In most cases, you won't want to cite the encyclopedia article itself in your final composition. Instead, use it to make an initial list of facts.

If you use *World Book*, *Encyclopedia Britannica*, or another recognized encyclopedia, you can trust the facts you find there. If you use Wikipedia to make your initial list of facts, you must check every one of them with a published source before using it in your composition. Wikipedia can be a useful first stop when you're first investigating something unfamiliar. But unlike a recognized encyclopedia, Wikipedia doesn't require any sort of expertise or training for its contributors, and there is no systematic fact-checking. So always confirm all information discovered on Wikipedia with at least one independent source.

Now read through the following article and write down, in list form, the most important events in Marie Antoinette's life. Since the entire article comes from page 326, you do not need to put the page number next to each event.

Try to list *only* historical facts that can be classified as common knowledge.

Chambers's Encyclopedia: A Dictionary of Universal Knowledge, Vol. 6. London: W. & R. Chambers, 1886, p. 326.

MARIE ANTOINETTE DE LORRAINE, Josephine Jeanne, wife of Louis XVI of France, was the youngest daughter of Francis I, Emperor of Germany. Her mother was the famous Maria Theresa, queen of Austria. Marie was born at Vienna, November 2, 1755.

At the age of fourteen, she was betrothed to the Dauphin of France; and in the following year was married at the palace of Versailles. Her lack of ceremony and hatred for rigid etiquette scandalised the court at Versailles. Soon after the accession of Louis XVI (May 1774), libels were circulated by her enemies, accusing her of constant intrigues and sins, not one of which has ever been proved.

Her faults, as a queen. . . were a certain levity of disposition, a girlish love of pleasure, banquets, fine dress, an aristocratic indifference to general opinion, and a lamentable incapacity to see the actual misery of France. The affair of the diamond necklace, in 1785, hopelessly compromised her good name in the eye of the public, although, in point of fact, she was quite innocent of any grave offence.

Her political role was not more fortunate. Her two favorite ministers were de Brienne and Calonne, and she shared the condemnation called down on them by the people for their reckless squandering of the national finances. She strongly opposed the Assembly of the Notables (a group of French aristocrats convened by the king to discuss state issues) in 1788. She also opposed, the following year, the assembling of the States-General (the legislative assembly of pre-revolutionary France). She had good reason to dread their convocation, for one of the very first things the Assembly of Notables did was to declare the queen the cause of France's financial difficulty.

From the first hour of the Revolution (May 1789–1799), Marie was an object of fanatical hatred to the mob of Paris. Her life was attempted at Versailles by a band of assassins on the morning of October 6, 1789, and she narrowly escaped. After this, she made some spasmodic efforts to gain the goodwill of the populace by visiting the great factories of the capital and by seeming to take an interest in the labours of the workmen, but the time was gone by for such weak efforts to succeed. The relentless populace only hated her the more.

At last she resolved on flight. Her husband long refused to abandon his country, and she would not go without him. Louis XVI had a dim sense of kingly duty and honour, but after a mob stopped his coach in April 1791, and would not let him leave Paris, he consented.

The flight took place on the night of the 20th of June, 1791. Unfortunately, the royal fugitives were recognised, and captured at the town of Varennes, near the Austrian border. From this time, Marie's attitude became heroic; but the French people could not rid themselves of the suspicion that she was secretly plotting with the allies for the invasion of the country. She was confined in the fortress in Paris called the Temple, separated from her family and friends, and subjected to most sickening humiliations.

On Aug. 1, 1793, by order of the National Convention (the new legislative assembly of revolutionary France), she was taken to the prison known as La Conciergerie. She was condemned by the Revolutionary Tribunal on Oct. 15, and guillotined the next day.

When you're finished, show your notes to your instructor before going on.

STEP FOUR: Take additional notes from other sources

Now take additional notes on the aspects and events you intend to use in your sketch.

Remember, historical events are generally considered to be common knowledge. However, if you use the writer's specific interpretation of those events, be sure to use a direct quote.

In the encyclopedia article above, for example, you would not need to footnote the fact that Marie and Louis fled on June 20, 1791; that they were captured in Varennes; or that Marie was imprisoned in the Temple fortress. However, if you decided to write that Marie had a heroic attitude during all of this, you would be using the encyclopedia's own interpretation. Not everyone agrees that Marie was being heroic—but everyone agrees that she fled on June 20.

So your notes might look like this:

> Marie and Louis XVI fled on June 20, 1791.
> They were captured in Varennes.
> "Marie's attitude became heroic" during her imprisonment. (326)

(As noted above, it's usually better not to quote directly from an encyclopedia—this is just an example.)

Do not take more than 15 notes on any single source. You can always go back to the source while you're writing if you need more information.

When you are finished with your notes, show them to your instructor.

Source #1, published 1913.

NOTABLE WOMEN IN HISTORY

THE LIVES OF WOMEN WHO IN ALL AGES, ALL LANDS AND IN ALL WOMANLY OCCUPATIONS HAVE WON FAME AND PUT THEIR IMPRINT ON THE WORLD'S HISTORY

BY

WILLIS J. ABBOT

AUTHOR OF "THE BLUE JACKET" SERIES, "THE BATTLEFIELDS" SERIES, "THE STORY OF OUR NAVY," "AMERICAN MERCHANT SHIPS AND SAILORS," ETC.

Illustrated

PHILADELPHIA, PA.
THE JOHN C. WINSTON CO.
PUBLISHERS

MARIE ANTOINETTE

(1755–1793)

THE DIAMOND NECKLACE AND THE GUILLOTINE

ONCE upon a time a queen of France, when the people of Paris were literally starving, was reported to have said innocently: "If they have no bread why don't they eat cake?"

About this same time a clever swindler, calling herself Countess de la Motte de Valois and an earlier prototype of Mme. Humbert, used the name of the queen to swindle a trusting jeweler out of a diamond necklace, and in the enterprise duped the Cardinal de Rohan and dragged that proudest of French names in the dust.

Queen Marie Antoinette probably never made the heartless jest at the expense of a starving people. Certainly she was no party to the diamond necklace swindle. But the mob of Paris, maddened by oppression and privation, believed she could laugh at their misery. They had been taught that kings and queens were more than ordinary mortals, but here was a queen conspiring with the basest swindlers to rob a jeweler. For the jester they had hatred and execration; for the swindler they lost all reverence and fear. Save for the temper of the people the affair would have been trivial. But it proved all important. "Mind that miserable affair of the necklace," said Talleyrand.

(146)

"I should not be surprised if it should overturn the French monarchy." The wiliest of European diplomats foresaw correctly.

Marie Antoinette was born in 1755, and was accordingly fifteen years old when in 1770 she was married to the Dauphin of France, who became King Louis XVI and gave his head as tribute to the French revolution. Her mother, Maria Theresa, was not merely the wife of Francis I, and therefore empress of Austria —she was one of the great monarchs of history, a ruler fit to be ranked with Isabella of Castile, Elizabeth of England, and Catherine of Russia. The daughter possessed many of the mother's regal qualities, and had she not been impeded with a supine and flabby husband might have checked the revolution in its incipiency, thus averting an upheaval which, though fatal to her, has been of surpassing value to humanity in all succeeding generations.

The progress of the child bride across the provinces of France to the great palace at Versailles, where the nuptials were to be celebrated, was triumphant. The nobility and country folk turned out to do her honor. The roads were strewn with flowers and her nights were dream hours of music and poesy. Only when she reached Versailles did the air grow chill. Her bridegroom, indeed, was enraptured with her appearance and the king cordiality itself. But the ladies of the gayest and most intriguant court in all Europe looked askance upon this new factor in the life of the palace. Versailles, to-day the property of the French people, is a palace which could house a whole cityful. In the days of the last two Kings Louis it was thronged by thousands of idle, dissipated, immoral courtiers.

They looked on the prospective dauphiness as a new power, necessary to reckon with and most annoyingly likely to unsettle all their existing combinations. Saying she was too free in her manners, they turned from her to the courtesan Du Barry, who at the moment had the king under her influence, and whose manners and morals seemed quite in accord with the requirements of the court. Marie Antoinette had entered the most artificial society in all Europe, and her girlish sense of humor impelled her to laugh at its follies. Grand dames drew comfortable pensions for pulling off the queen's stockings at night or tying the ribbons of her night cap. To put on the king's coat of a morning required the salaried services of four noblemen in waiting. All this the dauphiness laughed at and was correspondingly hated by the parasites who feared lest she laugh their perquisites away.

The hostility of the people of Paris was equally marked and equally unfair. Upon the marriage of the royal pair the king ordered magnificent popular fetes at Versailles and Paris. Among the attractions was a display of fireworks, in the course of which a panic ensued and many of the spectators were killed or wounded. The people grumbled; 20,000,000 livres and thirty-two good French lives was a high price, they said, to pay for "La Petite l'Autrichienne" (the little Austrian). The prime trouble was that France and Austria were hereditary enemies, continually at war, and the people resented the king's bringing a princess of the latter land to be their future queen. One of the personal perquisites of a French queen was a tax levied every three years on bread and wine.

This tax was peculiarly hard on the French people, who called it "la ceinture de la reine," or "the queen's girdle." When in May, 1774, Louis XV died and Marie Antoinette became queen she remitted this tax, declaring she would never accept one sou of it. For a time the populace applauded her action, but speedily forgot it.

Then came the scandal of the diamond necklace—an affair of which the queen was both innocent and ignorant. Cardinal Rohan was grand almoner of France, a noble of the highest standing at court, and withal a true gentleman of the time, preying upon the earnings of the people for profit and upon the virtue of women of every estate for pleasure. To him came the pretended Countess de la Motte with a story of a necklace of fabulous value for which the queen yearned, but which she dared not purchase. But more. The envoy told the cardinal that Marie was in love with him, and were he to purchase the necklace for her would refuse him nothing. The heart of the voluptuary was stirred; the ambition of the practised courtier aroused. He agreed to buy the necklace, the queen to repay him later, and as its value exceeded even his command of ready cash, would pay for it in instalments.

But he wanted some evidence of the queen's participation in the affair. Whereupon La Motte presently produced an invoice indorsed "Appreuvé; Marie Antoinette de France." The signature was forged, but neither the amorous cardinal nor the jeweler, eager for his sale, seemed to doubt it. But De Rohan demanded even more assurance. He must have an

interview with the queen herself. Nothing easier. La Motte knew a woman having a singular resemblance to the queen. This girl, called d'Oliva, impersonated Marie in a midnight interview with De Rohan in the shrubbery of the Trianon. The necklace was bought and turned over to La Motte. The cardinal began to press his supposed advantage with Marie Antoinette, who, knowing nothing of the affair, was first puzzled and then brusque. Notes which the swindlers had given purporting to bear Marie's signature were unpaid, and the jeweler, facing bankruptcy, went in despair to the court for advice. It happened that the man he consulted was a bitter enemy of De Rohan, and gathering slowly all the evidence in the matter, he finally gave it the widest publicity in the way to do the most hurt.

Only the Dreyfus case in later days has stirred France as did this seeming revelation of the participation of a queen in a vulgar swindle. The mills of justice were set to work and ground swiftly, but though the evidence showed the queen wholly ignorant of the whole affair, the populace refused to believe in her innocence and the cabal in the court opposed to her kept the smouldering embers of scandal alive with whispered suggestions about her relations with Rohan—who by the way was deprived of all honors and posts and exiled to a monastery.

Under the strain Marie Antoinette broke down. Historians say that she became solitary, weeping by the hour in her chamber. It was in this broken and pathetic state that she was called upon to meet the early stages of the revolution; to take the first steps along the path that ended with the guillotine.

Source #2
The publication information for this source is:
Tytler, Sarah. *Marie Antoinette: The Woman and the Queen.* London: Marcus Ward & Co., 1883. The first excerpt begins on p. 32, with young Marie on her way to be married in 1770. The second begins with Marie on the way to the guillotine.

On the 21st of April, Marie Antoinette took leave of the mother she was never to see again, of her family and early friends, and turned her back for ever on the Prater and the Danube, Schönbrunn and moated Laxenburg. All the palace, all Vienna, was full of excitement—in the case of the city, of loyal affection and sentimental lamentation, reaching to the height of cries of grief. Their Empress's fair young daughter, in whose coming exaltation they had taken the utmost pride—who was to do them such honour and service at the French Court—she whose bright face was familiar to them in its readiness to beam with easily-called-forth smiles, or to cloud over with momentary gravity in sympathy with some poor man or woman's trouble—was departing on her long journey, and, as

The Parting. 33

many of the spectators must have perceived, without much prophetic insight, her difficult career. But there was more than loyal affection and sentimental lamentation in the sorrow of mother and daughter which Marie Antoinette did not care to hide. According to an eye-witness, when the great coach rolled out of the palace court, the girl-bride covered her face with her hands, which yet could not conceal the tears that streamed through her slender fingers. She turned again and again for a last farewell-look at home.

The same day the Empress wrote the first of her earnest, affectionate letters to her daughter. Maria Theresa had to take extraordinary precautions, and she urged her daughter to do the same, in conducting this correspondence. The letters were sent by special messengers and separate couriers; loose leaves were inserted, and additions made at the last moment, to prevent private communications being treated as public property. There was an imperative necessity that the letters should be burnt as soon as read. In constantly writing to her ambassador, Comte de Mercy-Argenteau, and requiring from him long replies in detail on her daughter's affairs, Maria Theresa guarded herself and her correspondent by the same ceaseless, elaborate manœuvres.

In the sweet spring-tide, Marie Antoinette drove on with her great train of nobles to meet her fate.

By the time the travellers—everywhere hailed with jubilant huzzas, and followed with fervent good wishes—reached the boundaries of Germany, though she might spare a lingering regret for the last German-speaking town, her rosy cheeks were dry, her blue eyes shining, her fair curls dancing, as she looked eagerly round on the country flushed with tender green, and returned, by continual acknowledgments, the endless *vivats* of the crowds which lined the roads.

Marie Antoinette crossed the bridge over the Rhine and made her public entrance into Strasburg in the most gorgeous of state carriages, flaming with crimson and gold, surmounted by wrought and tinted wreaths and nosegays of flowers. She was received into her adopted country with salutes from regiments of cavalry, salvoes of cannon from the ramparts, the loud clanging of bells, fountains playing with wine—all the insignia of joy on such occasions. There was a living soul given to it in this instance, by the fact that the excitable French people, *les gens de people*, forgot their immeasurable grievances and hard lot to shout with the best. They broke out into ecstacy over their beautiful young Dauphiness.

Marie Antoinette, quick, kind, and tender-hearted as she was, knew nothing—as how should she?—a girl of fourteen and a-half, granted that she was a princess, soon to be a wedded wife—of the black

shadow on the other side of the picture, when she spent her first day in France. It was literally crammed with ceremonies and festivities, ranging through her public entrance, her reception at the Episcopal Palace, her Court held for the first time for the benefit of the noble ladies of the province, the public dinner in state, the visit to the theatre, where the people generally might see and be seen, the drive through the illuminated streets, and, finally, the ball in her honour, which had to be deferred till midnight, so much had to come before it. A weary, as well as a dizzy young head rested on its laced pillow that night.

Second excerpt from Tytler:

widow. But she was more; she was Maria Theresa's daughter; she had once been the queen of a million of hearts.

As on the occasion of Louis's death, every house was closed, and every window shut. But along the entire route there was a tremendous crowd, from which came at intervals cries of "*Vive la Nation*," "*À bas la Tyrannie.*" Nevertheless most people uncovered, and the police had difficulty in hindering the citizens of Paris from putting themselves, with their wives and children, at the windows. The Queen did not heed the cries; she seemed to notice the tricolour decorations in the Rue de St. Honoré and other streets, and to read the inscriptions to *Liberté, Egalité, et Fraternité* on the fronts of the houses. Before St. Roche she was insulted by some miserable people; but at another point a little child kissed its hand to her, and it was thought she saw and was touched by the innocent greeting. As she passed the Tuileries—her home, where her children had lived—she took one last look, and was visibly moved.

The guillotine was in the Place de la Revolution, on the side of the Champs Elysées, at the foot of the pedestal which had been surmounted by a statue of Louis XV., where the obelisk stands to-day. The Queen was executed with her head turned to the Champs Elysées, on the Tuileries side, between the Tuileries railing and the pedestal on which

the people had placed a female figure of Liberty, wearing the red cap, and holding in her right hand a lance, and in her left a globe supported on her knees.

Some one, probably the priest Gérard, spoke to Marie Antoinette on the way, and told her now was the moment to arm her courage. "Courage!" she exclaimed; "I have served an apprenticeship to it for a long time; there is no fear of my losing it at this moment."

Alone, without the aid of her church, the Queen ascended the scaffold quickly, and knelt down. Some said she spoke in a firm voice, loud enough to be heard, "Lord, enlighten and soften my executioners. Farewell, my children; I go to rejoin your father" ("*Seigneur, éclairez et touchez mes bourreaux. Adieu, mes enfants; je vais rejoindre votre père*"), and received the blow. Her head was shown to the people. She was buried, like the King, in an open coffin among quick-lime, near where he lay, among many a victim of the Revolution, in the cemetery of the Madeleine. Her rags of clothes were carried away, in one of the sheets taken off her bed, from her cell in the Conciergerie, and confiscated to the nation. The last entry of her expenses was, "The widow Capet, for the coffin, six francs. Twenty-five francs for the grave and for the grave-diggers."

"Thus died, on the 16th October, 1793, Marie

Source #3

THE PRISON LIFE OF

MARIE ANTOINETTE

AND HER CHILDREN, THE DAUPHIN AND THE DUCHESSE D'ANGOULEME

BY

M. C. BISHOP

NEW AND REVISED EDITION
WITH PORTRAIT.

LONDON
KEGAN PAUL, TRENCH, TRÜBNER & CO., LTD.
1893.

172 *The Prison Life of Marie Antoinette.*

in a dirty cart along the streets of Paris to the place of execution.

Twenty-three years before she had made her first entry into the city, among an enthusiastic people, who could not sufficiently admire and love her. Marshal de Brissac, the Governor of Paris, had said to her, " Madam, you see before you two hundred thousand lovers ; " and now she was placed in a cart in which there was a plank for a seat, while the carter with a lowering face led the strong horse in the shafts slowly, for, as remarked a bystander, "The Queen must be made to drink long of death."

To estimate the contrast of what had been and what was, the reader can glance backward and picture the figure for whose triumphant passage soldiers had once otherwise lined the streets. Of her, the artist Madame le Brun, who several times painted her portrait, writes with an artist's appreciation, " Marie Antoinette was tall, admirably made, rather fat, without being too much so. Her hands were small, and perfect in shape, as were her feet. Of all women in France she walked the best. She carried her head gracefully, and with a majesty which revealed her as sovereign in the midst of the Court, though her dignity did not interfere at

Requiem Æternam. 173

all with the kindly sweetness of her aspect. It is difficult to render any idea of such united dignity and nobleness. Her features were not regular. From her family she inherited the long and narrow oval face, which is peculiar to it. Her eyes were not large, their colour was almost blue. Her expression was intelligent and soft; her nose was well cut; her mouth was not large, though the lips were rather full. But the remarkable beauty of her face was in its colouring. I never saw so brilliant a complexion. Brilliant is the correct epithet, for her skin was so transparent that it hardly took shadow. The last time I was at Fontainebleau I saw the Queen in her fullest dress, covered with diamonds, and as a bright sun shone on her she was quite dazzling. Her head was so set on her beautiful Greek throat that she had the imposing and majestic air of a goddess among attendant nymphs. I ventured to speak to her majesty of the impression I had received, and of the noble effect produced by the way her head was set on her throat. Jesting, she replied, 'Is it not true, if I were not Queen people would think I looked insolent?'"

Marie Antoinette was but thirty-eight when she died; but after her return from Varennes her splendid hair had suddenly lost its colour.

Day Three: Practicing the Topos, Part Two: Organizing the Biographical Sketch

Focus: Using notes to construct an outline

Today, you'll prepare to write your biographical sketch by turning your notes into an outline and dividing the outline into paragraphs. Tomorrow, you'll finish your assignment by writing the sketch, complete with footnotes and Works Cited page.

STEP ONE: Arrange notes in order

Now go back to the notes you took from the encyclopedia article about Marie Antoinette. These basic facts will serve as the skeleton of your outline. Copy them and paste them into a new word processing document (or arrange the 3x5 cards into order, one fact on each card).

You'll now put each one of the additional notes you took underneath the corresponding fact from the encyclopedia article. Copy and paste the additional notes into your document, or arrange the cards in order behind the correct note card from the encyclopedia article.

For example, imagine that the first six facts in your encyclopedia list are these:

Youngest daughter of the German emperor Francis I and the queen of Austria, Maria Theresa
Born at Vienna on Nov. 2, 1755
Betrothed to the dauphin at 14
Married at Versailles at 15
Dauphin became Louis XVI in May 1774.
Her enemies circulated rumors and stories about her.

Suppose that the first few notes you took from Sarah Tytler's *Marie Antoinette* and M. C. Bishop's *The Prison Life of Marie Antoinette* look like this:

Tytler, Sarah. *Marie Antoinette: The Woman and the Queen.* London: Marcus Ward & Co., 1883.
Marie left home in 1770 on April 21 to go to France. (32)
She "covered her face with her hands" and cried when she left. (33)
The Empress wrote her many "earnest, affectionate letters" by special messenger, and the letters were burned "as soon as read." (33)
She had blue eyes and fair hair. (34)
She rode in a state carriage "flaming with crimson and gold, surmounted by wrought and tinted wreaths and nosegays of flowers." (34)
Bishop, M. C. *The Prison Life of Marie Antoinette.* London: Kegan Paul, Trench, Trübner & Co., 1893.
When she first came to Paris the "enthusiastic people . . . could not sufficiently admire and love her." (172)
Now she was on a cart with a "plank for a seat." (172)
Madame le Brun said that she was "tall, admirably made, rather fat" with small hands and feet. (172)

Five of the notes give details about Marie's arrival in France for her wedding. You would place all of them underneath "Married at Versailles at 15," like this:

Married at Versailles at 15
Marie left home in 1770 on April 21 to go to France. (32)
She "covered her face with her hands" and cried when she left. (33)
The Empress wrote her many "earnest, affectionate letters" by special messenger, and the letters were burned "as soon as read." (33)

She rode in a state carriage "flaming with crimson and gold, surmounted by wrought and tinted wreaths and nosegays of flowers." (34)
When she first came to Paris the "enthusiastic people . . . could not sufficiently admire and love her." (172)
Dauphin became Louis XVI in May 1774

Because the detail about the Empress's letter happens *after* Marie arrives in France, you would want to move it to the end of the list.

The detail about the plank for the seat would go later in your list of facts, in the section dealing with Marie's execution.

You may notice that the details about Marie's appearance don't seem to be connected to any particular fact from the encyclopedia article. A personal description can come at several different places in the biographical sketch. Create a separate list called "Personal description" and assemble all the details about her appearance underneath that heading:

Personal description
She had blue eyes and fair hair. (34)
Madame le Brun said that she was "tall, admirably made, rather fat" with small hands and feet. (172)

If you're using a word processing program, it isn't necessary to put the last name of the author in front of every single page number as long as you can glance back at your original list and confirm which note belongs to which source. (That's why you *copy and paste* instead of *cut and paste*—you want to leave your original notes to use as reference.)

When you're finished assembling your notes in order, show them to your instructor.

STEP TWO: Divide notes into main points

Now look over your assembled list of notes. Your next step is to divide them into main points, as you did with your notes on Julius Caesar and the process of digestion.

At least three of the facts from the encyclopedia should be followed by three or more details taken from your additional sources. Other facts will have no details at all, as in the following example (the encyclopedia facts are bolded):

Marie was put in the Temple, a fortress in Paris.
She was moved to prison on August 1, 1793.
Her hair lost its color after she was taken prisoner. (173)
The Revolutionary Tribunal condemned her on Oct. 15, 1793.
She was guillotined on Oct. 16.
Now she was on a cart with a "plank for a seat." (172)
When she went to the guillotine, "every house was closed and every window shut." (213)

Some people insulted her, but others greeted her. (213)
She had "one last look" at her home and "was visibly moved." (213)

Your next task: Divide your list into main points.

Each encyclopedia fact that has three or more details after it should be a separate paragraph. But where there are lists of encyclopedia facts with no details, you will need to decide how many facts to put in the same paragraph. Sometimes the only uniting theme in a paragraph of a biographical sketch is that the events all happened within a certain span of time. Remember, from the first lesson this week, that "Between Year X and Year Y" can be a perfectly good way to organize a paragraph!

So as you work on organizing the list into main points, you can use your best judgment. How many facts should you put into a list? Should you organize them by timespan, or look for another way to tie them together?

Try to use between six and eight divisions—not more than eight. This does not include the personal description. For right now, leave the personal description alone at the bottom of your list. In Step Four, you'll decide where to place it.

If you have trouble, just use your best judgment.

STEP THREE: **Title the main points**

When you have finished dividing your list into main points, give each main point a name.

Everywhere that a fact from the encyclopedia and details from your other sources form a separate, single paragraph, give that main point the name of the encyclopedia fact: for example,

II. Married at Versailles at 15

for

Married at Versailles at 15
Marie left home in 1770 on April 21 to go to France. (32)
She "covered her face with her hands" and cried when she left. (33) . . .

But for main points that contain one or more encyclopedia facts, you will need to choose a name.

Choosing a name will often show you that you need to go back and rethink your divisions. For example, imagine that you had chosen the following division of main points:

V.
Her two favorite ministers were condemned for overspending.
She opposed the Assembly of Notables in 1788.
She opposed the assembling of the States General in 1789.

The Assembly of Notables said she had caused France's financial trouble.
The Revolution began in May 1789.

VI.
There was an attempted assassination on October 6, 1789, in Versailles.
She tried to make herself popular.
She decided to flee.

You could give Section V the title "Trouble in the government" or "Marie and the French government"—except that the French Revolution doesn't really fit in. But change your division slightly:

V. **Marie and the French government**
    Her two favorite ministers were condemned for overspending.
    She opposed the Assembly of Notables in 1788.
    She opposed the assembling of the States General in 1789.
    The Assembly of Notables said she had caused France's financial trouble.
VI.
    The Revolution began in May 1789.
    There was an attempted assassination on October 6, 1789, in Versailles.
    She tried to make herself popular.
    She decided to flee.

and it fits perfectly. (You can borrow this title and use it in your own assignment.)

You can use "Marie's life from Year X to Year Y" as one title—but *only one*. Your other titles should sum up the events or give the central event.

If you have difficulty, ask your instructor for help. When you're finished, show your work to your instructor before going on.

STEP FOUR: **Place the personal description**

As your final step in constructing this outline, decide where to place the description of Marie Antoinette. Cut and paste it into the outline. Give it the appropriate Roman numeral, and renumber the sections that follow. (If this isn't clear, ask your instructor.)

Now your outline is complete. Tomorrow, you'll use it to write the final biographical sketch.

Day Four: Practicing the Topos, Part Three: Writing the Biographical Sketch

Focus: Writing from notes organized into an outline

Try to work independently today. Your goal is to show your instructor a completely finished biographical sketch.

STEP ONE: **Write**

Using your notes, write your biographical sketch. Give it the simple title "Marie Antoinette" and follow these guidelines:

1. Write one paragraph for each main point on your outline.
2. Each paragraph should have at least two sentences.
3. The finished composition should be at least 450 words.
4. Use footnotes if you are quoting directly or using ideas from another writer. Historical facts do not need to be documented.
5. Use at least four direct quotes.
6. Quote at least once from each of your three sources.
7. In your descriptive paragraph, use verbs, adjectives, and adverbs to either slant the description in a positive or negative way, or to support a metaphor that you have chosen.

Remember that you do not have to include everything in your notes. Pick and choose among the details.

Make sure that your paper is double-spaced and that the pages are numbered.

STEP TWO: **Assemble Works Cited page**

On a separate sheet of paper, center the title "Works Cited" at the top of the page. List your sources below in alphabetical order, in proper format.

STEP THREE: **Proofread**

Read your composition out loud. If any sentences sound awkward or unclear, work on rewriting them. Check for correct spelling and punctuation. (If you use the name of a month, spell it out rather than abbreviating.) Check the format of your footnotes.

When you are finished, show your work to your instructor.

Part VI

BEGINNING LITERARY CRITICISM: POETRY WRITING ABOUT POEMS WEEKS 32–34

Overview of Weeks 32–34

In Part IV of this course, you practiced basic literary criticism by writing about stories. In the next three weeks, you'll practice the same skills on poetry.

Poetry is very different than fiction. In poetry, the writer pays just as much attention to the *form* of the words as to the *content*; the sound and rhythm of every single syllable are important. And the words the writer chooses are absolutely central to the poem's meaning. In poetry, the words can't be separated from the ideas.

Because poems are so much shorter than stories, each word becomes much more important. To pack as much meaning as possible into fewer words, poets use many different strategies: meter, rhyme, alliteration, metaphors, similes, and much more.

When you write about poems, you'll write about their meaning. But since meaning and words are so closely tied together, you'll also have to write about the words and techniques that the poet uses. In the next three weeks, you'll practice putting these elements together into short essays about poems.

Week 32: Sound

Day One: Read

Focus: Reading

Your first step—just as when you were doing literary criticism on short stories—is to read.

Turn to Appendix IV. The first poem you'll see is "The Bells" by Edgar Allan Poe. You should know something about Poe; you wrote a biographical sketch about him back in Week 19. However, you don't really need to know anything about Poe to understand this poem.

Start by reading "The Bells" four times from beginning to end, closely following these instructions.

STEP ONE: Read silently

Read the poem silently and slowly. Stop and look up the meanings and pronunciations of all words you don't know.

STEP TWO: Read out loud

Go to a private place and read the poem out loud, at a normal pace, listening to the sounds. (You can do this in front of a sibling or someone else if you'd rather, but most people prefer to be alone.)

STEP THREE: Read for punctuation

Read the poem out loud again. This time, pay attention to the punctuation marks. Pause briefly at each comma and dash. Pause for a longer time at each period. When there's an exclamation point, raise your voice.

STEP FOUR: Read for effect

Read the poem out loud one more time, as quickly as possible. If you can, record yourself and listen to the recording.

Day Two: Analyze

Focus: Understanding how sound is used in the poem

You will need four colored pencils for today's lesson.

STEP ONE: **Examine the overall form**

In poetry, words and meaning are tied together—so before you can write anything about the poem's meaning, you have to become familiar with the words and techniques the poet uses.

Let's start with the overall form of the poem. It's divided into four *stanzas,* or groups of lines. On your Literary Terms chart in the Reference section of your notebook, add the following definition.

stanza: a group of lines within a poem

"The Bells" is *free verse,* meaning that Edgar Allan Poe did not force the poem to follow a strict pattern of rhythm and rhyme. Look at the first three lines of the poem. In the margin next to the poem, write how many syllables each line has. (If you have trouble, ask your instructor for help.)

Do you see how unequal the lines are?

In the same way, Poe doesn't follow a particular pattern of rhyme. Look at the sounds that end the first five lines of the first stanza, and the sounds that end the first five lines of the second stanza:

I.	II.
bells	bells
bells	bells
foretells	foretells
tinkle	night
night	delight

There's plenty of rhyming here, but in the first stanza, lines 4 and 5 don't rhyme; in the second, they do. The pattern isn't the same.

Before moving on, show the number of syllables you came up with to your instructor.

STEP TWO: **Understand onomatopoeia**

Instead of regular rhythm and rhyme, this poem is all about sound—at least four different kinds of sound.

The first kind of sound that this poem uses is *onomatopoeia*—when a word sounds like its meaning. Say the word "groan" out loud and notice how the word itself sounds like the sound a groaning person would make. Read the following onomatopoeic words out loud, listening carefully to yourself: *pop, crunch, meow, boom, slurp, buzz.*

On your Literary Terms chart in the Reference section of your notebook, add the following definition.

onomatopoeia: when a word sounds like its meaning

It may help you remember the term to know that *onoma* is Greek for "name" and *poiein* is Greek for "to make," so an onomatopoeic word is a name that's been made to go along with its meaning. In the first stanza, Poe made up the word *tintinnabulation* to represent bells ringing. You can find it in the dictionary now—but Poe was the first to use it.

Go through "The Bells" now with your first colored pencil and underline each onomatopoeic word. If the word repeats within the same stanza, you only need to underline it the first time.

When you are finished, show your work to your instructor before going on.

STEP THREE: **Look for repetition**

The poem also uses *exact repetition*. When you repeat the same word several times in a row, you create a new sound effect.

The most obvious repetition in this poem is found in the final lines of each stanza, when Poe writes the word *bells* over and over again—seven times in the first stanza, ten in the second, eight in the third, and in the fourth stanza three times, three times again, and then seven times. And that's not even counting all the *other* times he writes the word *bells*.

Go through the poem with a second colored pencil and underline every place where words are repeated more than one time in a row—*not* including the word "bells." Some words may be underlined twice if you've already underlined them in the first step.

On the lines below, write the answer to these two questions:

What series of words occurs more than once?

Where does it occur, and how many times?

____

____

____

____

When you are finished, show your work to your instructor before going on.

STEP FOUR: **Look for repeated rhymes**

The poem uses *repeated rhymes*. These don't always come at the end of the lines; sometimes they occur in the middle, or in the next to last word. But the sameness of the sounds creates a third kind of sound effect.

Look at the first stanza. The first line ends with the word *bells*. With your third colored pencil, underline all occurences of the word *bells* as well as the words *foretells* and *wells*. The repetition of those rhyming sounds affects the meaning of the poem.

Go through the entire poem and with your third colored pencil underline all the words that have repeated rhyming sounds. Some words may end up being underlined twice. In the first stanza, for example, you would underline *tinkle, tinkle, tinkle* for a second time, as well as *oversprinkle* and *twinkle*—and the first occurence of *tinkle* should be underlined three times, since that word is also an example of onomatopoeia.

When you're finished, show your work to your instructor.

STEP FIVE: **Find examples of alliteration**

The poem uses *alliteration*. Alliteration happens when two or more words within a group of words begin with the same sound or sounds.

On your Literary Terms chart in the Reference section of your notebook, add the following definition.

alliteration: when words begin with the same sound or sounds

In the first stanza, "merriment" and "melody" show alliteration. So does the phrase "Runic rhyme." With your fourth colored pencil, circle the opening *m*'s and *r*'s of these words.

Now go through the next three stanzas and circle the opening letters of any words that show alliteration. Look for words that occur in the same line. Don't circle the opening letters of repeated words.

Now glance back over your underlinings and circles and notice how many words in this poem have been carefully chosen for their *sound*.

When you are finished, show your work to your instructor.

Day Three: Think

Focus: Connecting form and meaning

STEP ONE: **Understand the difference between stories and poems**

When you learned how to write about stories, you started out by writing a summary of events—a plot summary. But although some poems tell stories, many others do not. Instead, they describe experiences, places, sensations, objects, moods, emotions, feelings, ideas, and many other things.

Think about "Rikki-Tikki-Tavi," the first story you read when you were learning how to write about literature. That story had a very clear beginning (Rikki-tikki-tavi went to live with the family), middle (the cobras wanted the family out of the bungalow), and end (Rikki killed the cobras). Compare that with the first six lines of "The Daffodils," by the nineteenth-century poet William Wordsworth:

> I wander'd lonely as a cloud
> That floats on high o'er vales and hills,
> When all at once I saw a crowd,
> A host, of golden daffodils;
> Beside the lake, beneath the trees,
> Fluttering and dancing in the breeze.

How would you write a "plot summary" of that poem? You couldn't, because you can't really find a protagonist, antagonist, or conflict in "The Daffodils." The poet is, instead, just looking at the daffodils.

So how do you begin to write about a poem? Instead of asking "What happens?" ask yourself "How does this poem move forward?"

Most poems don't begin and end in the same place. Something happens, or *changes,* during the poem. For a very simple (and ridiculous) example, consider this:

> There was an old man from Peru,
> Who dreamed he was eating his shoe.
>   He woke in the night
>   With a terrible fright,
> And found it was perfectly true.

At the beginning of the poem, the old man from Peru doesn't know that he's eating his shoe. At the end, he does. Things have changed.

In the next two steps, your instructor will carry on a dialogue with you. During these dialogues, you'll fill out the charts below. These charts will help you construct your short essay tomorrow.

STEP TWO: Examine the movement of the poem

	I.	II.	III.	IV.
KIND	______	______	______	______
MATERIAL	______	______	______	______
EMOTION	______	______	______	______
TIME	______	______	______	______

STEP THREE: Understand the connection between form and meaning

I TIME: ____________ **VOWEL SOUND** ____________

WORDS USED ____________

EFFECT ____________

____

____

____

II TIME: ____________ **VOWEL SOUND** ____________

WORDS USED ____________

EFFECT ____________

____

____

____

III TIME: ______________ **VOWEL SOUND** ______________

WORDS USED ______________________________

EFFECT ______________________________

____

____

____

IV TIME: ______________ **VOWEL SOUND** ______________

WORDS USED ______________________________

EFFECT ______________________________

____

____

____

Day Four: Write

Focus: Writing about the poem

Now that you've done all your thinking and talking, it will be much easier for you to write.

STEP ONE: Understand proper form for quoting a poem

Before you begin to write, read carefully through the following instructions on how to quote poetry directly.

When you cite a classic poem—one that has been reprinted in many different places over many different years—you don't need to give an actual book title along with publication information and page numbers. Instead, you need to identify the poem clearly in the introduction to your essay (we'll cover that in Step Three) and then include, in parentheses after the quote, the number of the line within the poem that your quote is drawn from:

The poem describes the "moaning and the groaning of the bells" (113).

To the right of "The Bells" in your poetry appendix, you'll see line numbers that occur every five lines. In very long poems, you will often find line numbers printed in the text to make citatation easier. (For shorter poems, you'll have to count the lines yourself.)

Notice that the parentheses goes outside the closing quotation mark, but inside the closing punctuation mark.

If you quote two or three consecutive lines from a poem, use a forward slash mark followed by a space to show the division between the lines. Use exactly the same punctuation as the original except in the last line; you should just drop the punctuation on that line.

For example:

> "The Bells" describes the "people" who live in the steeple as "neither man nor woman—/ They are neither brute nor human—/ They are Ghouls" (86–88).

Notice that the quote keeps the dashes after *woman* and *human* but drops the semicolon after *Ghouls*.

If you quote four or more lines from a poem, double-space down, indent twice, and reproduce the lines exactly as they appear in the poem. This is called a "block quote" and looks like this:

> The king of the Ghouls tolls the bell and does much more:
>
> > And his merry bosom swells
> > With the paean of the bells!
> > And he dances and he yells;
> > Keeping time, time, time (93–96).

Notice that there are no quotation marks. Indenting twice shows that you are quoting, so the punctuation isn't needed.

In a block quote, you can drop the last punctuation mark, just as in a shorter quote. In the original, there is a comma after the last "time." That comma has been dropped. Since the quote ends after the line citation, a period goes after the closing parenthesis.

STEP TWO: **Write one paragraph for each stanza**

Put your two charts side by side with your marked-up copy of the poem. Use these to write four paragraphs about the poem, one for each stanza. Each paragraph should tell the reader (not necessarily in this order):

1. The type of bell/what the bell is made of/why this is important
2. The time of life the bell represents
3. The emotion/state of mind in the stanza
4. What words, sounds, and rhymes in the passage help to make this clear

Here is an example for you: the first paragraph, written about the first stanza. You can use this first paragraph in your own composition, and model your other three paragraphs after it.

> The bells in the first stanza are silver sleigh bells, which represent childhood. Silver isn't as expensive as gold, but it is still valuable—just as youth is valuable, but not as important as the next phase of life. The silver bells are merry and delighted, like children at play. The poem uses *i*-sounds, cheerful verbs such as "twinkle," and phrases like "jingling and tinkling" (14) to make us think about childhood.

Make a run at three paragraphs of your own. (You can also write your own first paragraph, if you'd rather.) Your paragraphs can be as simple as the example, or use much more detail.

In each paragraph, quote at least once from the stanza you are writing about. Your quote should have at least three words in it; you can quote single words (as in the example above) but this doesn't count towards your total. At least one of your quotes should be four or more lines and set as a block quote.

When you are finished, show your work to your instructor.

STEP THREE: Write an introduction and assemble your essay

You should now have four paragraphs discussing the four stanzas of "The Bells"—but you don't yet have an essay.

In order to have an essay, you need an introduction and conclusion.

Your introduction only needs to be one sentence long (although you can make it longer if you want to). It should include the following information:

1. The name and the author of the poem. Remember that the titles of poems are put in quotation marks, while the titles of books are italicized (or underlined, if you're writing by hand).
2. The main topic, idea, or theme of the poem.

If you have difficulty, ask your instructor for help.

When you are finished, put your introduction at the beginning of your essay. It can either stand as its own paragraph or else be the first line of your existing first paragraph. Read your composition out loud, listening for awkward phrases and sentences that might not make sense. Then read it one more time silently, looking for misspelled words and incorrect punctuation.

When you are finished, show your composition to your instructor.

Week 33: Meter

Day One: Read

Focus: Reading

This week, you'll write about the second poem in Appendix IV: "Ozymandias" by Percy Bysshe Shelley.

Like "The Bells," this poem can be understood perfectly well even if you know nothing about Shelley. Start by reading "Ozymandias" four times from beginning to end, closely following these instructions.

STEP ONE: **Read silently**

Read the poem silently and slowly. Stop and look up the meanings and pronunciations of all words you don't know.

STEP TWO: **Read out loud**

Go to a private place and read the poem out loud, at a normal pace, listening to the sounds. (You can do this in front of a sibling or someone else if you'd prefer.) Pause briefly at the end of each line so that you can hear the rhythm of the poem's individual lines.

STEP THREE: **Read for punctuation**

Read the poem out loud again. This time, pay attention to the punctuation marks. Pause briefly at each comma and dash. Pause for a longer time at each period. When there's an exclamation point, raise your voice.

Do not stop at the end of a line if there is no punctuation. So you would read "Near them on the sand, [PAUSE] half sunk, [PAUSE] a shattered visage lies." But you would read "Two vast and trunkless legs of stone Stand in the desert [NO PAUSE].

STEP FOUR: **Read for dialogue**

Read the poem out loud one more time. This time, use three different voices: one for the narrator (the "I" in the first line), a second for the traveller, and a third for the words on the pedestal (Ozymandias).

Day Two: Analyze

Focus: Understanding meter and sonnet form

Last week's poem was free verse; the lines did not follow a regular pattern of rhythm or rhyme. This week, you'll study the opposite: a poem with an extremely *strict* pattern of both rhythm *and* rhyme.

STEP ONE: **Understand meter**

The rhythm that a poem follows is called its *meter.* The word "meter" means "measure," and to find the meter of a poem you measure each line by counting the syllables.

That's not all you do, though. To find meter, you also have to learn the difference between *stressed* and *unstressed* syllables.

Say the following words out loud. Emphasize the bolded syllables by making your voice just a little more forceful, but use a normal tone of voice on the syllables in regular type.

an a lyze
hum ming bird
to **ma** to
fan **tas** tic
mem **or** i al
vo lun **teer**
po li **ti** cian

The bolded syllables above are stressed syllables—places where your voice naturally wants to put more emphasis. Most English words have one syllable that should be stressed. If you stress the wrong syllable, the word sounds odd. Read these words again, once more emphasizing the bolded syllable.

an **a** lyze
hum **ming** bird
to ma to

fan tas **tic**
mem or **i** al
vo **lun** teer
po **li** ti cian

When you put the stress on a different syllable, the word sounds awkward and wrong.

The meter of a line of poetry is created by a particular pattern of stressed and unstressed syllables. Read the lines of the following poems out loud, stressing each bolded syllable.

Come **live** with **me** and **be** my **love**	(Christopher Marlowe)
Now **came** still **eve**ning **on,** and **twi**light **gray**	(John Milton)
What a **world** of **mer**riment their **mel**ody fore**tells**	(Edgar Allan Poe)
Like the **leaves** of the **for**est when **Sum**mer is **green**	(Lord Byron)

In the first two lines, the syllables fall into this pattern:

unstressed **stressed**   unstressed **stressed**   unstressed **stressed**

Each one of these pairs of syllables is called a **foot.** The first line has four feet, and the second line has five.

foot foot foot foot
(Come **live**) (with **me**) (and **be**) (my **love**)

foot foot foot foot foot
(Now **came**) (still **eve**) (ning **on**), (and **twi**) (light **gray**)

If all of the feet in a line of poetry have the pattern of unstressed **stressed**, the meter of the poem is **iambic**.

Iambic is one of the most common meters, but there are many others. In the third line of poetry above, each foot has the pattern

stressed unstressed   **stressed** unstressed   **stressed** unstressed

If all of the feet have this pattern of **stressed** unstressed, the meter of the poem is **trochaic.**

The last line above is in **anapestic** meter, which has this pattern:

unstressed unstressed **stressed**   unstressed unstressed **stressed**

As you can see, a foot can have either two or three syllables in it.

So far, you've learned the following two definitions:

meter: the rhythmical pattern of a poem
foot: a set of syllables that follows a certain pattern of stress and unstress

Write both definitions on your Literary Terms chart.

STEP TWO: **Understand iambic pentameter**

On the copy of the poem printed below, mark the stressed and unstressed syllables in each line. Use an accent mark (ˊ) to show a stressed syllable and a circumflex (ˇ) to show an unstressed syllable, like this:

> Come **live** with **me** and **be** my **love**

These are the most common marks used to show meter.

The first line is done for you. If you have difficulty, ask your instructor for help.

"Ozymandias"
Percy Bysshe Shelley

I met a traveller from an antique land
Who said: "Two vast and trunkless legs of stone
Stand in the desert. Near them on the sand,
Half sunk, a shattered visage lies, whose frown
And wrinkled lip and sneer of cold command
Tell that its sculptor well those passions read
Which yet survive, stamped on these lifeless things,
The hand that mocked them and the heart that fed.
And on the pedestal these words appear:
'My name is Ozymandias, King of Kings:
Look on my works, ye mighty, and despair!'
Nothing beside remains. Round the decay

Of that colossal wreck, boundless and bare, ________________

The lone and level sands stretch far away." ________________

Each line in this poem has five feet (pairs of stressed and unstressed syllables):

(I met) (a trav) (eller from) (an an) (tique land)
1 2 3 4 5

This meter is called *iambic pentameter.* "Iambic" tells you that each foot has two syllables that follow the pattern (unstressed **stressed**). "Pentameter" tells you that there are five feet in each line, for a total of ten syllables. (*Penta* comes from the Greek word for "five.")

Iambic pentameter often just sounds like natural speech, which is why Shakespeare uses iambic pentameter for so much of the dialogue in his plays. Read these four lines from *Henry V,* Act IV, Scene iii out loud, stressing the syllables with accent marks.

We few, we happy few, we band of brothers:

For he today that sheds his blood with me,

Shall be my brother: be he ne're so vile,

This day shall gentle his condition.

(You might notice that there's an extra syllable at the end of the first line and a missing syllable at the end of the fourth. Because iambic pentameter sounds so natural, poets often expand or shorten the lines where necessary.)

When a poet writes in iambic pentameter, you can usually assume that he wants you to pay more attention to the meaning than to the rhythm. The rhythm of the poem is very regular, but it fades into the background so that you can concentrate on the words and images themselves.

When you are finished with this lesson, show your poem marked with stresses and unstressses to your instructor.

STEP THREE: Understand rhyme scheme

Last week's poem had irregular rhythm; this week's poem has extremely regular rhythm. Last week's poem also had irregular rhyme; plenty of words in it rhymed, but there was no way to predict where those rhymes would be.

This week's poem has a very particular *rhyme scheme.* A rhyme scheme is a pattern of repeating rhymes. You find a rhyme scheme by giving the ending sound in each line of the poem a different letter of the alphabet.

Look at this example, from Edward Lear's *Book of Nonsense:*

There was an Old Man with a beard, A
Who said, "It is just as I feared! A
  Two Owls and a Hen, B
  Four Larks and a Wren, B
Have all built their nests in my beard!" A

The first line of the poem ends with the sound *-eard,* so we give that sound the letter A. Every time a line ends with *-eard,* no matter what the word itself is, we give that line the same letter.

The first two lines have the same rhyme, but the third line ends with a different sound: *-en*. This is the second ending sound in the poem, so we give it the second letter of the alphabet: B.

Turn back to your marked copy of the poem and assign each ending sound a letter of the alphabet. Write those letters at the end of each line on the blank provided.

When you are finished, write the following definition of rhyme scheme on your Literary Terms chart.

rhyme scheme: a pattern of repeating rhyme marked with letters of the alphabet

Then check your work with your instructor.

STEP FOUR: **Understand sonnet form**

"Ozymandias" is a *sonnet*. On your Literary Terms chart, write the following definition:

sonnet: a 14-line poem written in iambic pentameter

All sonnets are 14-line poems written in iambic pentameter, but there are several different variations on this pattern. The two most common variations are known as the Italian and English sonnet forms.

You don't have to memorize the following definitions and information; just read it carefully.

An "Italian sonnet" has two parts. The first eight lines ("octet") present a problem, an idea, an argument, or a situation. The last six lines ("sestet") give a solution, offer an answer, or complete the idea. Usually, the ninth line contains an obvious change, or shift, between the two parts of the poem; this is called a "turn."

The rhyme scheme for the Italian sonnet is almost always ABBAABBA for the first eight lines. The last six lines can be rhymed in a number of different ways (for example, CDCDCD or CDCEDC), but they never have more than three total rhymes.

An "English sonnet" has three parts. Like an Italian sonnet, an English sonnet has an octet (first eight lines) which goes in one direction. The "turn" that introduces a new direction for the poem comes in the next four lines ("quatrain"). Then the poem ends with two lines (a "couplet") that sums up the poem with a rhyming conclusion.

The rhyme scheme for an English sonnet is most often ABABCDCD EFEF GG.

These are just general rules, and poets often do not follow them exactly. However, when a poet decides to break the rules, you should always pay attention. The change often is a signal to you that you should look more closely at the lines that depart from the regular pattern.

With this in mind, look at "Ozymandias" again. Write brief answers to the following questions on the lines provided. If you have difficulty, ask your instructor for help.

In what line does the change of meaning happen?

____

Does the poem follow the English or Italian rhyme scheme more closely?

____

Which lines break the pattern?

____

Looking only at the meaning of the sonnet, not the rhyme scheme, how would you classify this sonnet? Is it closer to an Italian or English sonnet?

____

What makes the sonnet *different* from the form you did *not* choose?

____

____

When you are finished, show your answers to your instructor.

Day Three: Think

Focus: Connecting form and meaning

In the two steps of today's lesson, your instructor will carry on a dialogue with you. During these dialogues, you'll write brief answers in the spaces below. These answers will help you construct your short essay tomorrow.

STEP ONE: **Identify the voices within the poem**

#1 ____

#2 ____

#3 ____

____

____

STEP TWO: **Examine the movement of the poem**

The physical movement of the poem: ______________________

____

____

____

____

The movement of meaning in the poem: ____________________

Day Four: Write

Focus: Writing about the poem

STEP ONE: Write one paragraph for each aspect of the poem

Put all your answers in front of you, along with your copy of the poem. Use these to write three paragraphs about the poem.

In the first paragraph, explain in what way the poem is like an English sonnet, and in what way the poem is like an Italian sonnet. (You do not need to explain what English and Italian sonnets are—you can assume that your reader will know this.)

In the second paragraph, describe the two kinds of movement that are in the poem. Use at least two direct quotes.

In the third paragraph, explain the three different voices in the poem and who they belong to. Explain what this tells us about Ozymandias.

STEP TWO: Write an introduction and conclusion

The introduction to the poem should sum the story of the poem up briefly; it should tell you what the basic storyline, or plot, or subject matter of the poem is. A conclusion is a little different. Conclusions tell you what you've *learned* about the poem.

Think of it this way: An introduction just gives you a surface acquaintance with the poem (like an introduction to a person doesn't tell you much more than what the person looks and sounds like). But a conclusion looks beneath the surface of the poem and tells you what *message* the poet is giving you.

Now write one sentence that introduces the poem by giving its name, author, and overall meaning. Your sentence can begin like this:

"Ozymandias," by Percy Bysshe Shelley, tells about . . .

This sentence will stand on its own as the introductory paragraph to your brief essay. (In a short assignment like this, it is acceptable to have a one-sentence paragraph.)

Then write a concluding sentence that begins like this:

The form of the poem, the movement of the poem, and the voices of the poem all point out . . .

If you have difficulty, ask your instructor for help.

STEP THREE: Assemble and proofread your essay

Put your introduction at the beginning of your essay and your conclusion at the end. Read the composition out loud, listening for awkward phrases and sentences that might not make sense. Then read it one more time silently, looking for misspelled words and incorrect punctuation. Be sure that you have quoted from the poem directly at least twice in the essay.

Give the essay a title. ("Ozymandias" is fine!)

When you are finished, show your composition to your instructor.

Week 34: Narrative

Day One: Read

Focus: Reading

This week, you'll write about the final poem in Appendix IV: "The Charge of the Light Brigade" by Alfred, Lord Tennyson.

This poem is based on a historical event. Before you can write about this poem, you'll need to know something about the story behind it. But you can *read* the poem before learning about the historical background. When a poet writes about a historical event, he wants you to *experience* it (otherwise he would just write an essay or story). So today, you'll read the poem as a way of experiencing it; on Day Three, you'll learn about the historical background.

Read "The Charge of the Light Brigade" four times from beginning to end, closely following these instructions.

STEP ONE: **Read silently**

Read the poem silently and slowly. Stop and look up the meanings and pronunciations of all words you don't know.

STEP TWO: **Read out loud**

Go to a private place and read the poem out loud, at a normal pace, listening to the sounds. (You can do this in front of someone else if you'd prefer.) Pause briefly at the end of each line so that you can hear the rhythm of the poem's individual lines.

STEP THREE: **Read for rhythm**

Read the poem out loud again. This time, pay attention to the rhythm of the poem.

You'll learn more about the poem's meter in the next lesson, but for the purposes of reading the poem out loud, all you need to remember is that much of the poem is in 3/4 time.

If you play an instrument, you already know what this means—the rhythm of the poem is 1–2–3, 1–2–3, 1–2–3, 1–2–3. Even if you don't take music lessons, though, 3/4 time is easy to understand. All you need to do is sway back and forth. Sway to the right and say "One, two, three!" Then sway to the left and say "One, two, three!" Do this a few more times and you'll be chanting in 3/4 time.

If you still can't quite hear 3/4 time, try listening to a piece of music. There are plenty of classical music pieces written in 3/4 time: "The Blue Danube" by Johann Strauss and "Morning Mood" by Edvard Grieg are just two. The folk songs "Greensleeves" (same tune as the hymn "What Child Is This"), "Take Me Out to the Ballgame," "Waltzing with Bears," "The Tennessee Waltz," and "How Much Is That Doggie in the Window?" are all 3/4 time. So are "Edelweiss" and "My Favorite Things," from the movie *The Sound of Music*. The 1960s classic "The Times They Are a-Changin' " is in 3/4 time; so are the 1970s songs "Time in a Bottle" and "You Light Up My Life." (If you don't know these, your parents probably do.)

When you read the poem this time, try to chant it in regular 3/4 time. (Sway back and forth if necessary.) You'll notice that every once in a while, a line will be missing the last beat or two. Just count the last one or two beats silently in your head. (In music, this would be like a rest.)

For example, here's how the first four lines should sound:

(Sway left for a count of 1–2–3) (Sway right for a count of 1–2–3)
Half a league, half a league
(Sway left, 1–2–3) (Sway right, 1–2–3; the third beat will be silent)
Half a league onward,
(Sway left, 1–2–3) (Sway right, 1–2–3) (Sway left, 1–2–3; the second and third beats will be silent)
All in the valley of Death
(Sway right, 1–2–3) (Sway left, 1–2–3; the third beat will be silent)
Rode the six hundred

STEP FOUR: **Read for motion**

The rhythm of the poem mimics the galloping rhythm of a horse (a gallop also has three beats). For your final reading of the poem, you don't have to gallop, but you do have to get up and move.

Once again, read the poem in regular 3/4 time. But this time, walk around the room (or your house, or your yard), taking one step for each beat. Whenever you get to the end of a line that's missing a beat or two, stop dead in your tracks and count the remaining beats in your head. Then begin again.

Here's how the first four lines would work:

(Take three steps) (Take three steps)
Half a league, half a league
(Take three steps) (Take two steps and then pause for one beat)
Half a league onward,

(Take three steps) (Take three steps) (Take one step and then pause for two beats)
All in the valley of Death
(Take three steps) (Take two steps and then pause for one beat)
Rode the six hundred

Day Two: Analyze

Focus: Understanding ballad form

STEP ONE: Identify complete and incomplete dactyls

If you did yesterday's reading carefully, you already know what the metrical pattern of this poem is from the following feet:

(**Half** a league), (**half** a league) . . .

(**All** in the) (**vall**ey of) . . .

Each complete foot in the poem has three syllables and follows this pattern:

(**stressed** unstressed unstressed)

Remember, last week you learned about the following meters:

iambic (unstressed **stressed**)
trochaic (**stressed** unstressed)
anapestic (unstressed unstressed **stressed**)

The meter of this poem is a new one:

dactylic (**stressed** unstressed unstressed)

Dactylic meter is one of the most rhymic poetic patterns. (In fact, the word **po-**e-try itself is dactylic!) Say the following phrases out loud and listen to the dactylic pattern in each:

higgledy-piggledy
patty cake, patty cake
honor and glory and power and
I was out walking one morning

In "The Charge of the Light Brigade," Tennyson uses the dactylic meter very regularly—and when he leaves a dactyl incomplete (like at the end of the line "**Rode** the six **hund**red [missing beat]), he does so on purpose.

Your first step today will be to mark the stressed and unstressed syllables in each line of the poem. (This may seem tedious, but it forces you to read slowly and analytically, paying attention to each syllable.) As you mark the syllables, look for incomplete feet (feet with fewer than three syllables). Circle each incomplete foot.

The first four lines are done for you.

1
Half a league, half a league,

Half a league **onward**,

All in the valley of **Death**

Rode the six **hundred**.

"Forward, the Light Brigade!

"Charge for the guns!" he said:

Into the valley of Death

Rode the six hundred.

2
"Forward, the Light Brigade!"

Was there a man dismay'd?

Not tho' the soldier knew

Someone had blunder'd:

Theirs not to make reply,

Theirs not to reason why,

Theirs but to do and die:

Into the valley of Death

Rode the six hundred.

3
Cannon to right of them,

Cannon to left of them,

Cannon in front of them

Volley'd and thunder'd;

Storm'd at with shot and shell,

Boldly they rode and well,

Into the jaws of Death,

Into the mouth of Hell

Rode the six hundred.

4
Flash'd all their sabres bare,

Flash'd as they turn'd in air,

Sabring the gunners there,

Charging an army, while

All the world wonder'd:

Plunged in the battery-smoke

Right thro' the line they broke;

Cossack and Russian

Reel'd from the sabre stroke

Shatter'd and sunder'd.

Then they rode back, but not

Not the six hundred.

5
Cannon to right of them,

Cannon to left of them,

Cannon behind them
    Volley'd and thunder'd;
Storm'd at with shot and shell,
While horse and hero fell,
They that had fought so well
Came thro' the jaws of Death
Back from the mouth of Hell,
All that was left of them,
    Left of six hundred.

6
When can their glory fade?
O the wild charge they made!
    All the world wondered.
Honor the charge they made,
Honor the Light Brigade,
    Noble six hundred.

STEP TWO: **Identify rhyme scheme**

"The Charge of the Light Brigade" has an irregular rhyme scheme. There is a pattern to the rhymes—but the pattern changes from stanza to stanza.

Go back to the copy of the poem you marked up in the previous step. Look at the ending words of each line. Some of those ending words rhyme with other words in the same stanza. Some of the ending words don't have *any* matching rhyme within the stanza.

Underline the ending words that rhyme with at least one other ending word within the stanza. (Don't do anything to the ending words that have no match.) Then, give each rhyming sound a letter. Write that letter after each line that ends with the sound.

For example, Stanza 2 would look like this:

"Forward, the Light Brigade!"	A
Was there a man dismay'd?	A
Not tho' the soldier knew	
Someone had blunder'd:	B
Theirs not to make reply,	C
Theirs not to reason why,	C
Theirs but to do and die:	C
Into the valley of Death	
Rode the six hundred.	B

"Brigade" and "dismay'd" rhyme with each other and have the same ending sound. "Brigade" is the first rhyming word in the stanza, so the "-aid" sound at the end is given the letter A.

"Knew" doesn't rhyme with any other word, so it is neither underlined nor given a letter.

"Blunder'd" and "hundred" rhyme. (Well, close enough. Sometimes the ending sounds of words are *so* close that you *think* the poet intended a rhyme—but there's a tiny bit of difference. You can decide whether or not these "near rhymes" are *actual* rhymes. There isn't necessarily a right answer; this is a judgment call.) "Blunder'd" is the second rhyming word in the stanza, so the sound at the end is given the letter "B."

"Reply," "why," and "die" all rhyme and are given the letter C.

"Death" doesn't rhyme with anything, so it isn't underlined or given a letter.

Now do this with the other stanzas in the poem (you can copy our answers for Stanza 2). Note: when a word rhymes only with itself, such as the repetition of *Death* in Stanza 1, this is generally not considered part of a rhyme scheme. If three lines ended with *Death, breath, Death,* that would be considered part of a rhyme scheme.

When you are finished, fill out the following chart by listing the rhyme scheme for each stanza beneath the stanza number. (Leave out the unrhymed lines.) The second stanza is done for you.

Show your work to your instructor.

1	2	3	4	5	6
	A A B C C C B				

STEP THREE: **Understand ballad form**

You've already studied one poem written in free verse and one sonnet—two forms you'll see very often as you continue to write about poetry. This week's poem is another very common form: a *ballad.*

A ballad is a poem that tells a story, usually a heroic or tragic one. Ballads don't have one particular form, which makes them different from sonnets. A sonnet always has the same form (14 lines, iambic pentameter), but the *content* of the sonnet can be anything the poet chooses. A ballad always has the same *content* (a heroic or tragic story), but the poet can use different *forms* to tell that story.

Many ballads are written in sets of four lines called *quatrains*, from the Latin word for "four." These stanzas are from "The Rime of the Ancient Mariner," a ballad written by Samuel Taylor Coleridge:

The fair breeze blew, the white foam flew,
The furrow followed free;
We were the first that ever burst
Into that silent sea.

Down dropped the breeze, the sails dropped down,
'Twas sad as sad could be;
And we did speak only to break
The silence of the sea!

All in a hot and copper sky,
The bloody sun, at noon,
Right up above the mast did stand,
No bigger than the moon.

Day after day, day after day,
We stuck, nor breath nor motion;
As idle as a painted ship
Upon a painted ocean.

Water, water, every where,
And all the boards did shrink;
Water, water, every where,
Nor any drop to drink.

This ballad also has one of the most common rhyme schemes for ballads; the second and fourth lines of each quatrain rhyme with each other, while the first and third lines don't rhyme at all. We describe this rhyme scheme as ABCB.

Here's a stanza from another famous ballad, "Paul Revere's Ride" by Henry Wadsworth Longfellow:

You know the rest. In the books you have read
How the British regulars fired and fled;
How the farmers gave them ball for ball,
From behind each fence and farmyard wall,
Chasing the redcoats down the lane,
Then crossing the fields to emerge again
Under the trees at the turn of the road,
And only pausing to fire and load.

In this ballad, the stanzas are made up of *two* quatrains, and the rhyme scheme is AABBCCDDEE—each pair of lines rhymes.

Many ballads also have a refrain—a line that is repeated exactly, or with slight variation, throughout the poem. Sometimes this refrain is part of the quatrain, and sometimes it is an extra, fifth line. These stanzas are from "The Lady of Shalott" by Tennyson; the refrain lines are underlined.

She left the web, she left the loom,
She made three paces through the room,
She saw the water-lily bloom,
She saw the helmet and the plume,
    She looked down to Camelot.
Out flew the web and floated wide;
The mirror cracked from side to side;
"The curse is come upon me," cried
    The Lady of Shalott.

In the stormy east-wind straining,
The pale yellow woods were waning,
The broad stream in his banks complaining,
Heavily the low sky raining
    Over towered Camelot;
Down she came and found a boat
Beneath a willow left afloat,
And round about the prow she wrote
    The Lady of Shalott.

In each stanza, the first refrain is an additional, fifth line. The second refrain is just the fourth line of the quatrain.

Notice that this ballad uses yet another rhyme scheme: AAAABCCCB.

Now that you've seen three examples of ballads, look back at the poem you marked up in Steps One and Two. First, go through the copy of the poem below and draw a square bracket around each quatrain that you can find. Not every line in the poem belongs to a four-line quatrain, but many do. The first quatrain is done for you.

Second, circle every repeated line or phrase that you can find in the poem. The repetition may be exact (as in "The Lady of Shalott") or have a variation ("down to Camelot" "towered Camelot"). The first set of repetitions in Stanza 1 is circled for you.

Finally, write the following definition in your Literary Terms chart:

ballad: a poem that tells a story, usually a heroic or tragic one

When you are finished, check your work with your instructor.

1

Half a league, half a league,
    Half a league onward,
All in the valley of Death
    Rode the six hundred.
"Forward, the Light Brigade!
"Charge for the guns!" he said:
Into the valley of Death
    Rode the six hundred.

2

"Forward, the Light Brigade!"
Was there a man dismay'd?
Not tho' the soldier knew
    Someone had blunder'd:
Theirs not to make reply,
Theirs not to reason why,
Theirs but to do and die:
Into the valley of Death
    Rode the six hundred.

3

Cannon to right of them,
Cannon to left of them,
Cannon in front of them
    Volley'd and thunder'd;
Storm'd at with shot and shell,
Boldly they rode and well,
Into the jaws of Death,
Into the mouth of Hell
    Rode the six hundred.

4

Flash'd all their sabres bare,
Flash'd as they turn'd in air,
Sabring the gunners there,
Charging an army, while
    All the world wonder'd:
Plunged in the battery-smoke
Right thro' the line they broke;
Cossack and Russian
Reel'd from the sabre stroke
    Shatter'd and sunder'd.
Then they rode back, but not
    Not the six hundred.

5

Cannon to right of them,
Cannon to left of them,
Cannon behind them
    Volley'd and thunder'd;
Storm'd at with shot and shell,
While horse and hero fell,
They that had fought so well
Came thro' the jaws of Death
Back from the mouth of Hell,
All that was left of them,
    Left of six hundred.

6

When can their glory fade?
O the wild charge they made!
    All the world wondered.
Honor the charge they made,
Honor the Light Brigade,
    Noble six hundred.

Day Three: Think

Focus: Connecting form and meaning

In the first two steps of today's lesson, your instructor will carry on a dialogue with you. During these dialogues, you'll write brief answers in the spaces below. These answers will help you construct your short essay tomorrow.

STEP ONE: **Examine the movement of the poem**

Stanzas 1 and 2:

"Half a league, half a league, Half a league onward" shows ______________________.

Where? ______________________.

In what direction? ______________________.

Stanza 3

The Light Brigade has now ______________________

____

They are trapped in the ______________________

The jaws of Death are also ______________________

____

Most people ______________________

Stanza 4

The ______________________ shows that the Light Brigade has arrived at the center of the poem.

Two things happen there: ______________________

____

Stanza 5

Finally, they ____.

The repetition shows this pattern:

____

______________________________ ______________________________

Stanza 6

Physically, the Light Brigade moved ______________________________

and then ______________________________. In the eyes of others, they moved from being

______________________________ to ______________________________.

STEP TWO: Understand the relationship between form and meaning

____

______________________________ ______________________________

Incomplete feet:

Stanza 1: ______________________________

Stanza 2: ______________________________

Stanza 6: ______________________________

STEP THREE: Investigate the historical background

The charge of the Light Brigade took place during the Battle of Balaklava, during the Crimean War (1853–1856). The Crimean War was fought between Russia and the allied armies of Turkey, England, and France.

Read through the following account of the Battle of Balaklava, from Dorothy Donnell Calhoun's *The Book of Brave Adventures*. You will see from the tone of the book that it's intended for slightly younger readers, but Calhoun gives the clearest and most readable account of the battle that I could find.

After you read the account, go back and take notes on the events of the Battle of Balaklava. Tomorrow, when you write your composition, you will write one paragraph on the historical background of the poem. Prepare for this by first listing 14–15 events leading to and during the battle. Be sure to focus on the Battle of Balaklava itself, rather than on details of the Crimean War.

These events should not use the exact wording of the text. Historical events are common knowledge, so if you do not use the exact wording of the text, you do not need to use quotation marks or document the information. For example, you might write:

> The Light Brigade was a British cavalry regiment. (125)

Then go back and list three or four details that you can use to make your paragraph more vivid. These details may use the exact words of the source. Your paragraph will need to include at least one direct quote, so be sure to use quotation marks to surround the exact words of the text.

The publication information for the book is:

Calhoun, Dorothy Donnell. *The Book of Brave Adventures.* New York: The Macmillan Company, 1915.

If you need help, ask your instructor. When you're finished, show your work to your instructor.

THE CHARGE OF THE LIGHT BRIGADE

Crimea, Cri-me'a (pronounced cri-mī'a): territory north of the Black Sea.

Balaklava, Ba'la-kla'va (pronounced bä'lä-klä'va): a part of the Crimea.

IT seems strange that no matter how much land a nation owns, it is always trying to get more. Sometimes it buys land from another country, but more often it goes to war and takes what it wishes by force. You would suppose that Russia had as much land as she could possibly use. She is such a great bare country with thousands of miles of land where no one lives. Yet big as she was, she wished to be bigger. In 1853 the Czar of Russia thought that he saw a way to help himself to part of Turkey.

If you will look Russia up on the map, you will see that she has no very good seaports. There are ports into the Baltic, the Black Sea, and the Caspian Sea, but not into the Mediterranean,

where most of the trading is done. The Czar thought that it would be a very fine thing for Russia to have some of Turkey's harbors. He knew that Turkey had a small army and that he had a very large one. Considering this, he thought it would be easy for him to win a war with her.

The Czar did not know, however, that England, France, and Austria would try to protect Turkey. These nations did not wish Russia to get any more land; they were afraid for their own safety if Russia became too powerful. To protect themselves, in a way, when the Czar declared war on Turkey, England, France, and Austria declared war on the Czar.

In southern Russia lies a small province, sometimes called Crim Tartary, sometimes known as the Crimea. It was here that the Allies, the nations that were banded together against Russia, landed their troops. Among the British forces was a cavalry regiment called the Light Brigade.

Russia was taken by surprise and had very little time to gather troops together to meet the enemy. For some days, therefore, the Allies pushed on into the Crimea, winning victories and driving back the Russian troops. Then suddenly everything was changed. A great Russian army arrived. The French and English troops soon saw that they were in a dangerous place. The forces of the enemies came together in a place called Balaklava. Low hills surrounded a green plain here. On the top of these hills the Allies had dug trenches and placed small cannon. But they had left very few men in charge of the trenches, and the Russians soon captured the earthworks and the cannon.

The French and English regiments, however, managed to drive the Russians from the valley, down the plain toward the sea. They swept down the valley, through the hills, taking twelve of the captured English cannon with them.

The general at the head of the English army was Lord Raglan, a brave man who had lost an arm in the battle of Waterloo. Seeing the Russians who had taken the trenches on the hill beginning to remove the cannon from these places also, he wrote a hasty note to Lord Lucern who was directing the battle in the valley. In this note he told him to prevent the Russians from

taking away the rest of the cannon from the hills. At least that is what Lord Raglan meant to say; but Lord Lucern did not understand the order in that way. He thought the general was telling him to send his men after the main body of Russian troops, who were retreating down the valley with several English cannon. He was amazed at such an order.

Ahead lay a narrow valley with the hills on either side covered with Russian troops. At the farther end of the valley the Russians who had just been defeated had halted and taken up a position behind their guns. It would be like sending his men into a death trap to obey the order that the general had sent him. They would be shot at from three sides at once. He knew very well that they would most of them never reach the end of the valley alive.

The division which was ordered into this terrible danger was the cavalry regiment known as the Light Brigade. Six hundred soldiers sat in their saddles looking out over the hills that were dotted with the gray uniforms of the Russian troops; they were thinking probably of their homes, and their little boys and girls. Soon, perhaps, the war would be over, and they could go back to England. Suddenly they saw Lord Lucern riding rapidly toward them. Their captain, Lord Cardigan, went to meet him. The soldiers saw a piece of paper in Lord Lucern's hand and the troubled expression of his face. The two men talked earnestly together and pointed down the valley where the Russian troops had just fled.

What did it mean? they wondered. Surely they could not be planning to follow the enemy! After a moment's talk the two captains separated. Lord Cardigan rode toward his men. He drew his sword, pointed to the valley, and cried loudly: —

"The Brigade will now advance!"

Not one of the six hundred soldiers hesitated. Every man knew that a mistake must have been made somewhere. Every man knew that he would probably be killed. After they had once started down that narrow valley there would be no escape. Yet they had been taught to obey orders without questioning them. At the word,

"Advance," every horse started forward at a steady trot.

The first shell fired at the Light Brigade from the Russians on the hillside struck the leader. His horse turned around and carried his lifeless master back through the ranks of horsemen. In a moment a rain of bullets was upon them. From the hillsides on both sides of the valley came the shriek of bullets and the roar of shells. Horses and soldiers toppled to the ground, and their companions rode on over their bodies. The Light Brigade had been ordered to advance and they were advancing. They would keep on as long as there was a man left alive.

Ahead at the end of the valley were the defeated Russians. They were drawn up behind twelve powerful guns. When the Light Brigade was a hundred yards away, these guns began firing.

For five minutes the terrible ride had been going on. More than half of the Brigade lay dead or wounded on the ground. The guns in front increased the slaughter. Yet those who were still left rode on, into the clouds of cannon smoke which hid them from view. Behind them, friends and enemies watched in amazement. They had never seen such bravery before.

Of course the unequal battle could end only one way. After a few moments' brave attack on the Russians, in which the enemy's gunners were driven from their guns, the few who were left of the Light Brigade rode back. Their red uniforms were black with dust and powder smoke. They rode slowly, by twos and threes. Now and then they stopped to help a friend. Some dragged along on foot. Two regiments of the Light Brigade had kept some sort of order. These now rode back in a body, fighting their way through a Russian force that came down from one of the hillsides to capture them.

One hundred and ninety-five men came back where six hundred had ridden before. They had done no good to the cause, captured no guns, won no victory. But they had given the world a sight of men who were not afraid to do their duty in the face of certain death. Their heroic ride will never be forgotten.

Day Four: Write

Focus: Writing about the poem

Arrange your copy of the poem, your answers to the Day Three exercises, and your list of historical events and details in front of you.

You do not need to show your composition to your instructor until you are finished with all of the steps, but you may ask for help at any time.

STEP ONE: **Write a chronological narrative describing the Battle of Balaklava**

Your first paragraph will give the historical background of "The Charge of the Light Brigade." (Notice that although you experienced the poem *first,* the reader of your essay will not have the poem in front of him; he is relying solely on your interpretation. He can't understand your interpretation unless he knows the background, so you will present this information first.)

This paragraph will simply be a brief chronological narrative of a past event—something you've had plenty of practice in writing. Glance back at your Chronological Narrative of a Past Event chart and your list of time words. Then write a paragraph of at least 120 but not more than 200 words, explaining the events of "The Charge of the Light Brigade." Try to use at least two time words. You must include at least one direct quote, properly footnoted.

You will need an introductory sentence that tells the reader the connection between the poem and the historical background. You may use this introductory sentence:

> "The Charge of the Light Brigade" tells the story of a battle that took place during the Crimean War.

or else write your own.

STEP TWO: **Explain the movement of the poem**

Now write either two or three more short paragraphs, explaining the movement of the poem. These paragraphs should total at least 175 but not more than 300 words. Use the poem itself and your answers from Step One of yesterday's lesson. You may also glance back over your Day Two work if you need additional ideas.

You will need a sentence that connects this paragraph with the historical background. You may use this introductory sentence:

> When writing his poem about the Light Brigade, Tennyson chose to use the rhythm of a horse galloping.

or else write your own.

Your paragraphs should describe what happens in each stanza, and should tell how the repetitions of the poem help show the movement of the Light Brigade.

Your paragraphs should quote directly from the poem at least three times, using properly formatted line numbers.

If you have trouble getting started, ask your instructor to prompt you.

STEP THREE: **Explain how the meter and rhyme scheme of the poem support its meaning**

Your composition will conclude with a paragraph describing how Tennyson uses meter and rhyme scheme. Begin with rhyme scheme, and then explain how the incomplete feet in the poem add to the poem's meaning. This paragraph should be at least 120 and not more than 200 words.

You will need a transitional sentence at the beginning of this paragraph. You may use this sentence:

> Tennyson uses both rhyme and meter to add extra levels of meaning to the poem.

or else write your own.

In your paragraph, explain how the rhyme schemes in Stanzas 3, 4, and 5 reinforce the central position of Stanza 4. Also tell the reader that the poem is written in dactylic meter and that some feet are incomplete. Then, explain what these incomplete feet do.

STEP FOUR: **Assemble and proofread the composition**

Give the composition a title ("'The Charge of the Light Brigade,' by Alfred, Lord Tennyson" is fine). Proofread it for spelling and grammar mistakes. Check to see that your footnotes and poem line numbers are properly formatted.

Since this composition has only one citation, it is not necessary to do a separate Works Cited page.

When you are ready, give your composition to your instructor to read.

Part VII

FINAL PROJECT
WEEKS 35–36

Overview of Weeks 35–36

Over the past 34 weeks, you've practiced many separate skills: outlining; putting together narrations, descriptions, and sequences; writing basic literary essays on both stories and poems; and changing sentences around by transforming nouns, adjectives, and verbs.

In these last two weeks, you'll put the skills you've learned to use by writing an actual composition—on any topic you choose. You will decide on the form of the composition, pick the subject, find your own resources, read up on your topic, take notes, write your composition, and add the footnotes. You know how to do all of these things; this is your chance to put them all together.

Instead of giving you four days' worth of assigments, each week will be divided up into a number of steps, with a suggestion of how many hours you should spend on each step. You and your instructor can decide whether to spread these hours over several days, or concentrate them into one or two days of single-minded work. You can always spend more hours (but not fewer!) and go more deeply into your subject. You can take additional time to illustrate your final composition with drawings, graphs, charts—or not.

But however you decide to approach this final project, it must follow these guidelines.

Your final composition must:

1. Put together at least two of the topoi you've learned to write.
2. Be at least 1000 words in length.
3. Make use of at least three sources.
4. Include footnotes and a Works Cited page.

WEEK 35: FINDING AND RESEARCHING YOUR TOPIC

The Final Project, Part One: Finding and Researching Your Topic

This week, you should work independently as much as possible. You do not need to show your work to your instructor until the end of the week, but you may ask your instructor for help at any time.

STEP ONE: **Decide which topoi to include** — 1/2 hour

Turn to the Reference section of your Composition Notebook and review the forms of the seven topoi you have learned this year. They are:

Chronological Narrative of a Past Event
Chronological Narrative of a Scientific Discovery
Description of a Place
Scientific Description
Description of a Person
Biographical Sketch
Sequence: Natural Processes

Before going on, read the columns under "Procedure" and "Remember" for each topos.

✦

Now, make a tentative decision about which topoi you will use for your paper. You *must* use a minimum of two (but don't try to include more than four, even if you're feeling ambitious).

You've already practiced combining a chronological narrative of past events with a description of a place (Week 11, Ivan the Terrible and St. Basil's Cathedral), combining a chronological narrative of a scientific discovery with a scientific description (Week 15, the discovery and description of deep-ocean hydrothermal vents), a chronological narrative of past events that includes a personal description and a description of a place (Week 29, Julius Caesar), and a sequence of natural events that includes a scientific description (Week 30, digestion). You've also learned that a biographical sketch can include a personal description as one of the aspects covered (Week 31, Marie Antoinette). You can use one of these combinations, or choose your own.

As you choose the topoi, also make a decision about the subject you'll write about. If possible, choose a subject that's related to your other studies.

> *Example: I might like to write about X-rays, which were discovered in 1895 by Wilhelm Roentgen. I could combine a chronological narrative of a scientific discovery with a description of Roentgen, or with a biographical sketch of Roentgen. Or I could combine the chronological narrative with a sequence, describing exactly how X-rays work. Or I could write a biographical sketch of Roentgen that includes a sequence describing how X-rays work. I pick the combination of chronological narrative and sequence—but I might change my mind once I start researching, if I find out that writing a sequence will require me to know a lot more about physics than I do. In that case I might decide to do a biographical sketch of Roentgen instead.*

Your instructor can help you if you're having trouble deciding on your topoi or coming up with a subject. And remember: you can always change your mind when you start researching.

STEP TWO: **Collect resources** 2 hours

Your next task is to collect at least five books that deal generally with your subject. You won't need to use all five when you write, but you'll probably find that at least one or two of the books turns out to be unsuitable, so choosing five makes it more likely that you'll end up with three good resources.

For this assignment, you may not use websites. A published book may have errors in it, but it has been inspected and edited by professionals who are *not* the author. A website, on the other hand, doesn't have to be inspected or edited by anyone. A writer can put anything up on a website, and unless you're an expert yourself, you won't be able to tell what's true and what's false. (You'll learn more about this in future levels of this course.)

The only exception: you *may* use e-book versions of standard published works. These have been edited and proofread in the same way as the print versions.

Here are a few suggestions to help you find your five resources.

1. Start by reading encyclopedia articles on your subject. These will give you a useful overview and alert you to the topics you should cover as you write. Note down two or three important names, places, or details.

Remember that you may use online versions of standard encyclopedias such as Britannica or World Book. You may *not* use Wikipedia. Wikipedia is not professionally edited or fact-checked. Anyone can post anything on Wikipedia. Usually, other users will identify and remove mistakes—but if you happen to use Wikipedia five minutes after someone has posted bad information (which people sometimes do just for fun), you won't realize that you're writing down false facts.

Example: I look up Wilhelm Roentgen in the Encyclopedia Britannica and find out that he won the first Nobel prize for physics in 1901; that a unit of radiation called a roentgen *is named after him; and that he called his discovery "X-rays." I jot down "Nobel prize," "roentgen," and "X-rays."*

2. Visit your library. Look up the names, places, or details in the library catalog. (Ask the reference librarian for help if you don't know how to use the catalog. Reference librarians *want* to help you. That's why they became reference librarians.) Then go and pull at least ten books off the shelves.

Example: I search for "Wilhelm Roentgen" in the catalog of the York County Library. I see one title that might be useful—it's described as "juvenile literature," which means it won't be a complicated college-level text:

Gherman, Beverly. *The Mysterious Rays of Dr. Röntgen*

When I look over to the left of the catalog page, I see that I can find out more about three different subjects:

Roentgen, Wilhelm Conrad, 1845–1923—Juvenile literature
X-rays — Juvenile literature
Physicists—Germany—Biography—Juvenile literature

I click on each link to find more books, but the same book keeps coming up again and again. So I type "X-ray" into the search box and find:

McClafferty, Carla Killough. *The Head Bone's Connected to the Neck Bone: The Weird, Wacky, and Wonderful X-Ray*

When I type "roentgen" in the search box, I find:

Adler, Robert E. *Medical First: From Hippocrates to the Human Genome*

And when I type "Nobel prize" into the search box I find:

Worek, Michael, editor. *Nobel: A Century of Prize Winners*

That's only four books, but it's a start. I go find each book and look on either side of them on their shelves to find books on related topics. I look in the index of these surrounding books for "Roentgen" *and* "X-ray." *If I find a reference in the index, I take the surrounding books as well.*

3. Flip through the books. Eliminate those that are too complicated (remember, you're just writing a short essay, not a research paper—you don't want to end up with an overwhelming amount of information) or only have a sentence or two on your topic. Try to end up with five that you can check out and take home.

STEP THREE: **Do initial reading** — 4–5 hours

Sit down with your five books and read them. If the entire book is on your topic, try to read the whole thing. If there is only a chapter or page on your topic, only read that chapter or page. Don't take notes yet. If you take notes too early, you end up writing down a lot of information you won't need. This week's task is to get an overview of your topic.

STEP FOUR: **Choose final resources** 1/2 hour

Pick the two or three books that you will find useful. If necessary, change your topoi so that they match the information available to you. For example, if your library has lots of biographical information about Roentgen but nothing on your level about X-rays, you'll probably want to do a biographical sketch and a description—even if you had originally planned to do a sequence and a scientific description.

You'll finish your work next week. It is always easier to write about a topic if you've read about it first—and then let the information sit in your mind for a few days. Researching at the last minute often makes your paper sound rushed and superficial. (Remember this when you get to college!)

Show your collected books to your instructor.

Week 36: Writing Your Final Composition

The Final Project, Part Two: Taking Notes and Writing the Composition

STEP ONE: **Make a preliminary plan** — **1/2 hour**

Now that you've settled on a subject and two or three topoi, you're almost ready to start taking notes. But unless you know exactly what information you're looking for, you'll be tempted to take too many notes on too many different details. So before you go on to the note-taking step, stop for a minute and make a preliminary plan.

Making a preliminary plan means that you decide what *sorts* of details you'll need to fill out your composition. You've practiced making a preliminary plan in several previous lessons. For this project, glance down the list below. Choose the topoi you'll be using and make decisions about the information you'll need to complete them successfully. Answer each question by jotting down phrases or short sentences on a piece of paper. (Do *not* simply answer the questions in your head!)

If necessary, go back to the lessons listed to review the meaning of each question.

Chronological narrative of a past event
Week 4, Days Three–Four; Week 6, Days Three–Four
What is the theme of the narrative—its focus?
What are its beginning and ending points?
Will you use dialogue? Who will speak?

Chronological narrative of a scientific discovery
Week 5, Days Three–Four; Week 7, Days Three–Four;
Will you need a background paragraph explaining the circumstances before the discovery?
Can you quote from the scientist's own words?

Description of a place

Week 8, Days Three–Four; Week 9, Days Three–Four; Week 10, Days Three–Four

What purpose will this description fulfill?

What is your point of view?

What metaphors or similes will make the description more vivid?

Scientific description

Week 12, Days Three–Four; Week 13, Days Three–Four; Week 14, Days Three–Four

What are the parts of the object or phenomenon?

What is your point of view? Will you use more than one?

What figurative language can make the description more visual?

Description of a person

Week 16, Days Two–Three; Week 17, Days Two–Three; Week 18, Days Two–Three

What aspects will be included?

Will you slant the description in a positive or negative direction?

Will you use an overall metaphor to give clues about the person's character?

Biographical sketch

Week 19, Days Two–Three; Week 20, Days Two–Three

What will the focus be—life events, or the subject's accomplishments/work?

If life events, which ones will be included?

If accomplishments/work, will they be listed chronologically or by topic?

What aspects from the Description of a Person chart should be included?

Sequence: natural process

Week 21, Days Two–Three; Week 22, Days Two–Three

What other elements will you include?

Introduction/summary?

Scientific background?

Repetition of the process?

STEP TWO: **Take notes** 3–4 hours

Keeping your answers to Step One nearby, take notes from at least three of your resources. If you need to review the correct form, reread Week 28, Days Two–Four.

The number of notes you will take will vary. However, for a short composition you should try never to take more than 20 notes from any individual source.

STEP THREE: **Write the topoi** — 3 hours

Place your notes in order. If you need to review this process, reread Week 29, Days Two–Three. You may also want to reread Week 30, Days Two–Three, and Week 31, Days Two–Four.

Use your notes to write each topos. Write the topoi one at a time; you will assemble them in the final step.

You should quote directly from each of your three sources at least one time. If you need to review proper documentation, reread Week 28, Day Two.

STEP FOUR: **Assemble the composition** — 1/2 hour

Put your topoi together into a complete composition.

Read your composition out loud. Listen for awkward phrases and abrupt transitions. You may need to insert sentences linking the topoi together.

Read your composition one more time silently, looking for mistakes in spelling, grammar, and punctuation.

Make sure that all direct quotes and anything which is not common knowledge is footnoted.

Assemble your Works Cited page. If you need to review the form, reread Week 28, Day Two.

Give your composition a simple title (the name of the event, person, place, or process is fine).

Make sure your composition has page numbers.

Show your completed work to your instructor.

Certificate of Completion

This certifies that

____

Has successfully completed Level One
of Writing with Skill
and is now able to research and write
chronological narratives, descriptions,
biographical sketches, and sequences,
with proper documentation and mechanics.

______________ ______________

DATE SUSAN WISE BAUER

Appendix I

TIME AND SEQUENCE WORDS

For chronological narratives

Words for events that happen before any others
First
At first
In the beginning
Before

Words for events that happen at the same time
When
At that point
At that moment
While

Words for an event that happens very soon after a previous event
When
As soon as
Soon
Shortly/shortly afterwards
Presently
Before long
Not long after
Immediately

Words for an event that happens after a previous event—but you're not exactly sure whether a long or short period of time elapsed first
Next
Afterwards
After
After some time
Subsequently
Following/following that
Furthermore
Then

Words for an event that happened long after another event
Eventually
Later/later on
Finally

Words for an event that happened after another event—AND was caused by the previous event
As a result
As a consequence
Since
Because
Seeing that

Space and Distance Words/ Phrases For descriptions

Orientation
To (on) the right (side)
To (on) the left (side)
Above
Below
To/From the north/south/east/west of
On the one side/On the other side
In/at the middle of
In/at the center of
Around

Close relationship
By
Near (by)
Close (by)
Next to
At

Distant relationship
At a (in the) distance
Off
Far off (away)
Around (round)
About
Beyond
Further (farther)
Further away (on)
Until

Vertical relationship
Above
Below
Beyond
On
Up/upon
Over
Under
Up from (to/into)
Down
Down from (on/to/into)
Higher/higher than
Lower/lower than

Horizontal relationship
Back
Forward
Past
Before
In front of
From
Across
On (to/onto/on and on)
Into
Out (of)
By
Between
On either side (of)
Opposite

Interlocking relationship
Through
Into
In
Inside
With
Within
Without
Outside (outside of/outside)
Filled with
Around
Surrounding/surrounded by

Indeterminate relationship
Where
There
With
Without
A distance from
On the one/other side
On and on

APPENDIX II

POINTS OF VIEW

FOR PLACE DESCRIPTIONS

1. From above (impersonal)
2. From inside
3. From one side or angle
4. Moving through or around

FOR SCIENTIFIC DESCRIPTIONS

1. Removed from the object or phenomenon
2. Present with the object or phenomenon

Appendix III

Literature

Rikki-Tikki-Tavi

From *The Jungle Book*
by Rudyard Kipling

At the hole where he went in
Red-Eye called to Wrinkle-Skin.
Hear what little Red-Eye saith:
"Nag, come up and dance with death!"
Eye to eye and head to head,
    (Keep the measure, Nag.)
This shall end when one is dead;
    (At thy pleasure, Nag.)
Turn for turn and twist for twist—
    (Run and hide thee, Nag.)
Hah! The hooded Death has missed!
    (Woe betide thee, Nag!)

This is the story of the great war that Rikki-tikki-tavi fought single-handed, through the bath-rooms of the big bungalow in Segowlee cantonment.

Darzee, the Tailorbird, helped him, and Chuchundra, the musk-rat, who never comes out into the middle of the floor, but always creeps round by the wall, gave him advice, but Rikki-tikki did the real fighting.

He was a mongoose, rather like a little cat in his fur and his tail, but quite like a weasel in his head and his habits. His eyes and the end of his restless nose were pink. He could scratch himself anywhere he pleased with any leg, front or back, that he chose to use. He could fluff up his tail till it looked like a bottle brush, and his war cry as he scuttled through the long grass was: "Rikk-tikk-tikki-tikki-tchk!"

One day, a high summer flood washed him out of the burrow where he lived with his father and mother, and carried him, kicking and clucking, down a roadside ditch. He found a little wisp of grass floating there, and clung to it till he lost his senses. When he revived, he was lying in the hot sun on the middle of a garden path, very draggled indeed, and a small boy was saying, "Here's a dead mongoose. Let's have a funeral."

"No," said his mother, "let's take him in and dry him. Perhaps he isn't really dead."

They took him into the house, and a big man picked him up between his finger and thumb and said he was not dead but half choked. So they wrapped him in cotton wool, and warmed him over a little fire, and he opened his eyes and sneezed.

"Now," said the big man (he was an Englishman who had just moved into the bungalow), "don't frighten him, and we'll see what he'll do."

It is the hardest thing in the world to frighten a mongoose, because he is eaten up from nose to tail with curiosity. The motto of all the mongoose family is "Run and find out," and Rikki-tikki was a true mongoose. He looked at the cotton wool, decided that it was not good to eat, ran all round the table, sat up and put his fur in order, scratched himself, and jumped on the small boy's shoulder.

"Don't be frightened, Teddy," said his father. "That's his way of making friends."

"Ouch! He's tickling under my chin," said Teddy.

Rikki-tikki looked down between the boy's collar and neck, snuffed at his ear, and climbed down to the floor, where he sat rubbing his nose.

"Good gracious," said Teddy's mother, "and that's a wild creature! I suppose he's so tame because we've been kind to him."

"All mongooses are like that," said her husband. "If Teddy doesn't pick him up by the tail, or try to put him in a cage, he'll run in and out of the house all day long. Let's give him something to eat."

They gave him a little piece of raw meat. Rikki-tikki liked it immensely, and when it was finished he went out into the veranda and sat in the sunshine and fluffed up his fur to make it dry to the roots. Then he felt better.

"There are more things to find out about in this house," he said to himself, "than all my family could find out in all their lives. I shall certainly stay and find out."

He spent all that day roaming over the house. He nearly drowned himself in the bathtubs, put his nose into the ink on a writing table, and burned it on the end of the big man's cigar, for he climbed up in the big man's lap to see how writing was done. At nightfall he ran into Teddy's nursery to watch how kerosene lamps were lighted, and when Teddy went to bed Rikki-tikki climbed up too. But he was a restless companion, because he had to get up and attend to every noise all through the night, and find out what made it. Teddy's mother and father came in, the last thing, to look at their boy, and Rikki-tikki was awake on the pillow. "I don't like that," said Teddy's mother. "He may bite the child." "He'll do no such thing," said the father. "Teddy's safer with that little beast than if he had a bloodhound to watch him. If a snake came into the nursery now—"

But Teddy's mother wouldn't think of anything so awful.

Early in the morning Rikki-tikki came to early breakfast in the veranda riding on Teddy's shoulder, and they gave him banana and some boiled egg. He sat on all their laps one after the other, because every well-brought-up mongoose always hopes to be a house mongoose some day and have rooms to run about in; and Rikki-tikki's mother (she used to live in the general's house at Segowlee) had carefully told Rikki what to do if ever he came across white men.

Then Rikki-tikki went out into the garden to see what was to be seen. It was a large garden, only half cultivated, with bushes, as big as summer-houses, of Marshal Niel roses, lime and orange trees, clumps of bamboos, and thickets of high grass. Rikki-tikki licked his lips. "This is a splendid hunting-ground," he said, and his tail grew bottle-brushy at the thought of it, and he scuttled up and down the garden, snuffing here and there till he heard very sorrowful voices in a thorn-bush.

It was Darzee, the Tailorbird, and his wife. They had made a beautiful nest by pulling two big leaves together and stitching them up the edges with fibers, and had filled the hollow with cotton and downy fluff. The nest swayed to and fro, as they sat on the rim and cried.

"What is the matter?" asked Rikki-tikki.

"We are very miserable," said Darzee. "One of our babies fell out of the nest yesterday and Nag ate him."

"H'm!" said Rikki-tikki, "that is very sad—but I am a stranger here. Who is Nag?"

Darzee and his wife only cowered down in the nest without answering, for from the thick grass at the foot of the bush there came a low hiss—a horrid cold sound that made Rikki-tikki jump back two clear feet. Then inch by inch out of the grass rose up the head and spread hood of Nag, the big black cobra, and he was five feet long from tongue to tail. When he had lifted one-third of himself clear of the ground, he stayed balancing to and fro exactly as a dandelion tuft balances in the wind, and he looked at Rikki-tikki with the wicked snake's eyes that never change their expression, whatever the snake may be thinking of.

"Who is Nag?" said he. "I am Nag. The great God Brahm put his mark upon all our people, when the first cobra spread his hood to keep the sun off Brahm as he slept. Look, and be afraid!"

He spread out his hood more than ever, and Rikki-tikki saw the spectacle-mark on the back of it that looks exactly like the eye part of a hook-and-eye fastening. He was afraid for the minute, but it is impossible for a mongoose to stay frightened for any length of time, and though Rikki-tikki had never met a live cobra before, his mother had fed him on dead ones, and he knew that all a grown mongoose's business in life was to fight and eat snakes. Nag knew that too and, at the bottom of his cold heart, he was afraid.

"Well," said Rikki-tikki, and his tail began to fluff up again, "marks or no marks, do you think it is right for you to eat fledglings out of a nest?"

Nag was thinking to himself, and watching the least little movement in the grass behind Rikki-tikki. He knew that mongooses in the garden meant death sooner or later for him and his family, but he wanted to get Rikki-tikki off his guard. So he dropped his head a little, and put it on one side.

"Let us talk," he said. "You eat eggs. Why should not I eat birds?"

"Behind you! Look behind you!" sang Darzee.

Rikki-tikki knew better than to waste time in staring. He jumped up in the air as high as he could go, and just under him whizzed by the head of Nagaina, Nag's wicked wife. She had crept up behind him as he was talking, to make an end of him. He heard her savage hiss as the stroke missed. He came down almost across her back, and if he had been an old mongoose he would have known that then was the time to break her back with one bite; but he was afraid of the terrible lashing return stroke of the cobra. He bit, indeed, but did not bite long enough, and he jumped clear of the whisking tail, leaving Nagaina torn and angry.

"Wicked, wicked Darzee!" said Nag, lashing up as high as he could reach toward the nest in the thorn-bush. But Darzee had built it out of reach of snakes, and it only swayed to and fro.

Rikki-tikki felt his eyes growing red and hot (when a mongoose's eyes grow red, he is angry), and he sat back on his tail and hind legs like a little kangaroo, and looked all round him, and chattered with rage. But Nag and Nagaina had disappeared into the grass. When a snake misses its stroke, it never says anything or gives any sign of what it means to do next. Rikki-tikki did not care to follow them, for he did not feel sure that he could manage two snakes at once. So he trotted off to the gravel path near the house, and sat down to think. It was a serious matter for him.

If you read the old books of natural history, you will find they say that when the mongoose fights the snake and happens to get bitten, he runs off and eats some herb that cures him. That is not true. The victory is only a matter of quickness of eye and quickness of foot—snake's blow against mongoose's jump—and as no eye can follow the motion of a snake's head when it strikes, this makes things much more wonderful than any magic herb. Rikki-tikki knew he was a young mongoose, and it made him all the more pleased to think that he had managed to escape a blow from behind. It gave him confidence in himself, and when Teddy came running down the path, Rikki-tikki was ready to be petted.

But just as Teddy was stooping, something wriggled a little in the dust, and a tiny voice said: "Be careful. I am Death!" It was Karait, the dusty brown snakeling that lies for choice on the dusty earth; and his bite is as dangerous as the cobra's. But he is so small that nobody thinks of him, and so he does the more harm to people.

Rikki-tikki's eyes grew red again, and he danced up to Karait with the peculiar rocking, swaying motion that he had inherited from his family. It looks very funny, but it is so perfectly balanced a gait that you can fly off from it at any angle you please, and in dealing with snakes this is an advantage. If Rikki-tikki had only known, he was doing a much more dangerous thing than fighting Nag, for Karait is so small, and can turn so quickly, that unless Rikki bit him close to the back of the head, he would get the return stroke in his eye or his lip. But Rikki did not know. His eyes were all red, and he rocked back and forth, looking for a good place to hold. Karait struck out. Rikki jumped sideways and tried to run in, but the wicked little dusty gray head lashed within a fraction of his shoulder, and he had to jump over the body, and the head followed his heels close.

Teddy shouted to the house: "Oh, look here! Our mongoose is killing a snake." And Rikki-tikki heard a scream from Teddy's mother. His father ran out with a stick, but by the time he came up, Karait had lunged out once too far, and Rikki-tikki had sprung, jumped on the snake's back, dropped his head far between his forelegs, bitten as high up the back as he could get hold, and rolled away. That bite paralyzed Karait, and Rikki-tikki was just going to eat him up from the tail, after the custom of his family at dinner, when he remembered that a full meal makes a slow mongoose, and if he wanted all his strength and quickness ready, he must keep himself thin.

He went away for a dust bath under the castor-oil bushes, while Teddy's father beat the dead Karait. "What is the use of that?" thought Rikki-tikki. "I have settled it all"; and then Teddy's mother picked him up from the dust and hugged him, crying that he had saved Teddy from death, and Teddy's father said that he was a providence, and Teddy looked on with big scared eyes. Rikki-tikki was rather amused at all the fuss, which, of course, he did not understand. Teddy's mother might just as well have petted Teddy for playing in the dust. Rikki was thoroughly enjoying himself.

That night at dinner, walking to and fro among the wine-glasses on the table, he might have stuffed himself three times over with nice things. But he remembered Nag and Nagaina, and though it was very pleasant to be patted and petted by Teddy's mother, and to sit on Teddy's shoulder, his eyes would get red from time to time, and he would go off into his long war cry of "Rikk-tikk-tikki-tikki-tchk!"

Teddy carried him off to bed, and insisted on Rikki-tikki sleeping under his chin. Rikki-tikki was too well bred to bite or scratch, but as soon as Teddy was asleep he went off for his nightly walk round the house, and in the dark he ran up against Chuchundra, the musk-rat, creeping around by the wall. Chuchundra is a broken-hearted little beast. He whimpers and cheeps all the night, trying to make up his mind to run into the middle of the room. But he never gets there.

"Don't kill me," said Chuchundra, almost weeping. "Rikki-tikki, don't kill me!"

"Do you think a snake-killer kills muskrats?" said Rikki-tikki scornfully.

"Those who kill snakes get killed by snakes," said Chuchundra, more sorrowfully than ever. "And how am I to be sure that Nag won't mistake me for you some dark night?"

"There's not the least danger," said Rikki-tikki. "But Nag is in the garden, and I know you don't go there."

"My cousin Chua, the rat, told me—" said Chuchundra, and then he stopped.

"Told you what?"

"H'sh! Nag is everywhere, Rikki-tikki. You should have talked to Chua in the garden."

"I didn't—so you must tell me. Quick, Chuchundra, or I'll bite you!"

Chuchundra sat down and cried till the tears rolled off his whiskers. "I am a very poor man," he sobbed. "I never had spirit enough to run out into the middle of the room. H'sh! I mustn't tell you anything. Can't you hear, Rikki-tikki?"

Rikki-tikki listened. The house was as still as still, but he thought he could just catch the faintest scratch-scratch in the world—a noise as faint as that of a wasp walking on a window-pane—the dry scratch of a snake's scales on brick-work.

"That's Nag or Nagaina," he said to himself, "and he is crawling into the bath-room sluice. You're right, Chuchundra; I should have talked to Chua."

He stole off to Teddy's bath-room, but there was nothing there, and then to Teddy's mother's bathroom. At the bottom of the smooth plaster wall there was a brick pulled out to make a sluice for the bath water, and as Rikki-tikki stole in by the masonry curb where the bath is put, he heard Nag and Nagaina whispering together outside in the moonlight.

"When the house is emptied of people," said Nagaina to her husband, "he will have to go away, and then the garden will be our own again. Go in quietly, and remember that the big man who killed Karait is the first one to bite. Then come out and tell me, and we will hunt for Rikki-tikki together."

"But are you sure that there is anything to be gained by killing the people?" said Nag.

"Everything. When there were no people in the bungalow, did we have any mongoose in the garden? So long as the bungalow is empty, we are king and queen of the garden; and remember that as soon as our eggs in the melon bed hatch (as they may tomorrow), our children will need room and quiet."

"I had not thought of that," said Nag. "I will go, but there is no need that we should hunt for Rikki-tikki afterward. I will kill the big man and his wife, and the child if I can, and come away quietly. Then the bungalow will be empty, and Rikki-tikki will go."

Rikki-tikki tingled all over with rage and hatred at this, and then Nag's head came through the sluice, and his five feet of cold body followed it. Angry as he was, Rikki-tikki was very frightened as he saw the size of the big cobra. Nag coiled himself up, raised his head, and looked into the bathroom in the dark, and Rikki could see his eyes glitter.

"Now, if I kill him here, Nagaina will know; and if I fight him on the open floor, the odds are in his favor. What am I to do?" said Rikki-tikki-tavi.

Nag waved to and fro, and then Rikki-tikki heard him drinking from the biggest water-jar that was used to fill the bath. "That is good," said the snake. "Now, when Karait was killed, the big man had a stick. He may have that stick still, but when he comes in to bathe in the morning he will not have a stick. I shall wait here till he comes. Nagaina—do you hear me?—I shall wait here in the cool till daytime."

There was no answer from outside, so Rikki-tikki knew Nagaina had gone away. Nag coiled himself down, coil by coil, round the bulge at the bottom of the water jar, and Rikki-tikki stayed still as death. After an hour he began to move, muscle by muscle, toward the jar. Nag was asleep, and Rikki-tikki looked at his big back, wondering which would be the best place for a good hold. "If I don't break his back at the first jump," said Rikki, "he can still fight. And if he fights—O Rikki!" He looked at the thickness of the neck below the hood, but that was too much for him; and a bite near the tail would only make Nag savage.

"It must be the head," he said at last; "the head above the hood. And, when I am once there, I must not let go."

Then he jumped. The head was lying a little clear of the water jar, under the curve of it; and, as his teeth met, Rikki braced his back against the bulge of the red earthenware to hold down the head. This gave him just one second's purchase, and he made the most of it. Then he was battered to and fro as a rat is shaken by a dog—to and fro on the floor, up and down, and around in great circles, but his eyes were red and he held on as the body cart-whipped over the floor, upsetting the tin dipper and the soap dish and the flesh brush, and banged against the tin side of the bath. As he held he closed his jaws tighter and tighter, for he made sure he would be banged to death, and, for the honor of his family, he preferred to be found with his teeth locked. He was dizzy, aching, and felt shaken to pieces when something went off like a thunderclap just behind him. A hot wind knocked him senseless and red fire singed his fur. The big man had been wakened by the noise, and had fired both barrels of a shotgun into Nag just behind the hood.

Rikki-tikki held on with his eyes shut, for now he was quite sure he was dead. But the head did not move, and the big man picked him up and said, "It's the mongoose again, Alice. The little chap has saved our lives now."

Then Teddy's mother came in with a very white face, and saw what was left of Nag, and Rikki-tikki dragged himself to Teddy's bedroom and spent half the rest of the night shaking himself tenderly to find out whether he really was broken into forty pieces, as he fancied.

When morning came he was very stiff, but well pleased with his doings. "Now I have Nagaina to settle with, and she will be worse than five Nags, and there's no knowing when the eggs she spoke of will hatch. Goodness! I must go and see Darzee," he said.

Without waiting for breakfast, Rikki-tikki ran to the thornbush where Darzee was singing a song of triumph at the top of his voice. The news of Nag's death was all over the garden, for the sweeper had thrown the body on the rubbish-heap.

"Oh, you stupid tuft of feathers!" said Rikki-tikki angrily. "Is this the time to sing?"

"Nag is dead—is dead—is dead!" sang Darzee. "The valiant Rikki-tikki caught him by the head and held fast. The big man brought the bang-stick, and Nag fell in two pieces! He will never eat my babies again."

"All that's true enough. But where's Nagaina?" said Rikki-tikki, looking carefully round him.

"Nagaina came to the bathroom sluice and called for Nag," Darzee went on, "and Nag came out on the end of a stick—the sweeper picked him up on the end of a stick and threw him upon the rubbish heap. Let us sing about the great, the red-eyed Rikki-tikki!" And Darzee filled his throat and sang.

"If I could get up to your nest, I'd roll your babies out!" said Rikki-tikki. "You don't know when to do the right thing at the right time. You're safe enough in your nest there, but it's war for me down here. Stop singing a minute, Darzee."

"For the great, the beautiful Rikki-tikki's sake I will stop," said Darzee. "What is it, O Killer of the terrible Nag?"

"Where is Nagaina, for the third time?"

"On the rubbish heap by the stables, mourning for Nag. Great is Rikki-tikki with the white teeth."

"Bother my white teeth! Have you ever heard where she keeps her eggs?"

"In the melon bed, on the end nearest the wall, where the sun strikes nearly all day. She hid them there weeks ago."

"And you never thought it worth while to tell me? The end nearest the wall, you said?"

"Rikki-tikki, you are not going to eat her eggs?"

"Not eat exactly; no. Darzee, if you have a grain of sense you will fly off to the stables and pretend that your wing is broken, and let Nagaina chase you away to this bush. I must get to the melon-bed, and if I went there now she'd see me."

Darzee was a feather-brained little fellow who could never hold more than one idea at a time in his head. And just because he knew that Nagaina's children were born in eggs like his own, he didn't think at first that it was fair to kill them. But his wife was a sensible bird, and she knew that cobra's eggs meant young cobras later on. So she flew off from the nest, and left Darzee to keep the babies warm, and continue his song about the death of Nag. Darzee was very like a man in some ways.

She fluttered in front of Nagaina by the rubbish heap and cried out, "Oh, my wing is broken! The boy in the house threw a stone at me and broke it." Then she fluttered more desperately than ever.

Nagaina lifted up her head and hissed, "You warned Rikki-tikki when I would have killed him. Indeed and truly, you've chosen a bad place to be lame in." And she moved toward Darzee's wife, slipping along over the dust.

"The boy broke it with a stone!" shrieked Darzee's wife.

"Well! It may be some consolation to you when you're dead to know that I shall settle accounts with the boy. My husband lies on the rubbish heap this morning, but before night the boy in the house will lie very still. What is the use of running away? I am sure to catch you. Little fool, look at me!"

Darzee's wife knew better than to do that, for a bird who looks at a snake's eyes gets so frightened that she cannot move. Darzee's wife fluttered on, piping sorrowfully, and never leaving the ground, and Nagaina quickened her pace.

Rikki-tikki heard them going up the path from the stables, and he raced for the end of the melon patch near the wall. There, in the warm litter above the melons, very cunningly hidden, he found twenty-five eggs, about the size of a bantam's eggs, but with whitish skin instead of shell.

"I was not a day too soon," he said, for he could see the baby cobras curled up inside the skin, and he knew that the minute they were hatched they could each kill a man or a mongoose. He bit off the tops of the eggs as fast as he could, taking care to crush the young cobras, and turned over the litter from time to time to see whether he had missed any. At last there were only three eggs left, and Rikki-tikki began to chuckle to himself, when he heard Darzee's wife screaming:

"Rikki-tikki, I led Nagaina toward the house, and she has gone into the veranda, and—oh, come quickly—she means killing!"

Rikki-tikki smashed two eggs, and tumbled backward down the melon-bed with the third egg in his mouth, and scuttled to the veranda as hard as he could put foot to the ground. Teddy and his mother and father were there at early breakfast, but Rikki-tikki saw that they were not eating anything. They sat stone-still, and their faces were white. Nagaina was coiled up on the matting by Teddy's chair, within easy striking distance of Teddy's bare leg, and she was swaying to and fro, singing a song of triumph.

"Son of the big man that killed Nag," she hissed, "stay still. I am not ready yet. Wait a little. Keep very still, all you three! If you move I strike, and if you do not move I strike. Oh, foolish people, who killed my Nag!"

Teddy's eyes were fixed on his father, and all his father could do was to whisper, "Sit still, Teddy. You mustn't move. Teddy, keep still."

Then Rikki-tikki came up and cried, "Turn round, Nagaina. Turn and fight!"

"All in good time," said she, without moving her eyes. "I will settle my account with you presently. Look at your friends, Rikki-tikki. They are still and white. They are afraid. They dare not move, and if you come a step nearer I strike."

"Look at your eggs," said Rikki-tikki, "in the melon bed near the wall. Go and look, Nagaina!"

The big snake turned half around, and saw the egg on the veranda. "Ah-h! Give it to me," she said.

Rikki-tikki put his paws one on each side of the egg, and his eyes were blood-red. "What price for a snake's egg? For a young cobra? For a young king cobra? For the last—the very last of the brood? The ants are eating all the others down by the melon bed."

Nagaina spun clear round, forgetting everything for the sake of the one egg. Rikki-tikki saw Teddy's father shoot out a big hand, catch Teddy by the shoulder, and drag him across the little table with the tea-cups, safe and out of reach of Nagaina.

"Tricked! Tricked! Tricked! Rikk-tck-tck!" chuckled Rikki-tikki. "The boy is safe, and it was I—I—I that caught Nag by the hood last night in the bathroom." Then he began to jump up and down, all four feet together, his head close to the floor. "He threw me to and fro, but he could not shake me off. He was dead before the big man blew him in two. I did it! Rikki-tikki-tck-tck! Come then, Nagaina. Come and fight with me. You shall not be a widow long."

Nagaina saw that she had lost her chance of killing Teddy, and the egg lay between Rikki-tikki's paws. "Give me the egg, Rikki-tikki. Give me the last of my eggs, and I will go away and never come back," she said, lowering her hood.

"Yes, you will go away, and you will never come back. For you will go to the rubbish heap with Nag. Fight, widow! The big man has gone for his gun! Fight!"

Rikki-tikki was bounding all round Nagaina, keeping just out of reach of her stroke, his little eyes like hot coals. Nagaina gathered herself together and flung out at him. Rikki-tikki jumped up and backward. Again and again and again she struck, and each time her head came with a whack on the matting of the veranda and she gathered herself together like a watch spring. Then Rikki-tikki danced in a circle to get behind her, and Nagaina spun round to keep her head to his head, so that the rustle of her tail on the matting sounded like dry leaves blown along by the wind.

He had forgotten the egg. It still lay on the veranda, and Nagaina came nearer and nearer to it, till at last, while Rikki-tikki was drawing breath, she caught it in her mouth, turned to the veranda steps, and flew like an arrow down the path, with Rikki-tikki behind her. When the cobra runs for her life, she goes like a whip-lash flicked across a horse's neck.

Rikki-tikki knew that he must catch her, or all the trouble would begin again. She headed straight for the long grass by the thorn-bush, and as he was running Rikki-tikki heard Darzee still singing his foolish little song of triumph. But Darzee's wife was wiser. She flew off her nest as Nagaina came along, and flapped her wings about Nagaina's head. If Darzee had helped they might have turned her, but Nagaina only lowered her hood and went on. Still, the instant's delay brought Rikki-tikki up to her, and as she plunged into the rat-hole where she and Nag used to live, his little white teeth were clenched on her tail, and he went down with her—and very few mongooses, however wise and old they may be, care to follow a cobra into its hole. It was dark in the hole; and Rikki-tikki never knew when it might open out and give Nagaina room to turn and strike at him. He held on savagely, and stuck out his feet to act as brakes on the dark slope of the hot, moist earth.

Then the grass by the mouth of the hole stopped waving, and Darzee said, "It is all over with Rikki-tikki! We must sing his death song. Valiant Rikki-tikki is dead! For Nagaina will surely kill him underground."

So he sang a very mournful song that he made up on the spur of the minute, and just as he got to the most touching part, the grass quivered again, and Rikki-tikki, covered with dirt, dragged himself out of the hole leg by leg, licking his whiskers. Darzee stopped with a little shout. Rikki-tikki shook some of the dust out of his fur and sneezed. "It is all over," he said. "The widow will never come out again." And the red ants that live between the grass stems heard him, and began to troop down one after another to see if he had spoken the truth.

Rikki-tikki curled himself up in the grass and slept where he was—slept and slept till it was late in the afternoon, for he had done a hard day's work.

"Now," he said, when he awoke, "I will go back to the house. Tell the Coppersmith, Darzee, and he will tell the garden that Nagaina is dead."

The Coppersmith is a bird who makes a noise exactly like the beating of a little hammer on a copper pot; and the reason he is always making it is because he is the town crier to every Indian garden, and tells all the news to everybody who cares to listen. As Rikki-tikki went up the path, he heard his "attention" notes like a tiny dinner gong, and then the steady "Ding-dong-tock! Nag is dead—dong! Nagaina is dead! Ding-dong-tock!" That set all the birds in the garden singing, and the frogs croaking, for Nag and Nagaina used to eat frogs as well as little birds.

When Rikki got to the house, Teddy and Teddy's mother (she looked very white still, for she had been fainting) and Teddy's father came out and almost cried over him; and that night he ate all that was given him till he could eat no more, and went to bed on Teddy's shoulder, where Teddy's mother saw him when she came to look late at night.

"He saved our lives and Teddy's life," she said to her husband. "Just think, he saved all our lives."

Rikki-tikki woke up with a jump, for the mongooses are light sleepers.

"Oh, it's you," said he. "What are you bothering for? All the cobras are dead. And if they weren't, I'm here."

Rikki-tikki had a right to be proud of himself. But he did not grow too proud, and he kept that garden as a mongoose should keep it, with tooth and jump and spring and bite, till never a cobra dared show its head inside the walls.

The Necklace

by Guy de Maupassant

She was one of those pretty and charming girls who are sometimes, as if by a mistake of destiny, born in a family of clerks. She had no dowry, no expectations, no means of being known, understood, loved, wedded, by any rich and distinguished man; and she let herself be married to a little clerk at the Ministry of Public Instruction.

She dressed plainly because she could not dress well, but she was as unhappy as though she had really fallen from her proper station; since with women there is neither caste nor rank; and beauty, grace, and charm act instead of family and birth. Natural fineness, instinct for what is elegant, suppleness of wit, are the sole hierarchy, and make from women of the people the equals of the very greatest ladies.

She suffered ceaselessly, feeling herself born for all the delicacies and all the luxuries. She suffered from the poverty of her dwelling, from the wretched look of the walls, from the worn-out chairs, from the ugliness of the curtains. All those things, of which another woman of her rank would never even have been conscious, tortured her and made her angry. The sight of the little Breton peasant who did her humble housework aroused in her regrets which were despairing, and distracted dreams. She thought of the silent antechambers hung with Oriental tapestry, lit by tall bronze candelabra, and of the two great footmen in knee breeches who sleep in the big armchairs, made drowsy by the heavy warmth of the hot-air stove. She thought of the long *salons* fatted up with ancient silk, of the delicate furniture carrying priceless curiosities, and of the coquettish perfumed boudoirs made for talks at five o'clock with intimate friends, with men famous and sought after, whom all women envy and whose attention they all desire.

When she sat down to dinner, before the round table covered with a tablecloth three days old, opposite her husband, who uncovered the soup tureen and declared with an enchanted air, "Ah, the good *pot-au-feu*! I don't know anything better than that," she thought of dainty dinners, of shining silverware, of tapestry which peopled the walls with ancient personages and with strange birds flying in the midst of a fairy forest; and she thought of delicious dishes served on marvelous plates, and of the whispered gallantries which you listen to with a sphinx-like smile, while you are eating the pink flesh of a trout or the wings of a quail.

She had no dresses, no jewels, nothing. And she loved nothing but that; she felt made for that. She would so have liked to please, to be envied, to be charming, to be sought after.

She had a friend, a former schoolmate at the convent, who was rich, and whom she did not like to go and see any more, because she suffered so much when she came back. But, one evening, her husband returned home with a triumphant air, and holding a large envelope in his hand.

"There," said he, "here is something for you."

She tore the paper sharply, and drew out a printed card which bore these words:

"The Minister of Public Instruction and Mme. Georges Ramponneau request the honor of M. and Mme. Loisel's company at the palace of the Ministry on Monday evening, January 18th."

Instead of being delighted, as her husband hoped, she threw the invitation on the table with disdain, murmuring:

"What do you want me to do with that?"

"But, my dear, I thought you would be glad. You never go out, and this is such a fine opportunity. I had awful trouble to get it. Everyone wants to go; it is very select, and they are not giving many invitations to clerks. The whole official world will be there."

She looked at him with an irritated eye, and she said, impatiently:

"And what do you want me to put on my back?"

He had not thought of that; he stammered:

"Why, the dress you go to the theater in. It looks very well, to me."

He stopped, distracted, seeing that his wife was crying. Two great tears descended slowly from the corners of her eyes toward the corners of her mouth. He stuttered:

"What's the matter? What's the matter?"

But, by a violent effort, she had conquered her grief, and she replied, with a calm voice, while she wiped her wet cheeks:

"Nothing. Only I have no dress, and therefore I can't go to this ball. Give your card to some colleague whose wife is better equipped than I."

He was in despair. He resumed:

"Come, let us see, Mathilde. How much would it cost, a suitable dress, which you could use on other occasions, something very simple?"

She reflected several seconds, making her calculations and wondering also what sum she could ask without drawing on herself an immediate refusal and a frightened exclamation from the economical clerk.

Finally, she replied, hesitatingly:

"I don't know exactly, but I think I could manage it with four hundred francs."

He had grown a little pale, because he was laying aside just that amount to buy a gun and treat himself to a little shooting next summer on the plain of Nanterre, with several friends who went to shoot larks down there of a Sunday.

But he said:

"All right. I will give you four hundred francs. And try to have a pretty dress."

The day of the ball drew near, and Mme. Loisel seemed sad, uneasy, anxious. Her dress was ready, however. Her husband said to her one evening:

"What is the matter? Come, you've been so queer these last three days."

And she answered:

"It annoys me not to have a single jewel, not a single stone, nothing to put on. I shall look like distress. I should almost rather not go at all."

He resumed:

"You might wear natural flowers. It's very stylish at this time of the year. For ten francs you can get two or three magnificent roses."

She was not convinced.

"No; there's nothing more humiliating than to look poor among other women who are rich."

But her husband cried:

"How stupid you are! Go look up your friend Mme. Forestier, and ask her to lend you some jewels. You're quite thick enough with her to do that."

She uttered a cry of joy:

"It's true. I never thought of it."

The next day she went to her friend and told of her distress.

Mme. Forestier went to a wardrobe with a glass door, took out a large jewel box, brought it back, opened it, and said to Mme. Loisel:

"Choose, my dear."

She saw first of all some bracelets, then a pearl necklace, then a Venetian cross, gold and precious stones of admirable workmanship. She tried on the ornaments before the glass, hesitated, could not make up her mind to part with them, to give them back. She kept asking:

"Haven't you any more?"

"Why, yes. Look. I don't know what you like."

All of a sudden she discovered, in a black satin box, a superb necklace of diamonds, and her heart began to beat with an immoderate desire. Her hands trembled as she took it. She fastened it around her throat, outside her high-necked dress, and remained lost in ecstasy at the sight of herself.

Then she asked, hesitating, filled with anguish:

"Can you lend me that, only that?"

"Why, yes, certainly."

She sprang upon the neck of her friend, kissed her passionately, then fled with her treasure.

The day of the ball arrived. Mme. Loisel made a great success. She was prettier than them all, elegant, gracious, smiling, and crazy with joy. All the men looked at her, asked her name, endeavored to be introduced. All the attachés of the Cabinet wanted to waltz with her. She was remarked by the minister himself.

She danced with intoxication, with passion, made drunk by pleasure, forgetting all, in the triumph of her beauty, in the glory of her success, in a sort of cloud of happiness composed of all this homage, of all this admiration, of all these awakened desires, and of that sense of complete victory which is so sweet to woman's heart.

She went away about four o'clock in the morning. Her husband had been sleeping since midnight, in a little deserted anteroom, with three other gentlemen whose wives were having a very good time.

He threw over her shoulders the wraps which he had brought, modest wraps of common life, whose poverty contrasted with the elegance of the ball dress. She felt this and wanted to escape so as not to be remarked by the other women, who were enveloping themselves in costly furs.

Loisel held her back.

"Wait a bit. You will catch cold outside. I will go and call a cab."

But she did not listen to him, and rapidly descended the stairs. When they were in the street they did not find a carriage; and they began to look for one, shouting after the cabmen whom they saw passing by at a distance.

They went down toward the Seine, in despair, shivering with cold. At last they found on the quay one of those ancient noctambulant coupés which, exactly as if they were ashamed to show their misery during the day, are never seen round Paris until after nightfall.

It took them to their door in the Rue des Martyrs, and once more, sadly, they climbed up homeward. All was ended for her. And as to him, he reflected that he must be at the Ministry at ten o'clock.

She removed the wraps, which covered her shoulders, before the glass, so as once more to see herself in all her glory. But suddenly she uttered a cry. She had no longer the necklace around her neck!

Her husband, already half undressed, demanded:

"What is the matter with you?"

She turned madly toward him:

"I have—I have—I've lost Mme. Forestier's necklace."

He stood up, distracted.

"What!—how?—Impossible!"

And they looked in the folds of her dress, in the folds of her cloak, in her pockets, everywhere. They did not find it.

He asked:

"You're sure you had it on when you left the ball?"

"Yes, I felt it in the vestibule of the palace."

"But if you had lost it in the street we should have heard it fall. It must be in the cab."

"Yes. Probably. Did you take his number?"

"No. And you, didn't you notice it?"

"No."

They looked, thunderstruck, at one another. At last Loisel put on his clothes.

"I shall go back on foot," said he, "over the whole route which we have taken, to see if I can't find it."

And he went out. She sat waiting on a chair in her ball dress, without strength to go to bed, overwhelmed, without fire, without a thought.

Her husband came back about seven o'clock. He had found nothing.

He went to Police Headquarters, to the newspaper offices, to offer a reward; he went to the cab companies—everywhere, in fact, whither he was urged by the least suspicion of hope.

She waited all day, in the same condition of mad fear before this terrible calamity.

Loisel returned at night with a hollow, pale face; he had discovered nothing.

"You must write to your friend," said he, "that you have broken the clasp of her necklace and that you are having it mended. That will give us time to turn round."

She wrote at his dictation.

At the end of a week they had lost all hope. And Loisel, who had aged five years, declared:

"We must consider how to replace that ornament."

The next day they took the box which had contained it, and they went to the jeweler whose name was found within. He consulted his books.

"It was not I, madame, who sold that necklace; I must simply have furnished the case."

Then they went from jeweler to jeweler, searching for a necklace like the other, consulting their memories, sick both of them with chagrin and with anguish.

They found, in a shop at the Palais Royal, a string of diamonds which seemed to them exactly like the one they looked for. It was worth forty thousand francs.

They could have it for thirty-six.

So they begged the jeweler not to sell it for three days yet. And they made a bargain that he should buy it back for thirty-four thousand francs in case they found the other one before the end of February.

Loisel possessed eighteen thousand francs which his father had left him. He would borrow the rest.

He did borrow, asking a thousand francs of one, five hundred of another, five louis here, three louis there. He gave notes, took up ruinous obligations, dealt with usurers, and all the race of lenders. He compromised all the rest of his life, risked his signature without even knowing if he could meet it; and, frightened by the pains yet to come, by the black misery which was about to fall upon him, by the prospect of all the physical privations and of all the moral tortures which he was to suffer, he went to get the new necklace, putting down upon the merchant's counter thirty-six thousand francs.

When Mme. Loisel took back the necklace, Mme. Forestier said to her, with a chilly manner:

"You should have returned it sooner, I might have needed it."

She did not open the case, as her friend had so much feared. If she had detected the substitution, what would she have thought, what would she have said? Would she not have taken Mme. Loisel for a thief?

Mme. Loisel now knew the horrible existence of the needy. She took her part, moreover, all on a sudden, with heroism. That dreadful debt must be paid. She would pay it. They dismissed their servant; they changed their lodgings; they rented a garret under the roof.

She came to know what heavy housework meant and the odious cares of the kitchen. She washed the dishes, using her rosy nails on the greasy pots and pans. She washed the dirty linen, the shirts, and the dish-cloths, which she dried upon a line; she carried the slops down to the street every morning, and carried up the water, stopping for breath at every landing.

And, dressed like a woman of the people, she went to the fruiterer, the grocer, the butcher, her basket on her arm, bargaining, insulted, defending her miserable money sou by sou.

Each month they had to meet some notes, renew others, obtain more time.

Her husband worked in the evening making a fair copy of some tradesman's accounts, and late at night he often copied manuscripts for five sous a page.

And this life lasted ten years.

At the end of ten years they had paid everything, everything, with the rates of usury, and the accumulations of the compound interest.

Mme. Loisel looked old now. She had become the woman of impoverished households—strong and hard and rough. With frowsy hair, skirts askew, and red hands, she talked loud while washing the floor with great swishes of water. But sometimes, when her husband was at the office, she sat down near the window, and she thought of that gay evening of long ago, of that ball where she had been so beautiful and so feted.

What would have happened if she had not lost that necklace? Who knows? who knows? How life is strange and changeful! How little a thing is needed for us to be lost or to be saved!

But, one Sunday, having gone to take a walk in the Champs Élysées to refresh herself from the labors of the week, she suddenly perceived a woman who was leading a child. It was Mme. Forestier, still young, still beautiful, still charming.

Mme. Loisel felt moved. Was she going to speak to her? Yes, certainly. And now that she had paid, she was going to tell her all about it. Why not?

She went up.

"Good day, Jeanne."

The other, astonished to be familiarly addressed by this plain good-wife, did not recognize her at all, and stammered:

"But—madame!—I do not know—You must have mistaken."

"No. I am Mathilde Loisel."

Her friend uttered a cry.

"Oh, my poor Mathilde! How you are changed!"

"Yes, I have had days hard enough, since I have seen you, days wretched enough—and that because of you!"

"Of me! How so?"

"Do you remember that diamond necklace which you lent me to wear at the ministerial ball?"

"Yes. Well?"

"Well, I lost it."

"What do you mean? You brought it back."

"I brought you back another just like it. And for this we have been ten years paying. You can understand that it was not easy for us, us who had nothing. At last it is ended, and I am very glad."

Mme. Forestier had stopped.

"You say that you bought a necklace of diamonds to replace mine?"

"Yes. You never noticed it, then! They were very like."

And she smiled with a joy which was proud and naïve at once.

Mme. Forestier, strongly moved, took her two hands.

"Oh, my poor Mathilde! Why, my necklace was paste. It was worth at most five hundred francs!"

The Ransom of Red Chief

by O. Henry

It looked like a good thing: but wait till I tell you. We were down South, in Alabama—Bill Driscoll and myself—when this kidnapping idea struck us. It was, as Bill afterward expressed it, "during a moment of temporary mental apparition"; but we didn't find that out till later.

There was a town down there, as flat as a flannel-cake, and called Summit, of course. It contained inhabitants of as undeleterious and self-satisfied a class of peasantry as ever clustered around a Maypole.

Bill and me had a joint capital of about six hundred dollars, and we needed just two thousand dollars more to pull off a fraudulent town-lot scheme in Western Illinois with. We talked it over on the front steps of the hotel. Philoprogenitiveness, says we, is strong in semi-rural communities; therefore and for other reasons, a kidnapping project ought to do better there than in the radius of newspapers that send reporters out in plain clothes to stir up talk about such things. We knew that Summit couldn't get after us with anything stronger than constables and maybe some lackadaisical bloodhounds and a diatribe or two in the Weekly Farmers' Budget. So, it looked good.

We selected for our victim the only child of a prominent citizen named Ebenezer Dorset. The father was respectable and tight, a mortgage fancier and a stern, upright collection-plate passer and forecloser. The kid was a boy of ten, with bas-relief freckles, and hair the colour of the cover of the magazine you buy at the news-stand when you want to catch a train. Bill and me figured that Ebenezer would melt down for a ransom of two thousand dollars to a cent. But wait till I tell you.

About two miles from Summit was a little mountain, covered with a dense cedar brake. On the rear elevation of this mountain was a cave. There we stored provisions. One evening after sundown, we drove in a buggy past old Dorset's house. The kid was in the street, throwing rocks at a kitten on the opposite fence.

"Hey, little boy!" says Bill, "would you like to have a bag of candy and a nice ride?"

The boy catches Bill neatly in the eye with a piece of brick.

"That will cost the old man an extra five hundred dollars," says Bill, climbing over the wheel.

That boy put up a fight like a welter-weight cinnamon bear; but, at last, we got him down in the bottom of the buggy and drove away. We took him up to the cave and I hitched the horse in the cedar brake. After dark I drove the buggy to the little village, three miles away, where we had hired it, and walked back to the mountain.

Bill was pasting court-plaster over the scratches and bruises on his features. There was a fire burning behind the big rock at the entrance of the cave, and the boy was watching a pot of boiling coffee, with two buzzard tail-feathers stuck in his red hair. He points a stick at me when I come up, and says:

"Ha! cursed paleface, do you dare to enter the camp of Red Chief, the terror of the plains?"

"He's all right now," says Bill, rolling up his trousers and examining some bruises on his shins. "We're playing Indian. We're making Buffalo Bill's show look like magic-lantern views of Palestine in the town hall. I'm Old Hank, the Trapper, Red Chief's captive, and I'm to be scalped at daybreak. By Geronimo! that kid can kick hard."

Yes, sir, that boy seemed to be having the time of his life. The fun of camping out in a cave had made him forget that he was a captive himself. He immediately christened me Snake-eye, the Spy, and announced that, when his braves returned from the warpath, I was to be broiled at the stake at the rising of the sun.

Then we had supper; and he filled his mouth full of bacon and bread and gravy, and began to talk. He made a during-dinner speech something like this:

"I like this fine. I never camped out before; but I had a pet 'possum once, and I was nine last birthday. I hate to go to school. Rats ate up sixteen of Jimmy Talbot's aunt's speckled hen's eggs. Are there any real Indians in these woods? I want some more gravy. Does the trees moving make the wind blow? We had five puppies. What makes your nose so red, Hank? My father has lots of money. Are the stars hot? I whipped Ed Walker twice, Saturday. I don't like girls. You dassent catch toads unless with a string. Do oxen make any noise? Why are oranges round? Have you got beds to sleep on in this cave? Amos Murray has got six toes. A parrot can talk, but a monkey or a fish can't. How many does it take to make twelve?"

Every few minutes he would remember that he was a pesky redskin, and pick up his stick rifle and tiptoe to the mouth of the cave to rubber for the scouts of the hated paleface. Now and then he would let out a war-whoop that made Old Hank the Trapper shiver. That boy had Bill terrorized from the start.

"Red Chief," says I to the kid, "would you like to go home?"

"Aw, what for?" says he. "I don't have any fun at home. I hate to go to school. I like to camp out. You won't take me back home again, Snake-eye, will you?"

"Not right away," says I. "We'll stay here in the cave a while."

"All right!" says he. "That'll be fine. I never had such fun in all my life."

We went to bed about eleven o'clock. We spread down some wide blankets and quilts and put Red Chief between us. We weren't afraid he'd run away. He kept us awake for three hours, jumping up and reaching for his rifle and screeching: "Hist! pard," in mine and Bill's ears, as the fancied crackle of a twig or the rustle of a leaf revealed to his young imagination the stealthy approach of the outlaw band. At last, I fell into a troubled sleep, and dreamed that I had been kidnapped and chained to a tree by a ferocious pirate with red hair.

Just at daybreak, I was awakened by a series of awful screams from Bill. They weren't yells, or howls, or shouts, or whoops, or yawps, such as you'd expect from a manly set of vocal organs—they were simply indecent, terrifying, humiliating screams, such as women emit when they see ghosts or caterpillars. It's an awful thing to hear a strong, desperate, fat man scream incontinently in a cave at daybreak.

I jumped up to see what the matter was. Red Chief was sitting on Bill's chest, with one hand twined in Bill's hair. In the other he had the sharp case-knife we used for slicing bacon; and he was industriously and realistically trying to take Bill's scalp, according to the sentence that had been pronounced upon him the evening before.

I got the knife away from the kid and made him lie down again. But, from that moment, Bill's spirit was broken. He laid down on his side of the bed, but he never closed an eye again in sleep as long as that boy was with us. I dozed off for a while, but along toward sun-up I remembered that Red Chief had said I was to be burned at the stake at the rising of the sun. I wasn't nervous or afraid; but I sat up and lit my pipe and leaned against a rock.

"What you getting up so soon for, Sam?" asked Bill.

"Me?" says I. "Oh, I got a kind of a pain in my shoulder. I thought sitting up would rest it."

"You're a liar!" says Bill. "You're afraid. You was to be burned at sunrise, and you was afraid he'd do it. And he would, too, if he could find a match. Ain't it awful, Sam? Do you think anybody will pay out money to get a little imp like that back home?"

"Sure," said I. "A rowdy kid like that is just the kind that parents dote on. Now, you and the Chief get up and cook breakfast, while I go up on the top of this mountain and reconnoitre."

I went up on the peak of the little mountain and ran my eye over the contiguous vicinity. Over toward Summit I expected to see the sturdy yeomanry of the village armed with scythes and pitchforks beating the countryside for the dastardly kidnappers. But what I saw was a peaceful landscape dotted with one man ploughing with a dun mule. Nobody was dragging the creek; no couriers dashed hither and yon, bringing tidings of no news to the distracted parents. There was a sylvan attitude of somnolent sleepiness pervading that section of the external outward surface of Alabama that lay exposed to my view. "Perhaps," says I to myself, "it has not yet been discovered that the wolves have borne away the tender lambkin from the fold. Heaven help the wolves!" says I, and I went down the mountain to breakfast.

When I got to the cave I found Bill backed up against the side of it, breathing hard, and the boy threatening to smash him with a rock half as big as a coconut.

"He put a red-hot boiled potato down my back," explained Bill, "and then mashed it with his foot; and I boxed his ears. Have you got a gun about you, Sam?"

I took the rock away from the boy and kind of patched up the argument. "I'll fix you," says the kid to Bill. "No man ever yet struck the Red Chief but what he got paid for it. You better beware!"

After breakfast the kid takes a piece of leather with strings wrapped around it out of his pocket and goes outside the cave unwinding it.

"What's he up to now?" says Bill, anxiously. "You don't think he'll run away, do you, Sam?"

"No fear of it," says I. "He don't seem to be much of a home body. But we've got to fix up some plan about the ransom. There don't seem to be much excitement around Summit on account of his disappearance; but maybe they haven't realized yet that he's gone. His folks may think he's spending the night with Aunt Jane or one of the neighbours. Anyhow, he'll be missed to-day. To-night we must get a message to his father demanding the two thousand dollars for his return.

Just then we heard a kind of war-whoop, such as David might have emitted when he knocked out the champion Goliath. It was a sling that Red Chief had pulled out of his pocket, and he was whirling it around his head.

I dodged, and heard a heavy thud and a kind of a sigh from Bill, like a horse gives out when you take his saddle off. A [smooth round] rock the size of an egg had caught Bill just behind his left ear. He loosened himself all over and fell in the fire across the frying pan of hot water for washing the dishes. I dragged him out and poured cold water on his head for half an hour.

By and by, Bill sits up and feels behind his ear and says: "Sam, do you know who my favourite Biblical character is?"

"Take it easy," says I. "You'll come to your senses presently."

"King Herod," says he. "You won't go away and leave me here alone, will you, Sam?"

I went out and caught that boy and shook him until his freckles rattled.

"If you don't behave," says I, "I'll take you straight home. Now, are you going to be good, or not?"

"I was only funning," says he sullenly. "I didn't mean to hurt Old Hank. But what did he hit me for? I'll behave, Snake-eye, if you won't send me home, and if you'll let me play the Black Scout to-day."

"I don't know the game," says I. "That's for you and Mr. Bill to decide. He's your playmate for the day. I'm going away for a while, on business. Now, you come in and make friends with him and say you are sorry for hurting him, or home you go, at once."

I made him and Bill shake hands, and then I took Bill aside and told him I was going to Poplar Cove, a little village three miles from the cave, and find out what I could about how the kidnapping had been regarded in Summit. Also, I thought it best to send a peremptory letter to old man Dorset that day, demanding the ransom and dictating how it should be paid.

"You know, Sam," says Bill, "I've stood by you without batting an eye in earthquakes, fire and flood—in poker games, dynamite outrages, police raids, train robberies and cyclones. I never lost my nerve yet till we kidnapped that two-legged skyrocket of a kid. He's got me going. You won't leave me long with him, will you, Sam?"

"I'll be back some time this afternoon," says I. "You must keep the boy amused and quiet till I return. And now we'll write the letter to old Dorset."

Bill and I got paper and pencil and worked on the letter while Red Chief, with a blanket wrapped around him, strutted up and down, guarding the mouth of the cave. Bill begged me tearfully to make the ransom fifteen hundred dollars instead of two thousand. "I ain't attempting," says he, "to decry the celebrated moral aspect of parental affection, but we're dealing with humans, and it ain't human for anybody to give up two thousand dollars for that forty-pound chunk of freckled wildcat. I'm willing to take a chance at fifteen hundred dollars. You can charge the difference up to me."

So, to relieve Bill, I acceded, and we collaborated a letter that ran this way:

Ebenezer Dorset, Esq.:

We have your boy concealed in a place far from Summit. It is useless for you or the most skilful detectives to attempt to find him. Absolutely, the only terms on which you can have him restored to you are these: We demand fifteen hundred dollars in large bills for his return; the money to be left at midnight to-night at the same spot and in the same box as your reply—as hereinafter described. If you agree to these terms, send your answer in writing by a solitary messenger to-night at half-past eight o'clock. After crossing Owl Creek, on the road to Poplar Cove, there are three large trees about a hundred yards apart, close to the fence of the wheat field on the right-hand side. At the bottom of the fence-post, opposite the third tree, will be found a small pasteboard box.

The messenger will place the answer in this box and return immediately to Summit.

If you attempt any treachery or fail to comply with our demand as stated, you will never see your boy again.

If you pay the money as demanded, he will be returned to you safe and well within three hours. These terms are final, and if you do not accede to them no further communication will be attempted.

TWO DESPERATE MEN.

I addressed this letter to Dorset, and put it in my pocket. As I was about to start, the kid comes up to me and says:

"Aw, Snake-eye, you said I could play the Black Scout while you was gone."

"Play it, of course," says I. "Mr. Bill will play with you. What kind of a game is it?"

"I'm the Black Scout," says Red Chief, "and I have to ride to the stockade to warn the settlers that the Indians are coming. I'm tired of playing Indian myself. I want to be the Black Scout."

"All right," says I. "It sounds harmless to me. I guess Mr. Bill will help you foil the pesky savages."

"What am I to do?" asks Bill, looking at the kid suspiciously.

"You are the hoss," says Black Scout. "Get down on your hands and knees. How can I ride to the stockade without a hoss?"

"You'd better keep him interested," said I, "till we get the scheme going. Loosen up."

Bill gets down on his all fours, and a look comes in his eye like a rabbit's when you catch it in a trap.

"How far is it to the stockade, kid?" he asks, in a husky manner of voice.

"Ninety miles," says the Black Scout. "And you have to hump yourself to get there on time. Whoa, now!"

The Black Scout jumps on Bill's back and digs his heels in his side.

"For Heaven's sake," says Bill, "hurry back, Sam, as soon as you can. I wish we hadn't made the ransom more than a thousand. Say, you quit kicking me or I'll get up and warm you good."

I walked over to Poplar Cove and sat around the post office and store, talking with the chawbacons that came in to trade. One whiskerando says that he hears Summit is all upset on account of Elder Ebenezer Dorset's boy having been lost or stolen. That was all I wanted to know. I bought some smoking tobacco, referred casually to the price of black-eyed peas, posted my letter surreptitiously and came away. The postmaster said the mail-carrier would come by in an hour to take the mail on to Summit.

When I got back to the cave Bill and the boy were not to be found. I explored the vicinity of the cave, and risked a yodel or two, but there was no response.

So I lighted my pipe and sat down on a mossy bank to await developments.

In about half an hour I heard the bushes rustle, and Bill wabbled out into the little glade in front of the cave. Behind him was the kid, stepping softly like a scout, with a broad grin on his face. Bill stopped, took off his hat and wiped his face with a red handkerchief. The kid stopped about eight feet behind him.

"Sam," says Bill, "I suppose you'll think I'm a renegade, but I couldn't help it. I'm a grown person with masculine proclivities and habits of self-defense, but there is a time when all systems of egotism and predominance fail. The boy is gone. I have sent him home. All is off. There was martyrs in old times," goes on Bill, "that suffered death rather than give up the particular graft they enjoyed. None of 'em ever was subjugated to such supernatural tortures as I have been. I tried to be faithful to our articles of depredation; but there came a limit."

"What's the trouble, Bill?" I asks him.

"I was rode," says Bill, "the ninety miles to the stockade, not barring an inch. Then, when the settlers was rescued, I was given oats. Sand ain't a palatable substitute. And then, for an hour I had to try to explain to him why there was nothin' in holes, how a road can run both ways and what makes the grass green. I tell you, Sam, a human can only stand so much. I takes him by the neck of his clothes and drags him down the mountain. On the way he kicks my legs black-and-blue from the knees down; and I've got to have two or three bites on my thumb and hand cauterized.

"But he's gone"—continues Bill—"gone home. I showed him the road to Summit and kicked him about eight feet nearer there at one kick. I'm sorry we lose the ransom; but it was either that or Bill Driscoll to the madhouse."

Bill is puffing and blowing, but there is a look of ineffable peace and growing content on his rose-pink features.

"Bill," says I, "there isn't any heart disease in your family, is there?"

"No," says Bill, "nothing chronic except malaria and accidents. Why?"

"Then you might turn around," says I, "and have a look behind you."

Bill turns and sees the boy, and loses his complexion and sits down plump on the ground and begins to pluck aimlessly at grass and little sticks. For an hour I was afraid for his mind. And then I told him that my scheme was to put the whole job through immediately and that we would get the ransom and be off with it by midnight if old Dorset fell in with our proposition. So Bill braced up enough to give the kid a weak sort of a smile and a promise to play the Russian in a Japanese war with him as soon as he felt a little better.

I had a scheme for collecting that ransom without danger of being caught by counterplots that ought to commend itself to professional kidnappers. The tree under which the answer was to be left—and the money later on—was close to the road fence with big, bare fields on all sides. If a gang of constables should be watching for any one to come for the note they could see him a long way off crossing the fields or in the road. But no, sirree! At half-past eight I was up in that tree as well hidden as a tree toad, waiting for the messenger to arrive.

Exactly on time, a half-grown boy rides up the road on a bicycle, locates the pasteboard box at the foot of the fence-post, slips a folded piece of paper into it and pedals away again back toward Summit.

I waited an hour and then concluded the thing was square. I slid down the tree, got the note, slipped along the fence till I struck the woods, and was back at the cave in another half an hour. I opened the note, got near the lantern and read it to Bill. It was written with a pen in a crabbed hand, and the sum and substance of it was this:

Two Desperate Men.

Gentlemen: I received your letter to-day by post, in regard to the ransom you ask for the return of my son. I think you are a little high in your demands, and I hereby make you a counter-proposition, which I am inclined to believe you will accept. You bring Johnny home and pay me two hundred and fifty dollars in cash, and I agree to take him off your hands. You had better come at night, for the neighbours believe he is lost, and I couldn't be responsible for what they would do to anybody they saw bringing him back. Very respectfully,

EBENEZER DORSET.

"Great pirates of Penzance!" says I; "of all the impudent—"

But I glanced at Bill, and hesitated. He had the most appealing look in his eyes I ever saw on the face of a dumb or a talking brute.

"Sam," says he, "what's two hundred and fifty dollars, after all? We've got the money. One more night of this kid will send me to a bed in Bedlam. Besides being a thorough gentleman, I think Mr. Dorset is a spendthrift for making us such a liberal offer. You ain't going to let the chance go, are you?"

"Tell you the truth, Bill," says I, "this little he ewe lamb has somewhat got on my nerves too. We'll take him home, pay the ransom and make our get-away."

We took him home that night. We got him to go by telling him that his father had bought a silver-mounted rifle and a pair of moccasins for him, and we were going to hunt bears the next day.

It was just twelve o'clock when we knocked at Ebenezer's front door. Just at the moment when I should have been abstracting the fifteen hundred dollars from the box under the tree, according to the original proposition, Bill was counting out two hundred and fifty dollars into Dorset's hand.

When the kid found out we were going to leave him at home he started up a howl like a calliope and fastened himself as tight as a leech to Bill's leg. His father peeled him away gradually, like a porous plaster.

"How long can you hold him?" asks Bill.

"I'm not as strong as I used to be," says old Dorset, "but I think I can promise you ten minutes."

"Enough," says Bill. "In ten minutes I shall cross the Central, Southern and Middle Western States, and be legging it trippingly for the Canadian border."

And, as dark as it was, and as fat as Bill was, and as good a runner as I am, he was a good mile and a half out of Summit before I could catch up with him.

Anne of Green Gables

by Lucy Maud Montgomery

CHAPTER III
Marilla Cuthbert Is Surprised

Marilla came briskly forward as Matthew opened the door. But when her eyes fell on the odd little figure in the stiff, ugly dress, with the long braids of red hair and the eager, luminous eyes, she stopped short in amazement.

"Matthew Cuthbert, who's that?" she ejaculated. "Where is the boy?"

"There wasn't any boy," said Matthew wretchedly. "There was only *her*."

He nodded at the child, remembering that he had never even asked her name.

"No boy! But there *must* have been a boy," insisted Marilla. "We sent word to Mrs. Spencer to bring a boy."

"Well, she didn't. She brought *her*. I asked the station-master. And I had to bring her home. She couldn't be left there, no matter where the mistake had come in."

"Well, this is a pretty piece of business!" ejaculated Marilla.

During this dialogue the child had remained silent, her eyes roving from one to the other, all the animation fading out of her face. Suddenly she seemed to grasp the full meaning of what had been said. Dropping her precious carpet-bag she sprang forward a step and clasped her hands.

"You don't want me!" she cried. "You don't want me because I'm not a boy! I might have expected it. Nobody ever did want me. I might have known it was all too beautiful to last. I might have known nobody really did want me. Oh, what shall I do? I'm going to burst into tears!"

Burst into tears she did. Sitting down on a chair by the table, flinging her arms out upon it, and burying her face in them, she proceeded to cry stormily. Marilla and Matthew looked at each other deprecatingly across the stove. Neither of them knew what to say or do. Finally Marilla stepped lamely into the breach.

"Well, well, there's no need to cry so about it."

"Yes, there *is* need!" The child raised her head quickly, revealing a tear-stained face and trembling lips. "*You* would cry, too, if you were an orphan and had come to a place you thought was going to be home and found that they didn't want you because you weren't a boy. Oh, this is the most *tragical* thing that ever happened to me!"

Something like a reluctant smile, rather rusty from long disuse, mellowed Marilla's grim expression.

"Well, don't cry any more. We're not going to turn you out-of-doors to-night. You'll have to stay here until we investigate this affair. What's your name?"

The child hesitated for a moment.

"Will you please call me Cordelia?" she said eagerly.

"*Call* you Cordelia? Is that your name?"

"No-o-o, it's not exactly my name, but I would love to be called Cordelia. It's such a perfectly elegant name."

"I don't know what on earth you mean. If Cordelia isn't your name, what is?"

"Anne Shirley," reluctantly faltered forth the owner of that name, "but, oh, please do call me Cordelia. It can't matter much to you what you call me if I'm only going to be here a little while, can it? And Anne is such an unromantic name."

"Unromantic fiddlesticks!" said the unsympathetic Marilla. "Anne is a real good plain sensible name. You've no need to be ashamed of it."

"Oh, I'm not ashamed of it," explained Anne, "only I like Cordelia better. I've always imagined that my name was Cordelia—at least, I always have of late years. When I was young I used to imagine it was Geraldine, but I like Cordelia better now. But if you call me Anne please call me Anne spelled with an E."

"What difference does it make how it's spelled?" asked Marilla with another rusty smile as she picked up the teapot.

"Oh, it makes *such* a difference. It *looks* so much nicer. When you hear a name pronounced can't you always see it in your mind, just as if it was printed out? I can; and A-n-n looks dreadful, but A-n-n-e looks so much more distinguished. If you'll only call me Anne spelled with an E I shall try to reconcile myself to not being called Cordelia."

"Very well, then, Anne spelled with an E, can you tell us how this mistake came to be made? We sent word to Mrs. Spencer to bring us a boy. Were there no boys at the asylum?"

"Oh, yes, there was an abundance of them. But Mrs. Spencer said *distinctly* that you wanted a girl about eleven years old. And the matron said she thought I would do. You don't know how delighted I was. I couldn't sleep all last night for joy. Oh," she added reproachfully, turning to Matthew, "why didn't you tell me at the station that you didn't want me and leave me there? If I hadn't seen the White Way of Delight and the Lake of Shining Waters it wouldn't be so hard."

"What on earth does she mean?" demanded Marilla, staring at Matthew.

"She—she's just referring to some conversation we had on the road," said Matthew hastily. "I'm going out to put the mare in, Marilla. Have tea ready when I come back."

"Did Mrs. Spencer bring anybody over besides you?" continued Marilla when Matthew had gone out.

"She brought Lily Jones for herself. Lily is only five years old and she is very beautiful and has nut-brown hair. If I was very beautiful and had nut-brown hair would you keep me?"

"No. We want a boy to help Matthew on the farm. A girl would be of no use to us. Take off your hat. I'll lay it and your bag on the hall table."

Anne took off her hat meekly. Matthew came back presently and they sat down to supper. But Anne could not eat. In vain she nibbled at the bread and butter and pecked at the crab-apple preserve out of the little scalloped glass dish by her plate. She did not really make any headway at all.

"You're not eating anything," said Marilla sharply, eying her as if it were a serious shortcoming. Anne sighed.

"I can't. I'm in the depths of despair. Can you eat when you are in the depths of despair?"

"I've never been in the depths of despair, so I can't say," responded Marilla.

"Weren't you? Well, did you ever try to *imagine* you were in the depths of despair?"

"No, I didn't."

"Then I don't think you can understand what it's like. It's a very uncomfortable feeling indeed. When you try to eat a lump comes right up in your throat and you can't swallow anything, not even if it was a chocolate caramel. I had one chocolate caramel once two years ago and it was simply delicious. I've often dreamed since then that I had a lot of chocolate caramels, but I always wake up just when I'm going to eat them. I do hope you won't be offended because I can't eat. Everything is extremely nice, but still I cannot eat."

"I guess she's tired," said Matthew, who hadn't spoken since his return from the barn. "Best put her to bed, Marilla."

Marilla had been wondering where Anne should be put to bed. She had prepared a couch in the kitchen chamber for the desired and expected boy. But, although it was neat and clean, it did not seem quite the thing to put a girl there somehow. But the spare room was out of the question for such a stray waif, so there remained only the east gable room. Marilla lighted a candle and told Anne to follow her, which Anne spiritlessly did, taking her hat and carpet-bag from the hall table as she passed. The hall was fearsomely clean; the little gable chamber in which she presently found herself seemed still cleaner.

Marilla set the candle on a three-legged, three-cornered table and turned down the bedclothes.

"I suppose you have a nightgown?" she questioned.

Anne nodded.

"Yes, I have two. The matron of the asylum made them for me. They're fearfully skimpy. There is never enough to go around in an asylum, so things are always skimpy—at least in a poor asylum like ours. I hate skimpy night-dresses. But one can dream just as well in them as in lovely trailing ones, with frills around the neck, that's one consolation."

"Well, undress as quick as you can and go to bed. I'll come back in a few minutes for the candle. I daren't trust you to put it out yourself. You'd likely set the place on fire."

When Marilla had gone Anne looked around her wistfully. The whitewashed walls were so painfully bare and staring that she thought they must ache over their own bareness. The floor was bare, too, except for a round braided mat in the middle such as Anne had never seen before. In one corner was the bed, a high, old-fashioned one, with four dark, low-turned posts. In the other corner was the aforesaid three-corner table adorned with a fat, red velvet pin-cushion hard enough to turn the point of the most adventurous pin. Above it hung a little six-by-eight mirror. Midway between table and bed was the window, with an icy white muslin frill over it, and opposite it was the wash-stand. The whole apartment was of a rigidity not to be described in words, but which sent a shiver to the very marrow of Anne's bones. With a sob she hastily discarded her garments, put on the skimpy nightgown and sprang into bed where she burrowed face downward into the pillow and pulled the clothes over her head. When Marilla came up for the light various skimpy articles of raiment scattered most untidily over the floor and a certain tempestuous appearance of the bed were the only indications of any presence save her own.

She deliberately picked up Anne's clothes, placed them neatly on a prim yellow chair, and then, taking up the candle, went over to the bed.

"Good night," she said, a little awkwardly, but not unkindly.

Anne's white face and big eyes appeared over the bedclothes with a startling suddenness.

"How can you call it a *good* night when you know it must be the very worst night I've ever had?" she said reproachfully.

Then she dived down into invisibility again.

Marilla went slowly down to the kitchen and proceeded to wash the supper dishes. Matthew was smoking—a sure sign of perturbation of mind. He seldom smoked, for Marilla set her face against it as a filthy habit; but at certain times and seasons he felt driven to it and then Marilla winked at the practice, realizing that a mere man must have some vent for his emotions.

"Well, this is a pretty kettle of fish," she said wrathfully. "This is what comes of sending word instead of going ourselves. Richard Spencer's folks have twisted that message somehow. One of us will have to drive over and see Mrs. Spencer tomorrow, that's certain. This girl will have to be sent back to the asylum."

"Yes, I suppose so," said Matthew reluctantly.

"You *suppose* so! Don't you know it?"

"Well now, she's a real nice little thing, Marilla. It's kind of a pity to send her back when she's so set on staying here."

"Matthew Cuthbert, you don't mean to say you think we ought to keep her!"

Marilla's astonishment could not have been greater if Matthew had expressed a predilection for standing on his head.

"Well, now, no, I suppose not—not exactly," stammered Matthew, uncomfortably driven into a corner for his precise meaning. "I suppose—we could hardly be expected to keep her."

"I should say not. What good would she be to us?"

"We might be some good to her," said Matthew suddenly and unexpectedly.

"Matthew Cuthbert, I believe that child has bewitched you! I can see as plain as plain that you want to keep her."

"Well now, she's a real interesting little thing," persisted Matthew. "You should have heard her talk coming from the station."

"Oh, she can talk fast enough. I saw that at once. It's nothing in her favour, either. I don't like children who have so much to say. I don't want an orphan girl and if I did she isn't the style I'd pick out. There's something I don't understand about her. No, she's got to be despatched straight-way back to where she came from."

"I could hire a French boy to help me," said Matthew, "and she'd be company for you."

"I'm not suffering for company," said Marilla shortly. "And I'm not going to keep her."

"Well now, it's just as you say, of course, Marilla," said Matthew rising and putting his pipe away. "I'm going to bed."

To bed went Matthew. And to bed, when she had put her dishes away, went Marilla, frowning most resolutely. And up-stairs, in the east gable, a lonely, heart-hungry, friendless child cried herself to sleep.

The Bowmen

by Arthur Machen

It was during the Retreat of the Eighty Thousand, and the authority of the Censorship is sufficient excuse for not being more explicit. But it was on the most awful day of that awful time, on the day when ruin and disaster came so near that their shadow fell over London far away; and, without any certain news, the hearts of men failed within them and grew faint; as if the agony of the army in the battlefield had entered into their souls.

On this dreadful day, then, when three hundred thousand men in arms with all their artillery swelled like a flood against the little English company, there was one point above all other points in our battle line that was for a time in awful danger, not merely of defeat, but of utter annihilation. With the permission of the Censorship and of the military expert, this corner may, perhaps, be described as a salient, and if this angle were crushed and broken, then the English force as a whole would be shattered, the Allied left would be turned, and Sedan would inevitably follow.

All the morning the German guns had thundered and shrieked against this corner, and against the thousand or so of men who held it. The men joked at the shells, and found funny names for them, and had bets about them, and greeted them with scraps of music-hall songs. But the shells came on and burst, and tore good Englishmen limb from limb, and tore brother from brother, and as the heat of the day increased so did the fury of that terrific cannonade. There was no help, it seemed. The English artillery was good, but there was not nearly enough of it; it was being steadily battered into scrap iron.

There comes a moment in a storm at sea when people say to one another, "It is at its worst; it can blow no harder," and then there is a blast ten times more fierce than any before it. So it was in these British trenches.

There were no stouter hearts in the whole world than the hearts of these men; but even they were appalled as this seven-times-heated hell of the German cannonade fell upon them and overwhelmed them and destroyed them. And at this very moment they saw from their trenches that a tremendous host was moving against their lines. Five hundred of the thousand remained, and as far as they could see the German infantry was pressing on against them, column upon column, a grey world of men, ten thousand of them, as it appeared afterwards.

There was no hope at all. They shook hands, some of them. One man improvised a new version of the battlesong, "Good-bye, good-bye to Tipperary," ending with "And we shan't get there." And they all went on firing steadily. The officers pointed out that such an opportunity for high-class, fancy shooting might never occur again; the Germans dropped line after line;

the Tipperary humorist asked, "What price Sidney Street?" And the few machine guns did their best. But everybody knew it was of no use. The dead grey bodies lay in companies and battalions, as others came on and on and on, and they swarmed and stirred and advanced from beyond and beyond.

"World without end. Amen," said one of the British soldiers with some irrelevance as he took aim and fired. And then he remembered—he says he cannot think why or wherefore—a queer vegetarian restaurant in London where he had once or twice eaten eccentric dishes of cutlets made of lentils and nuts that pretended to be steak. On all the plates in this restaurant there was printed a figure of St. George in blue, with the motto, *Adsit Anglis Sanctus Georgius*—May St. George be a present help to the English. This soldier happened to know Latin and other useless things, and now, as he fired at his man in the grey advancing mass—300 yards away—he uttered the pious vegetarian motto. He went on firing to the end, and at last Bill on his right had to clout him cheerfully over the head to make him stop, pointing out as he did so that the King's ammunition cost money and was not lightly to be wasted in drilling funny patterns into dead Germans.

For as the Latin scholar uttered his invocation he felt something between a shudder and an electric shock pass through his body. The roar of the battle died down in his ears to a gentle murmur; instead of it, he says, he heard a great voice and a shout louder than a thunder-peal crying, "Array, array, array!"

His heart grew hot as a burning coal, it grew cold as ice within him, as it seemed to him that a tumult of voices answered to his summons. He heard, or seemed to hear, thousands shouting: "St. George! St. George!"

"Ha! messire; ha! sweet Saint, grant us good deliverance!"

"St. George for merry England!"

"Harow! Harow! Monseigneur St. George, succour us."

"Ha! St. George! Ha! St. George! a long bow and a strong bow."

"Heaven's Knight, aid us!"

And as the soldier heard these voices he saw before him, beyond the trench, a long line of shapes, with a shining about them. They were like men who drew the bow, and with another shout their cloud of arrows flew singing and tingling through the air towards the German hosts.

The other men in the trench were firing all the while. They had no hope; but they aimed just as if they had been shooting at Bisley. Suddenly one of them lifted up his voice in the plainest English, "Gawd help us!" he bellowed to the man next to him, "but we're blooming marvels! Look at those grey . . . gentlemen, look at them! D'ye see them? They're not going down in dozens, nor in 'undreds; it's thousands, it is. Look! look! there's a regiment gone while I'm talking to ye."

"Shut it!" the other soldier bellowed, taking aim, "what are ye gassing about!"

But he gulped with astonishment even as he spoke, for, indeed, the grey men were falling by the thousands. The English could hear the guttural scream of the German officers, the crackle of their revolvers as they shot the reluctant; and still line after line crashed to the earth. All the while the Latin-bred soldier heard the cry: "Harow! Harow! Monseigneur, dear saint, quick to our aid! St. George help us!"

"High Chevalier, defend us!"

The singing arrows fled so swift and thick that they darkened the air; the heathen horde melted from before them.

"More machine guns!" Bill yelled to Tom.

"Don't hear them," Tom yelled back. "But, thank God, anyway; they've got it in the neck."

In fact, there were ten thousand dead German soldiers left before that salient of the English army, and consequently there was no Sedan. In Germany, a country ruled by scientific principles, the Great General Staff decided that the contemptible English must have employed shells containing an unknown gas of a poisonous nature, as no wounds were discernible on the bodies of the dead German soldiers. But the man who knew what nuts tasted like when they called themselves steak knew also that St. George had brought his Agincourt Bowmen to help the English.

Appendix IV

Poetry

The Bells
Edgar Allan Poe

I
Hear the sledges with the bells—
Silver bells!
What a world of merriment their melody foretells!
How they tinkle, tinkle, tinkle,
In the icy air of night!
While the stars that oversprinkle
All the heavens, seem to twinkle
With a crystalline delight;
Keeping time, time, time,
In a sort of Runic rhyme,
To the tintinnabulation that so musically wells
From the bells, bells, bells, bells,
Bells, bells, bells—
From the jingling and the tinkling of the bells.

II
Hear the mellow wedding bells,
Golden bells!
What a world of happiness their harmony foretells!
Through the balmy air of night
How they ring out their delight!
From the molten-golden notes,
And all in tune,
What a liquid ditty floats
To the turtle-dove that listens, while she gloats

On the moon!
Oh, from out the sounding cells,
What a gush of euphony voluminously wells!
How it swells!
How it dwells
On the Future! how it tells
Of the rapture that impels
To the swinging and the ringing
Of the bells, bells, bells,
Of the bells, bells, bells, bells,
Bells, bells, bells—
To the rhyming and the chiming of the bells!

III
Hear the loud alarum bells—
Brazen bells!
What a tale of terror, now, their turbulency tells!
In the startled ear of night
How they scream out their affright!
Too much horrified to speak,
They can only shriek, shriek,
Out of tune,
In a clamorous appealing to the mercy of the fire,

In a mad expostulation with the deaf and frantic fire,
Leaping higher, higher, higher,
With a desperate desire,
And a resolute endeavor,
Now—now to sit or never,
By the side of the pale-faced moon.
Oh, the bells, bells, bells!
What a tale their terror tells
Of Despair!
How they clang, and clash, and roar!
What a horror they outpour
On the bosom of the palpitating air!
Yet the ear it fully knows,
By the twanging,
And the clanging,
How the danger ebbs and flows:
Yet the ear distinctly tells,
In the jangling,
And the wrangling,
How the danger sinks and swells,
By the sinking or the swelling in the anger of the bells—
Of the bells—
Of the bells, bells, bells, bells,
Bells, bells, bells—
In the clamor and the clangor of the bells!

IV
Hear the tolling of the bells—
Iron Bells!
What a world of solemn thought their monody compels!
In the silence of the night,
How we shiver with affright
At the melancholy menace of their tone!
For every sound that floats
From the rust within their throats
Is a groan.
And the people—ah, the people—
They that dwell up in the steeple,
All Alone
And who, tolling, tolling, tolling,
In that muffled monotone,
Feel a glory in so rolling

On the human heart a stone—
They are neither man nor woman—
They are neither brute nor human—
They are Ghouls:
And their king it is who tolls;
And he rolls, rolls, rolls,
Rolls
A paean from the bells!
And his merry bosom swells
With the paean of the bells!
And he dances, and he yells;
Keeping time, time, time,
In a sort of Runic rhyme,
To the paean of the bells—
Of the bells:
Keeping time, time, time,
In a sort of Runic rhyme,
To the throbbing of the bells—
Of the bells, bells, bells—
To the sobbing of the bells;
Keeping time, time, time,
As he knells, knells, knells,
In a happy Runic rhyme,
To the rolling of the bells—
Of the bells, bells, bells:
To the tolling of the bells,
Of the bells, bells, bells, bells—
Bells, bells, bells—
To the moaning and the groaning of the bells.

Ozymandias
Percy Bysshe Shelley

I met a traveller from an antique land
Who said: "Two vast and trunkless legs of stone
Stand in the desert. Near them on the sand,
Half sunk, a shattered visage lies, whose frown
And wrinkled lip and sneer of cold command
Tell that its sculptor well those passions read
Which yet survive, stamped on these lifeless things,
The hand that mocked them and the heart that fed.
And on the pedestal these words appear:
'My name is Ozymandias, King of Kings:
Look on my works, ye mighty, and despair!'
Nothing beside remains. Round the decay
Of that colossal wreck, boundless and bare,
The lone and level sands stretch far away."

The Charge of the Light Brigade
Alfred, Lord Tennyson

1
Half a league, half a league,
Half a league onward,
All in the valley of Death
Rode the six hundred.
"Forward, the Light Brigade!
"Charge for the guns!" he said:
Into the valley of Death
Rode the six hundred.

2
"Forward, the Light Brigade!"
Was there a man dismay'd?
Not tho' the soldier knew
Someone had blunder'd:
Theirs not to make reply,
Theirs not to reason why,
Theirs but to do and die:
Into the valley of Death
Rode the six hundred.

3
Cannon to right of them,
Cannon to left of them,
Cannon in front of them
Volley'd and thunder'd;
Storm'd at with shot and shell,
Boldly they rode and well,
Into the jaws of Death,
Into the mouth of Hell
Rode the six hundred.

4
Flash'd all their sabres bare,
Flash'd as they turn'd in air,
Sabring the gunners there,
Charging an army, while
All the world wonder'd:

Plunged in the battery-smoke
Right thro' the line they broke;
Cossack and Russian
Reel'd from the sabre stroke
    Shatter'd and sunder'd.
Then they rode back, but not
    Not the six hundred.

5
Cannon to right of them,
Cannon to left of them,
Cannon behind them
    Volley'd and thunder'd;
Storm'd at with shot and shell,
While horse and hero fell,
They that had fought so well
Came thro' the jaws of Death
Back from the mouth of Hell,
All that was left of them,
    Left of six hundred.

6
When can their glory fade?
O the wild charge they made!
    All the world wondered.
Honor the charge they made,
Honor the Light Brigade,
    Noble six hundred.

WORKS CITED

1000 Wonders of Nature. New York: Reader's Digest Association, 1994. [Week 21]

Abbott, Jacob. *History of King Charles the First of England*. Philadelphia: Henry Altemus Company, 1900. [Week 28]

Abbot, Willis J. *Notable Women in History*. Philadelphia, Penn.: John C. Winston, 1913 [Week 31]

Adkins, Roy. *Nelson's Trafalgar: The Battle That Changed the World*. New York: Viking, 2005. [Week 11]

Aiken, Joan. *The Wolves of Willoughby Chase*. New York: Yearling, 1962. [Week 1]

The American Heritage Science Dictionary. Boston: Houghton Mifflin, 2005. [Week 21]

Appleton's Journal, Vol. 11. New York: D. Appleton & Company 1874. [Week 22]

Arnold, Isaac Newton. *The History of Abraham Lincoln and the Overthrow of Slavery*. Chicago: Clarke & Co., 1866. [Week 17]

Balachandran, K., *Critical Essays on American Literature*. New Delhi: Sarup & Sons, 2005. [Week 25]

Banks, Louis Albert. *The Story of the Hall of Fame*. New York: The Christian Herald, 1902. [Week 20]

Bauer, Susan Wise. *The Story of the World, Volume 3: Early Modern Times*. Charles City, Va.: Peace Hill Press, 2004. [Week 1]

Baum, L. Frank. *Tik-Tok of Oz*. Chicago: Reilly & Britton, 1914. [Week 7]

Birds and Nature in Natural Colors. Chicago: A. W. Mumford, 1914. [Week 2]

Bishop, M. C. *The Prison Life of Marie Antoinette*. London: Keegan Paul, Trench, Trübner & Co., 1893. [Week 31]

Blackwood, Gary L. *Life in a Medieval Castle*. New York: Lucent Books, 2000. [Week 9]

Blake, Stephen P. *Shahjahanabad: The Sovereign City in Mughal India 1639–1739*. Cambridge: Cambridge University Press, 2002. [Week 9]

Bodmer, Rudolph John. *The Book of Wonders*. Washington, D.C.: Bureau of Industrial Education, 1916. [Week 21]

Bourne, Henry Eldridge, and Elbert Jay Benton. *A History of the United States.* Boston: D. C. Heath and Co., 1913. [Week 2]

Bova, Ben. *Venus.* New York: Tor, 2000. [Week 14]

Brawley, Benjamin Griffith. *A Short History of the English Drama.* New York: Harcourt, Brace & Company, 1921. [Week 20]

Brown, Billye Walker, and Walter R. Brown. *Historical Catastrophes: Hurricanes and Tornadoes.* Reading, Mass.: Addison-Wesley, 1972. [Week 6]

Bryson, Bill. *A Short History of Nearly Everything.* New York: Random House, 2004. [Weeks 12, 14]

Burroughs, William James. *The Climate Revealed.* Cambridge: Cambridge University Press, 1999. [Week 22]

Burton, Maurice, and Robert Burton. *The International Wildlife Encyclopedia,* Vol. 1. London: BCP Publications, 1969. [Week 22]

Cadell, W. A. *A Journey in Carniola, Italy, and France in the Years 1817, 1818,* Vol. 2. Edinburgh: Archibald Constable and Co., 1820. [Week 29]

Calhoun, Dorothy Donnell. *The Book of Brave Adventures.* New York: The Macmillan Company, 1915. [Week 34]

Capaccio, George. *Mars.* Tarrytown, N.Y.: Marshall Cavendish Benchmark, 2010. [Week 14]

Card, Orson Scott. *How to Write Science Fiction and Fantasy.* Cincinnati, Ohio: Writers Digest Books, 2001. [Week 26]

Casey, Susan. *The Wave: In Pursuit of the Rogues, Freaks, and Giants of the Ocean.* New York: Doubleday, 2010. [Weeks 4, 15]

Caspar, Max, and Clarisse Doris Hellman. *Kepler.* New York: Dover, 1993. [Week 7]

Chambers's Encyclopedia: A Dictionary of Universal Knowledge, Vol. 6. London: W. & R. Chambers, 1886. [Week 31]

Chrisley, Ronald, and Sander Begeer. *Artificial Intelligence: Critical Concepts,* Vol. 1. New York: Routledge, 2000. [Week 25]

Compton's Learning Company. *Earth's Changing Environment.* Chicago: Encyclopedia Britannica, 2008. [Week 27]

Comstock, Anna Botsford. *Handbook of Nature Study,* rev. ed. Ithaca, N.Y.: Cornell University Press, 1986. [Week 14]

Costain, Thomas. *The Mississippi Bubble.* New York: Random House, 1955. [Week 8]

Couvares, Francis G. *Interpretations of American History: Through Reconstruction.* New York: Simon & Schuster, 2000. [Week 17]

Cunningham, George Godfrey. *Lives of Eminent and Illustrious Englishmen: From Alfred the Great,* Vol. 4. Glasgow: A. Fullarton & Co., 1833. [Week 17]

Cwiklik, Robert. *Albert Einstein and the Theory of Relativity.* Hauppage, N.Y.: Barron's Educational Series, Inc., 1987. [Week 4]

Daniel, John Franklin. *Animal Life of Malaysia.* Indianapolis, Ind.: Bobbs-Merrill, 1908. [Week 22]

Decker, Robert Wayne, and Barbara Decker. *Volcanoes.* San Francisco: W. H. Freeman, 1981 [Week 12]

Dell, Pamela. *Hatshepsut: Egypt's First Female Pharaoh.* Minneapolis, Minn.: Compass Point Books, 2009. [Week 2]

Delphian Society. *The Delphian Course.* Chicago: The Society, 1913. [Week 29]

Dempsey, Michael. *The Round World: Foundations of Geology and Geomorphology.* London: Sampson Low, Marston & Co., 1966. [Week 2]

Denny, Mark W., and Steven Dean Gaines. *Encyclopedia of Tidepools and Rocky Shores.* Berkeley: University of California Press, 2007. [Week 22]

De Pree, Christopher Gordon, and Alan Axelrod. *The Complete Idiot's Guide to Astronomy.* Indianapolis, Ind.: Alpha, 2001. [Week 21]

Derry, Gregory Neil. *What Science Is and How It Works.* Princeton, N.J.: Princeton University Press, 1999. [Week 21]

Dickens, Charles. *A Christmas Carol in Prose, Being a Ghost Story of Christmas.* London: Chapman & Hall, 1845. [Weeks 9, 10, 18]

Doak, Robin Santos. *Galileo: Astronomer and Physicist.* Minneapolis, Minn.: Compass Point Books, 2005. [Week 15]

Doyle, Arthur Conan. *The Hound of the Baskervilles: Another Adventure of Sherlock Holmes.* New York: Mclure, Phillips & Co., 1902. [Week 12]

Dunford, Martin, and Phil Lee. *Belgium and Luxembourg.* London: Rough Guides, 2002. [Week 26]

Ebrey, Patricia Buckley, Anne Walthall, and James B. Palais, *Pre-Modern East Asia to 1800: A Cultural, Social, and Political History.* Boston: Houghton Mifflin, 2006. [Week 27]

Edmonds, George. *Facts and Falsehoods Concerning the War on the South, 1861–1865.* Memphis, Tenn.: A. R. Taylor & Co., 1904. [Week 17]

Elkins-Tanton, Linda T. *Mars.* New York: Chelsea House, 2006. [Week 14]

Ellis, Richard. *Monsters of the Sea.* New York: Knopf, 1994. [Week 22]

Erasmus, Desiderius. *Copia: Foundations of the Abundant Style: De duplici copia verborum ac rerum Commentarii duo*, trans and ed. Betty I. Knott, in C*ollected Works of Erasmus:*

Literary and Educational Writings 2, ed. Craig R. Thompson, vol. 28. University of Toronto Press, 1978, ch. 33. [Week 15]

Facklam, Margery, and Howard Facklam. *Changes in the Wind: Earth's Shifting Climate.* Harcourt Brace Jovanovich, 1986. [Week 15]

Foreman, Laura. *Alexander the Conqueror: The Epic Story of the Warrior King.* Cambridge, Mass.: Da Capo, 2004. [Week 28]

Frost, J., ed. *The Class Book of Nature*. Hartford, Conn.: Belknap & Hamersley, 1839. [Week 30]

Gaddis, Vincent H. *The Wide World of Magic*. New York: Criterion Books, 1967. [Week 2]

Gandhi, M. K., and Homer Alexander Jack. *The Gandhi Reader: A Source Book of His Life and Writings.* Bloomington: Indiana University Press, 1956. [Week 16]

Gates, Alexander E., and David Ritchie, *Encyclopedia of Earthquakes and Volcanoes.* New York: Facts on File, 2007. [Week 12]

Geikie, Archibald. *Textbook of Geology.* New York: P. F. Collier, 1902. [Week 12]

Gibson, R. N., R. J. A. Atkinson, and J. D. M. Gordon. *Oceanography and Marine Biology.* Boca Raton, La.: CRC Press, 2008. [Week 22]

Gingerich, Owen. *The Eye of Heaven: Ptolemy, Copernicus, Kepler.* College Park, Md.: American Institute of Physics, 1993. [Week 7]

Goebel, Stefan. *The Great War and Medieval Memory: War, Remembrance, and Medievalism in Britain and Germany, 1914–1940.* Cambridge: Cambridge University Press, 2007. [Week 26]

Goldsworthy, Adrian Keith. *Caesar: Life of a Colossus.* New Haven, Conn.: Yale University Press, 2006. [Week 29]

Goleman, Daniel, and Richard J. Davidson. *Consciousness: the Brain, States of Awareness, and Alternate Realities.* New York: Irvington Publishers, 1979. [Week 12]

Good, Gerry A. *Observing Variable Stars.* New York: Springer, 2003. [Week 21]

Greely, A. W., George L. Barclay, and Winfield Scott Schley. *The Greely Arctic Expedition: As Fully Narrated by Lieut. Greely, U.S.A., and Other Survivors.* Philadelphia: Barclay & Co, 1884. [Week 13]

Greenburg, Dan. *Attack of the Giant Octopus.* Edina, Minn.: Spotlight, 2009. [Week 22]

Griffin, L. R. F. "Study of Giant Trees." In *The School Journal,* Vol. LX, Jan.–June 1900, pp. 550–551. [Week 27]

Grove, George. *Grove's Dictionary of Music and Musicians,* Vol. 1. London: Macmillan & Co., 1904. [Week 16]

Haines, Catharine M. C. *International Women in Science: A Biographical Dictionary to 1950.* Santa Barbara, Calif.: ABC-CLIO, 2001. [Week 31]

Harkness, Albert. *Caesar's Commentaries on the Gallic War: Notes, Dictionary, and a Map of Gaul.* New York: American Book Company, 1901. [Weeks 28, 29]

Harty, Kevin J. *Cinema Arthuriana.* Jefferson, N.C.: McFarland & Co., 2002. [Week 25]

Haven, Kendall. *100 Greatest Science Discoveries of All Time.* Westport, Conn.: Libraries Unlimited, 2007. [Week 5]

Hawks, Francis Lister. *The Adventures of Daniel Boone, The Kentucky Rifleman.* New York: D. Appleton, 1850. [Week 19]

Hayden, Robert C., and Richard Loehle. *Seven African-American Scientists.* Frederick, Md.: Twenty-First Century Books, 1992. [Week 5]

Heath, Thomas. *Archimedes.* London: Macmillan, 1920. [Week 20]

Henry, O. "The Ransom of Red Chief," *In Whirligigs.* New York: Double, Page and co., 1910 [Week 24]

Herodotus, *The Landmark Herodotus: The Histories,* trans. Robert B. Strassler. New York: Random House, 2009. [Week 9]

Hirschi, Ron. *Octopuses.* Minneapolis, Minn.: Carolrhoda Books, 2000. [Week 22]

Hitchins, Derek K. *Systems Engineering: A 21st Century Systems Methodology* (Hoboken, N.J.: John Wiley, 2007. [Week 22]

Holden, Edward Singleton. *Real Things in Nature: A Reading Book of Science for American Boys and Girls.* New York: Macmillan, 1921. [Week 2, 30]

Horowitz, Alexandra. *Inside of a Dog: What Dogs See, Smell, and Know.* New York: Scribner, 2009. [Week 2]

Horvath, Polly. *The Pepins and Their Problems.* New York: Square Fish, 2008. [Week 1]

Hosmer, James Kendall. *A Short History of Anglo-Saxon Freedom.* New York: Charles Scribner's Sons, 1890. [Week 8]

Hugo, Victor. *The Hunchback of Notre-Dame.* Philadelphia: Carey, Lea and Blanchard, 1834. [Week 18]

———. *Les Misérables.* New York: Carlton, 1862. [Week 18]

Jayapalan, N. *History of English Literature.* New Delhi: Atlantic Publishers, 2001. [Week 20]

Jerrold, Blanchard, and Gustave Dore. *London: A Pilgrimage.* Boston: Anthem Press, 2005. [Week 10]

Johnson, Rebecca L. *Plate Tectonics.* New York: Lerner Publications, 2006. [Week 14]

Keller, Helen. *The Story of My Life.* New York: Doubleday, Page & Company, 1903. [Week 3]

Kendall, Calvin N., and Marion Paine Stevens. *Fourth Reader.* Boston: D. C. Heath and Co., 1920. [Week 13]

Kepler, Johannes, and Charles G. Wallis. *The Harmonies of the World.* Charleston, S.C.: BiblioBazaar, 2008. [Week 7]

Kershaw, Ian. *Hitler: A Biography.* New York: W. W. Norton, 2008. [Week 17]

Kheirabadi, Masoud. *Islam.* Philadelphia: Chelsea House Publishers, 2004. [Week 20]

Kipling, Rudyard. "Rikki-Tikki-Tavi." In *The Jungle Book.* New York: The Century Co., 1894. [Week 23]

Kjelgaard, Jim. *Big Red.* New York: Holiday House, 1945. [Week 15]

Komaroff, Anthony L. *The Harvard Medical School Family Health Guide.* New York: Simon & Schuster, 1999. [Week 30]

Koupelis, Theo. *In Quest of the Universe,* 6th ed. Sudbury, Mass.: Jones and Bartlett, 2010. [Week 5]

Kozol, Jonathan. *Savage Inequalities.* New York: Harper Perennial, 1992. [Week 8]

Krakauer, Jon. *Into Thin Air.* New York: Anchor Books, 1999. [Week 9]

Kubba, Juman. *The First Evidence: A Memoir of Life in Iraq under Saddam Hussein.* Jefferson, N.C.: McFarland & Co., 2003. [Week 18]

Kubesh, Katie, Kimm Bellotto, and Niki McNeil, *Predators of the Deep.* Coloma, Mich.: In the Hands of a Child, 2007. [Week 22]

Kusky, Timothy. *Encyclopedia of Earth and Space Science, Vol. 1* (New York: Facts on File, 2010. [Week 21]

Lamb, Harold. *Genghis Khan and the Mongol Horde.* New York: Random House, 1954. [Week 6]

Lang, Andrew. *The Red Fairy Book.* London: Longmans, Green & Co., 1891. [Week 1]

Laycock, George. *The Complete Beginner's Guide to Photography.* Garden City, N.Y.: Doubleday, 1979. [Week 2]

Lee, Henry. *Aquarium Notes: The Octopus.* London: Chapman and Hall, 1875. [Week 22]

Lee, Rupert. *The Eureka! Moment: 100 Key Scientific Discoveries of the 20th Century.* New York: Routledge, 2002. [Week 15]

Leick, Gwendolyn. *Historical Dictionary of Mesopotamia.* Lanham, Md.: Scarecrow Press, 2003. [Week 19]

Leuchtenburg, William E. *The White House Looks South: Franklin D. Roosevelt, Harry S. Truman, Lyndon B. Johnson.* Baton Rouge: Louisiana State University Press, 2005. [Week 17]

Life Magazine. "America Loved the Roosevelts." Nov. 25, 1946 (Vol. 21, No. 22), pp. 110–111. [Week 16]

Locke, Gladys Edson. *Queen Elizabeth: Various Scenes and Events in the Life of Her Majesty*. Boston: Sherman French & Co., 1913. [Week 16]

Lofaro, Michael A. *Daniel Boone: An American Life*. Lexington, Ky.: University Press of Kentucky, 2003. [Week 19]

Lopez de Gomara, Francisco. *Cortes: The Life of the Conqueror by His Secretary,* trans. Lesley Byrd Simpson. Berkeley: University of California Press, 1964. [Week 9]

Lunn, Janet, and Christopher Moore. *The Story of Canada*. Toronto: Key Porter Books, 1992. [Weeks 2, 27]

Lusebrink, Hans-Jurgen. *The Bastille: A History of a Symbol of Despotism and Freedom,* trans. Rolf Reichardt. Durham, N.C.: Duke University Press, 1997. [Week 9]

MacDonald, George. *The Princess and the Goblin*. London: Blackie & Son, 1888. [Week 8]

Machen, Arthur. *The Angels of Mons: The Bowmen and Other Legends of the War*. New York: G. P. Putnam's Sons, 1915. [Week 26]

Martin, Robert E. "Sailors' Battle with Huge Octopus Revives Tales of Dread Sea Monsters." In *Popular Science,* Dec. 1922, p. 37, 39. [Week 22]

Mather, Jennifer A., Roland C. Anderson, and James B. Wood. *Octopus: The Ocean's Intelligent Invertebrate*. Portland, Oreg.: Timber Press, 2010. [Week 22]

Maupassant, Guy de. 1900. "The Necklace." In *A Coward and Other Stories*. New York: Barse & Hopkins, 1900. [Week 24]

McKinley, Albert E., Charles A. Coulomb, and Armand J. Gerson, *The World War: A School History of the Great War*. New York: American Book Co., 1919. [Week 27]

Miller, Ron. *Mars*. Minneapolis, Minn.: Twenty-First Century Books, 2006. [Week 14]

Milner, Cork. *The Everything Shakespeare Book*. Avon, Mass.: Adams Media, 2008. [Week 20]

Montgomery, Lucy Maud. *Anne of Green Gables*. Toronto: Seal Books, 1900. [Week 25]

Morgan, Robert. *Boone: A Biography*. Chapel Hill, N.C.: Algonquin, 2007. [Week 19]

Morse, John Torrey. *Thomas Jefferson*. Boston: Houghton Mifflin, 1898. [Week 17]

Morton, Ron L. *Music of the Earth: Volcanoes, Earthquakes, and Other Geological Wonders*. New York: Plenum Press, 1996. [Week 14]

Muir, John. *Nature Writings*. New York: Library of America, 1997. [Week 10]

———. *The Yosemite*. New York: Century, 1912. [Week 13]

Nesbit, Edith. "The Deliverers of Their Country." In *The Book of Dragons*. Mineola, N.Y.: Dover, 2004. [Week 4]

O'Brien, John Maxwell. *Alexander the Great: The Invisible Enemy*. New York: Routledge, 1992. [Week 28]

Ogilvie, Marilyn Bailey, and Joy Dorothy Harvey. *The Biographical Dictionary of Women in Science: Pioneering Lives from Ancient Times to the Mid-20th Century, Vol. 1, A–K.* New York: Routledge, 2000. [Week 19]

Oz, Mehmet. *Healing from the Heart.* New York: Dutton, 1998. [Week 14]

Parsons, Reuben. *A Biographical Dictionary: For the Use of Colleges, Schools, & Families.* New York: Sadlier & Co., 1872. [Week 19]

Payer, Julius. *New Lands Within the Arctic Circle.* New York: Macmillan & Co., 1876. [Week 10]

Perry, Walter Scott. *With Azir Girges in Egypt.* Chicago: Atkinson, Mentzer & Co., 1913. [Week 10]

Peters, Stephanie True. *The Battle against Polio.* New York: Benchmark Books, 2005. [Week 15]

Petersen, Carolyn Collins, and John C. Brandt. *Hubble Vision: Further Adventures with the Hubble Space Telescope.* New York: Cambridge University Press, 1995. [Week 21]

Pilkington, Matthew. *A General Dictionary of Painters,* rev. ed. London: Thomas Tegg, 1840. [Week 18]

Pliny the Younger. *The Letters of the Younger Pliny,* trans. and ed. Betty Radice. Harmondsworth, Middlesex, England: Penguin Books, 1963. [Week 13]

Poe, Edgar Allan. "The Fall of the House of Usher." In *Prose Tales of Mystery and Imagination,* by Edgar Allan Poe. London: Henry Frowde, 1903. [Week 8]

Pollard, Albert Frederick. *Henry VIII.* London: Longmans, 1919. [Week 18]

Polo, Marco, and John Masefield. *The Travels of Marco Polo, the Venetian.* London: J. M. Dent, 1908. [Week 10]

Ralston, Alma Payne. *Discoverer of the Unseen World: A Biography of Antoni van Leeuwenhoek.* New York: The World Publishing Company, 1966. [Weeks 7, 15]

Raspe, Rudolf Erich. *The Adventures of Baron Munchausen.* New York: Thomas Y. Crowell & Co., 1902. [Week 14]

Ricks, Delthia, and Marc Siegel. *100 Questions & Answers about Influenza.* Sudbury, Mass.: Jones & Bartlett Learning, 2008. [Week 13]

Ridpath, Ian, ed. *The Illustrated Encyclopedia of Astronomy and Space,* rev. ed. New York: Thomas Y. Crowell Publishers, 1979. [Week 12]

Riley, Franklin Lafayette. *General Robert E. Lee after Appomattox.* New York: The Macmillan Company, 1922. [Week 17]

Rogers, Julia Ellen. *Trees That Every Child Should Know: Easy Tree Studies for All Seasons of the Year.* New York: Doubleday, 1909. [Week 13]

Rozakis, Laurie. *Schaum's Quick Guide to Writing Great Research Papers*, 2nd ed. New York: McGraw-Hill, 2007. [Week 28]

Scalzi, John. *The Rough Guide to the Universe*. London: Rough Guides, 2003. [Week 14]

Schiff, Stacy. *Cleopatra: A Life*. New York: Little, Brown and Company, 2010. [Week 16]

Schom, Alan. *Napoleon Bonaparte*. New York: HarperCollins, 1997. [Week 18]

Seeds, Michael A. *The Solar System*, 6th ed. Belmont, Calif.: Thomson Brooks/Cole, 2008. [Week 14]

Shoumatoff, Nicholas, and Nina Shoumatoff. *The Alps: Europe's Mountain Heart*. Ann Arbor: University of Michigan Press, 2001. [Week 10]

Silcox, S. *Modern Nature Study*. Toronto: George N. Morang & Company, 1902. [Week 3]

Simmons, John G. *Doctors and Discoveries: Lives That Created Today's Medicine*. Boston: Houghton Mifflin, 2002. [Week 7]

Standard Classics, With Biographical Sketches and Helpful Notes. Boston: Educational Publishing Company, 1910. [Week 19]

Strickland, Agnes. *Life of Mary, Queen of Scots*, Vol. 1. London: George Bell and Sons, 1888. [Week 17]

Symonds, John Addington. *Sketches and Studies in Southern Europe*, Vol. 2. New York: Harper & Brothers, 1880. [Week 29]

Tannenbaum, Beulah, and Myra Stillman. *Understanding Light: The Science of Visible and Invisible Rays*. New York: McGraw-Hill, 1960. [Week 2]

Thwaites, Reuben Gold. *Daniel Boone*. New York: D. Appleton, 1902. [Week 19]

Timbs, John. *Eccentricities of the Animal Creation*. London: Seeley, Jackson and Halliday, 1869. [Week 22]

Tolkien, J. R. R. *The Hobbit*. New York: Random House, 1982. [Week 8]

Travers, P. L. *Mary Poppins in the Park*. New York: Harcourt Books, 1997. [Week 9]

Trefil, James, ed. *Encyclopedia of Science and Technology*. New York: Routledge, 2001. [Week 12]

Twain, Mark. *The Adventures of Tom Sawyer*. Hartford, Conn.: The American Publishing Company, 1881. [Week 11]

Tytler, Patrick Fraser. *Life of King Henry the Eighth*. Edinburgh: Oliver & Boyd, 1837. [Week 18]

Tytler, Sarah. *Marie Antoinette: The Woman and the Queen*. London: Marcus Ward & Co., 1883. [Week 31]

Ueberweg, Friedrich, George S. Morris, Henry B. Smith, Philip Schaff, Noah Porter, and Vincenzo Botta. *A History of Philosophy: From Thales to the Present Time.* New York: C. Scribner & Company, 1872. [Week 28]

Van Dyke, John Charles. *The Desert: Further Studies in Natural Appearances.* New York: Charles Scribner's Sons, 1913. [Week 10]

van Loon, Hendrik. *The Story of Mankind.* Boni and Liveright, 1921. [Week 4]

Van Middeldyk, Rudolph Adams. *The History of Puerto Rico: From the Spanish Discovery to the American Occupation.* New York: D. Appleton and Company, 1903. [Week 11]

Von Baeyer, Hans Christian. *Taming the Atom: The Emergence of the Visible Microworld.* Mineola, N.Y.: Dover Publications, 2000. [Week 13]

Weir, Alison. *Henry VIII: The King and His Court.* New York: Random House, 2002. [Week 18]

———. *The Six Wives of Henry VIII.* New York: Grove, 1991. [Week 18]

West, Willis Mason. *Ancient History to the Death of Charlemagne.* Boston, Mass.: Allyn and Bacon, 1902. [Week 29]

White, T. H. *The Once and Future King.* New York: Ace Books, 1958. [Week 6]

Wolpert, Lewis. *How We Live and Why We Die: The Secret Life of Cells.* New York: W. W. Norton, 2009. [Week 14]

Wynn-Williams, C. Gareth. *The Fullness of Space: Nebulae, Stardust, and the Interstellar Medium.* Cambridge: Cambridge University Press, 1992. [Week 2]

Zeilik, Michael. *Astronomy: The Evolving Universe.* Cambridge: Cambridge University Press, 2002. [Week 21].

PERMISSIONS

Chelsea House: Excerpt from *Islam*, by Masoud Kheirabadi, © 2004 by Chelsea House Publishers. All rights reserved.

Compass Point Books: Excerpt from *Galileo: Astronomer and Physicist*, by Robin S. Doak, © 2005 by Compass Point Books. All rights reserved.

Compass Point Books: *Hatshepsut: Egypt's First Female Pharaoh*, by Pamela Dell © 2009 by Compass Point Books. Text from pages 41-43. All rights reserved.

Compton's Learning Company. *Earth's Changing Environment*. Reprinted with permission from *Earth's Changing Environment*, © 2008 by Encyclopedia Britannica, Inc.

Copyright Clearance Center: Excerpt from *International Women in Science: A Biographical Dictionary to 1950*, by Catharine M. C. Haines, © 2001 ABC-CLIO. All rights reserved.

Copyright Clearance Center: *Historical Dictionary of Mesopotamia* by LEICK, GWENDOLYN. Copyright 2003 by SCARECROW PRESS, INC. Reproduced with permission of SCARECROW PRESS, INC. in the format Other Book via Copyright Clearance Center.

G.P. Putnam's Sons: "Part I, Chapter XVIII", from THE ONCE AND FUTURE KING by T.H. White, copyright © 1938, 1939, 1940 © 1958 by T.H. White renewed. Used by permission of G.P. Putnam's Sons, a division of Penguin Group (USA) Inc.

Houghton Mifflin Publishing Company: CHANGES IN THE WIND: EARTH'S SHIFTING CLIMATE copyright © 1986 by Margery Facklam & Howard Facklam. Used by permission of Houghton Mifflin Publishing Company.

Harcourt, Inc: MARY POPPINS IN THE PARK, copyrighted © 1952 and renewed 1980 by P. L. Travers. Excerpt used by permission of Harcourt, Inc.

Harcourt Brace Jovanovich: *Changes in the Wind: Earth's Shifting Climate*, by Margery and Howard Facklam copyright © 1986. Excerpt from pp. 5-6 used by permission of Harcourt Brace Jovanovich.

Harper Collins (UK) and Penguin (USA): THE ONCE AND FUTURE KING by T H White © 1958. Excerpt used with permission by Harper Collins (UK) and Penguin Inc. (USA)

Harvard Health Publications: Excerpt from *The Harvard Medical School Family Health Guide*, by Anthony L. Komaroff, © 1999 by Harvard Health Publications.

Holiday House, Inc: Excerpt from *Big Red* Copyright © 1945 by Jim Kjelgaard. Reprinted from BIG RED by permission of Holiday House, Inc. All rights reserved.

McGraw-Hill Material: *Understanding Light: The Science of Visible and Invisible Rays* © 1960 by Beulah Tannenbaum and Myra Stillman. Excerpt used with permission by McGraw-Hill Material.

Penguin: DISCOVERER OF THE UNSEEN WORLD: A BIOGRAPHY OF ANTONI VAN LEEUWENHOEK by Alma Smith Payne, copyright © 1996. Copyright renewal 1994 by Mr. William Robertson Ralston. Excerpt pp. 16-19 used by permission of Penguin Young Readers Group, A Member of Penguin Group (USA) Inc., 345 Hudson Street, New York, NY 10014. All rights reserved.

Random House, Inc.: From THE MISSISSIPPI BUBBLE by Thomas Costain, copyright © 1995 by Thomas Costain. Used by permission of Random House, Inc.

Random House, Inc.: *The Complete Beginner's Guide to Photography* by George Laycock copyright ©1979. Excerpt from pp. 58-61 used by permission of Random House, Inc.

Square Fish: Excerpt from *The Pepins and Their Problems*, by Polly Horvath, © 2008 by Square Fish Books. All rights reserved.

Viking Penguin: "Slaughter", from NELSON'S TRAFALGAR by Roy Adkins, copyright © 2004. Used by permission of Viking Penguin, a division of Penguin Group (USA) Inc.

Yearling Books: Excerpt from *The Wolves of Willoughby Chase*, by Joan Aiken, © 1962 by Yearling. All rights reserved.